ITIVE Boyfriend

2

story & art by
YOSHINEKO KITAFUKU

PRIMITIVE BOYFRIEND 2 CONTENTS

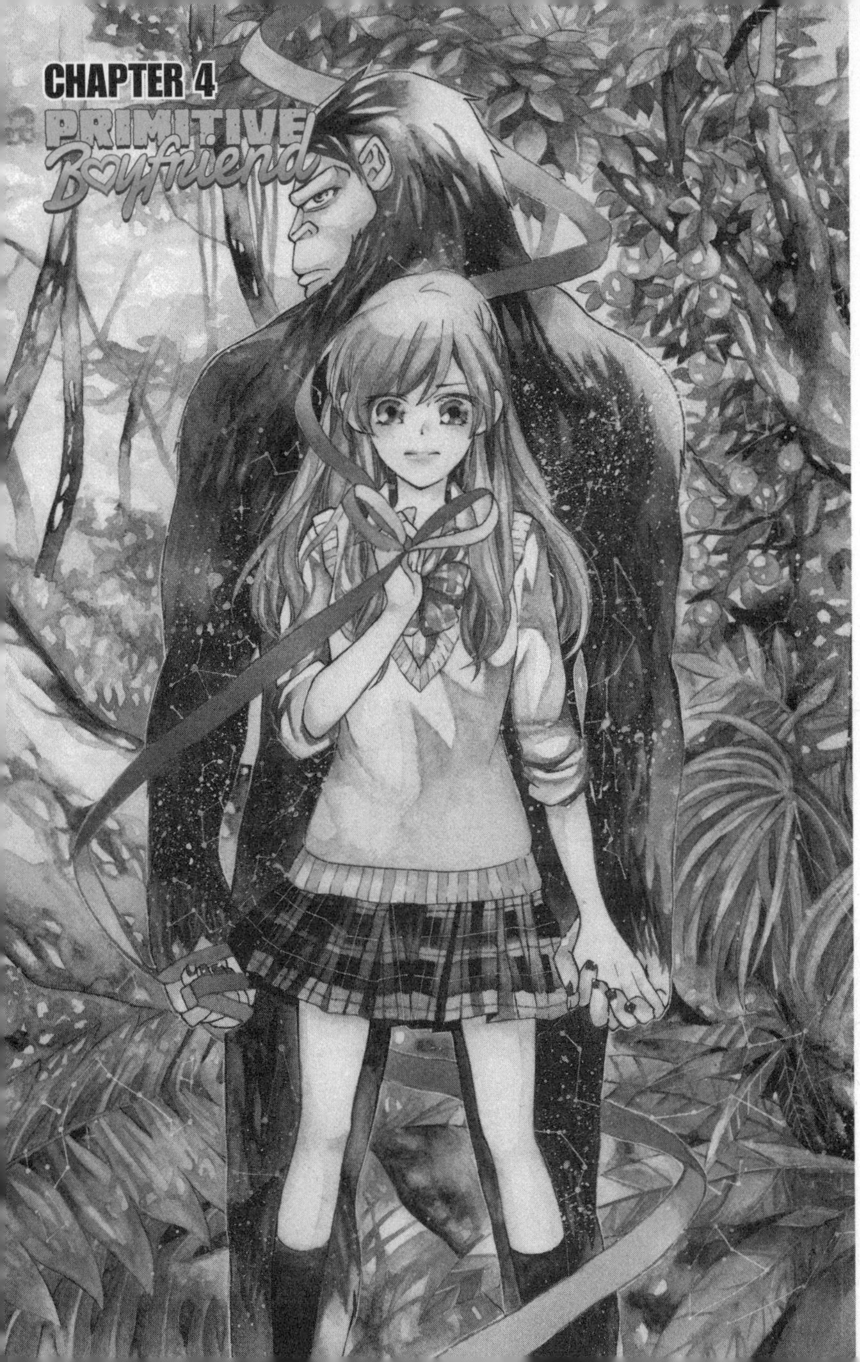
CHAPTER 4
PRIMITIVE Boyfriend

PRIMITIVE BOYFRIEND BY Yoshineko Kitafuku PRIMITIVE BOYFRIEND

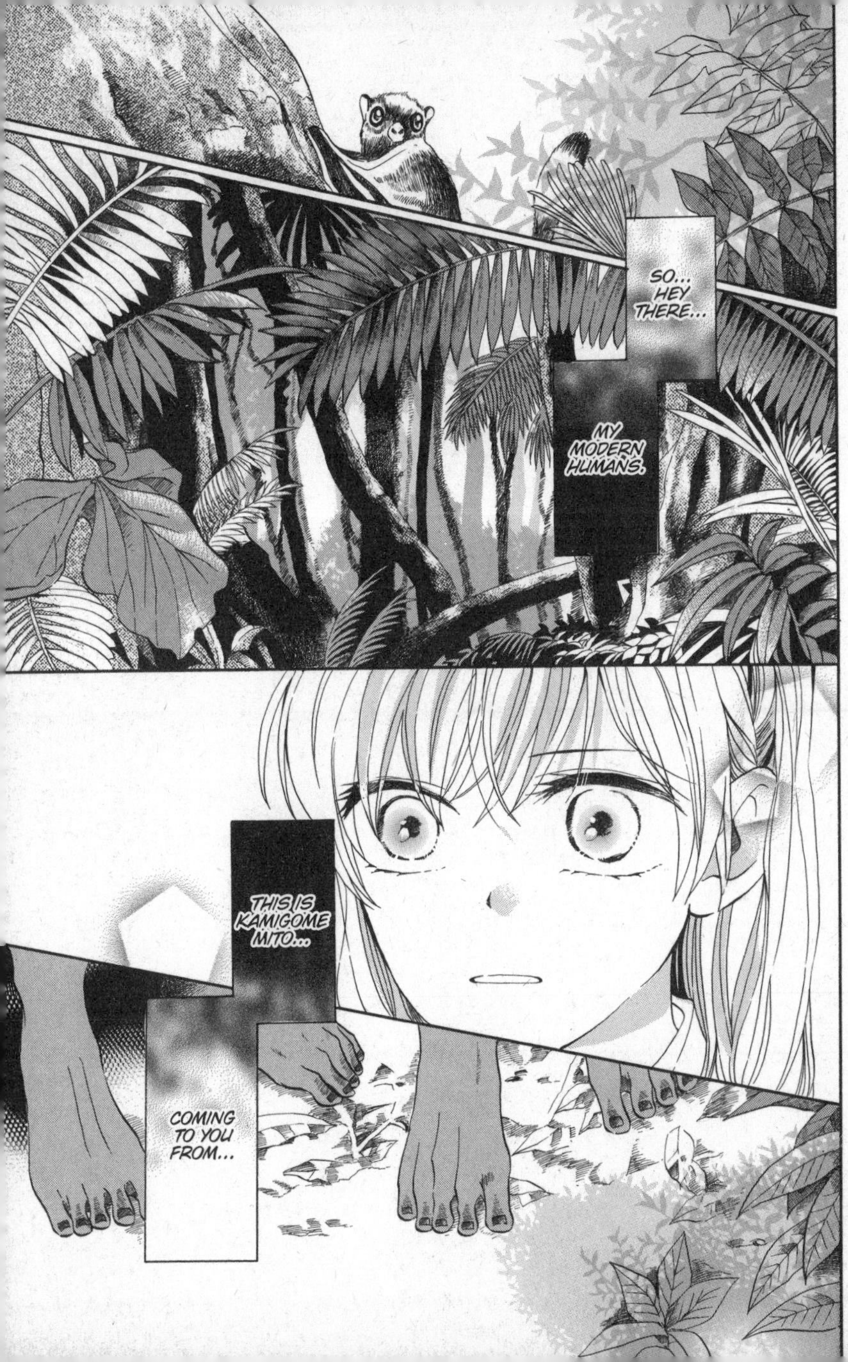
SO... HEY THERE...
MY MODERN HUMANS.
THIS IS KAMIGOME MITO...
COMING TO YOU FROM...

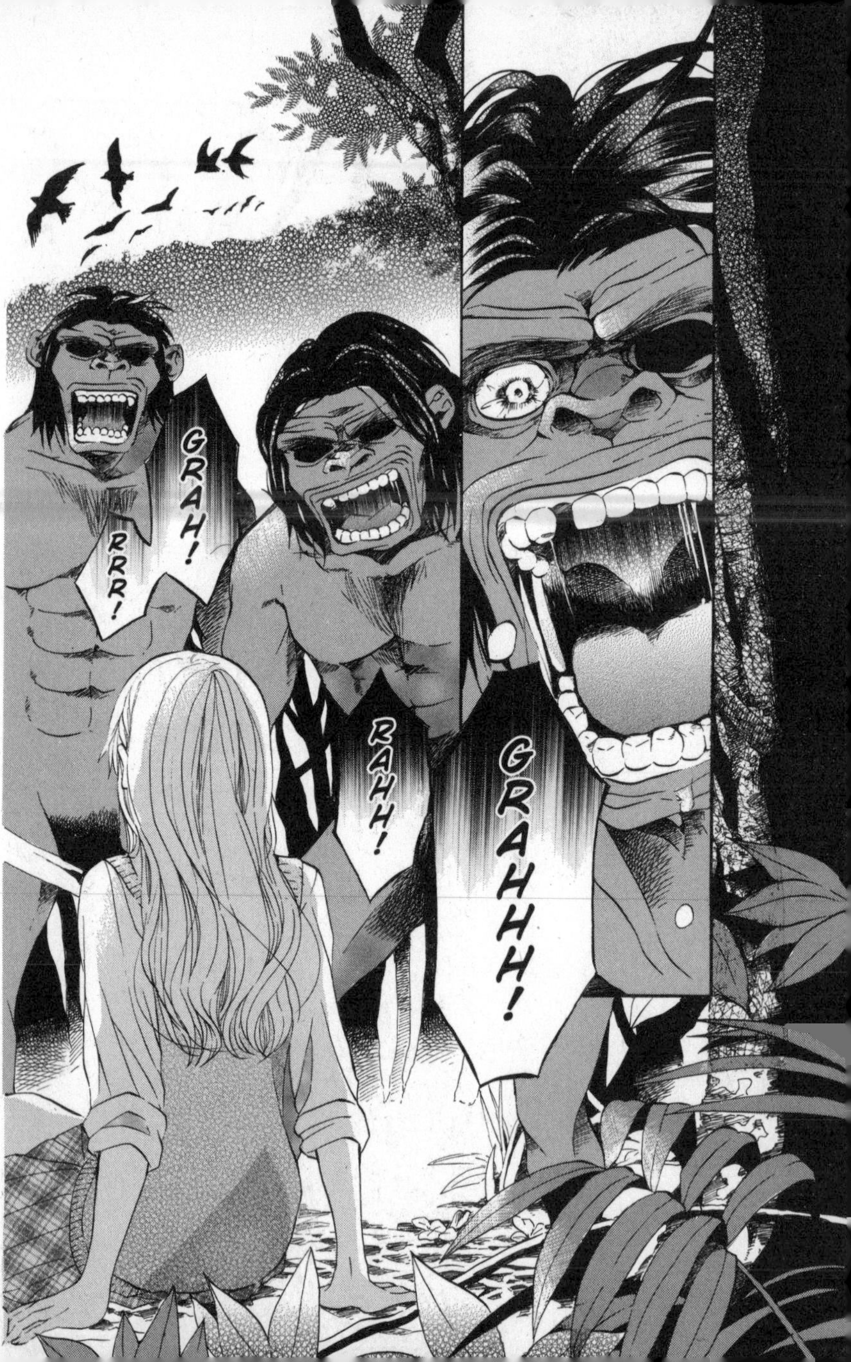
GRAHHHH!
GRAH!
RRR!
RAHH!

FLAP
FLAP
FLAP
GYAH!
GRAH!
NOW, YOU MAY BE ASKING YOUR-SELVES...
A RATHER HAIRY SITUATION.
HOW THE HECK DID I END UP HERE?

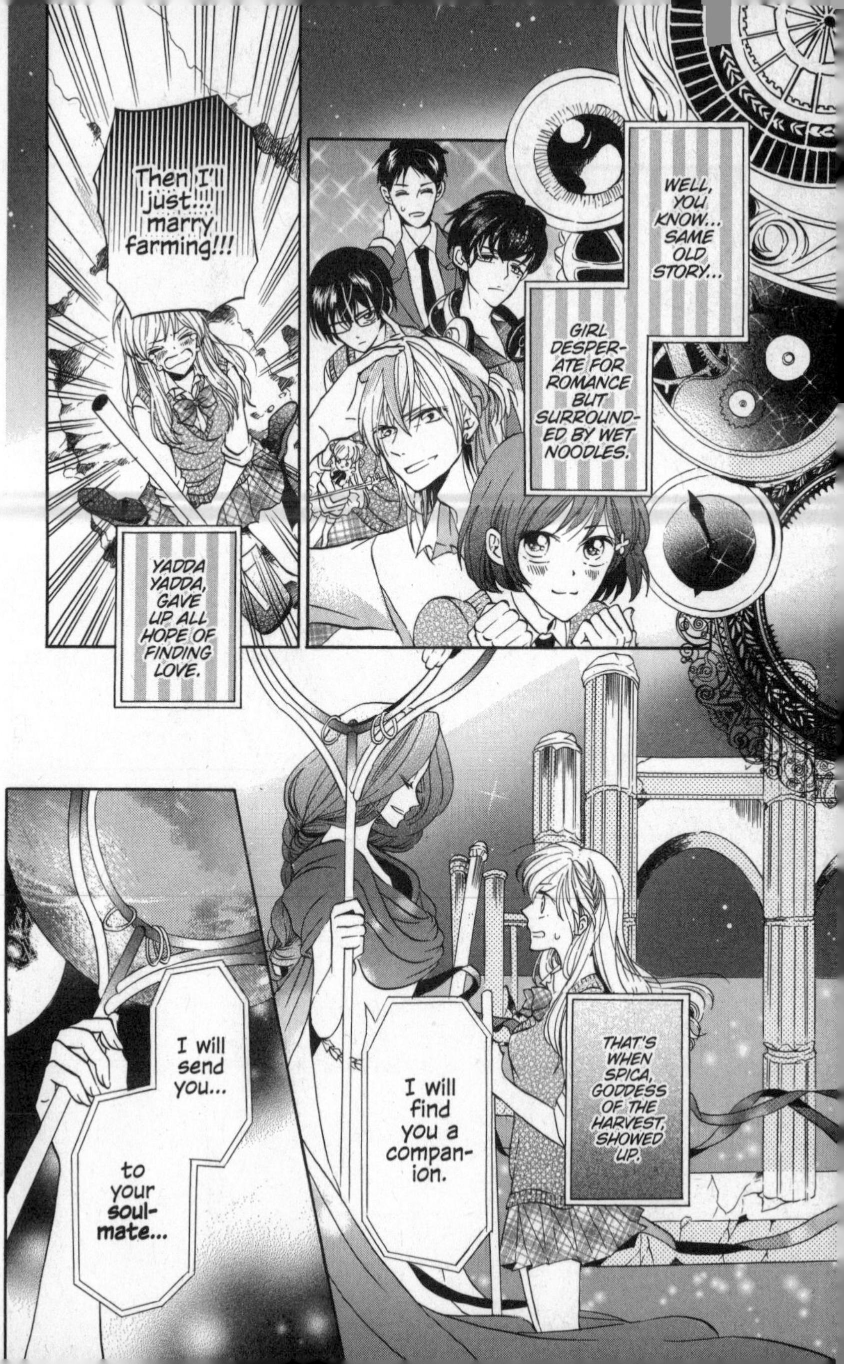
WELL, YOU KNOW... SAME OLD STORY...
GIRL DESPERATE FOR ROMANCE BUT SURROUNDED BY WET NOODLES.
Then I'll just... marry farming!!!
YADDA YADDA, GAVE UP ALL HOPE OF FINDING LOVE.
THAT'S WHEN SPICA, GODDESS OF THE HARVEST, SHOWED UP.
I will find you a companion.
I will send you...
to your soulmate...

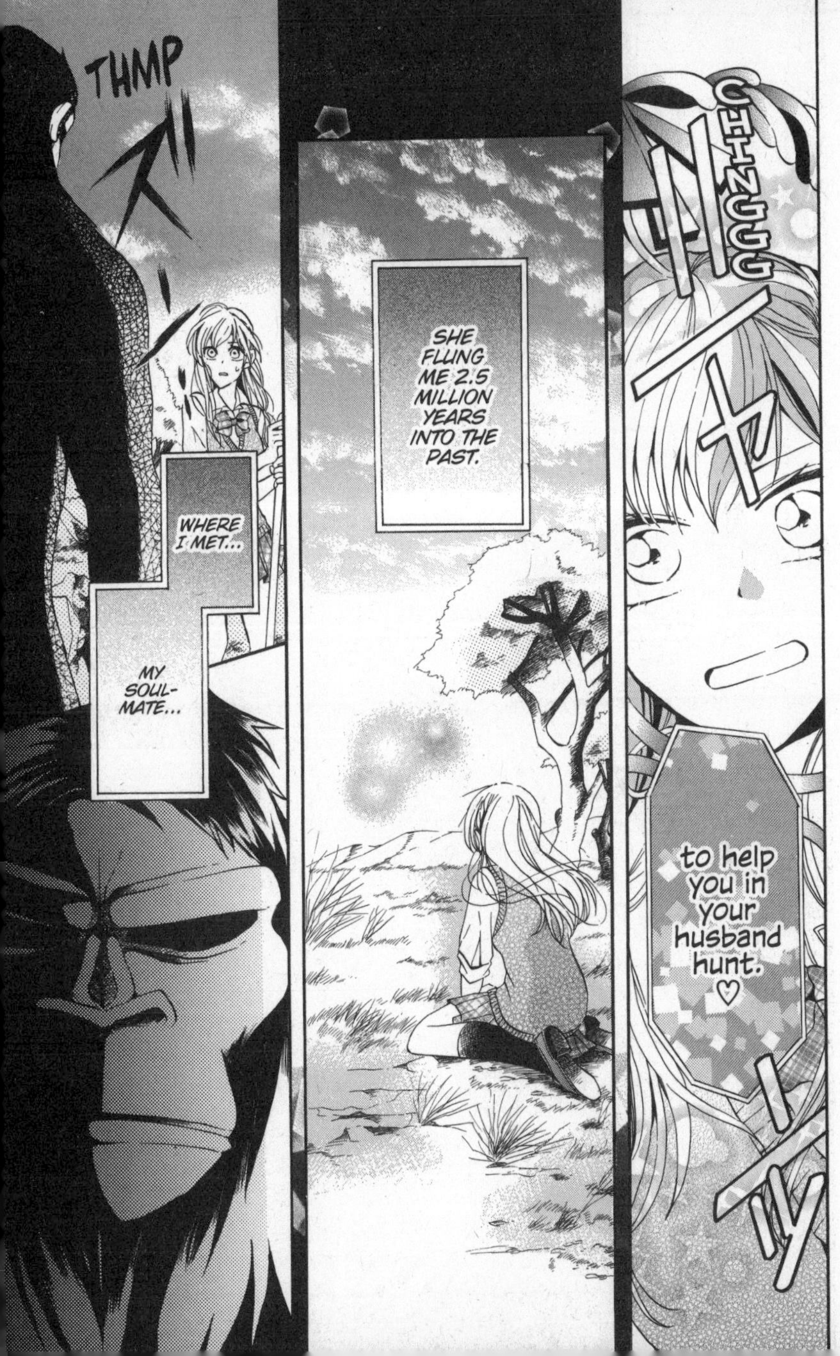
CHINGGG
to help you in your husband hunt. ♡
SHE FLUNG ME 2.5 MILLION YEARS INTO THE PAST.
THMP
WHERE I MET...
MY SOUL-MATE...

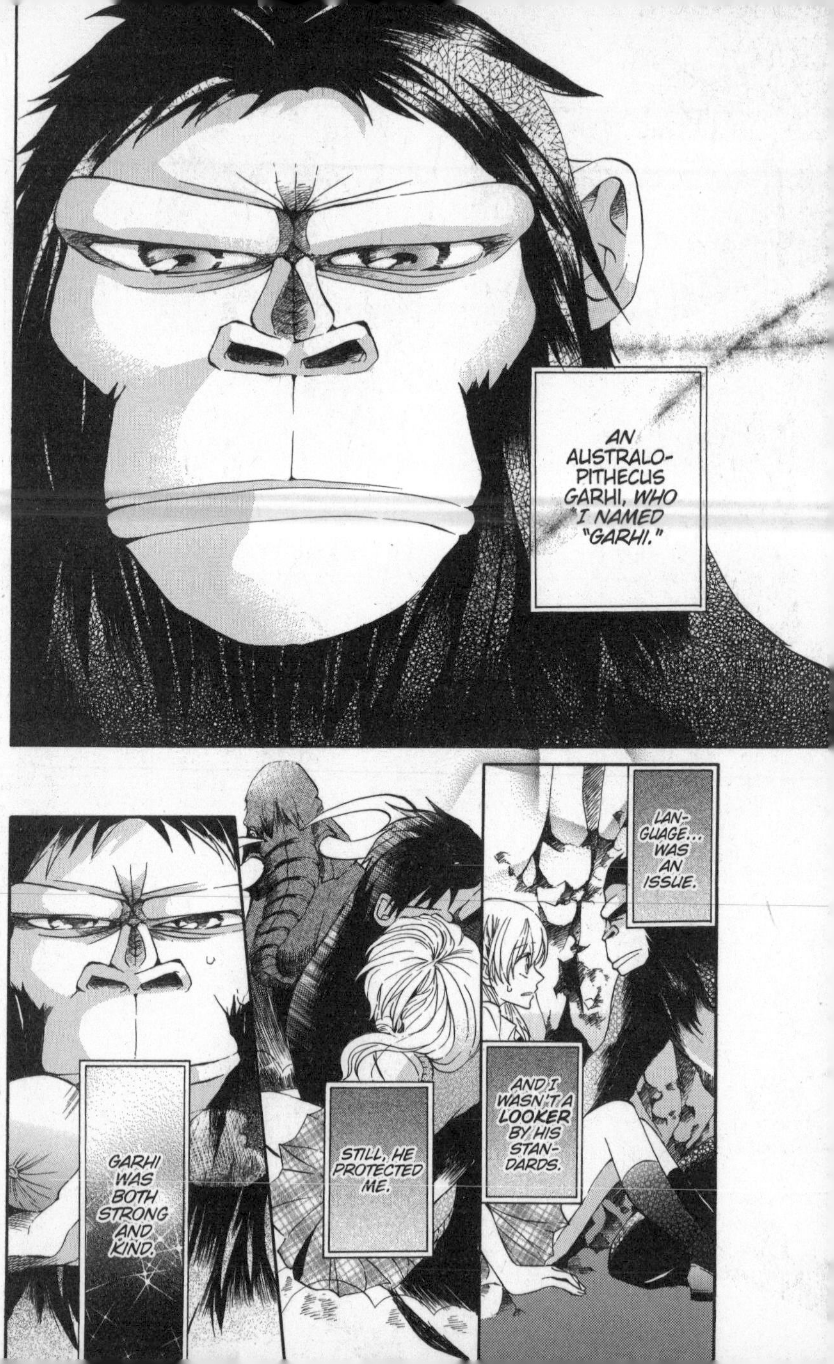
AN AUSTRALOPITHECUS GARHI, WHO I NAMED "GARHI."
LANGUAGE... WAS AN ISSUE.
AND I WASN'T A LOOKER BY HIS STANDARDS.
STILL, HE PROTECTED ME.
GARHI WAS BOTH STRONG AND KIND.

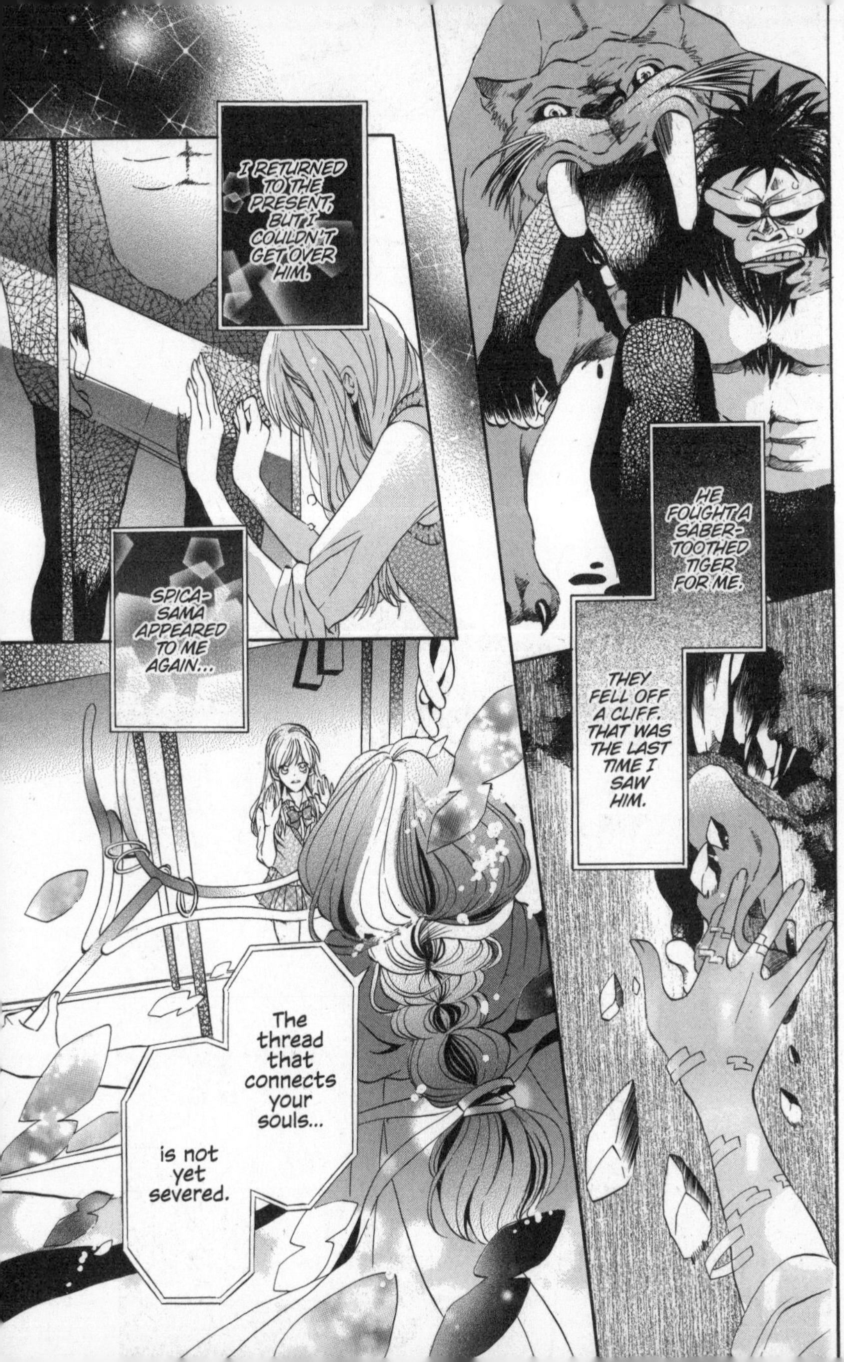
HE FOUGHT A SABER-TOOTHED TIGER FOR ME.
THEY FELL OFF A CLIFF. THAT WAS THE LAST TIME I SAW HIM.
I RETURNED TO THE PRESENT, BUT I COULDN'T GET OVER HIM.
SPICA-SAMA APPEARED TO ME AGAIN...
The thread that connects your souls...
is not yet severed.

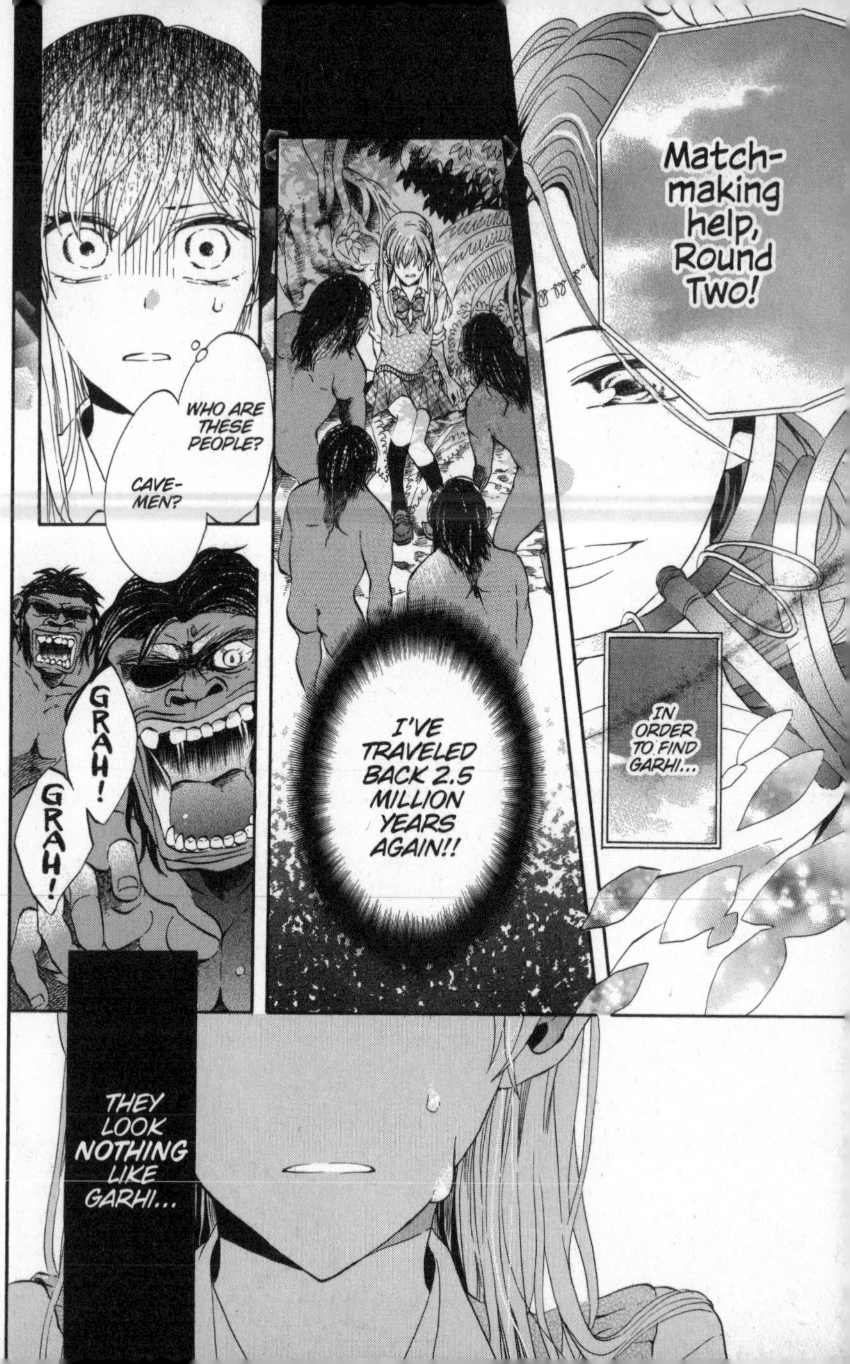

Match-making help, Round Two!
IN ORDER TO FIND GARHI...
I'VE TRAVELED BACK 2.5 MILLION YEARS AGAIN!!
WHO ARE THESE PEOPLE?
CAVE-MEN?
GRAH!
GRAH!
THEY LOOK NOTHING LIKE GARHI...

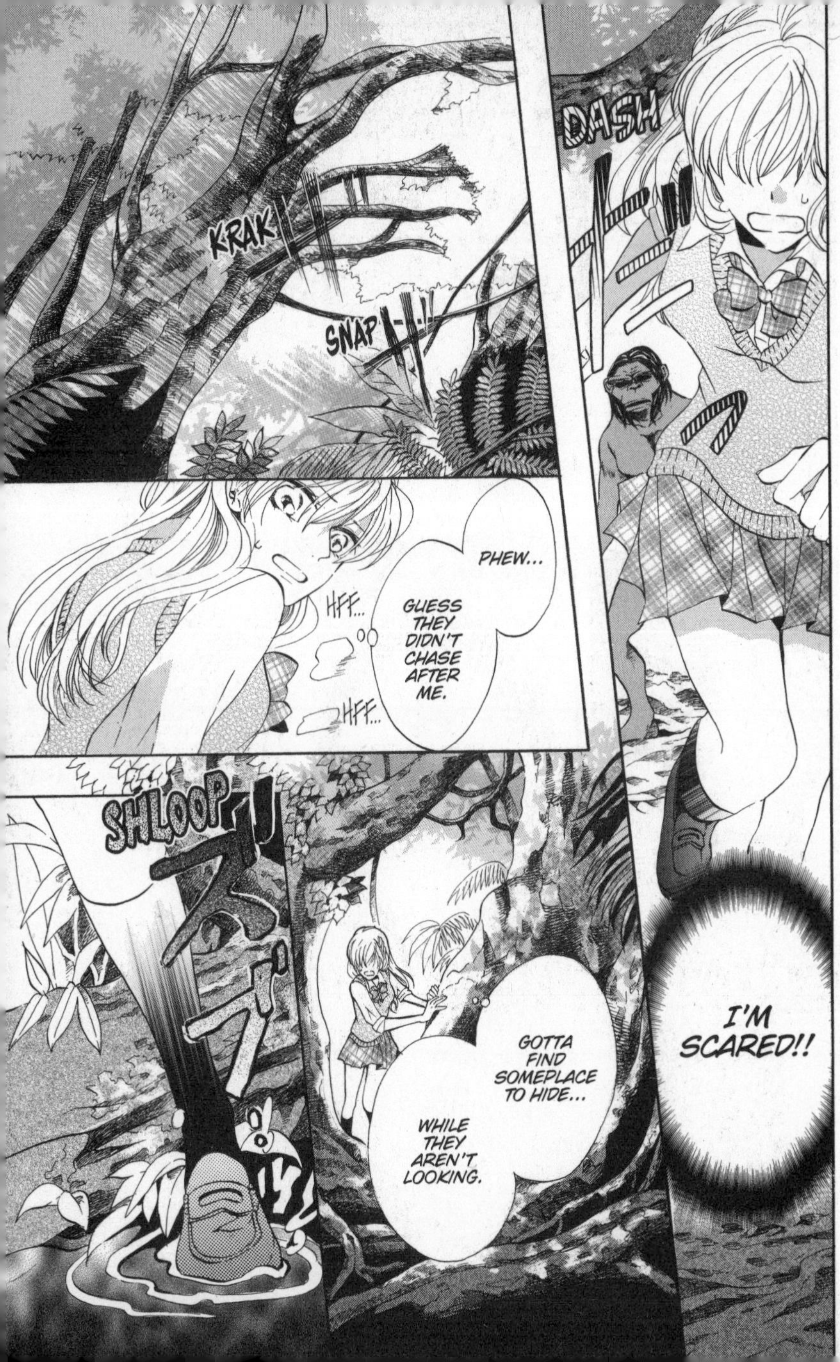

DASH
I'M SCARED!!
KRAK
SNAP
PHEW...
GUESS THEY DIDN'T CHASE AFTER ME.
HFF...
HFF...
GOTTA FIND SOMEPLACE TO HIDE...
WHILE THEY AREN'T LOOKING.
SHLOOP

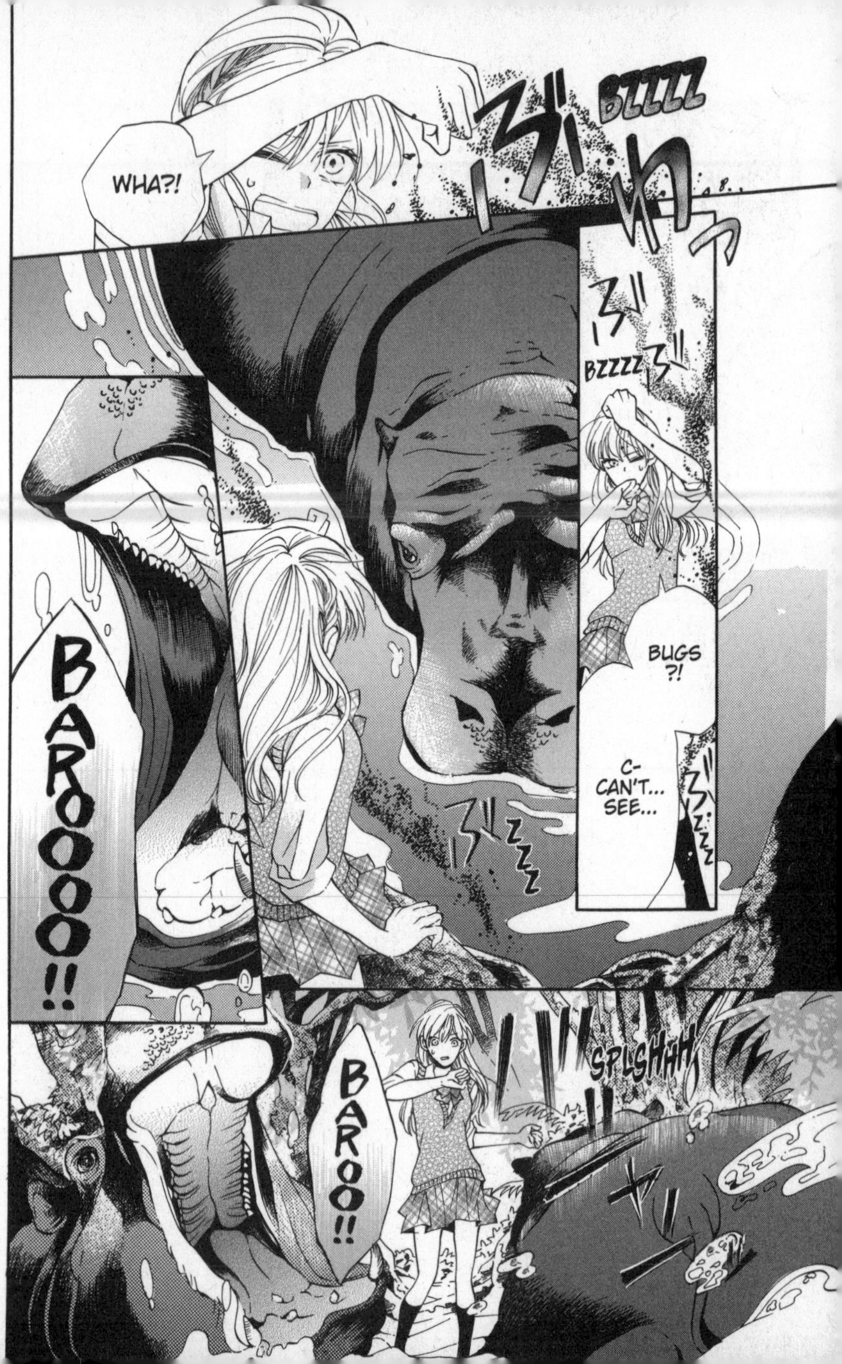
BZZZZ
WHA?!
BZZZZ
BUGS ?!
C-CAN'T... SEE...
BAROOOOOO!!
SPLSHHH
BAROO!!

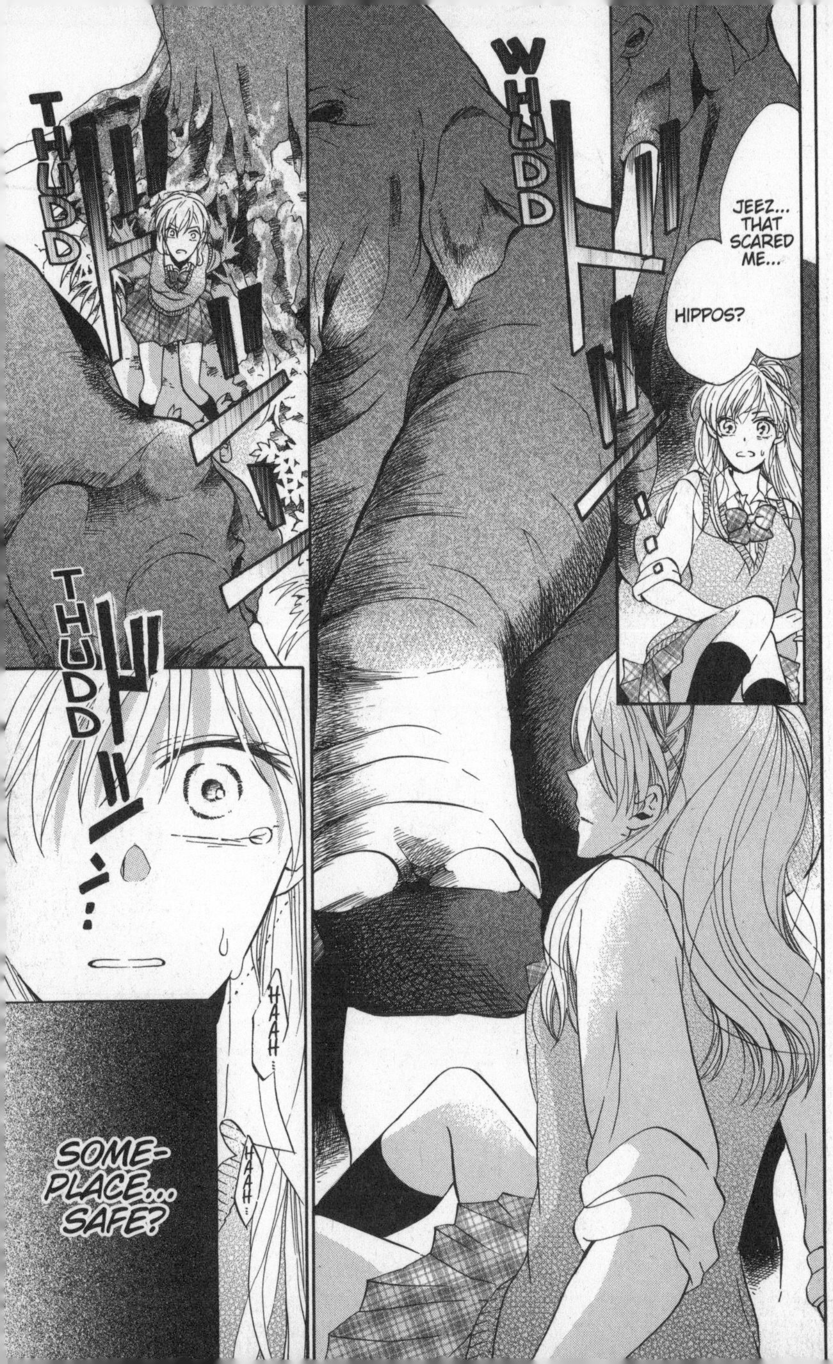
JEEZ... THAT SCARED ME...
HIPPOS?
WHUDD
THUDD
THUDD
HAAH...
HAAH...
SOME-PLACE... SAFE?

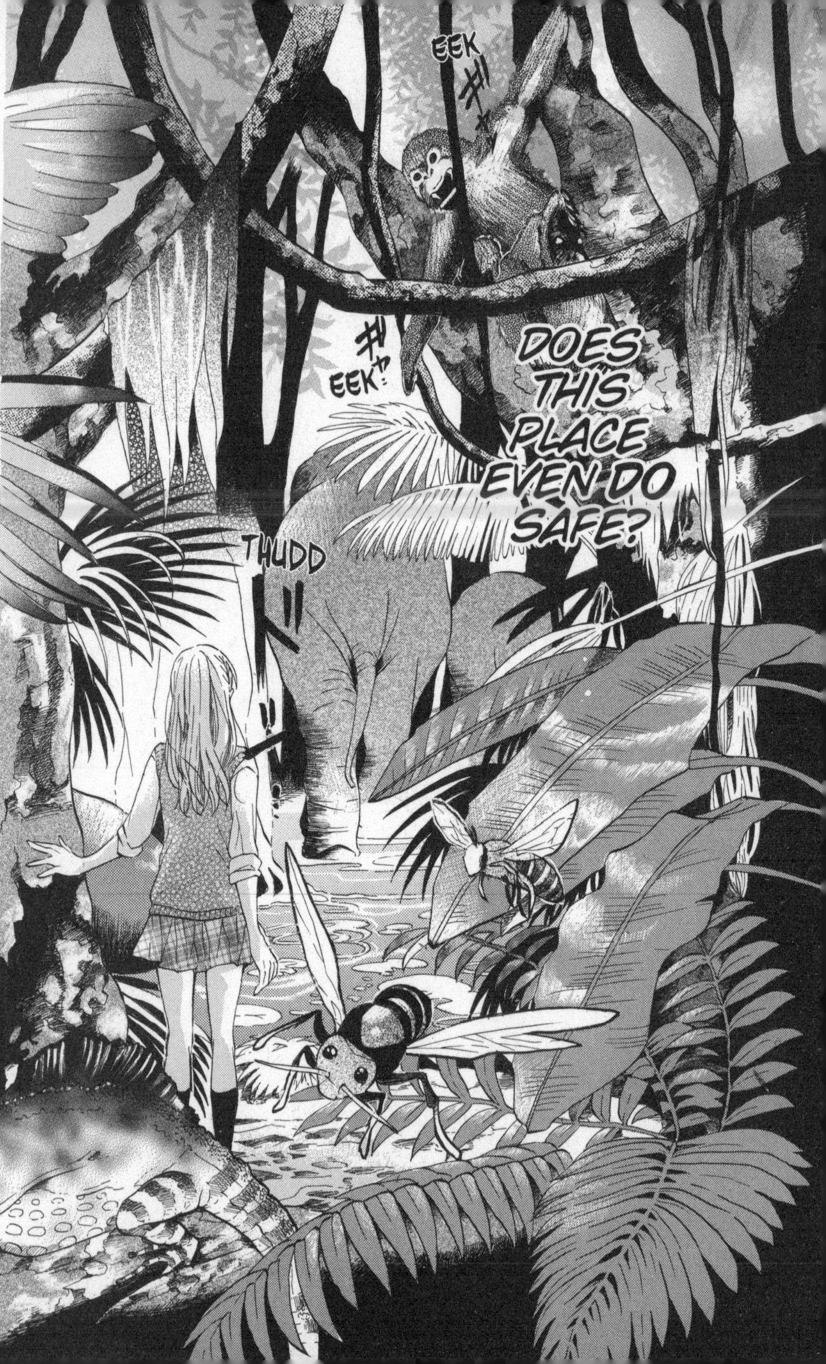
EEK
DOES THIS PLACE EVEN DO SAFE?
EEK
THUDD

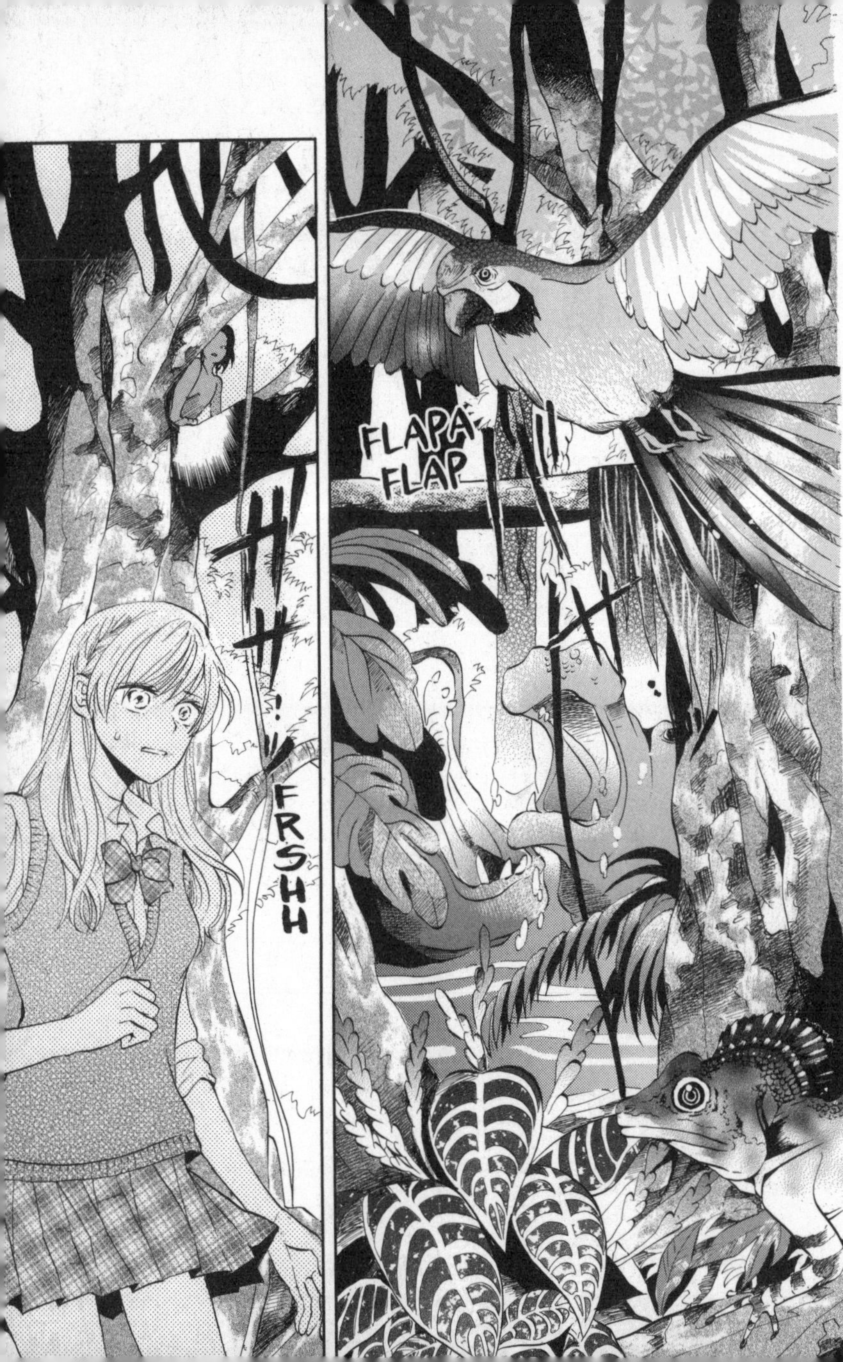
FLAPA FLAP
FRSHH

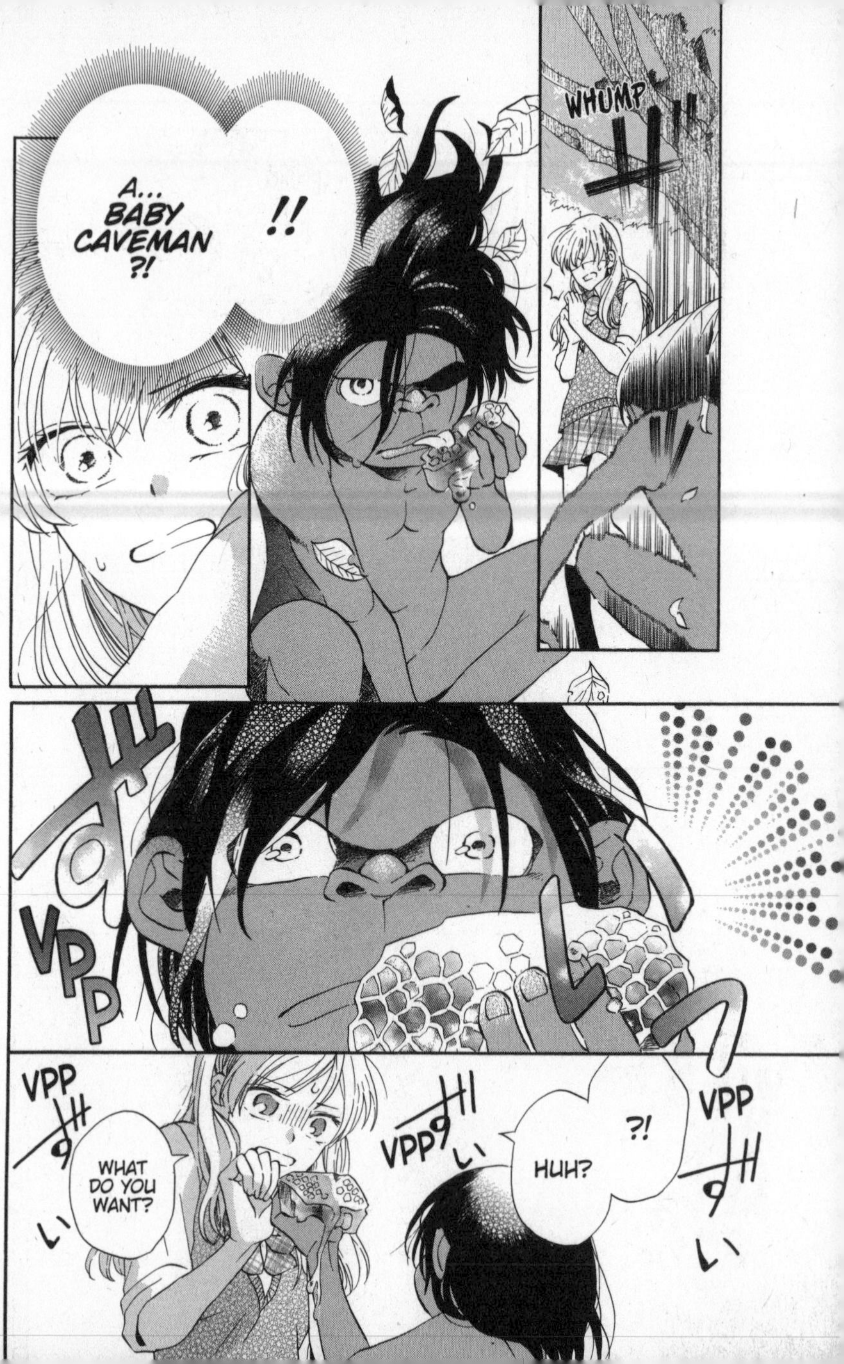
WHUMP
!!
A... BABY CAVEMAN?!
VPP
VPP
?!
HUH?
VPP
WHAT DO YOU WANT?
VPP

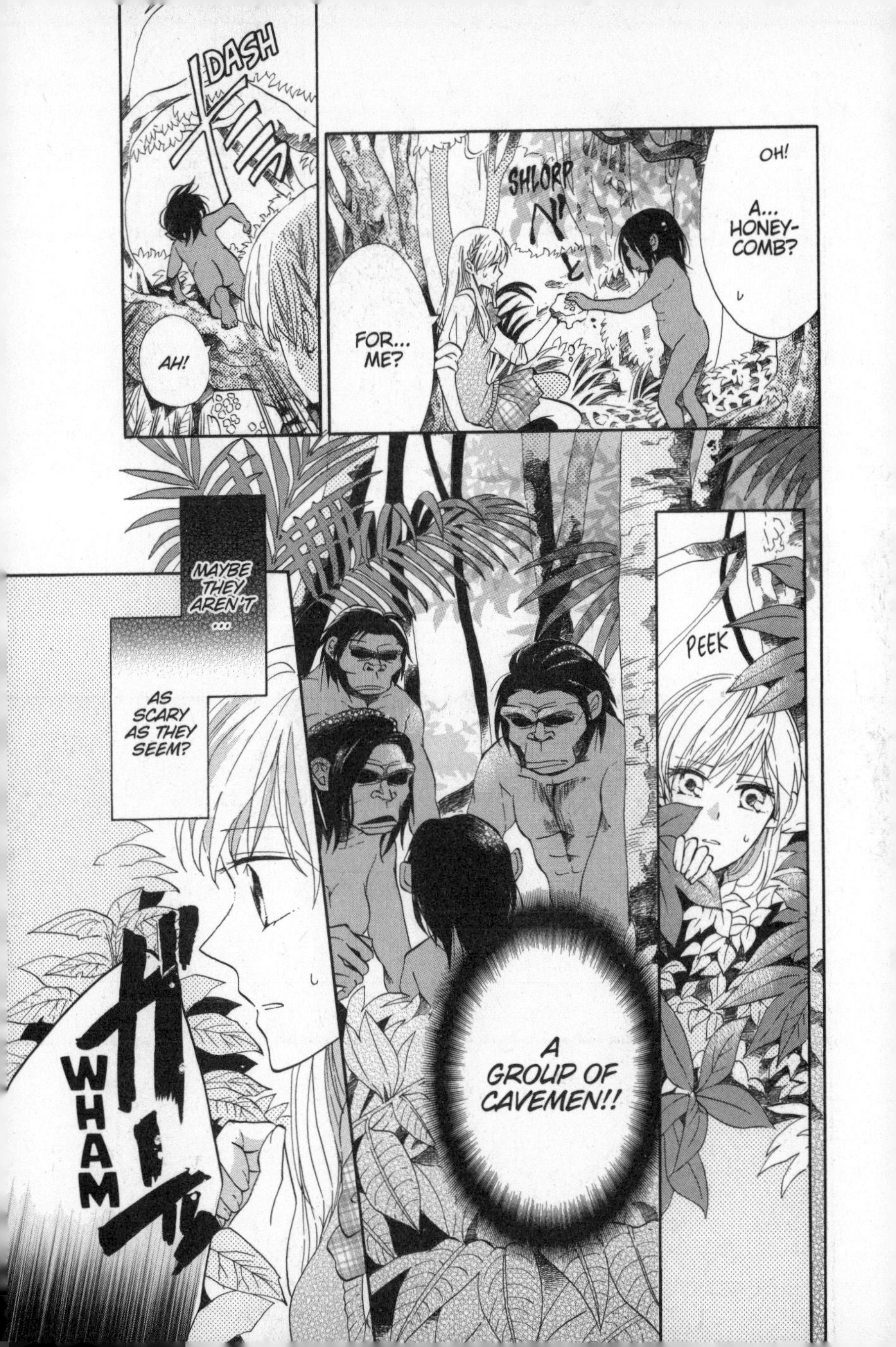
OH!
A... HONEY-COMB?
SHLORP
FOR... ME?
DASH
AH!
PEEK
A GROUP OF CAVEMEN!!
MAYBE THEY AREN'T...
AS SCARY AS THEY SEEM?
WHAM

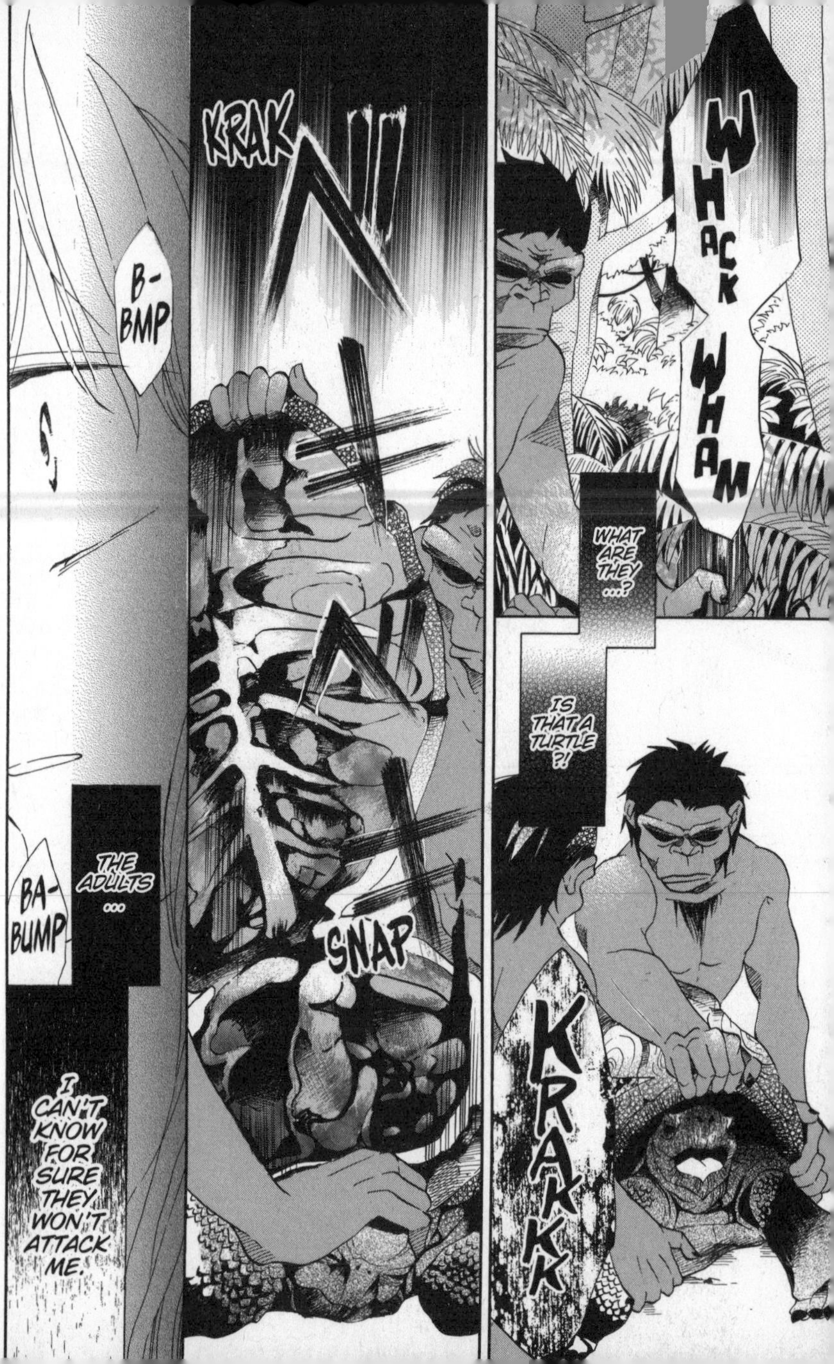
WHACK WHAM WHAM
WHAT ARE THEY ...?
IS THAT A TURTLE ?!
KRAKK
KRAK
SNAP
B-BMP
THE ADULTS ...
BA-BUMP
I CAN'T KNOW FOR SURE THEY WON'T ATTACK ME.

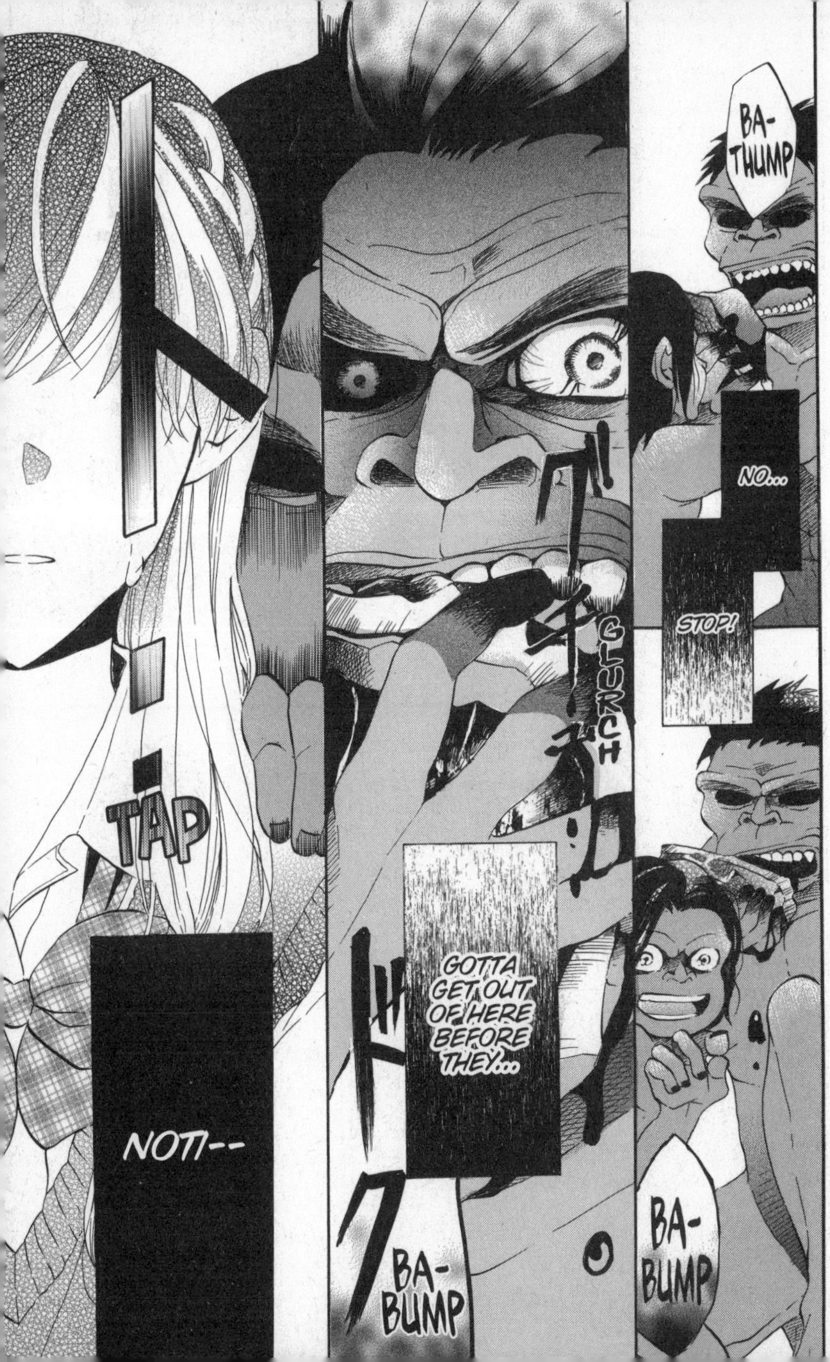
BA-THUMP
NO...
STOP!
BA-BUMP
GLURCH
GOTTA GET OUT OF HERE BEFORE THEY...
BA-BUMP
TAP
NOTI--

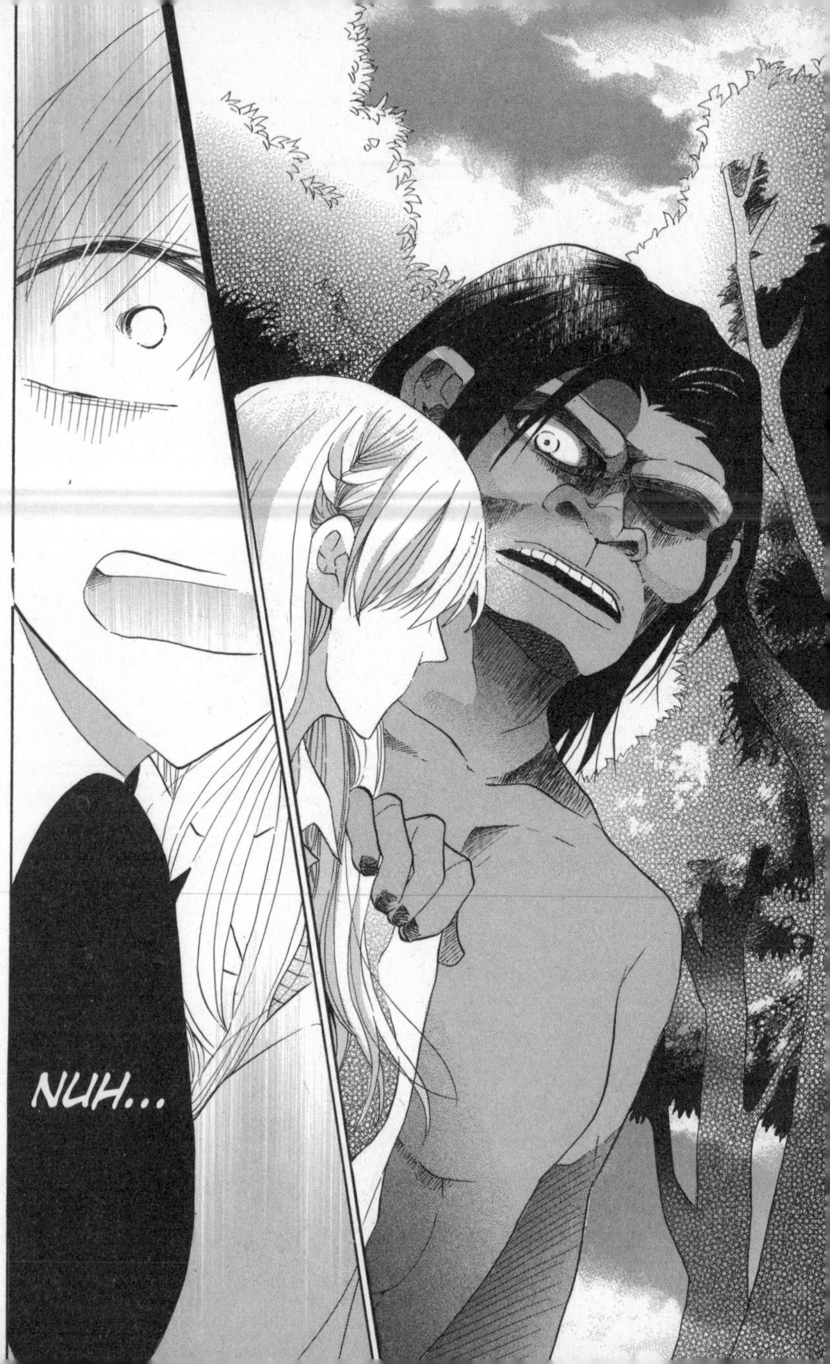
NUH...

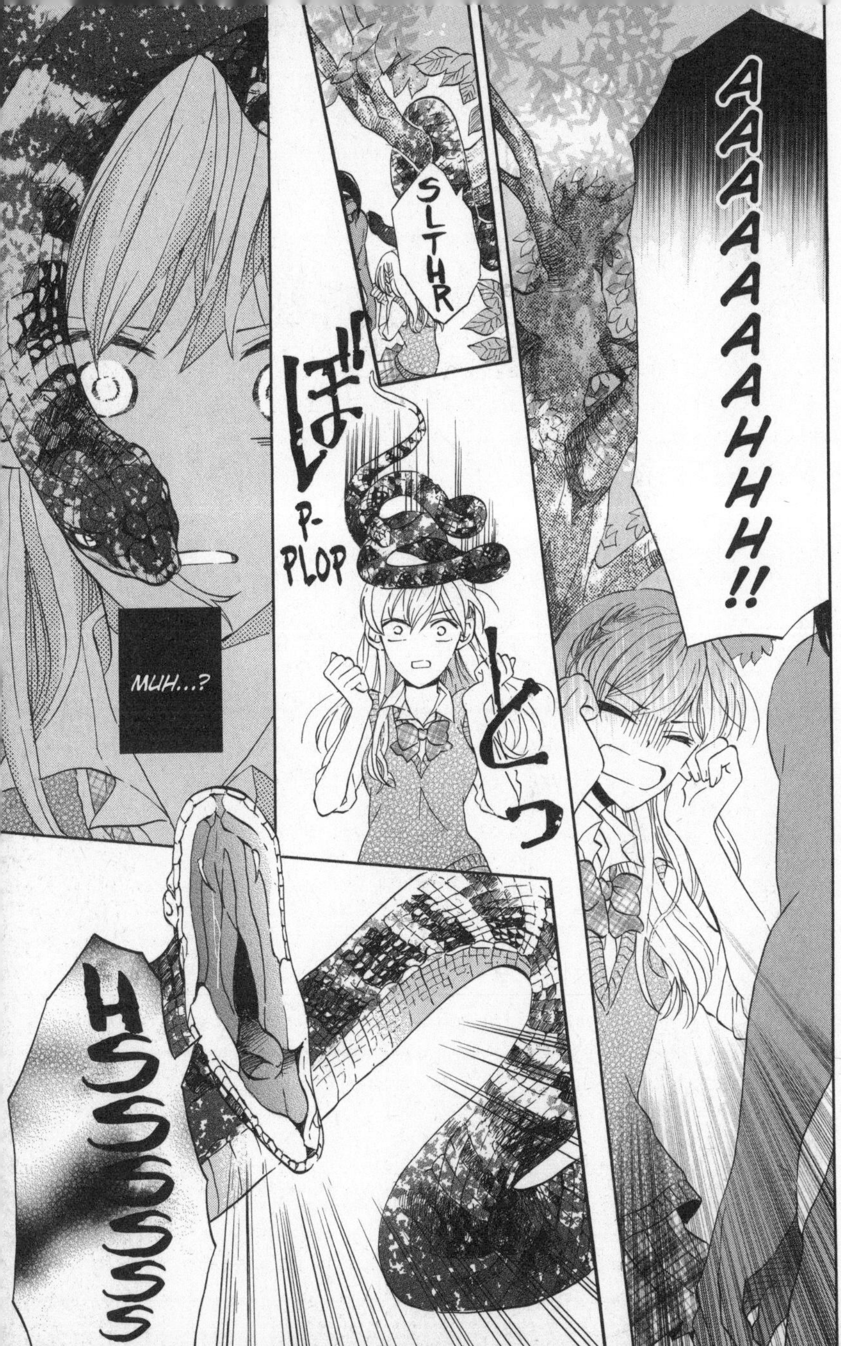
AAAAAAAHHH!!
SLTHR
ぽとっ
P-PLOP
MUH...?
HSSSSSS

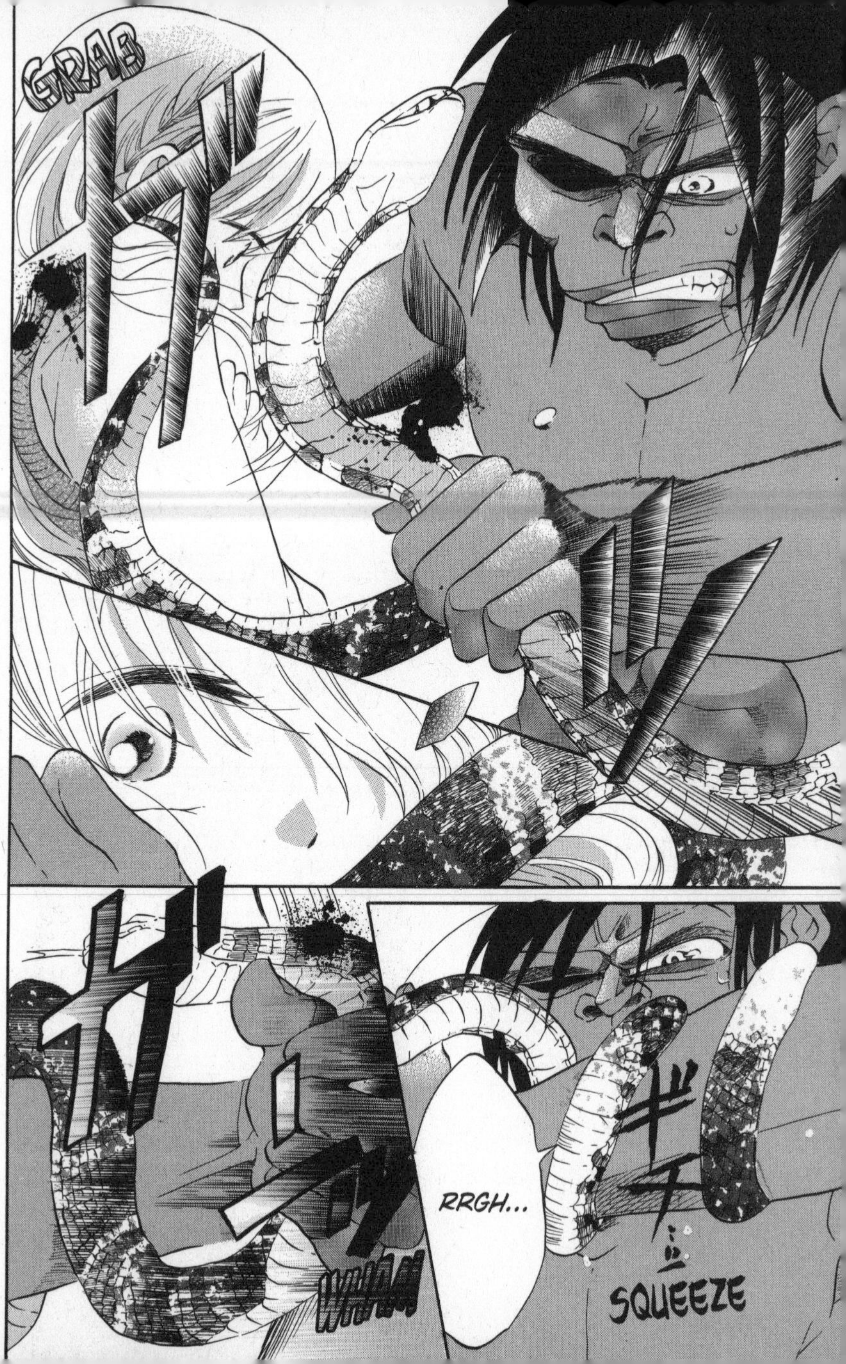
GRAB
RRGH...
SQUEEZE
WHAM!

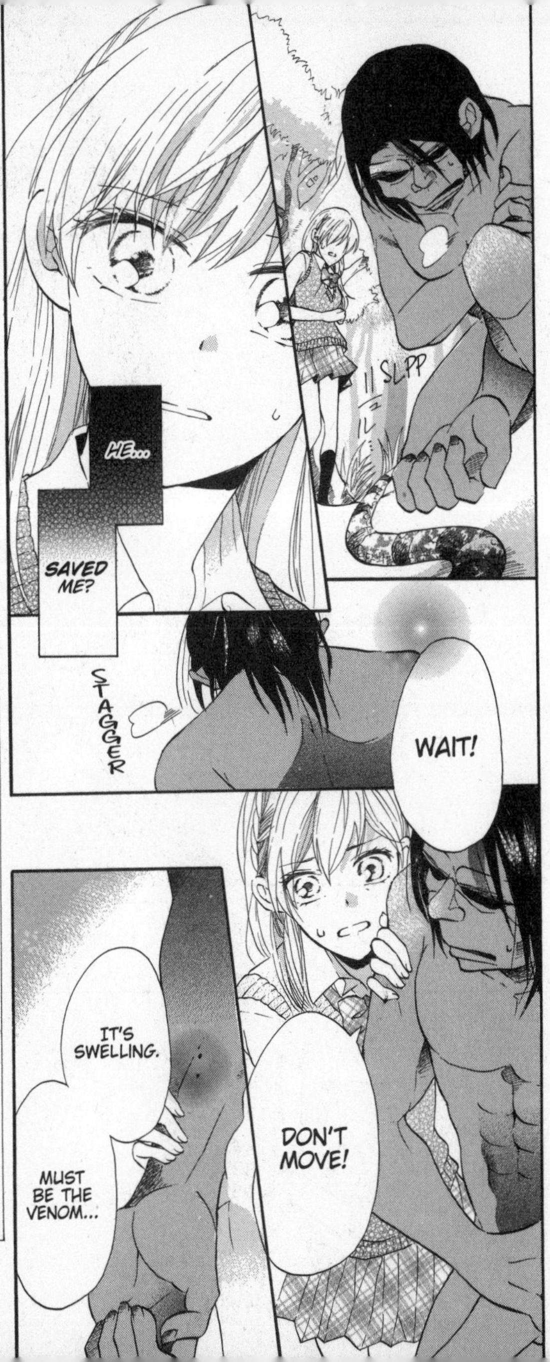
SLPP
HE...
SAVED ME?
STAGGER
WAIT!
DON'T MOVE!
IT'S SWELLING.
MUST BE THE VENOM...

1

GREETINGS

HELLO. I'M YOSHINEKO KITAFUKU.

THANK YOU SO MUCH FOR PICKING UP *PRIMITIVE BOYFRIEND*, VOLUME 2!

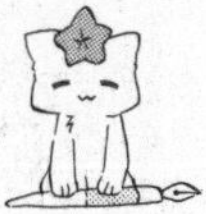

THOSE OF YOU WHO'VE BEEN READING SINCE VOLUME 1, AND THOSE OF YOU WHO JUST JOINED US, I HOPE YOU ENJOY IT WITH A NICE CUP OF TEA.

THIS WAY TO THE JUNGLE CRUISE!

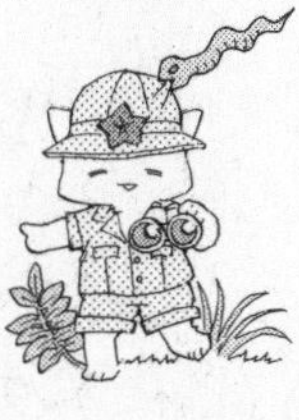

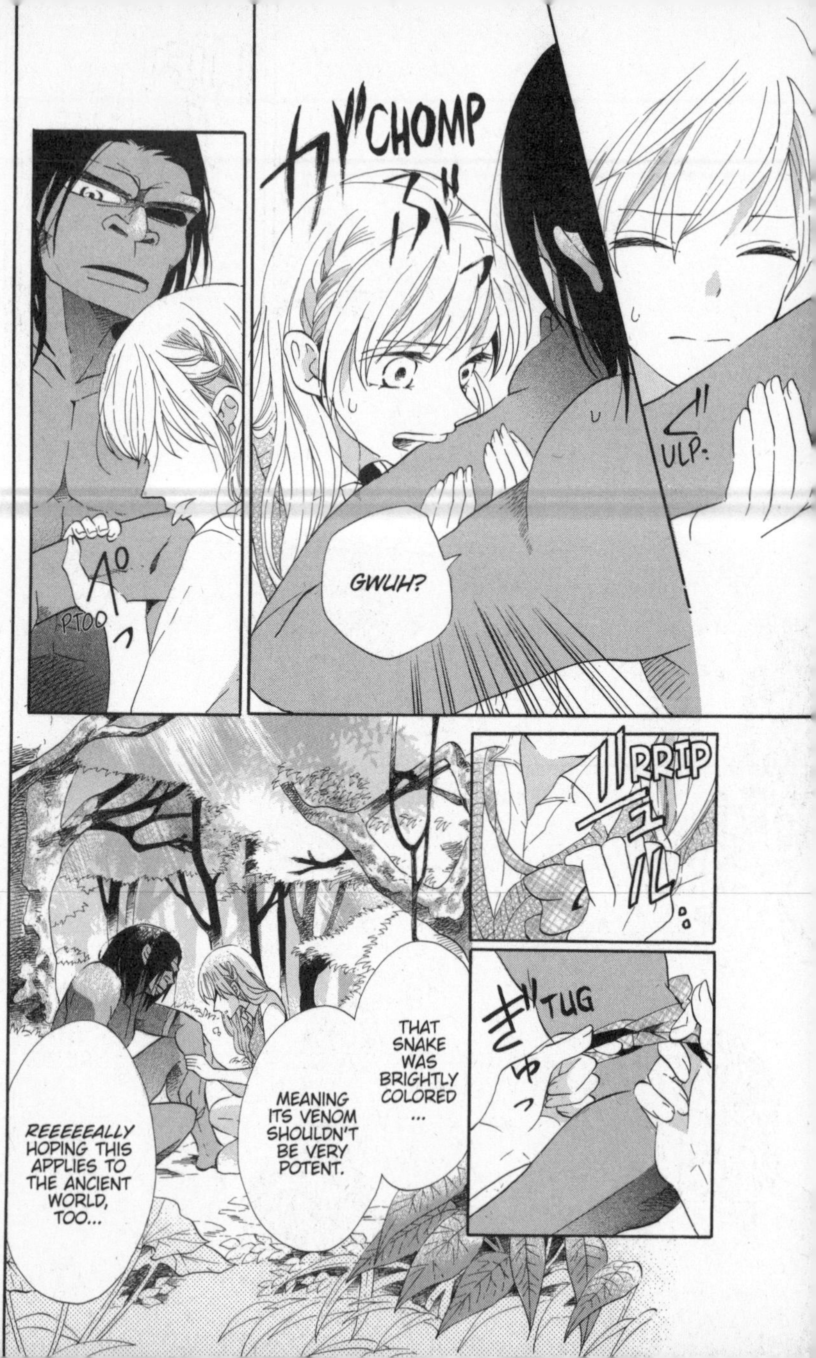
CHOMP
ULP
GWUH?
PTOO
RRIP
TUG
THAT SNAKE WAS BRIGHTLY COLORED...
MEANING ITS VENOM SHOULDN'T BE VERY POTENT.
REEEEEALLY HOPING THIS APPLIES TO THE ANCIENT WORLD, TOO...

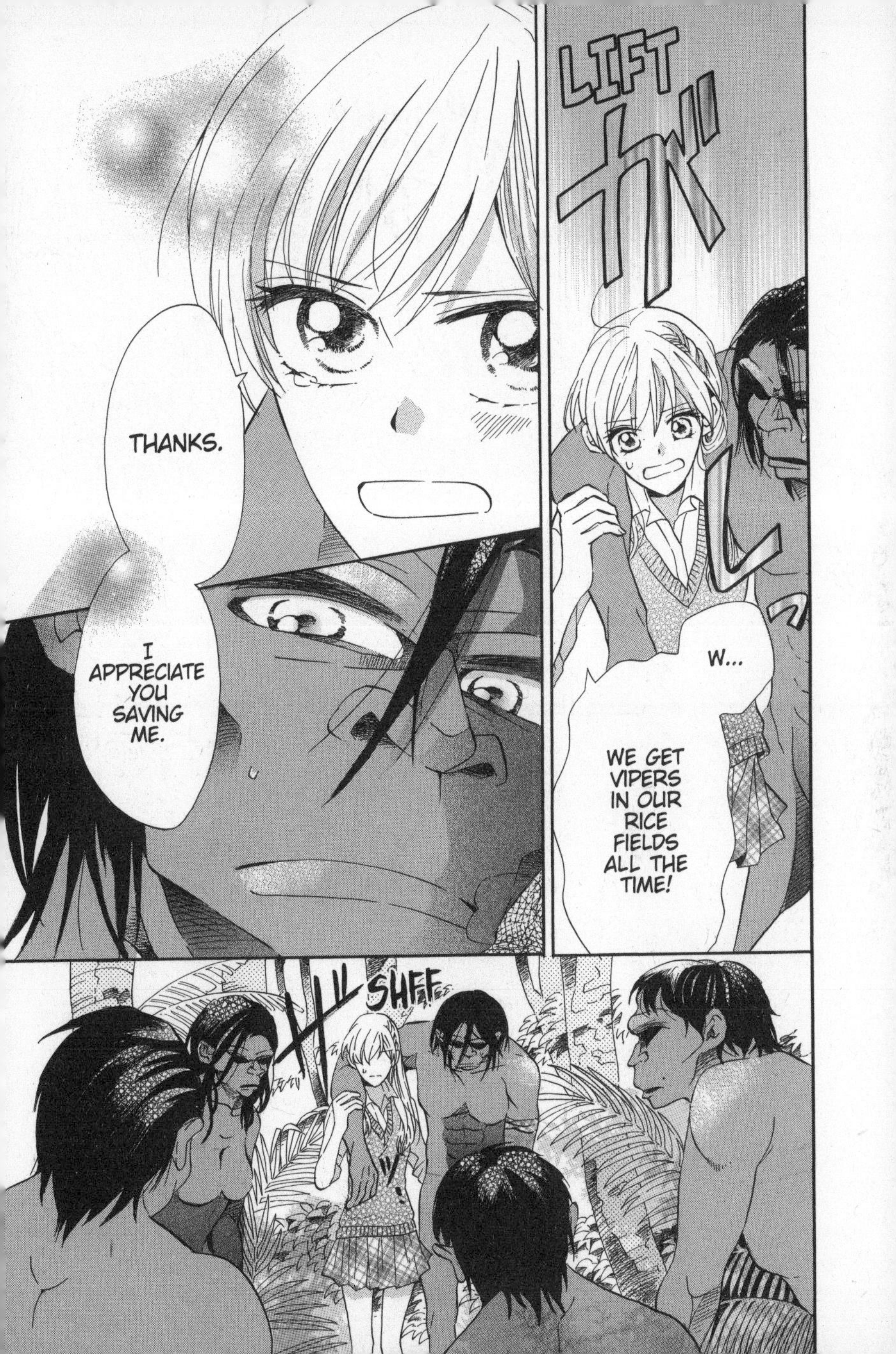
LIFT
W...
WE GET VIPERS IN OUR RICE FIELDS ALL THE TIME!
THANKS.
I APPRECIATE YOU SAVING ME.
SHFF

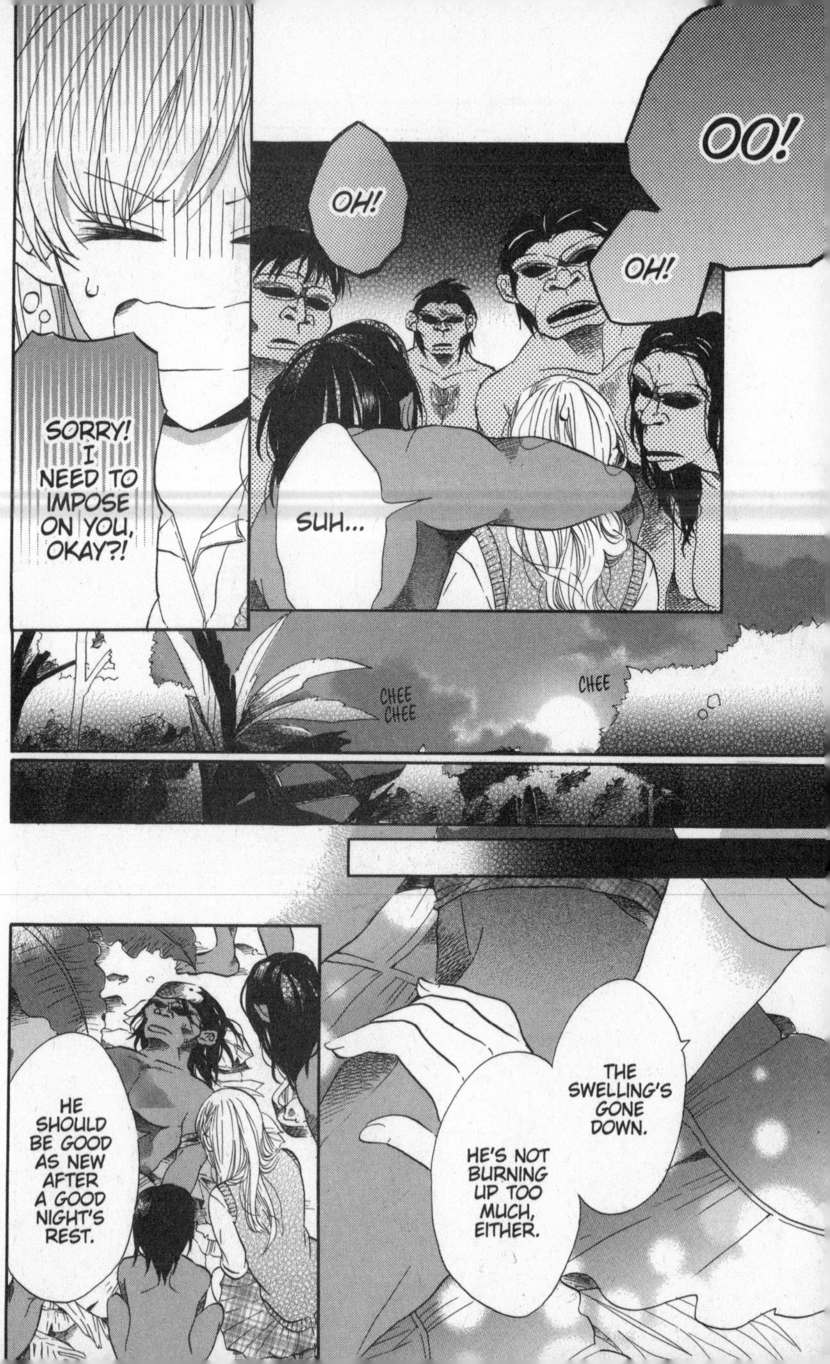
OO!
OH!
OH!
SUH...
SORRY! I NEED TO IMPOSE ON YOU, OKAY?!
CHEE
CHEE CHEE
THE SWELLING'S GONE DOWN.
HE'S NOT BURNING UP TOO MUCH, EITHER.
HE SHOULD BE GOOD AS NEW AFTER A GOOD NIGHT'S REST.

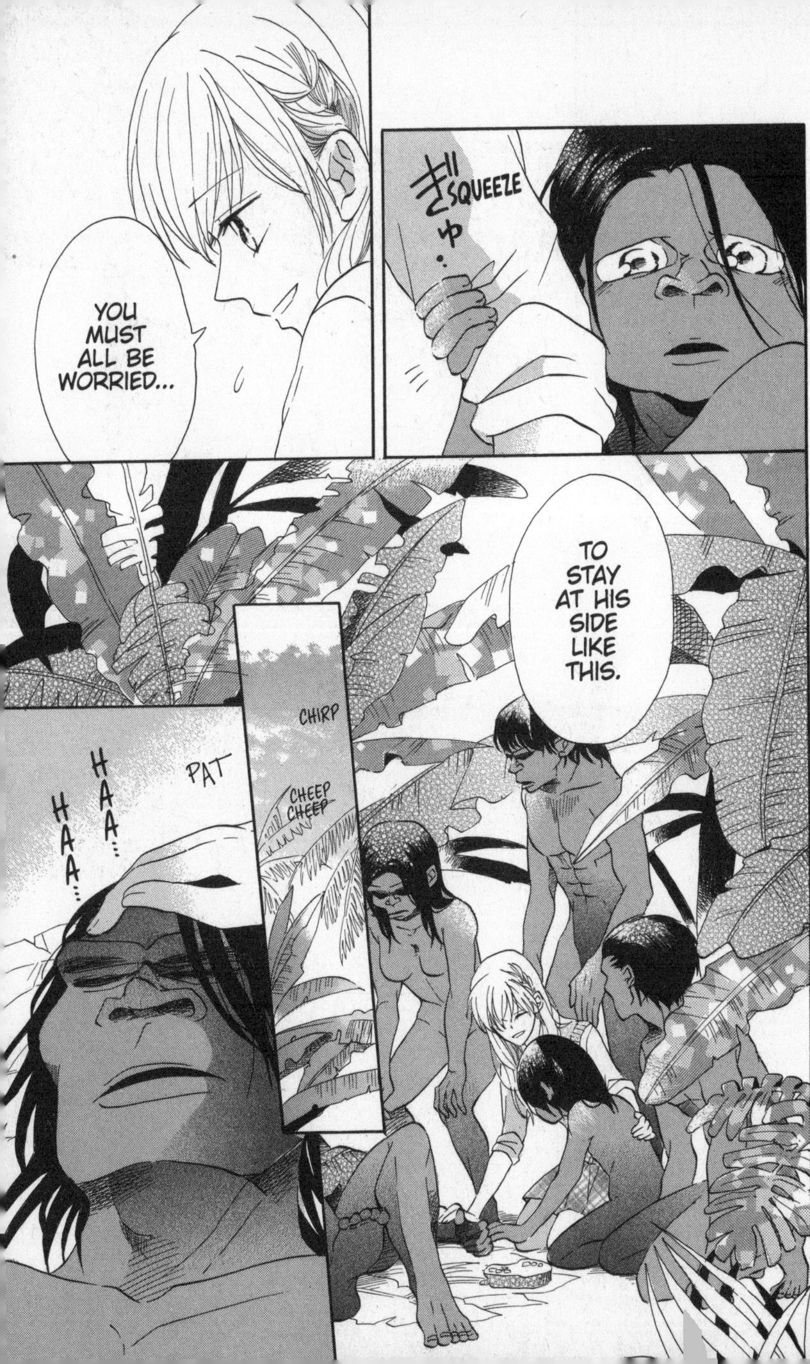
ぎゅ
SQUEEZE
YOU MUST ALL BE WORRIED...
TO STAY AT HIS SIDE LIKE THIS.
CHIRP
CHEEP CHEEP
HAA HAA...
HAA...
PAT

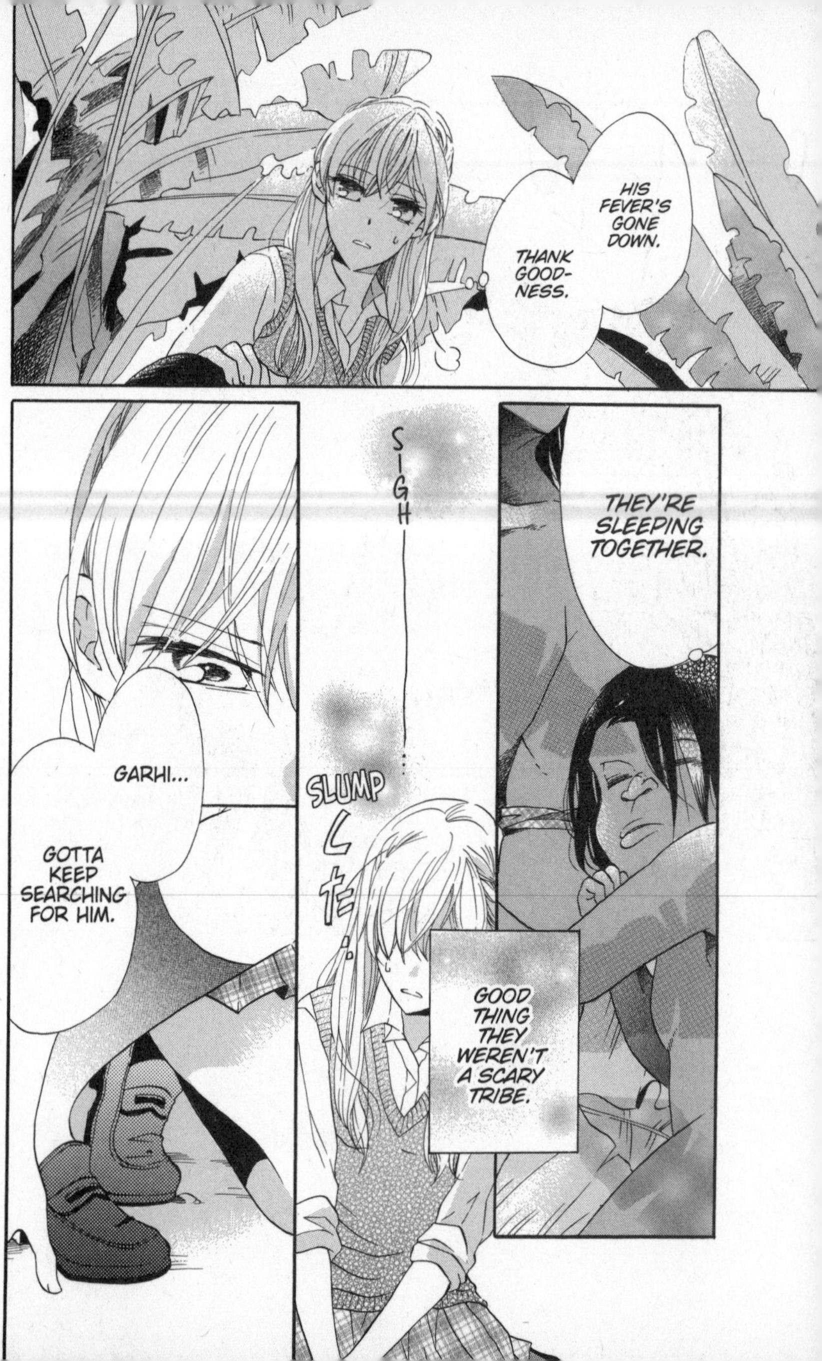
HIS FEVER'S GONE DOWN.
THANK GOODNESS.
THEY'RE SLEEPING TOGETHER.
GOOD THING THEY WEREN'T A SCARY TRIBE.
SIGH...
SLUMP
GARHI...
GOTTA KEEP SEARCHING FOR HIM.

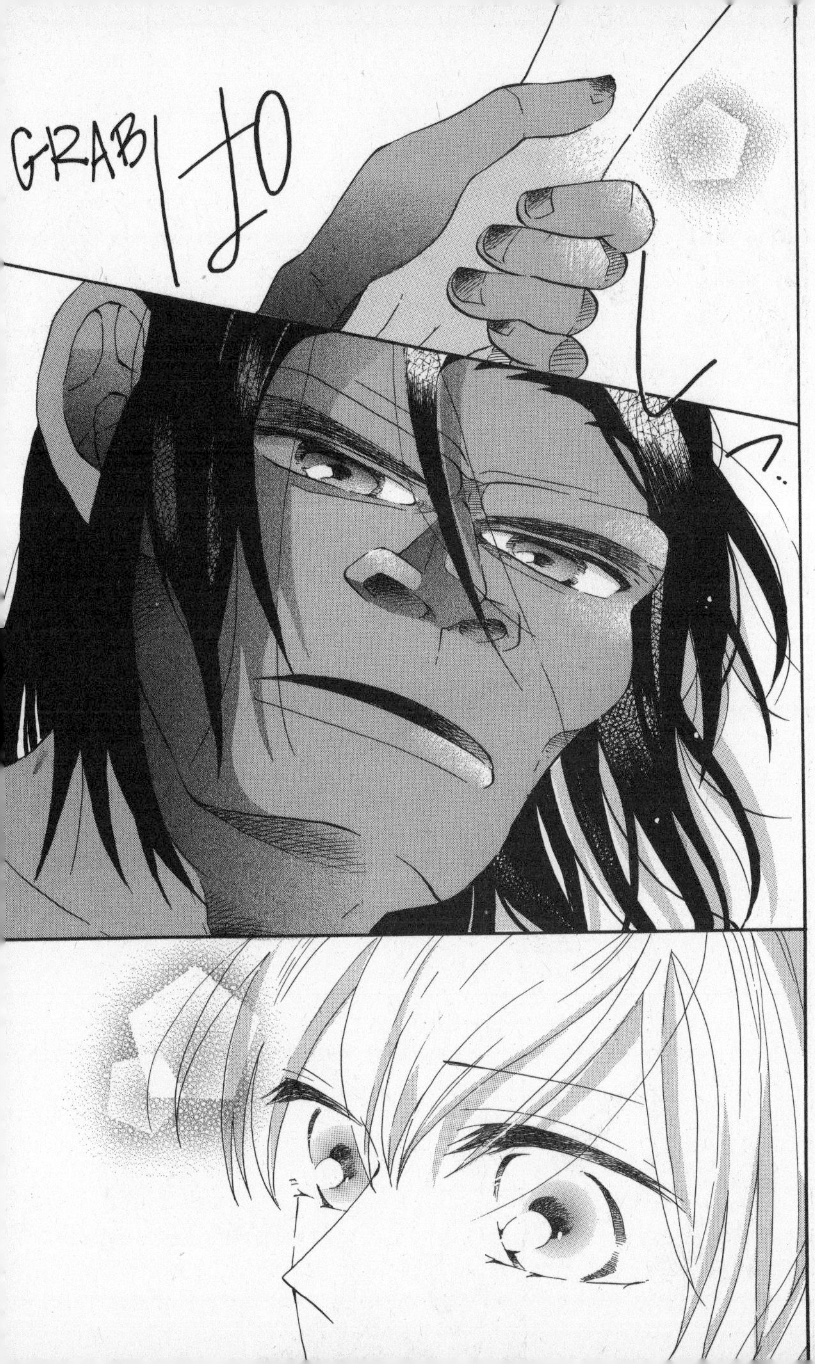
GRAB!

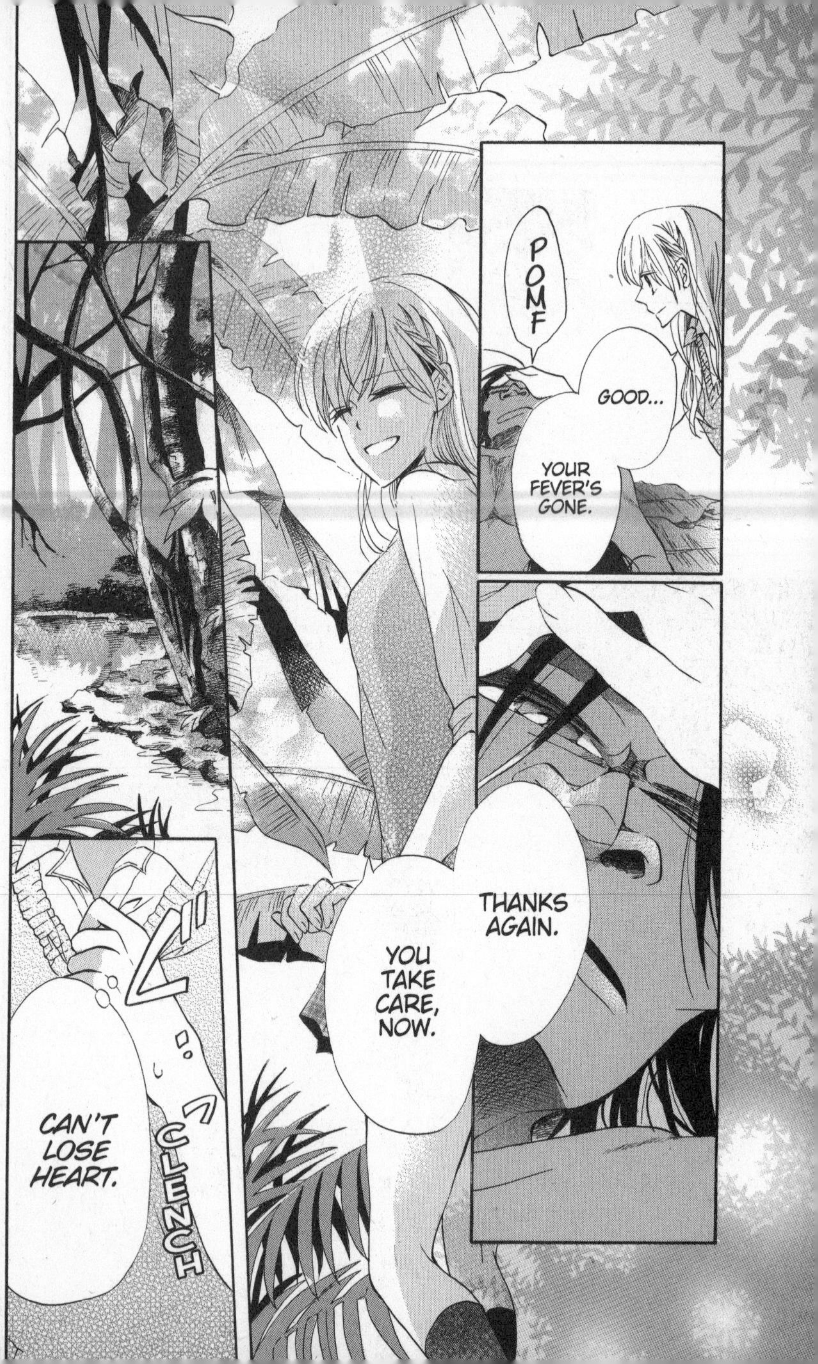
POMF
GOOD...
YOUR FEVER'S GONE.
THANKS AGAIN.
YOU TAKE CARE, NOW.
CLENCH
CAN'T LOSE HEART.

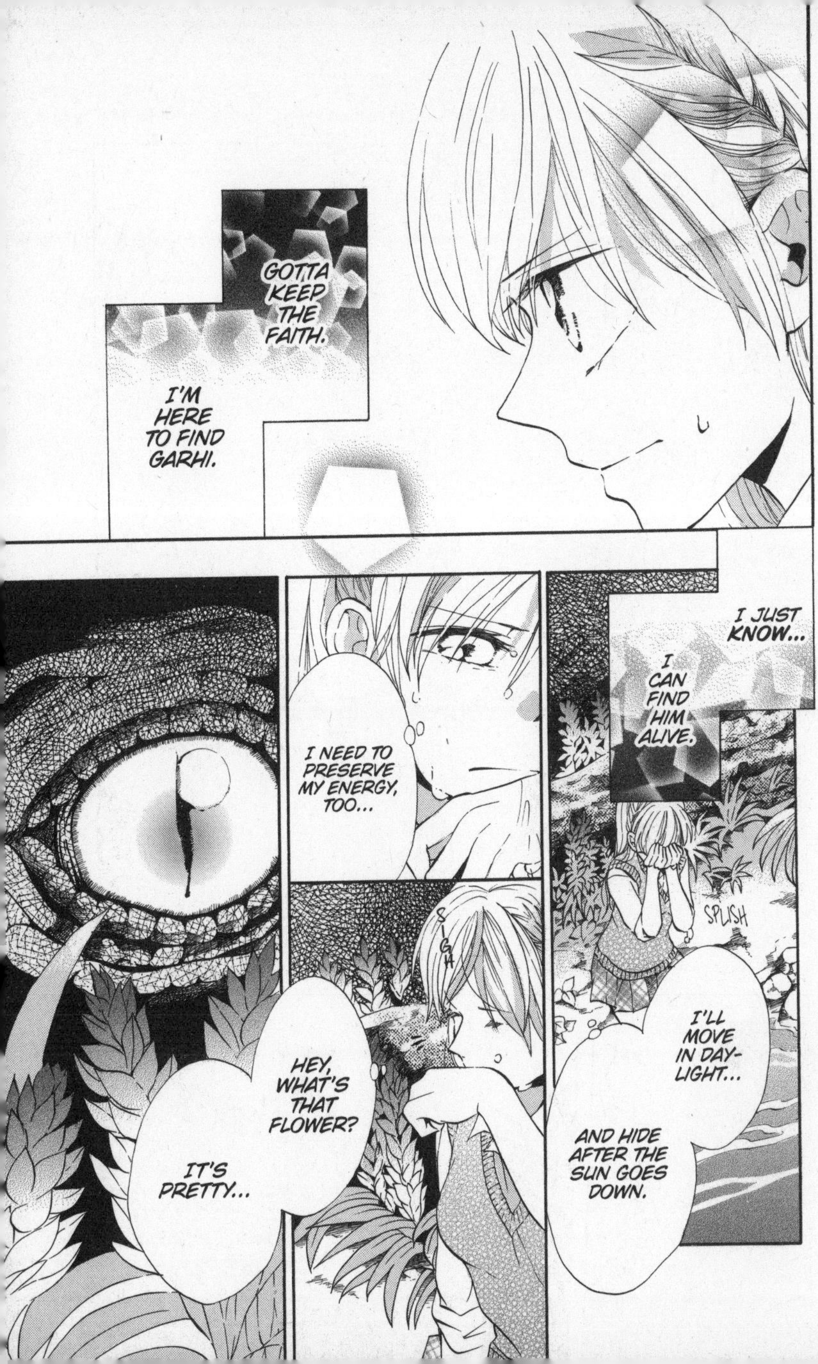
GOTTA KEEP THE FAITH.
I'M HERE TO FIND GARHI.
I JUST KNOW...
I CAN FIND HIM ALIVE.
SPLISH
I'LL MOVE IN DAY-LIGHT...
AND HIDE AFTER THE SUN GOES DOWN.
I NEED TO PRESERVE MY ENERGY, TOO...
SIGH
HEY, WHAT'S THAT FLOWER?
IT'S PRETTY...

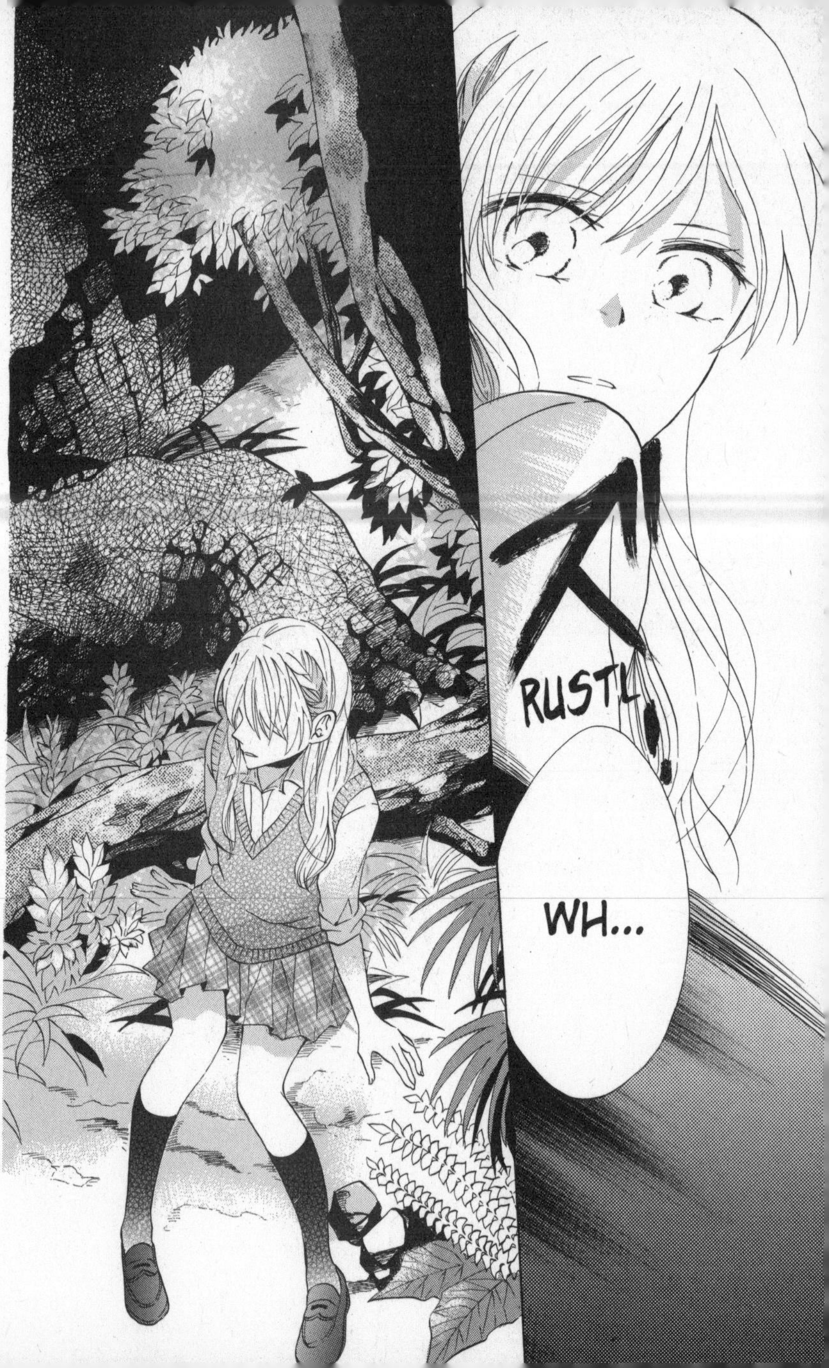
RUSTL
WH...

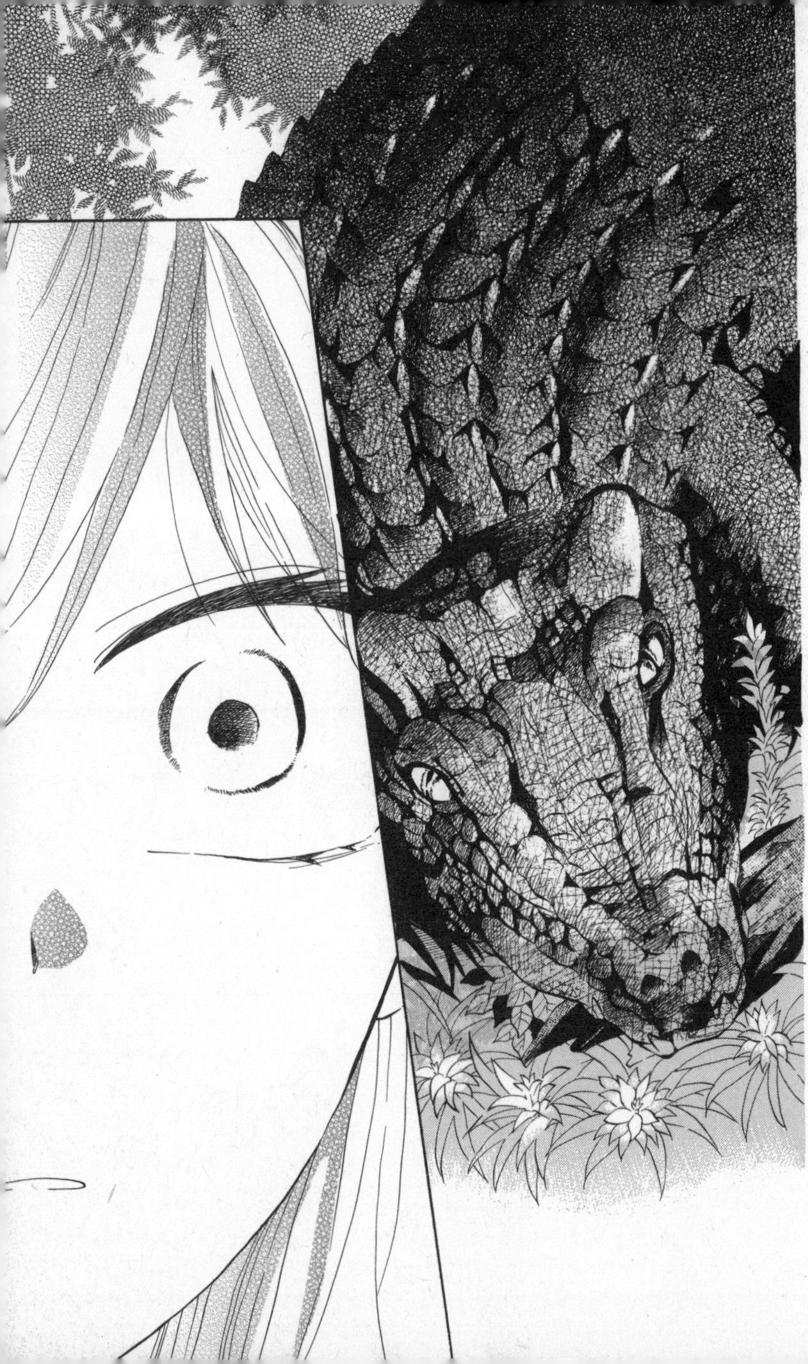

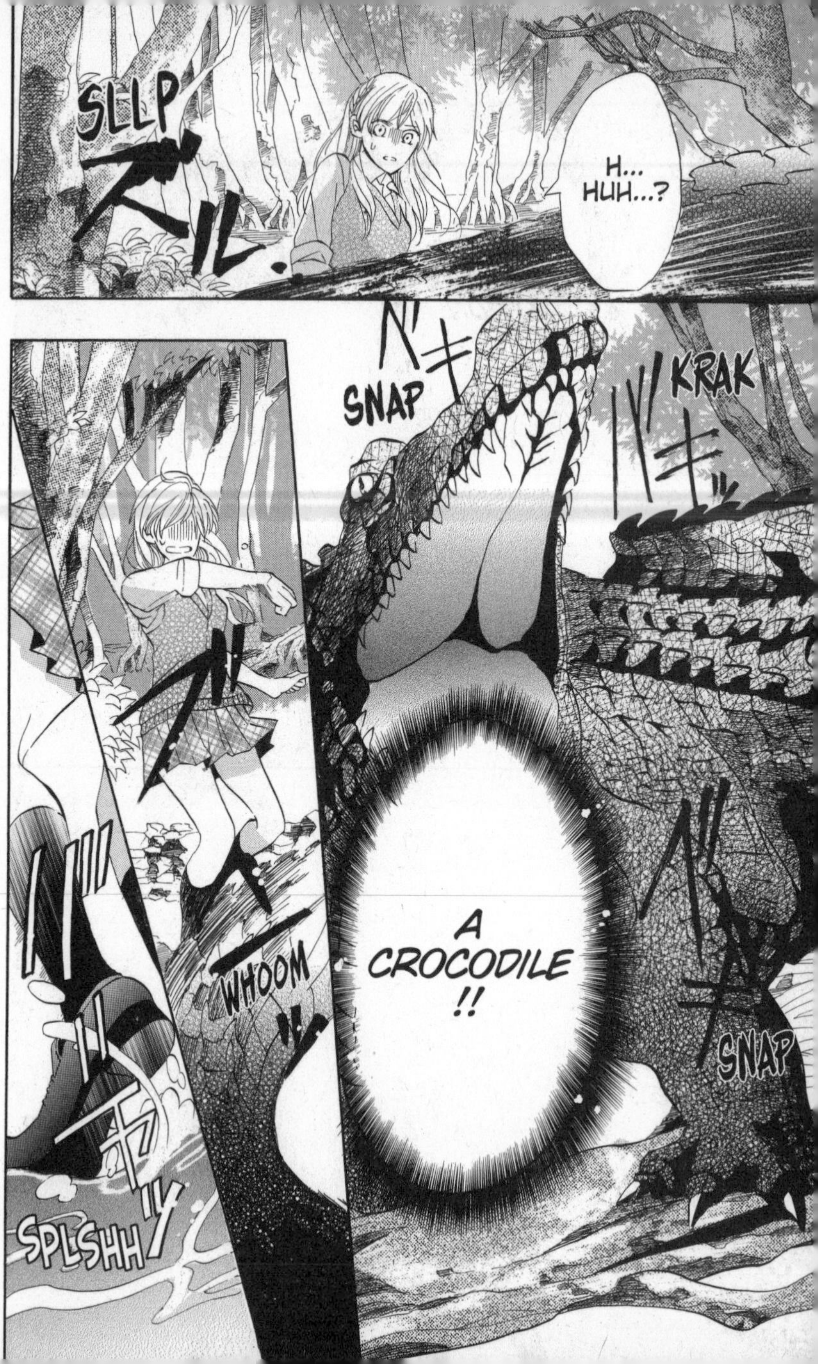
H... HUH...?
SLLP
SNAP
KRAK
A CROCODILE!!
SNAP
WHOOM
SPLSHH

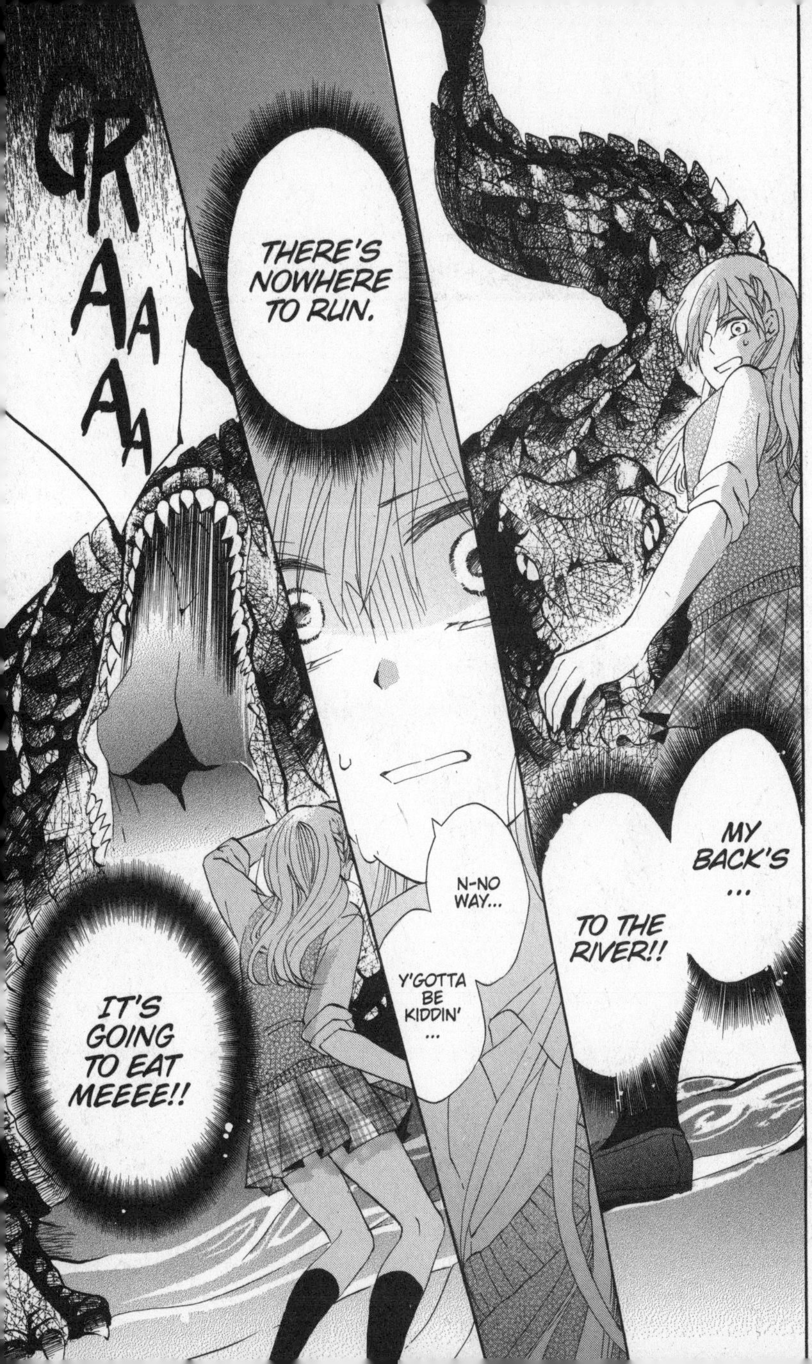
MY BACK'S ...
TO THE RIVER!!
THERE'S NOWHERE TO RUN.
N-NO WAY...
Y'GOTTA BE KIDDIN' ...
GRAAAAA
IT'S GOING TO EAT MEEEE!!

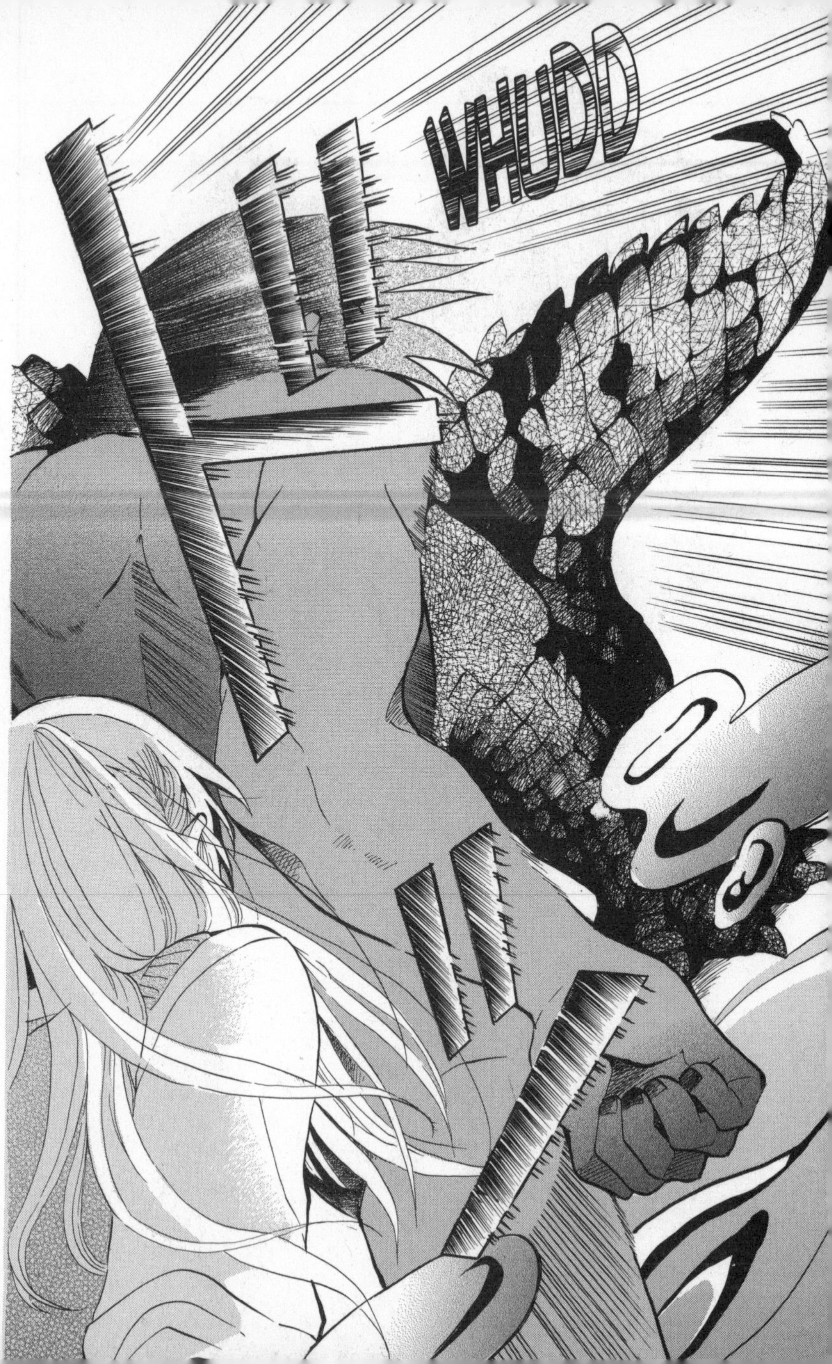
WHUDD

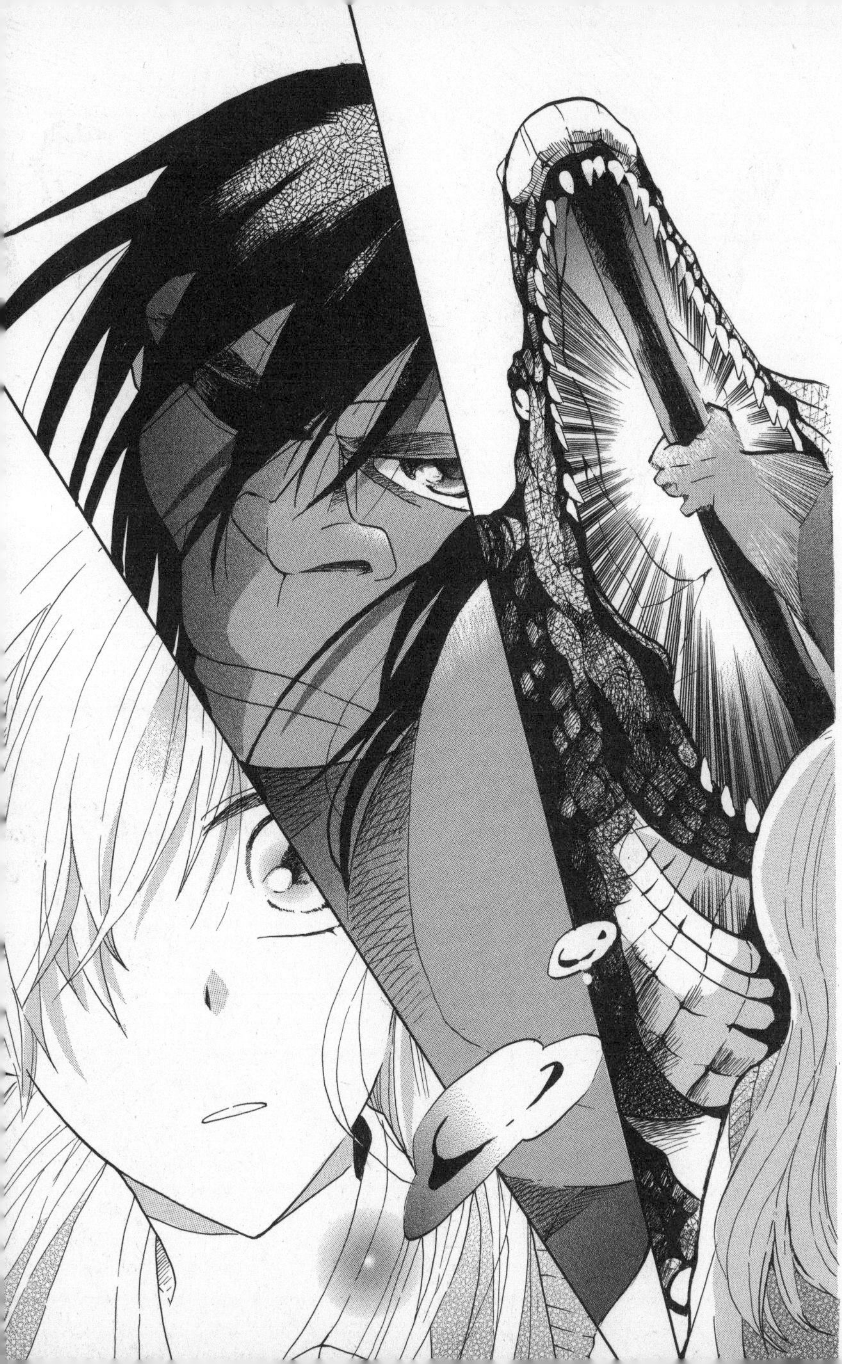

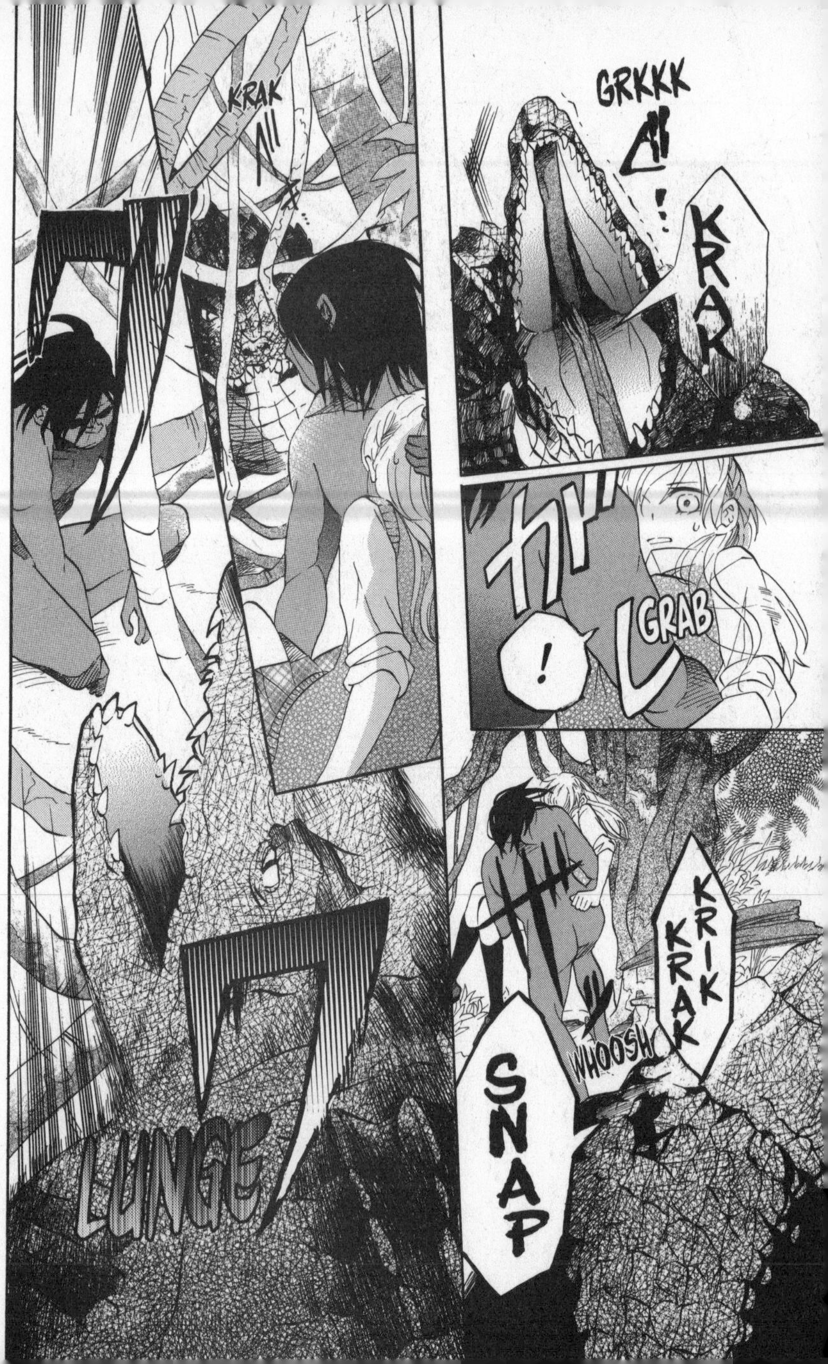
GRKKK
KRAK
!
GRAB
KRIK KRAK
WHOOSH
SNAP
KRAK
LUNGE

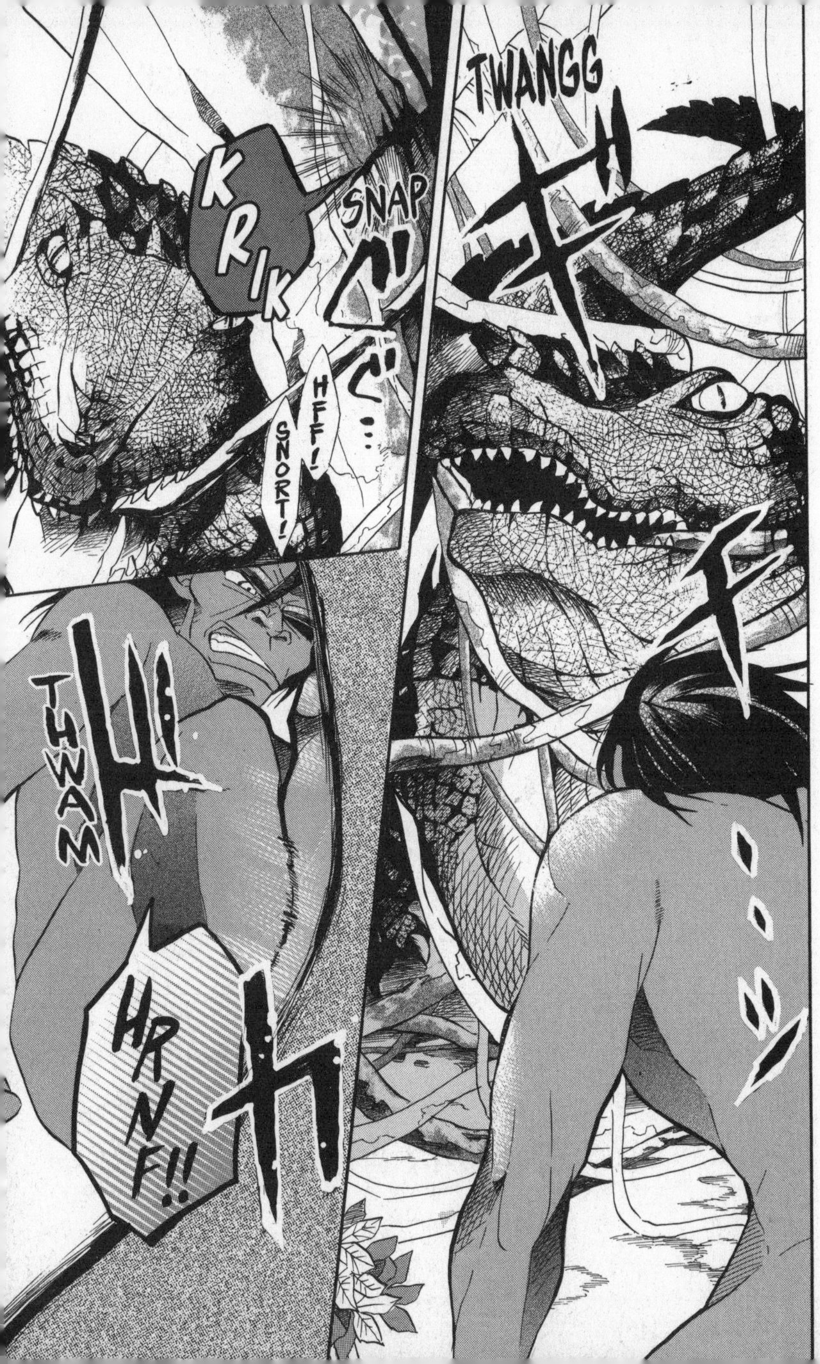
TWANGG
SNAP
KRIK
HFF!
SNORT!
THWAM
HRNF!!

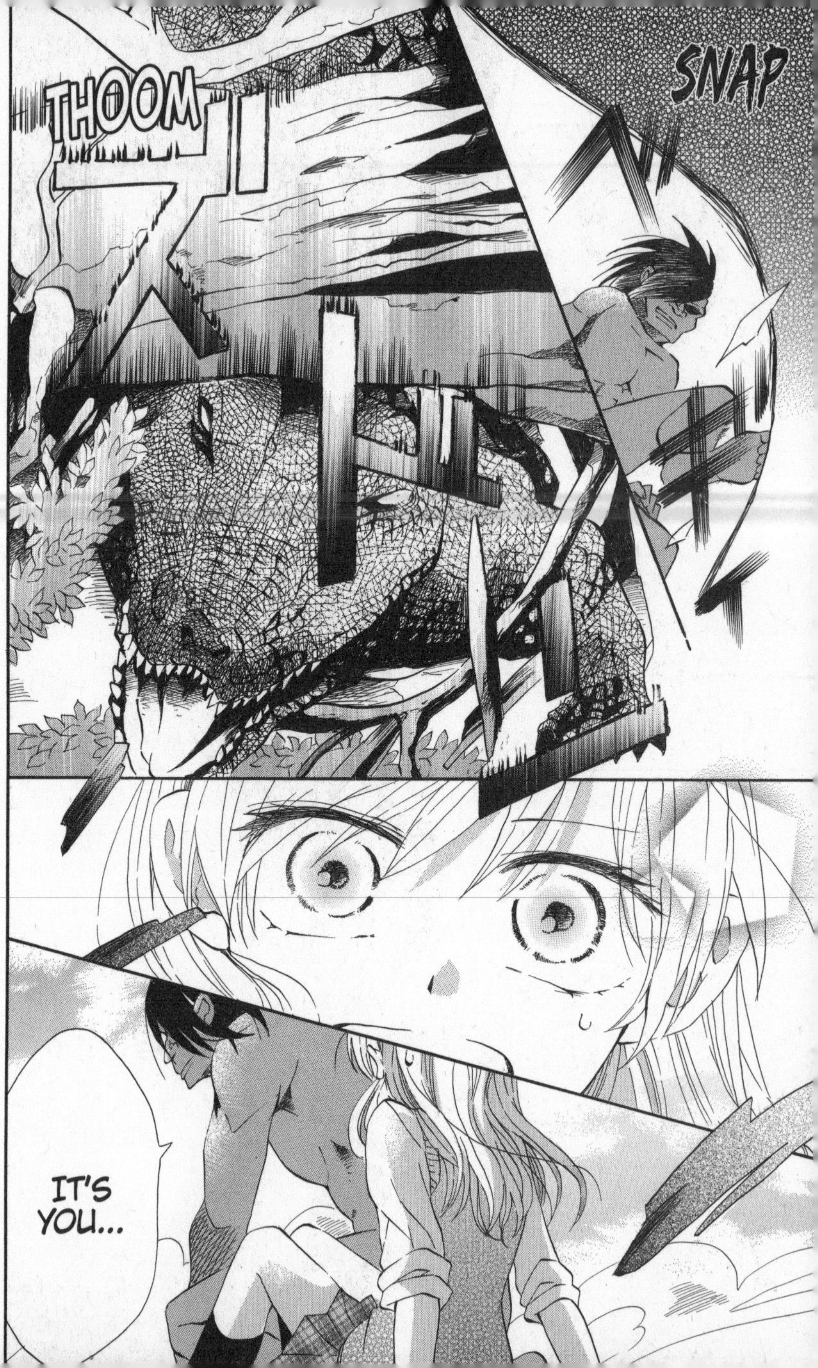
SNAP
THOOM
IT'S YOU...

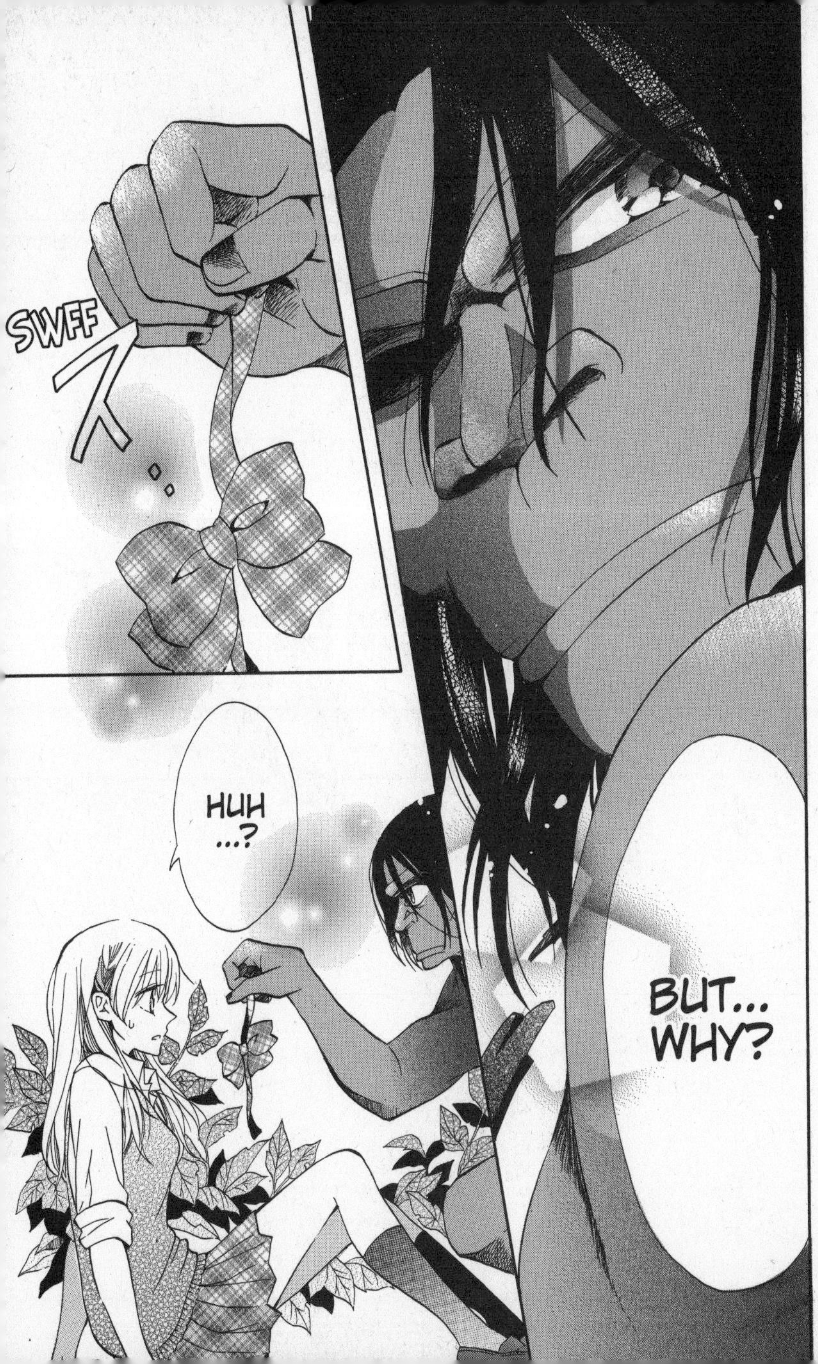
BUT... WHY?
SWFF
HUH ...?

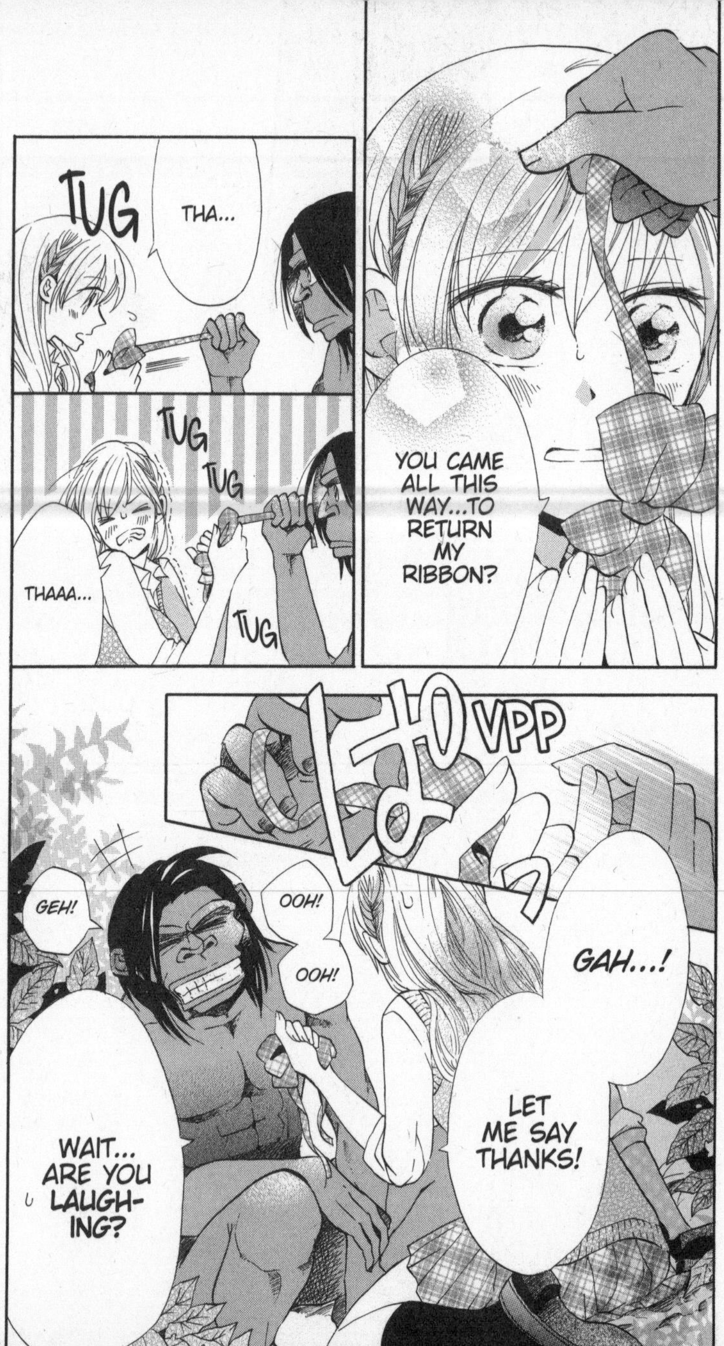
YOU CAME ALL THIS WAY...TO RETURN MY RIBBON?
TUG
THA...
TUG
TUG
THAAA...
TUG
VPP
GAH...!
LET ME SAY THANKS!
OOH!
OOH!
GEH!
WAIT... ARE YOU LAUGH-ING?

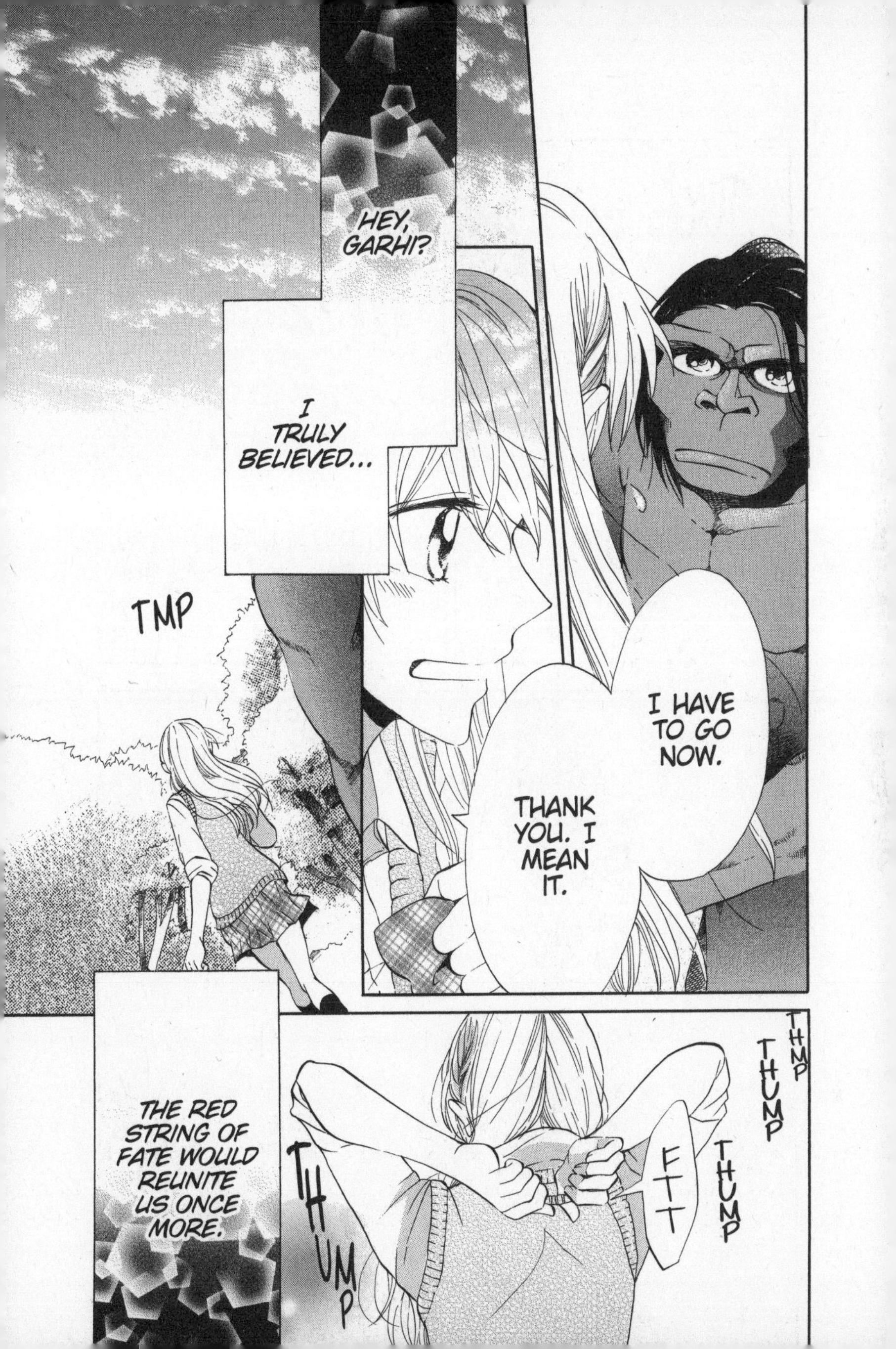
I HAVE TO GO NOW.
THANK YOU. I MEAN IT.
HEY, GARHI?
I TRULY BELIEVED...
TMP
THMP
THUMP
THUMP
FTT
THUMP
THE RED STRING OF FATE WOULD REUNITE US ONCE MORE.

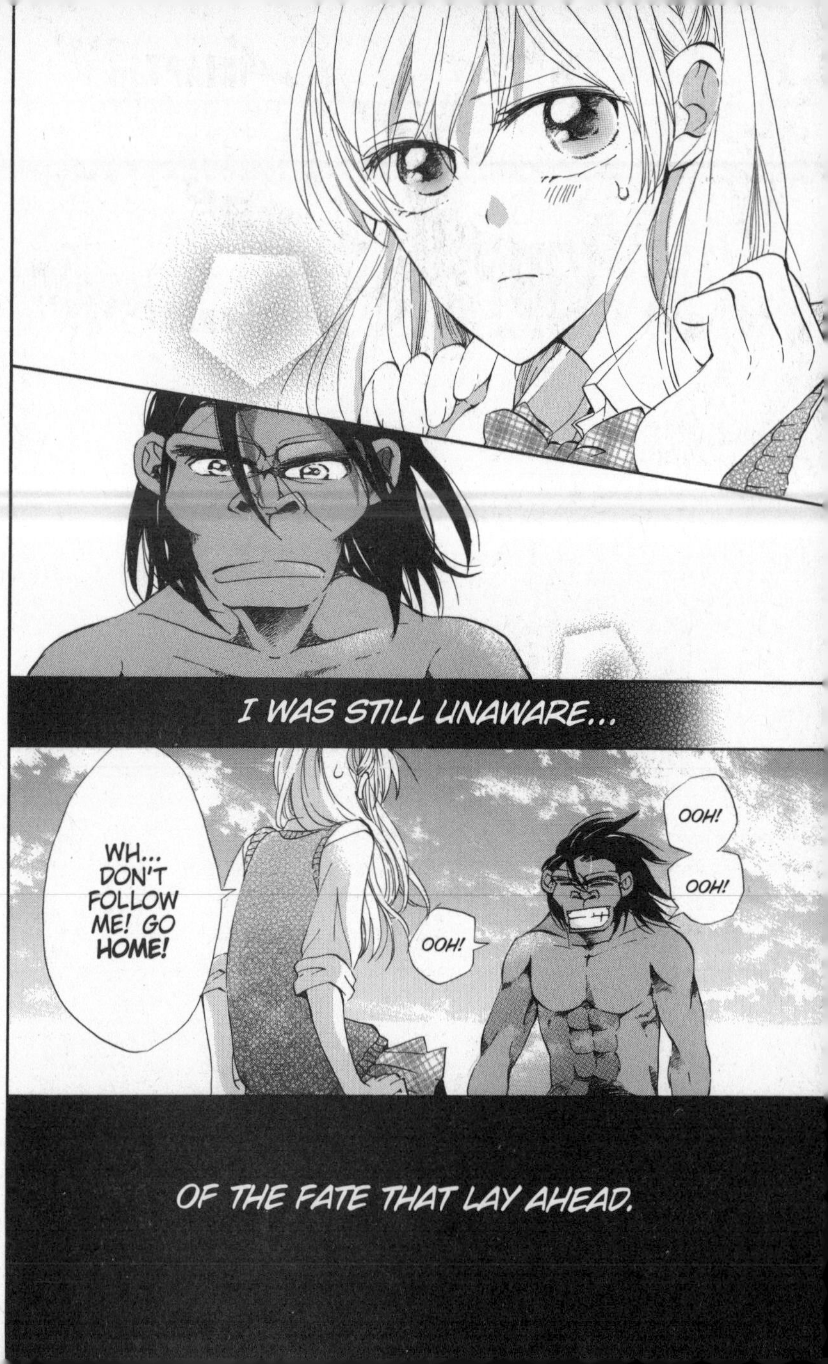
I WAS STILL UNAWARE...
OOH!
OOH!
OOH!
WH... DON'T FOLLOW ME! GO HOME!
OF THE FATE THAT LAY AHEAD.

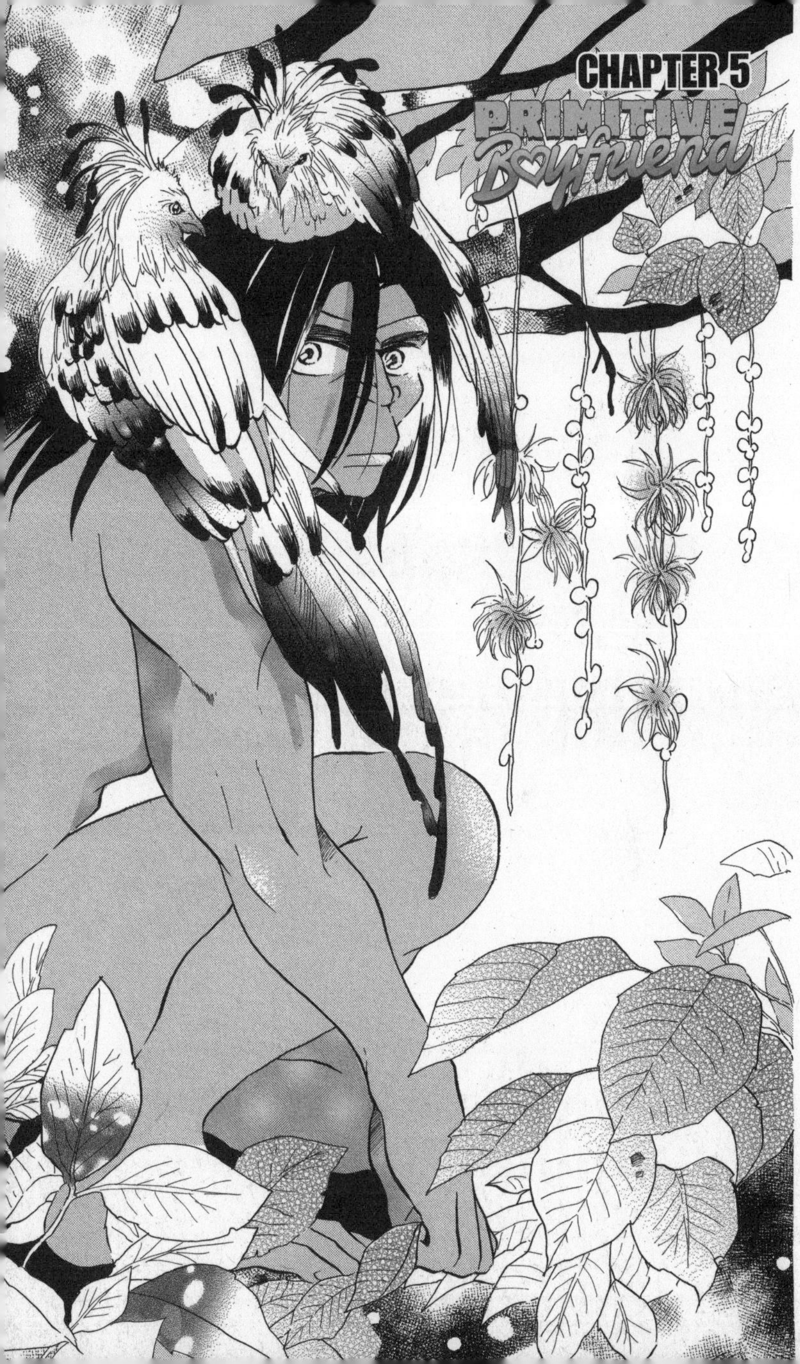
CHAPTER 5
PRIMITIVE
Boyfriend

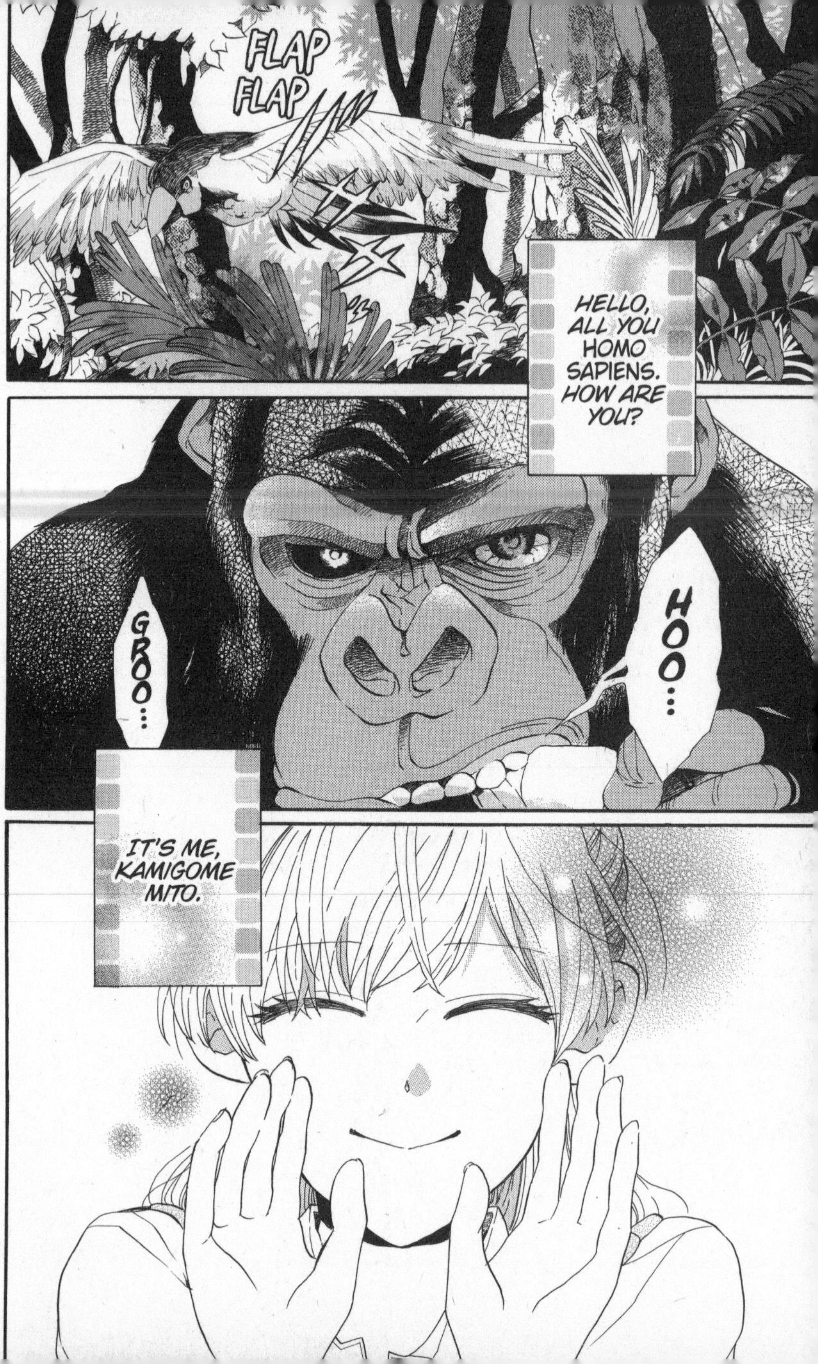
FLAP FLAP
HELLO, ALL YOU HOMO SAPIENS. HOW ARE YOU?
HOO...
GROO...
IT'S ME, KAMIGOME MITO.

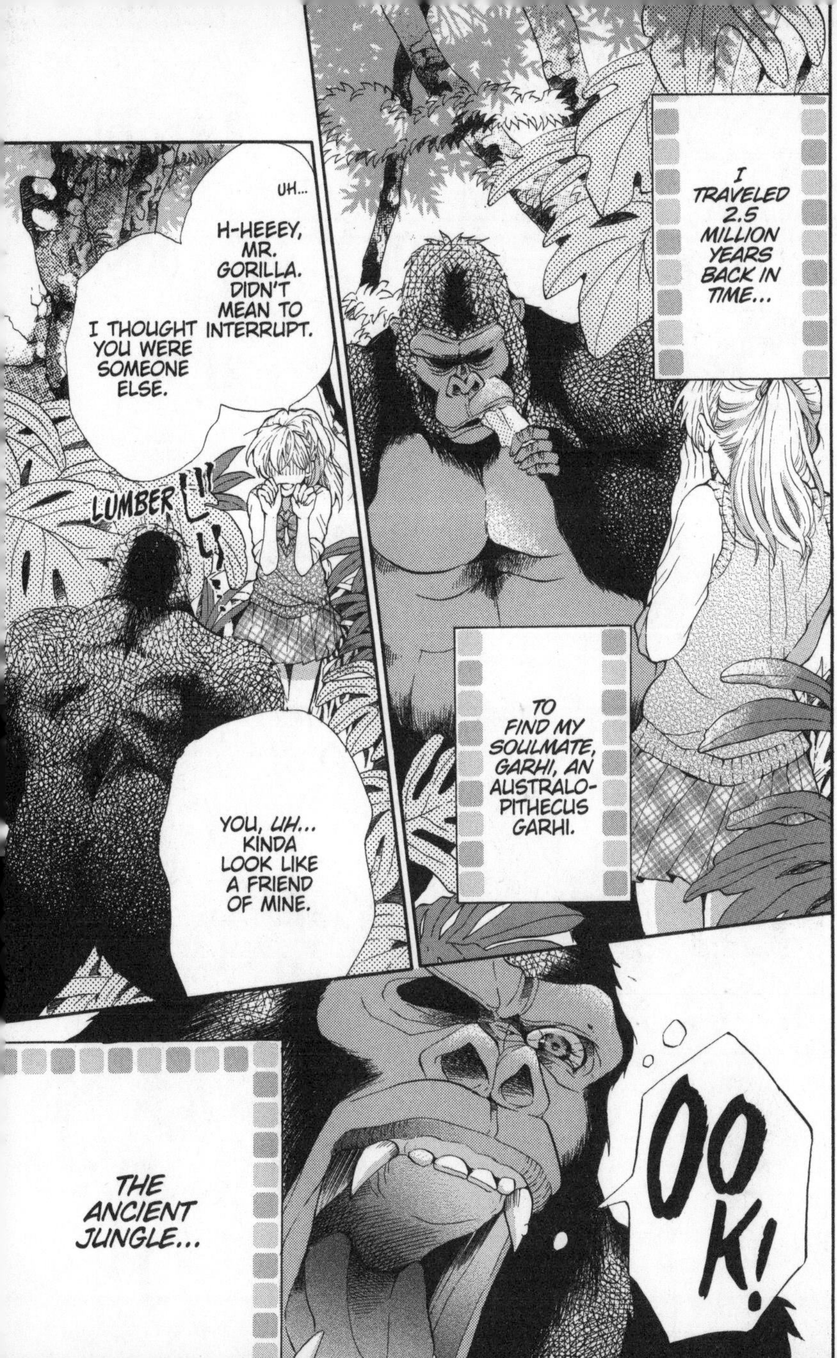
I TRAVELED 2.5 MILLION YEARS BACK IN TIME...
TO FIND MY SOULMATE, GARHI, AN AUSTRALOPITHECUS GARHI.
UH...
H-HEEEY, MR. GORILLA. DIDN'T MEAN TO INTERRUPT.
I THOUGHT YOU WERE SOMEONE ELSE.
LUMBER
YOU, UH... KINDA LOOK LIKE A FRIEND OF MINE.
OOK!
THE ANCIENT JUNGLE...

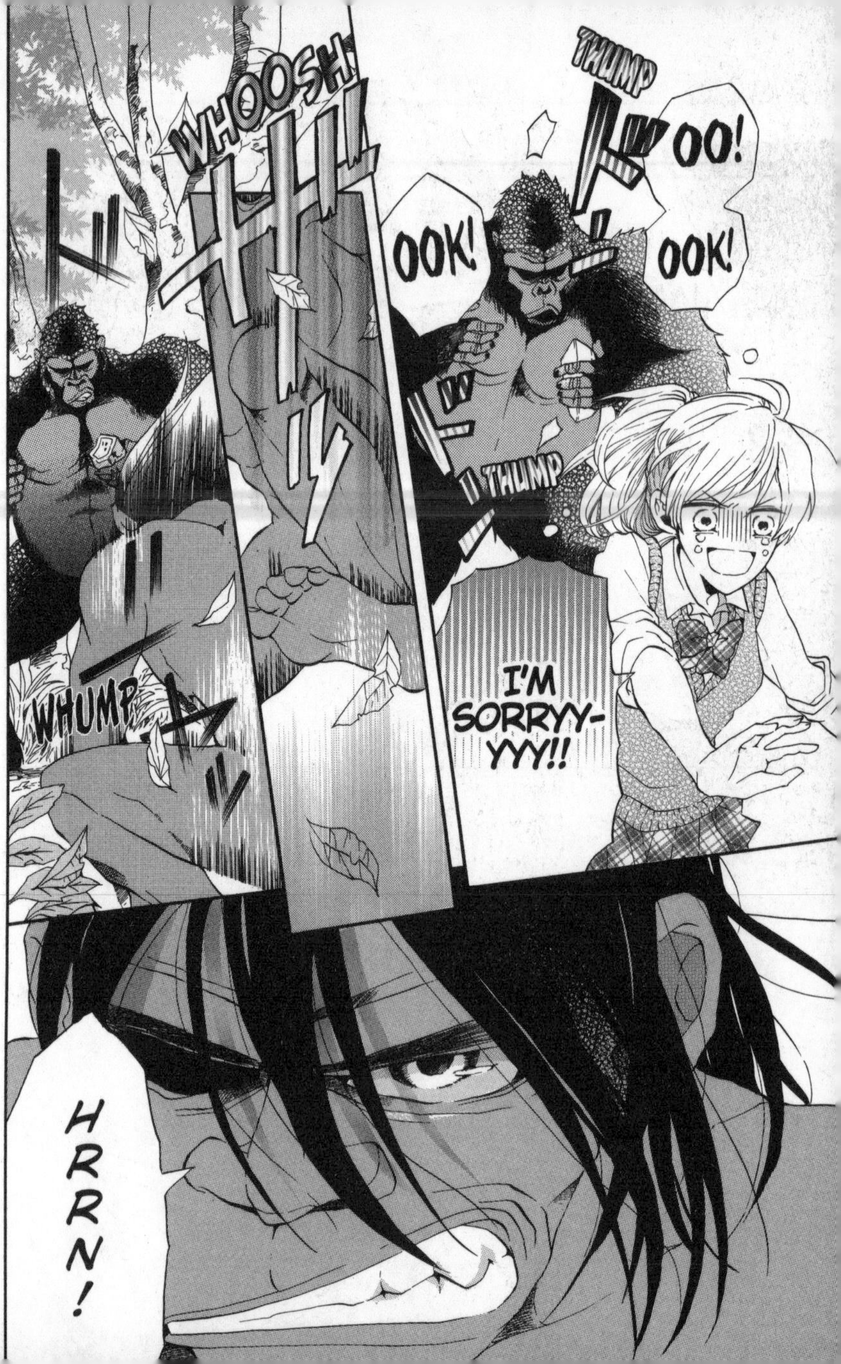
THUMP
OO!
OOK!
OOK!
THUMP
I'M SORRYY-YYY!!
WHOOSH
WHUMP
HRRN!

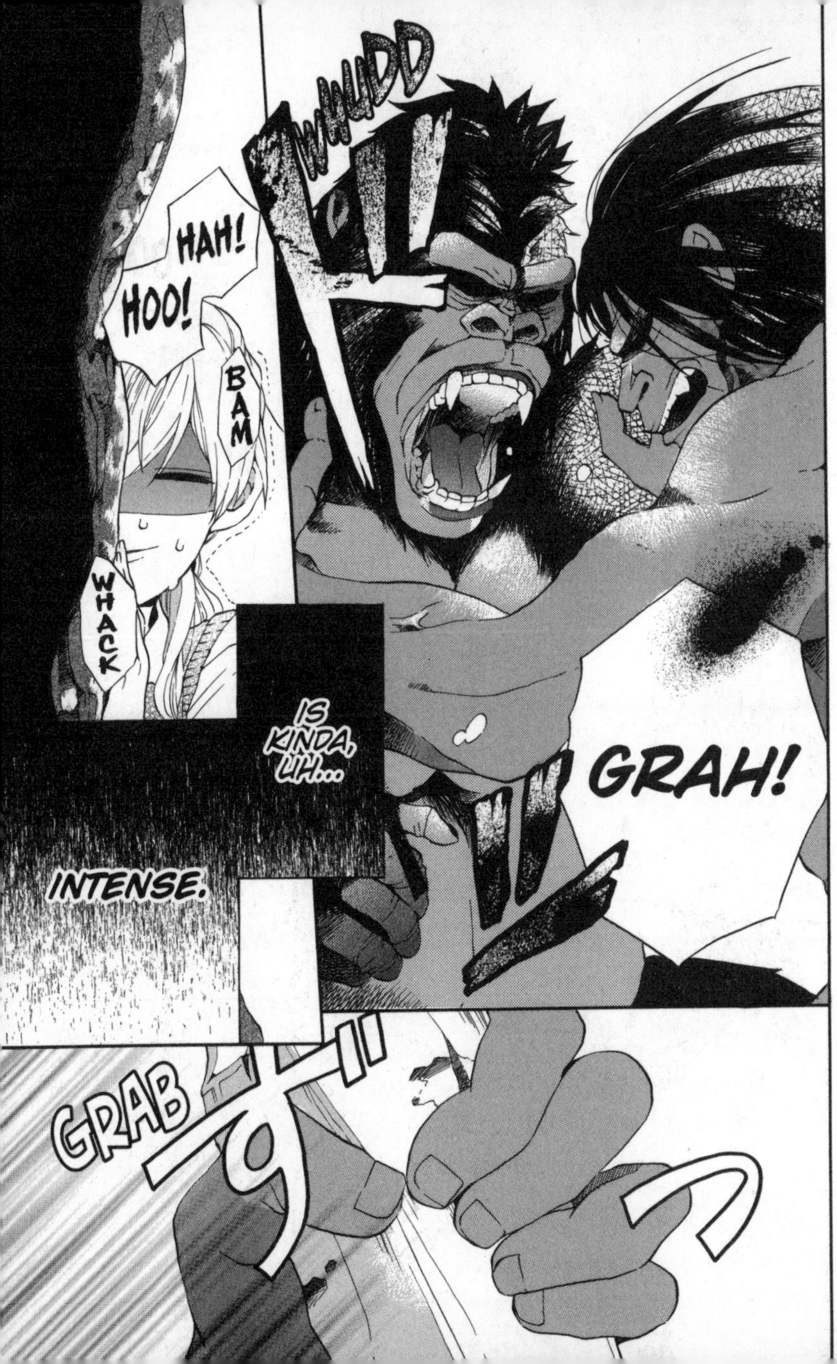
WHUDD
GRAH!
HAH!
HOO!
BAM
WHACK
IS KINDA, UH...
INTENSE.
GRAB

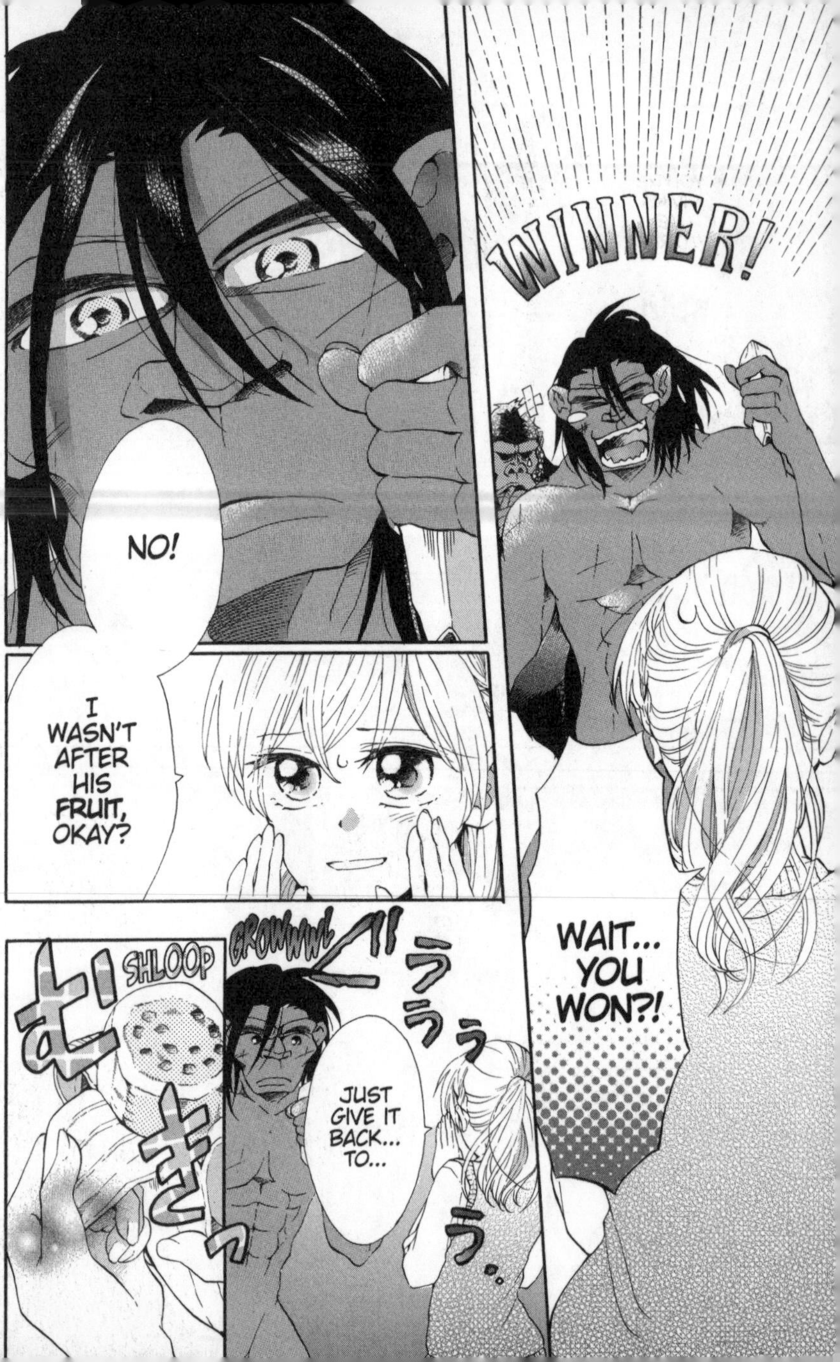
WINNER!
WAIT... YOU WON?!
NO!
I WASN'T AFTER HIS FRUIT, OKAY?
GROWWWL
うううう
JUST GIVE IT BACK... TO...
SHLOOP
むきっ

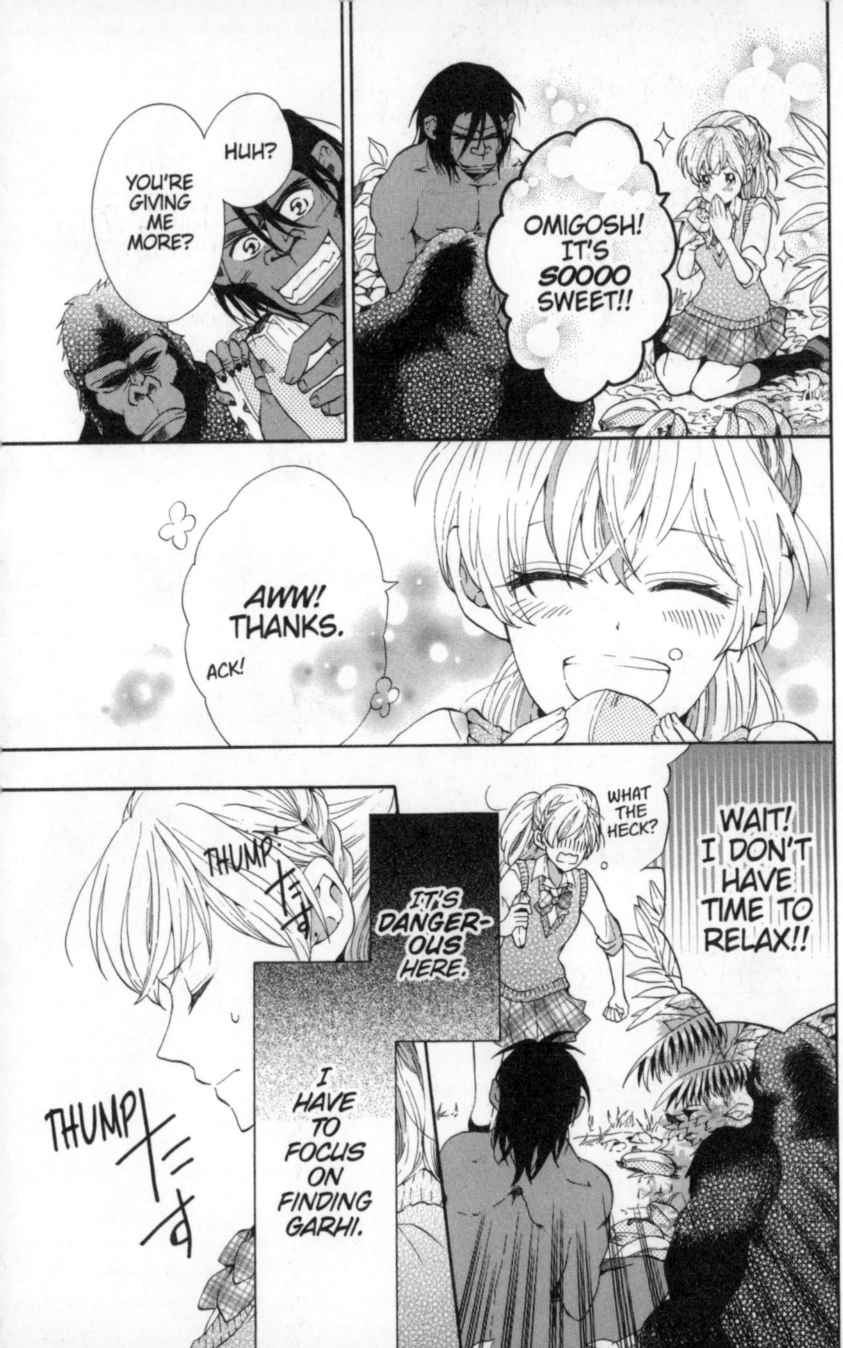

OMIGOSH! IT'S SOOOO SWEET!!
HUH?
YOU'RE GIVING ME MORE?
AWW! THANKS.
ACK!
WAIT! I DON'T HAVE TIME TO RELAX!!
WHAT THE HECK?
IT'S DANGER-OUS HERE.
I HAVE TO FOCUS ON FINDING GARHI.
THUMP
THUMP

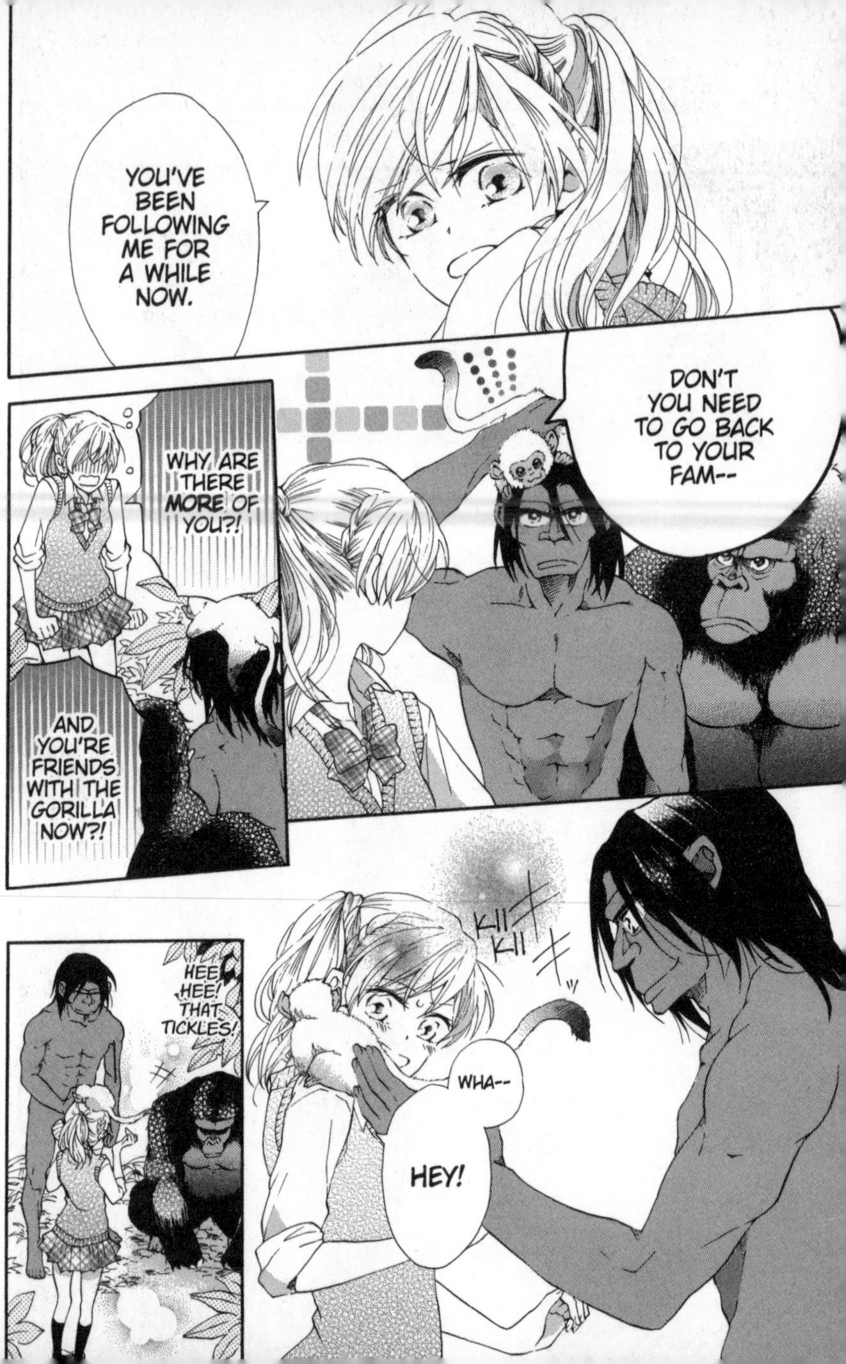
YOU'VE BEEN FOLLOWING ME FOR A WHILE NOW.
DON'T YOU NEED TO GO BACK TO YOUR FAM--
WHY ARE THERE MORE OF YOU?!
AND YOU'RE FRIENDS WITH THE GORILLA NOW?!
KII KII
WHA--
HEY!
HEE HEE! THAT TICKLES!

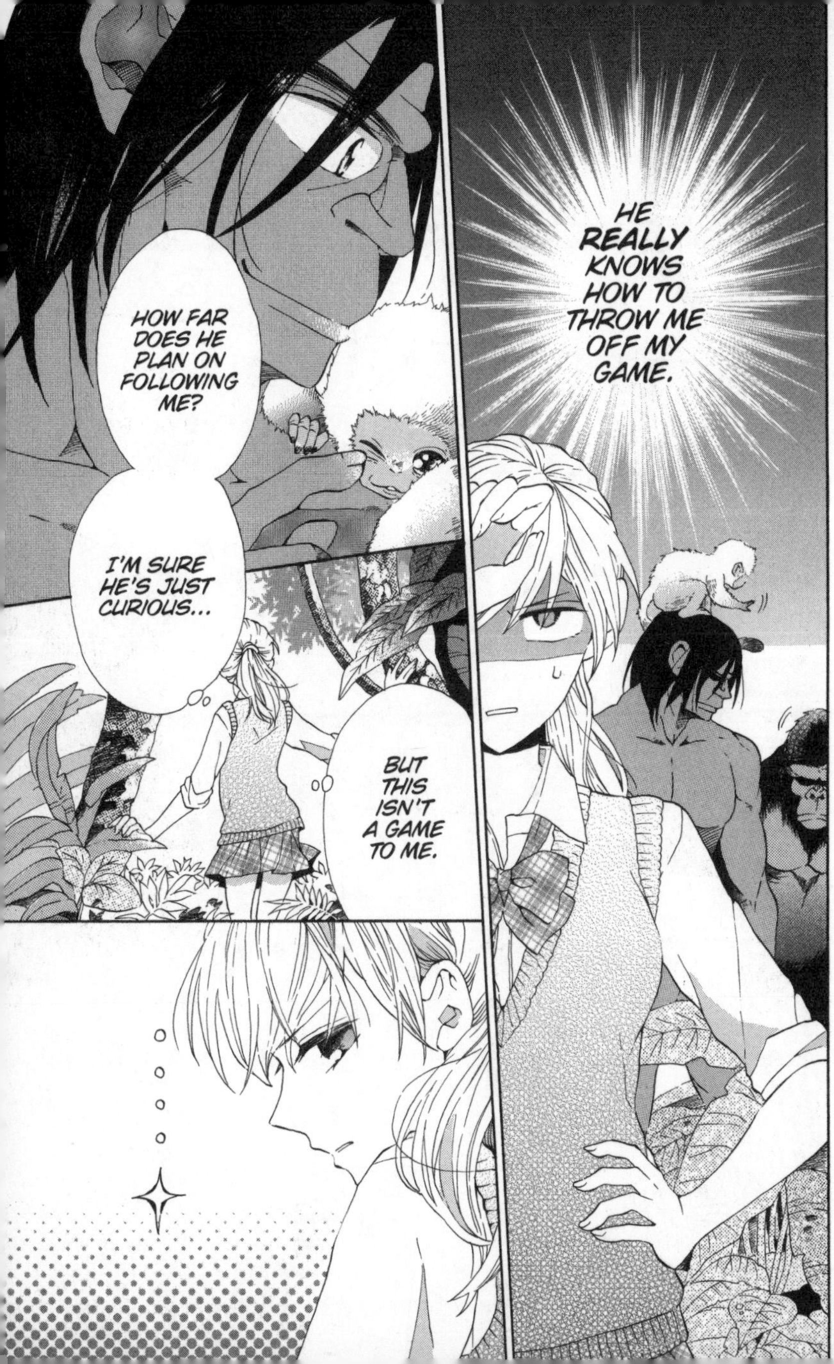
HE REALLY KNOWS HOW TO THROW ME OFF MY GAME.
HOW FAR DOES HE PLAN ON FOLLOWING ME?
I'M SURE HE'S JUST CURIOUS...
BUT THIS ISN'T A GAME TO ME.

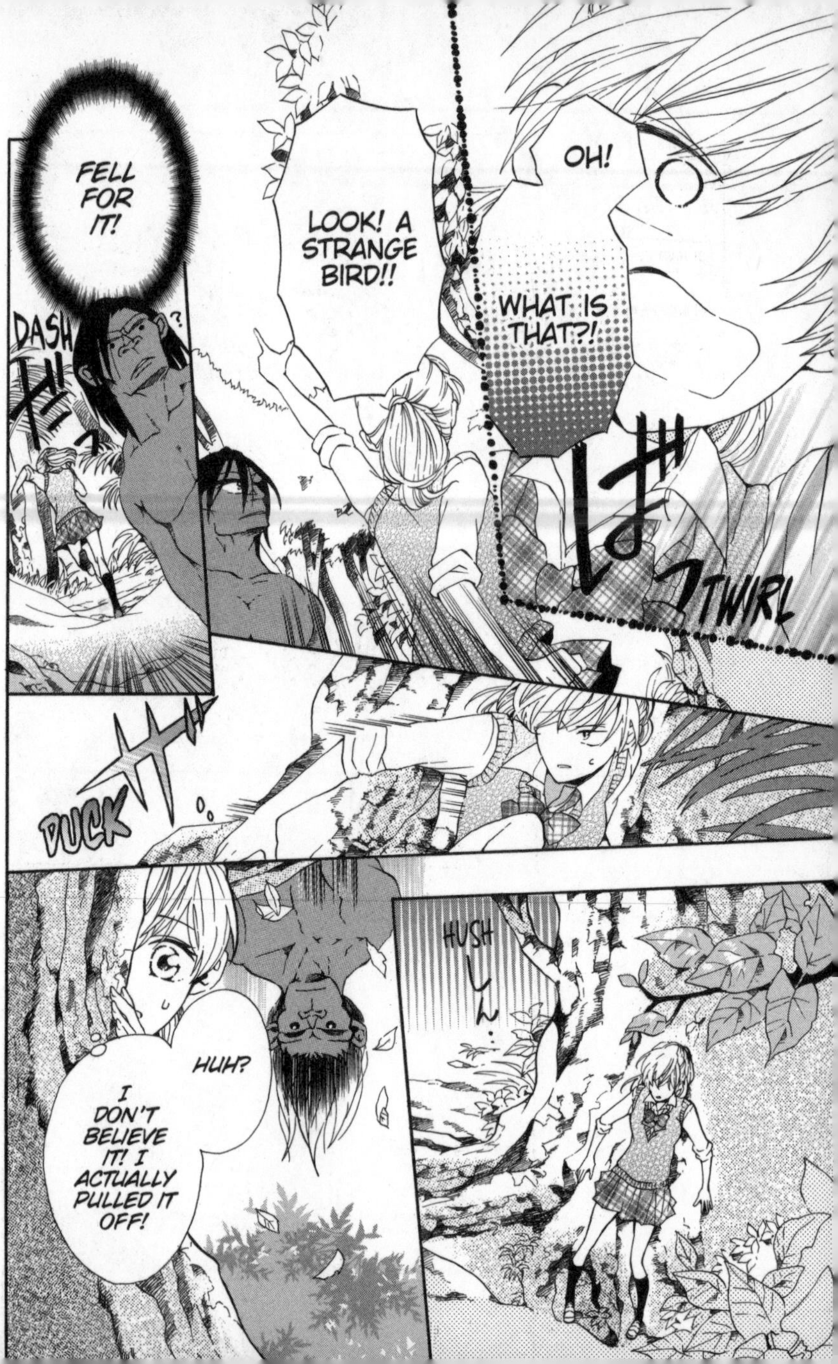
LOOK! A STRANGE BIRD!!
OH!
WHAT IS THAT?!
TWIRL
FELL FOR IT!
DASH
?
DUCK
HUSH
HUH?
I DON'T BELIEVE IT! I ACTUALLY PULLED IT OFF!

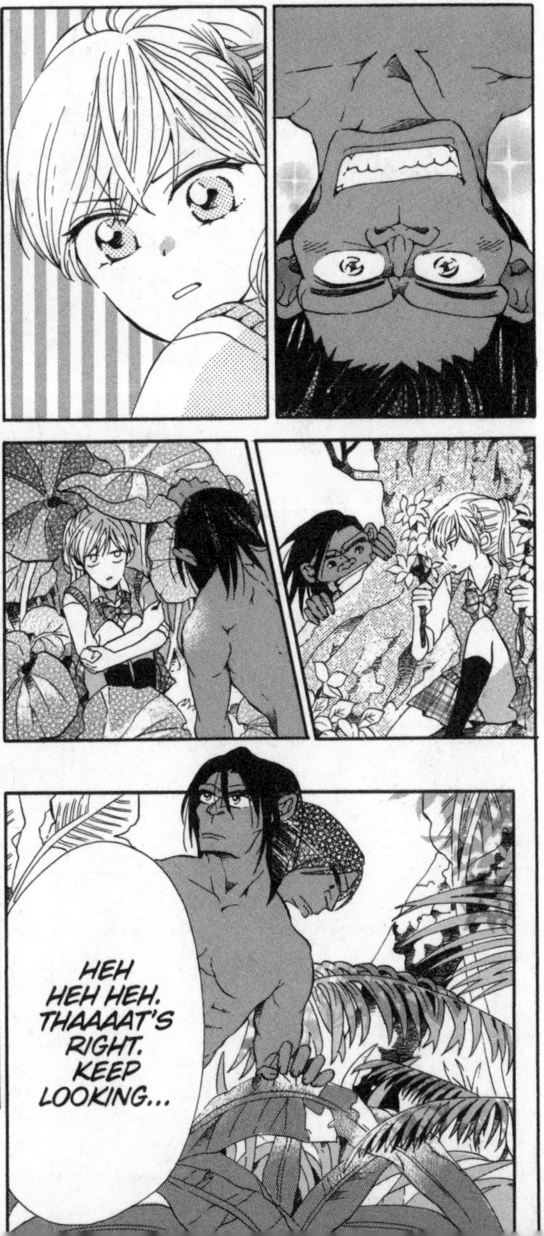
HEH HEH HEH. THAAAAT'S RIGHT. KEEP LOOKING...

2

BEHIND THE SCENES

CHAPTERS 4 + 5

WITH THESE CHAPTERS, THE SERIES MOVED FROM *LALA DX* TO MONTHLY *LALA*, AND MY PERSONAL WAR WITH PENCILING AND INKING INTENSIFIED.

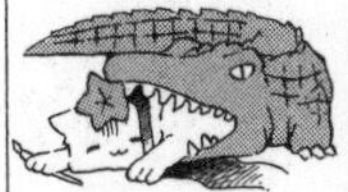

SINCE BOTH MOTHER NATURE AND WILD ANIMALS ARE VITAL TO *PRIMITIVE BOYFRIEND*...

MY ARTISTIC SKILLS

VS.

WHAT I NEED TO DRAW IN EVERY SCENE

I'M IN A CONSTANT LIFE-OR-DEATH BATTLE.

I'M FREQUENTLY IN AWE OVER WHAT AN INSIGNIFICANT BLIP I AM IN MOTHER NATURE'S GRAND SCHEME.

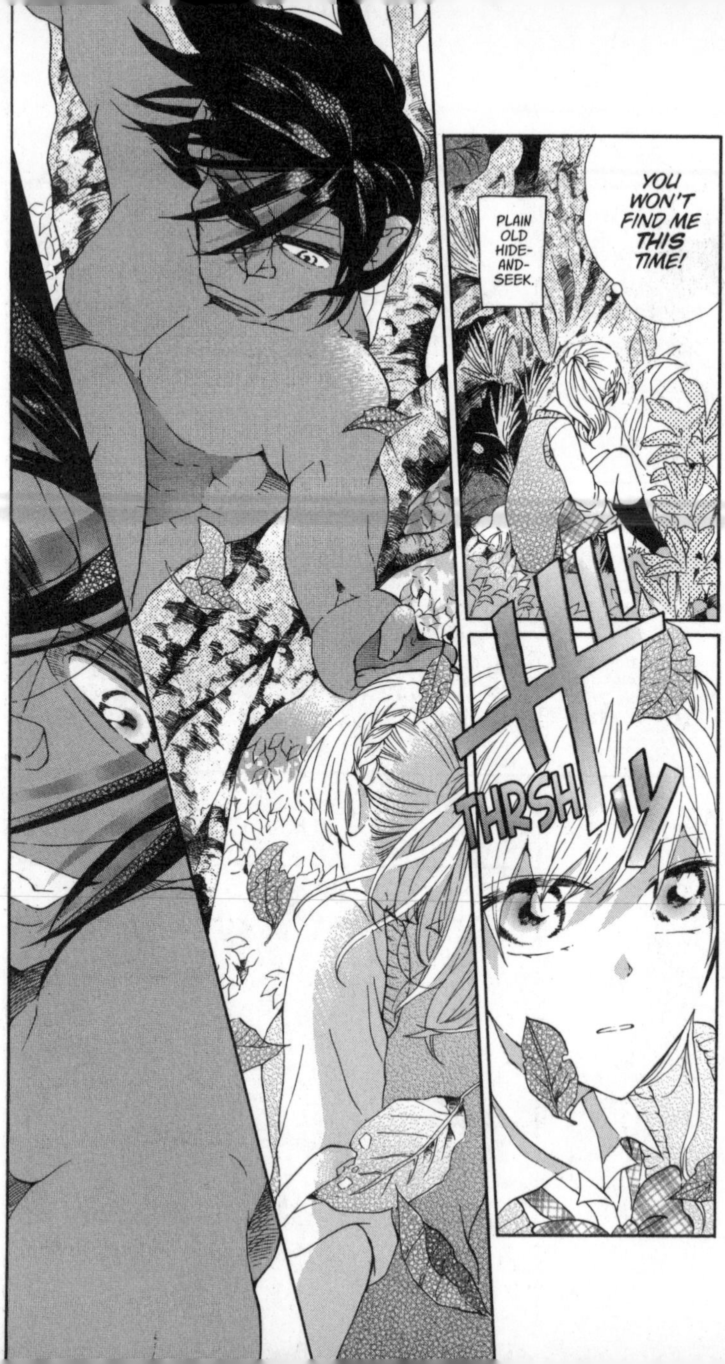
YOU WON'T FIND ME THIS TIME!
PLAIN OLD HIDE-AND-SEEK.
THRSH

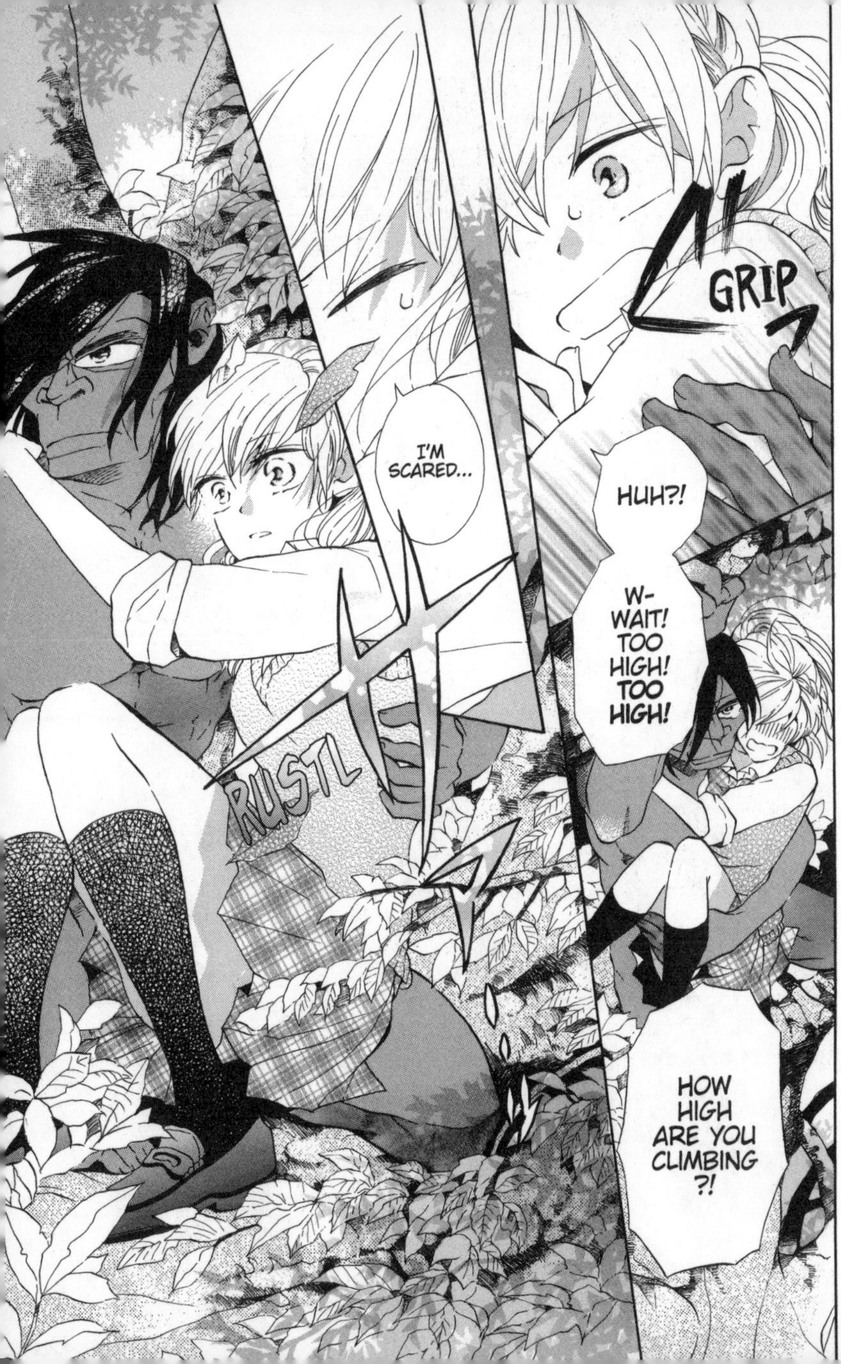
GRIP
HUH?!
W-WAIT! TOO HIGH! TOO HIGH!
HOW HIGH ARE YOU CLIMBING?!
I'M SCARED...
RUSTL

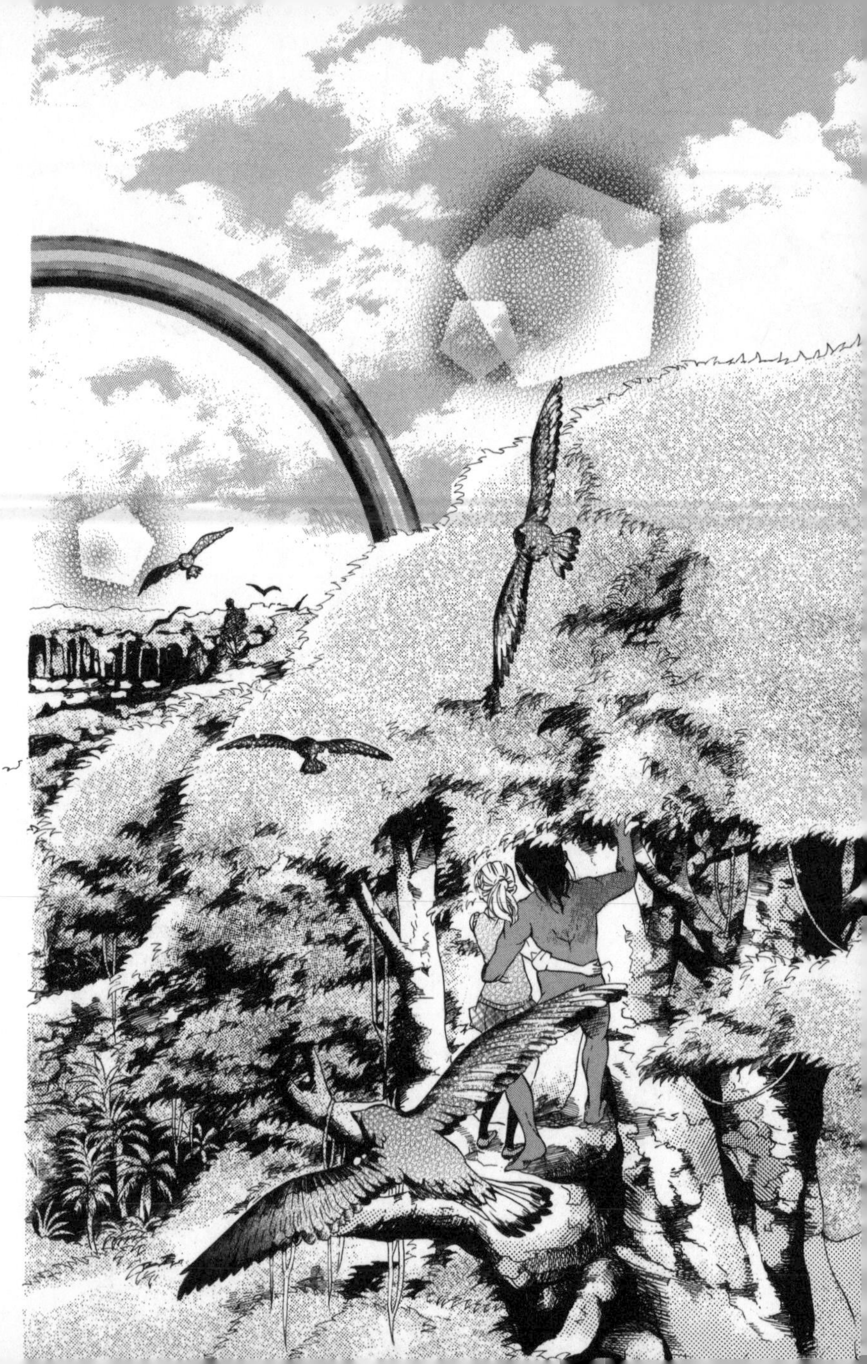

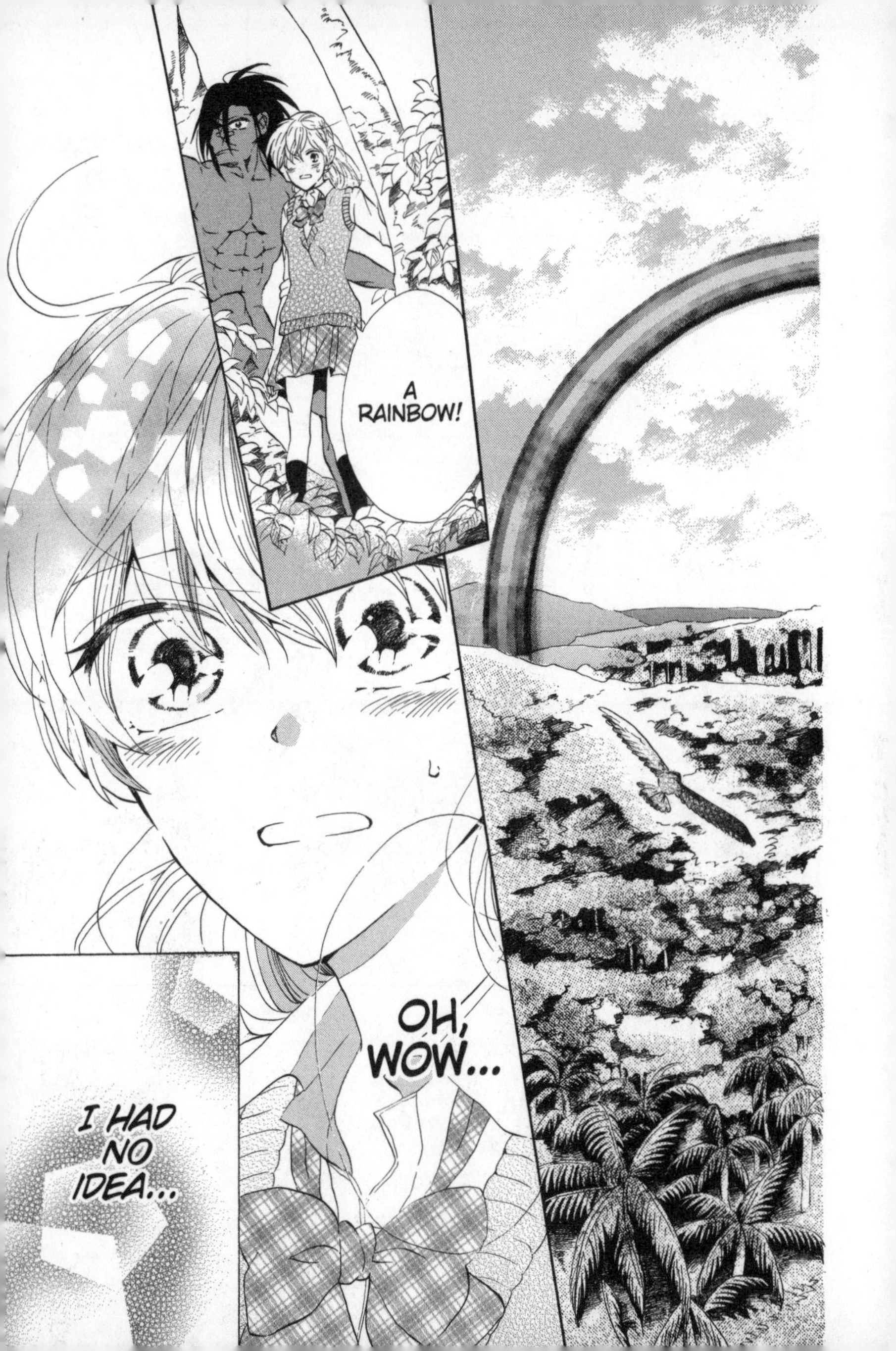
A RAINBOW!
OH, WOW...
I HAD NO IDEA...

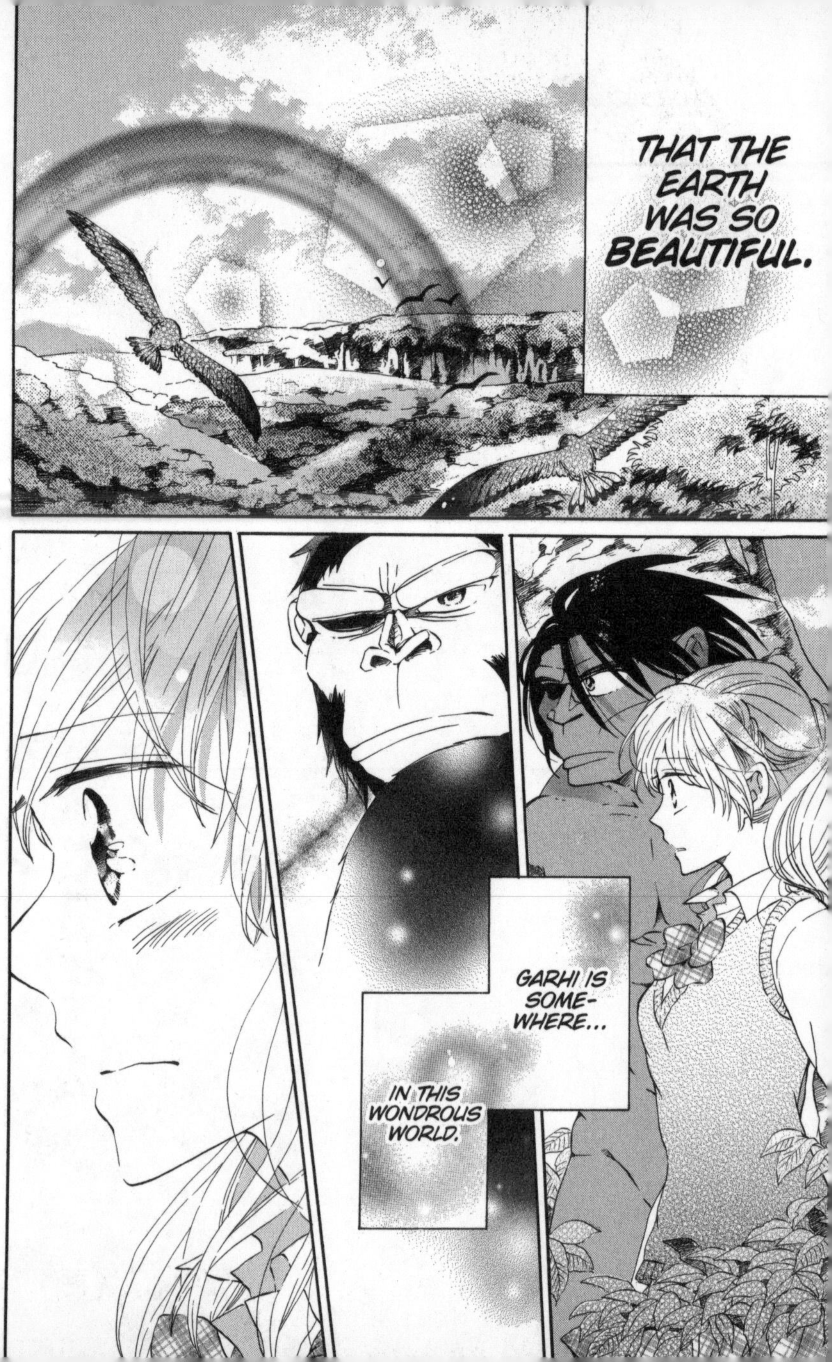
THAT THE EARTH WAS SO BEAUTIFUL.
GARHI IS SOME-WHERE...
IN THIS WONDROUS WORLD.

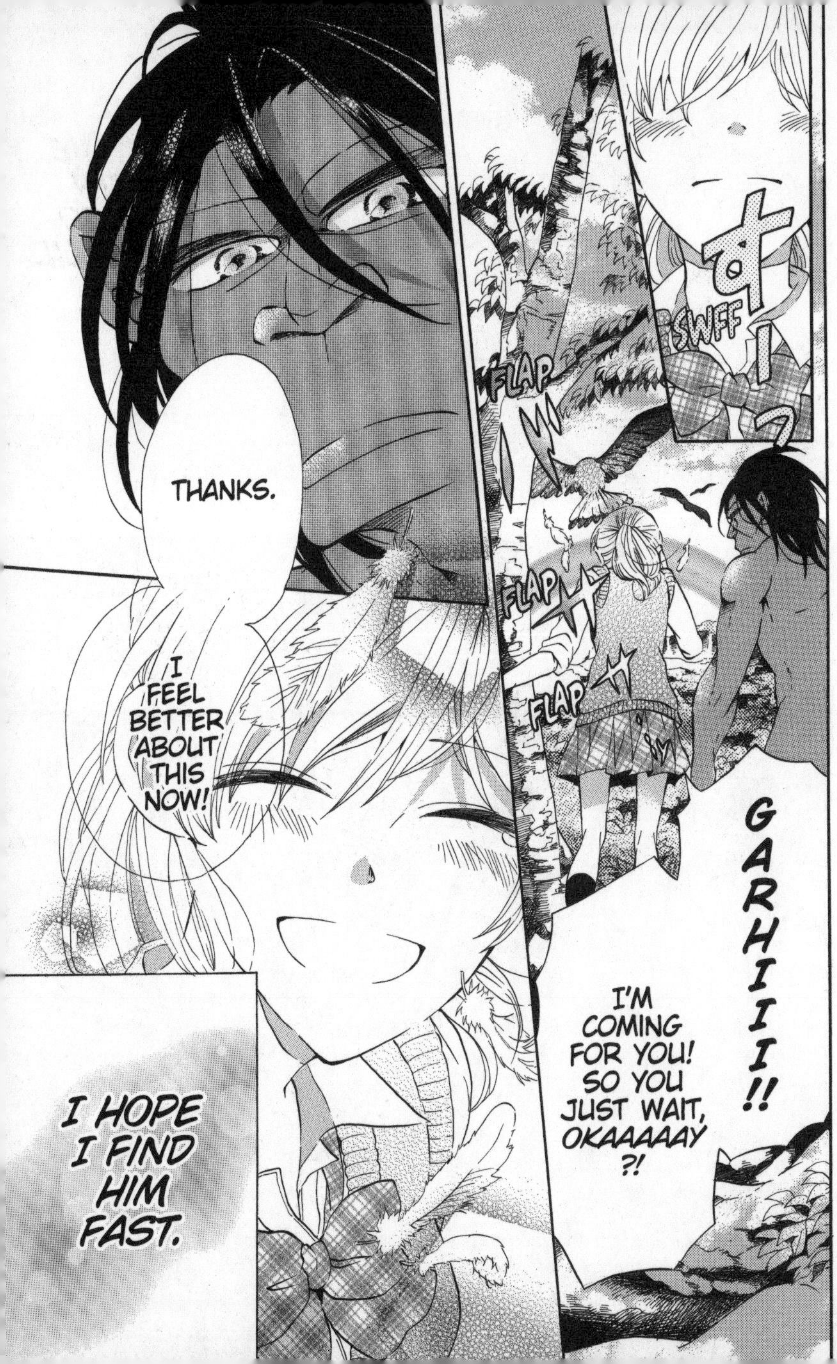

すーっ
SWFF
FLAP
FLAP
FLAP
GARHIIIII!!
I'M COMING FOR YOU! SO YOU JUST WAIT, OKAAAAAY?!
THANKS.
I FEEL BETTER ABOUT THIS NOW!
I HOPE I FIND HIM FAST.

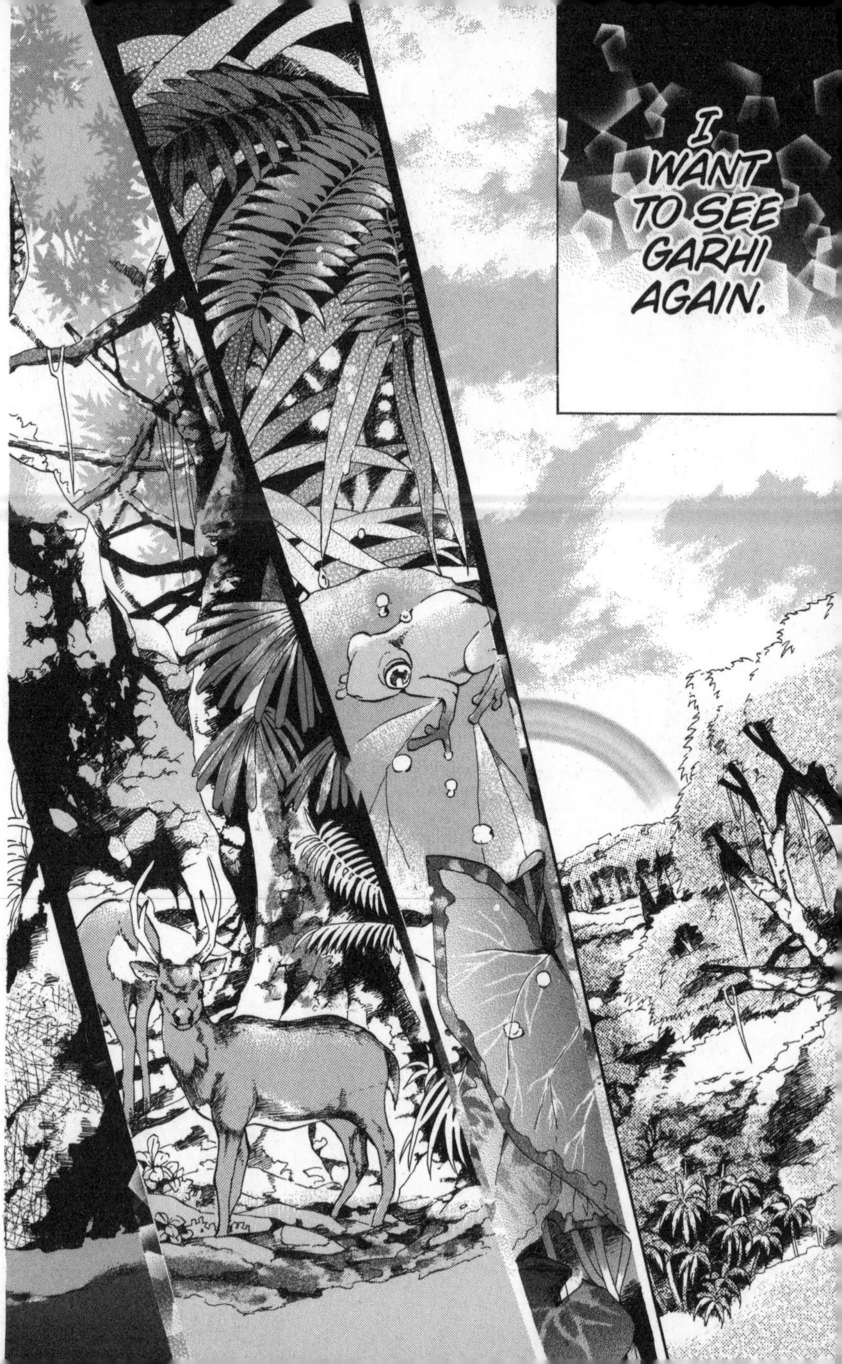
I WANT TO SEE GARHI AGAIN.

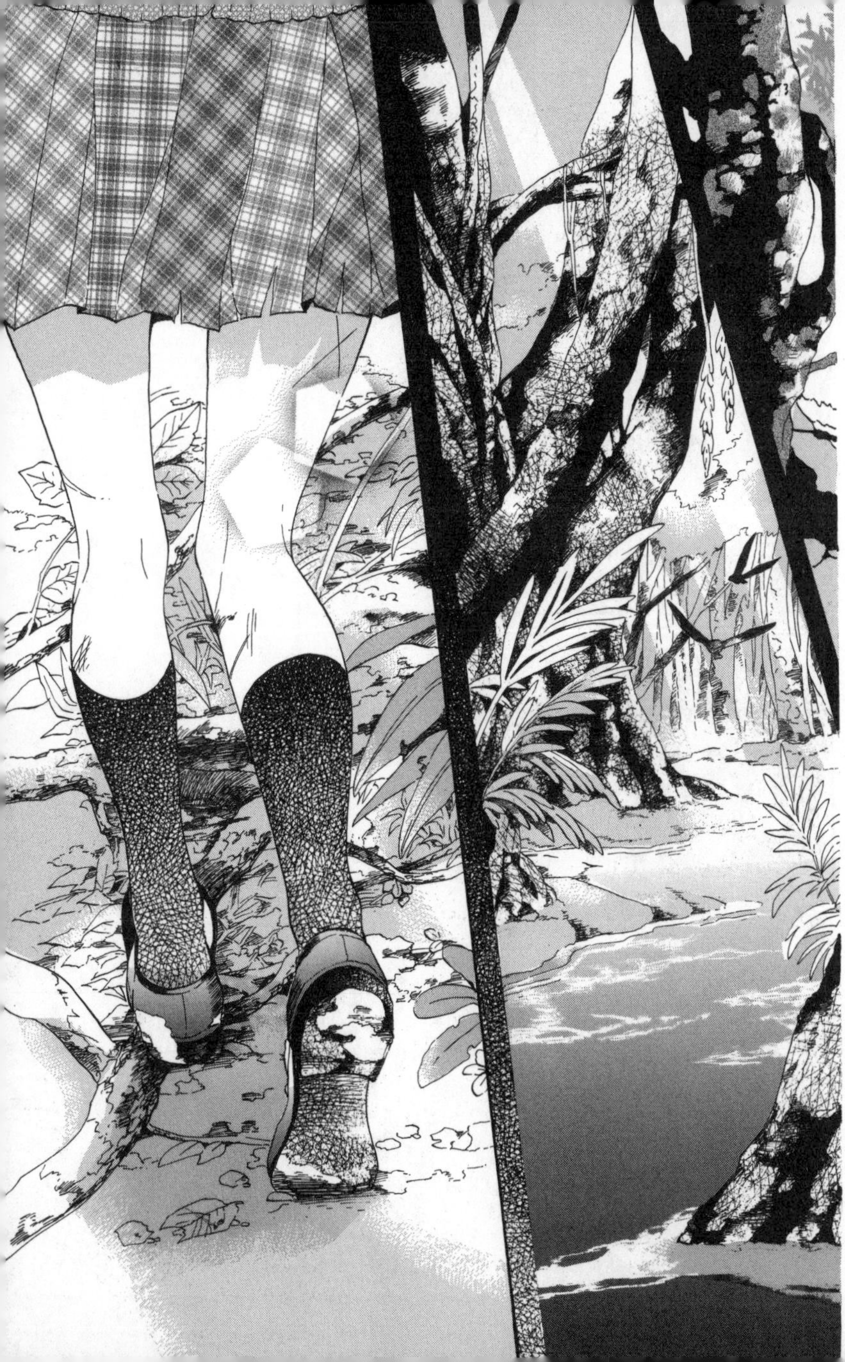

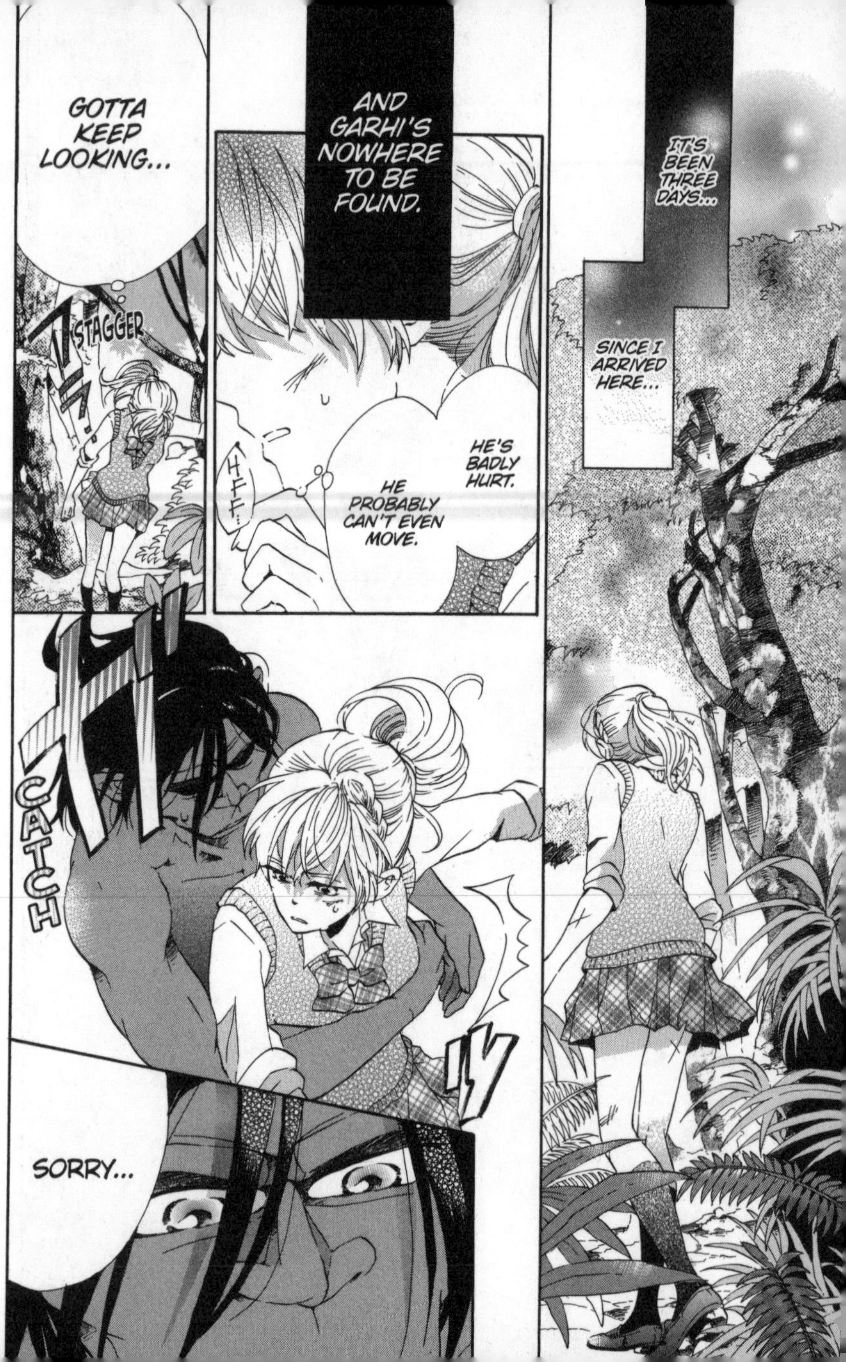
IT'S BEEN THREE DAYS...
SINCE I ARRIVED HERE...
AND GARHI'S NOWHERE TO BE FOUND.
HFF...
HE'S BADLY HURT.
HE PROBABLY CAN'T EVEN MOVE.
GOTTA KEEP LOOKING...
STAGGER
CATCH
SORRY...

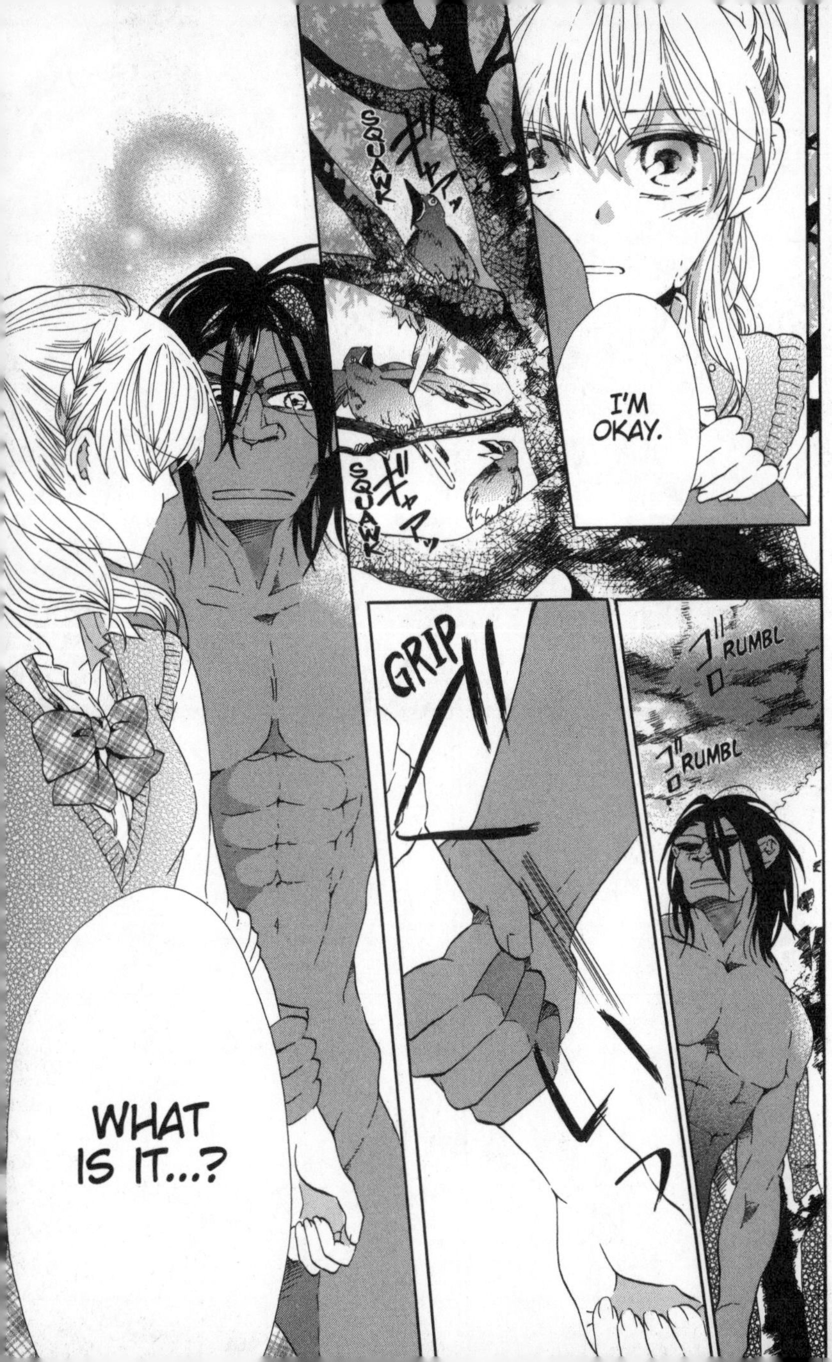
I'M OKAY.
SQUAWK
SQUAWK
RUMBL
RUMBL
GRIP
WHAT IS IT...?

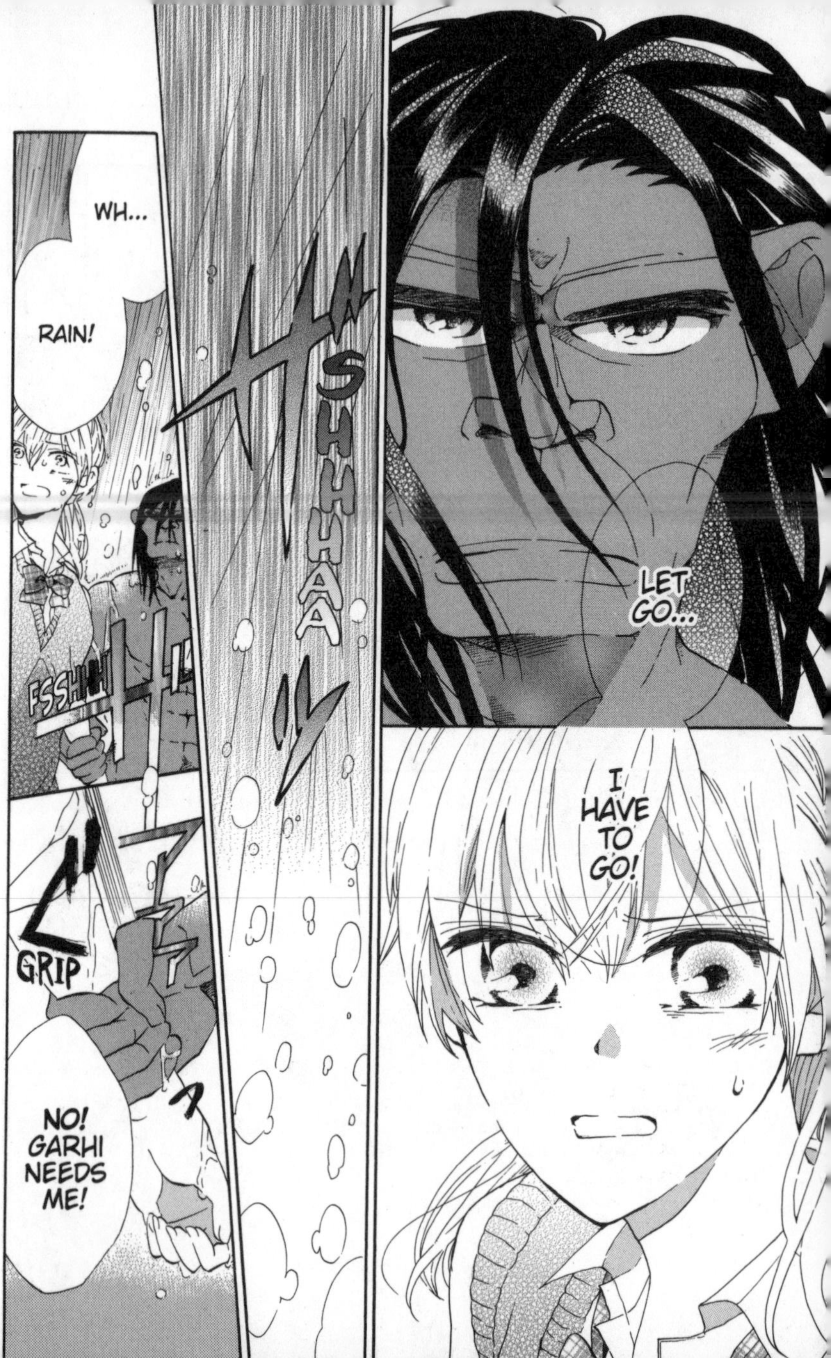
LET GO...
I HAVE TO GO!
SHHHAA
WH...
RAIN!
FSSHHH
GRIP
NO! GARHI NEEDS ME!

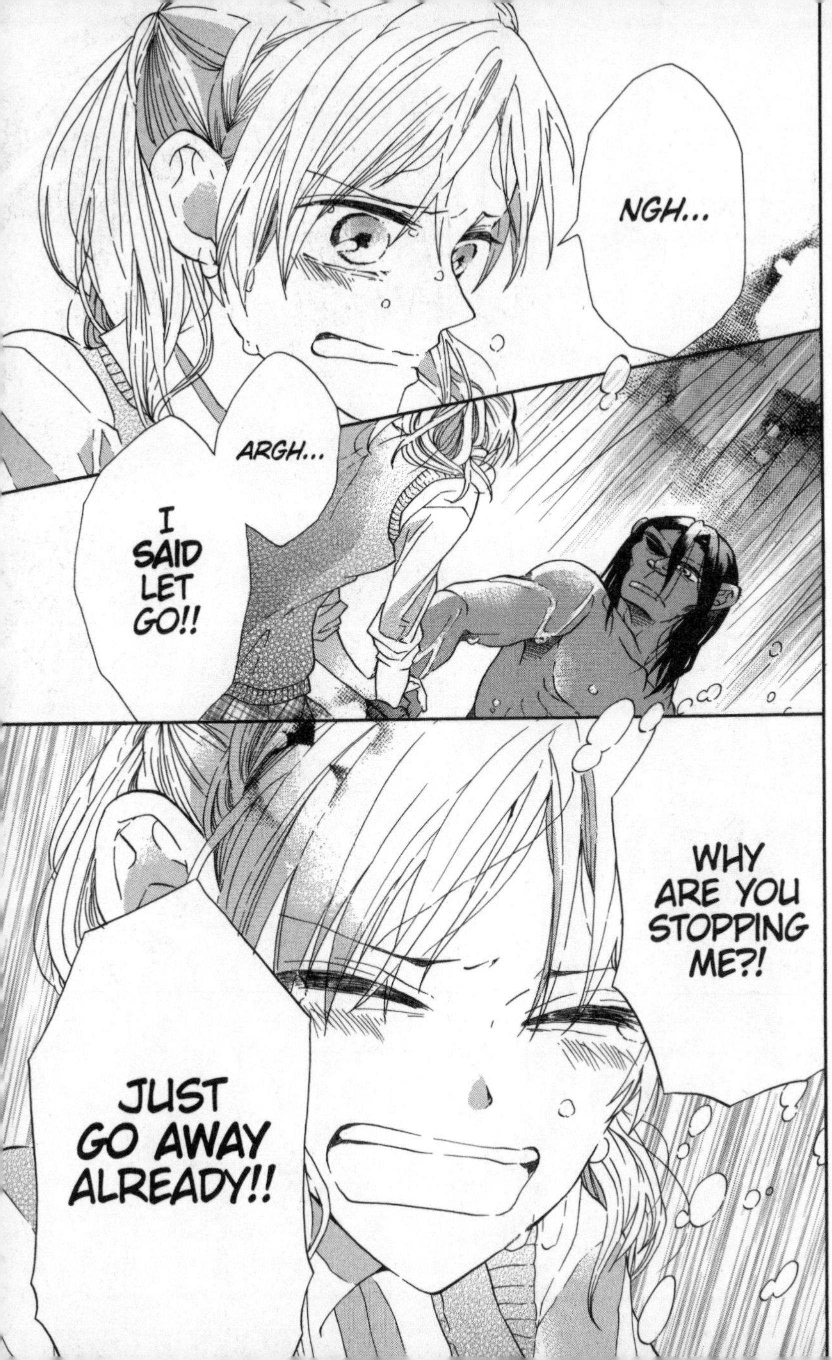
NGH...
ARGH...
I SAID LET GO!!
WHY ARE YOU STOPPING ME?!
JUST GO AWAY ALREADY!!

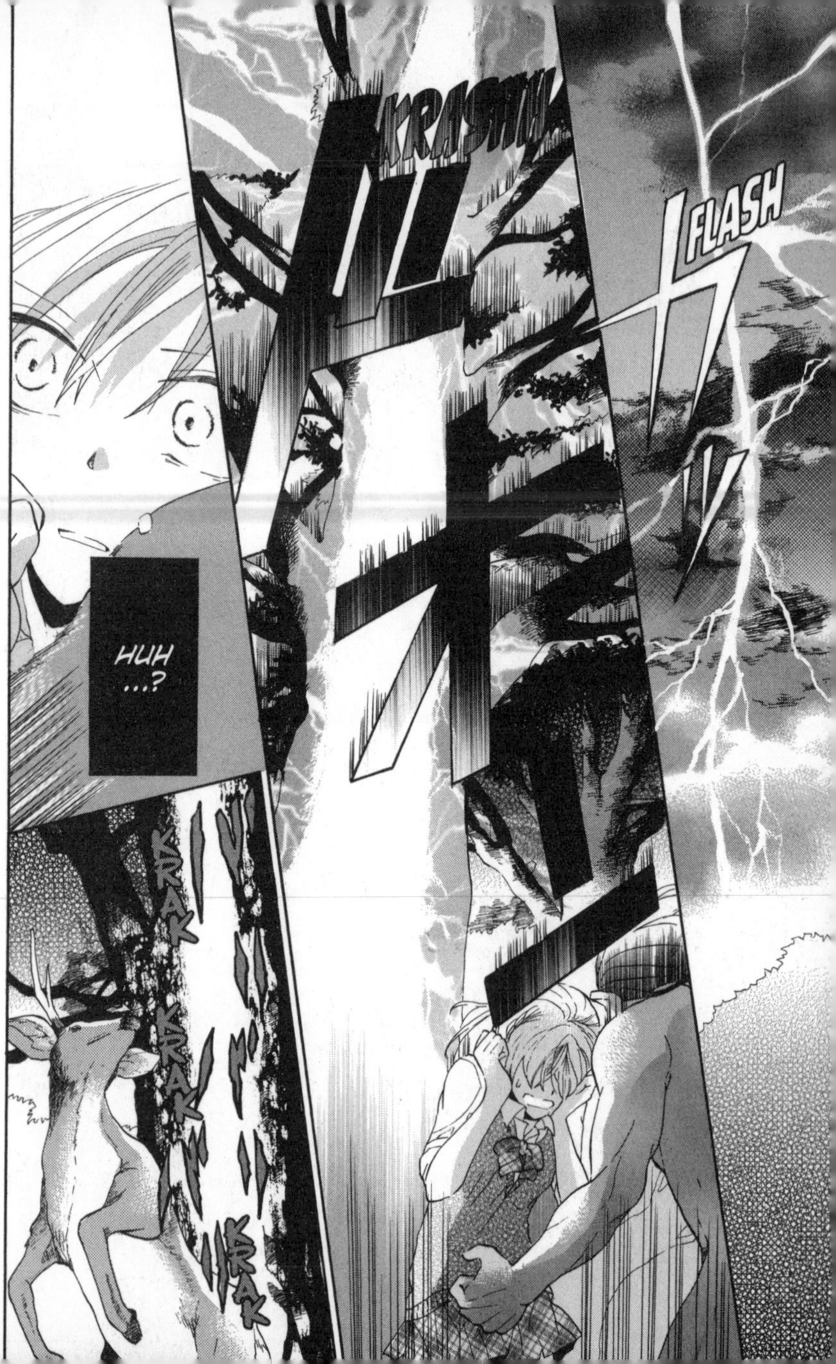
FLASH
KRASHH
HUH
...?
KRAK
KRAK
KRAK

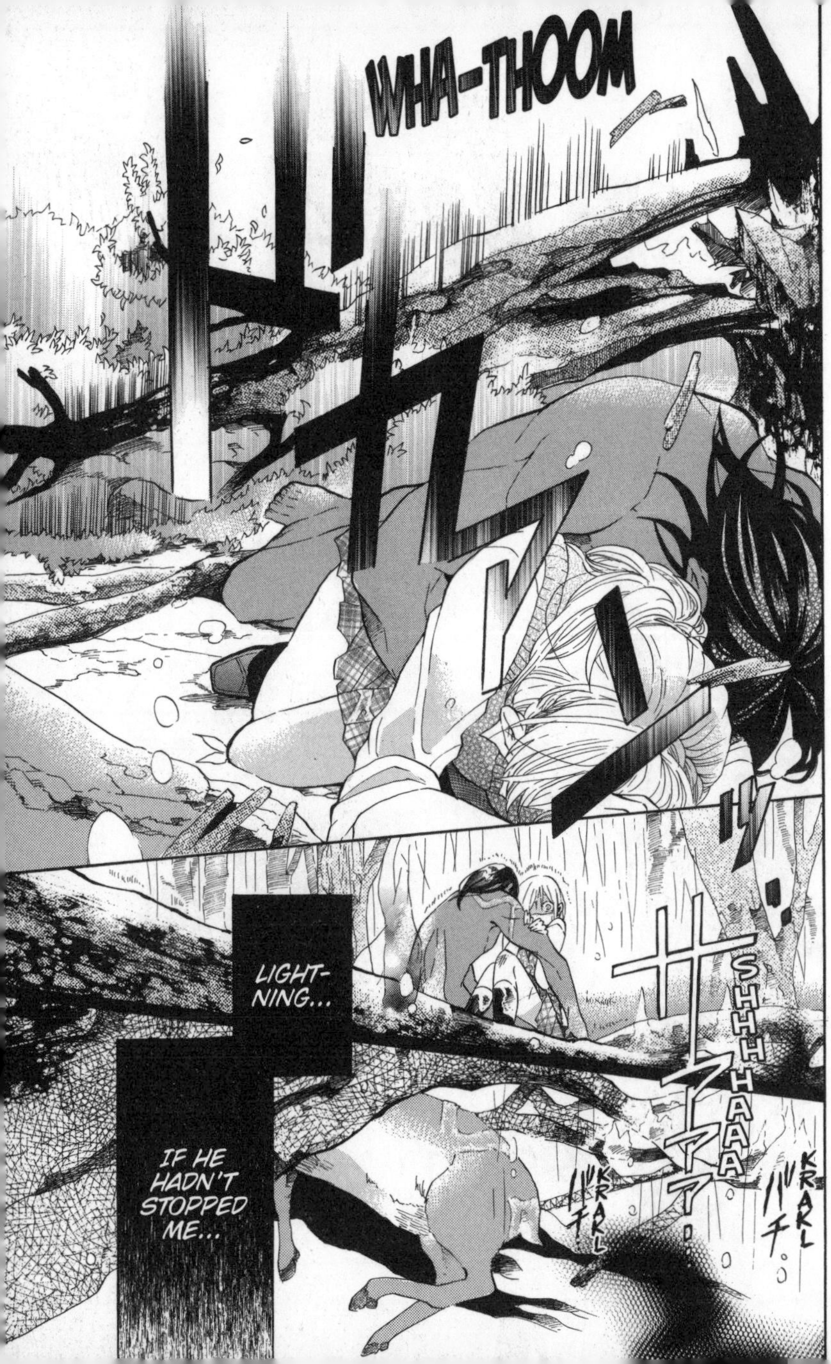
WHA-THOOM
SHHHHAAAA
LIGHT-NING...
KRAKL
KRAKL
IF HE HADN'T STOPPED ME...

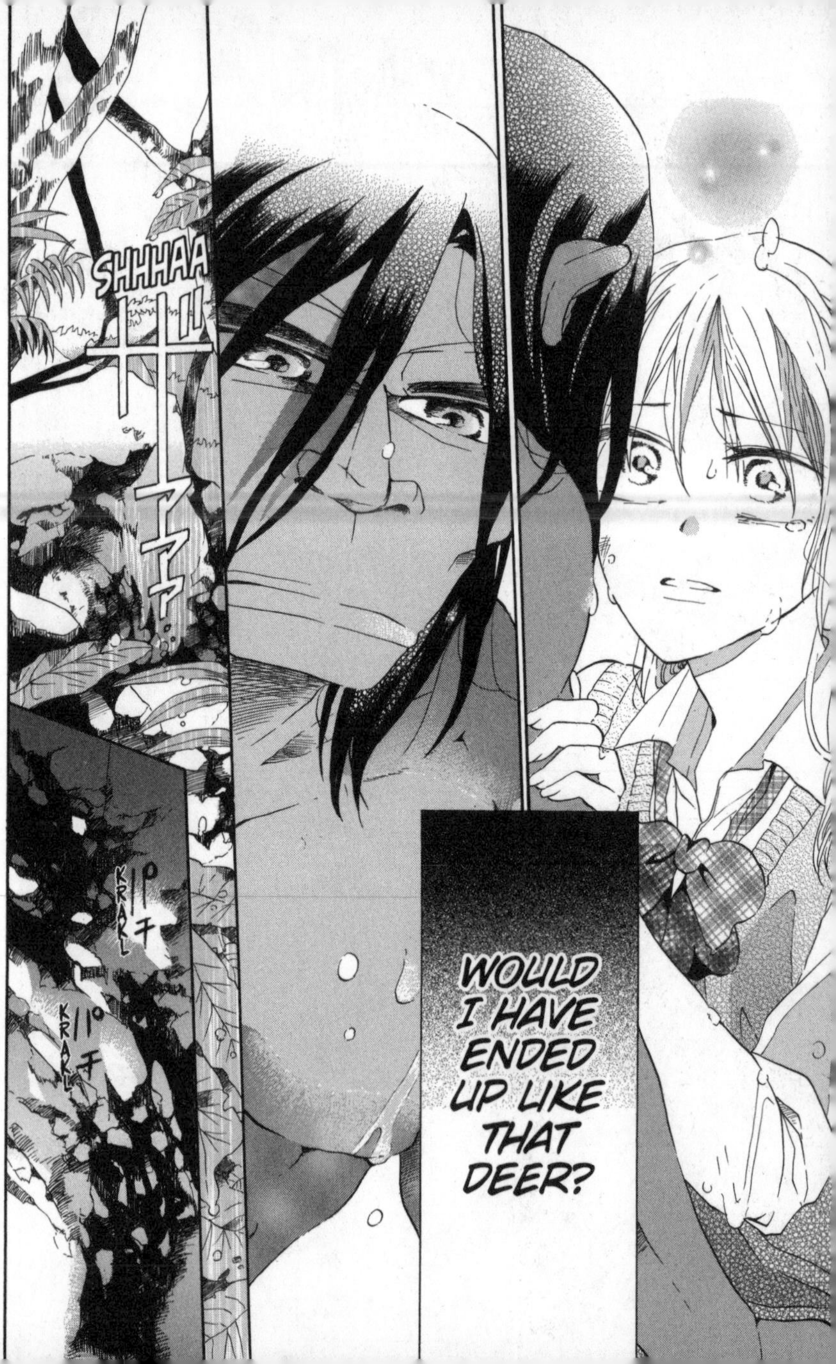
WOULD I HAVE ENDED UP LIKE THAT DEER?
SHHHAA
KRAKL
パチ
KRAKL
パチ

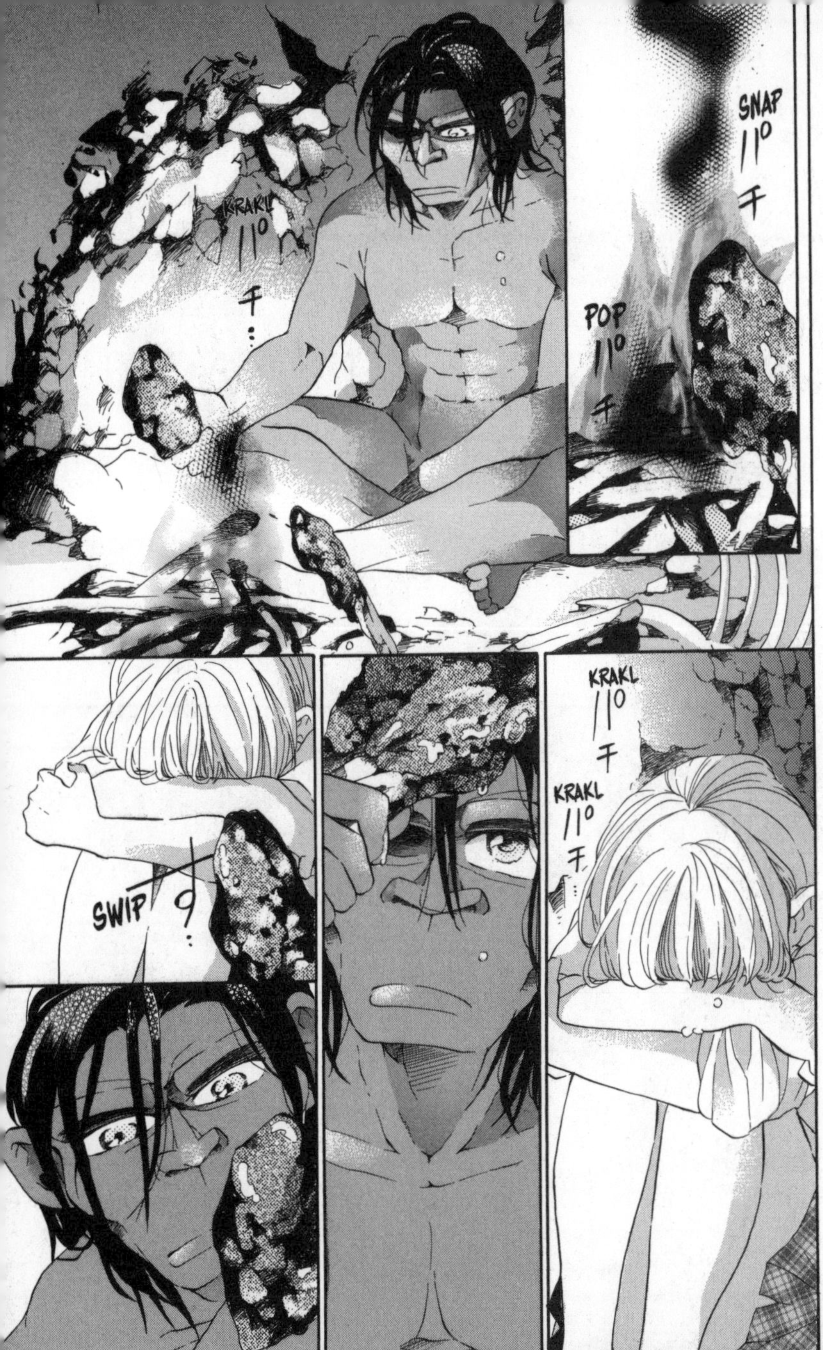
SNAP
POP
KRAKL
KRAKL
KRAKL
SWIP

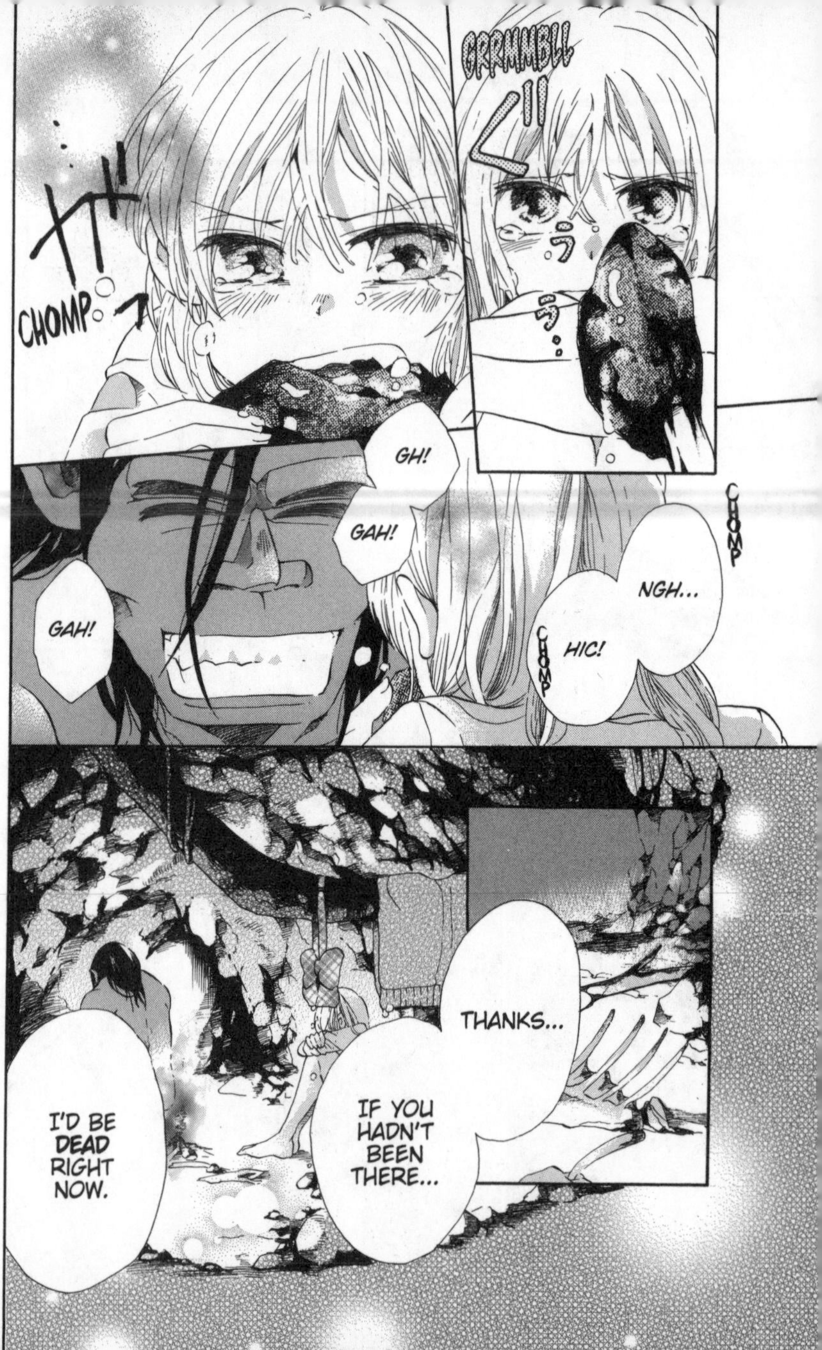
GRRMMBLL
CHOMP
CHOMP
CHOMP
NGH...
HIC!
GH!
GAH!
GAH!
THANKS...
IF YOU HADN'T BEEN THERE...
I'D BE **DEAD** RIGHT NOW.

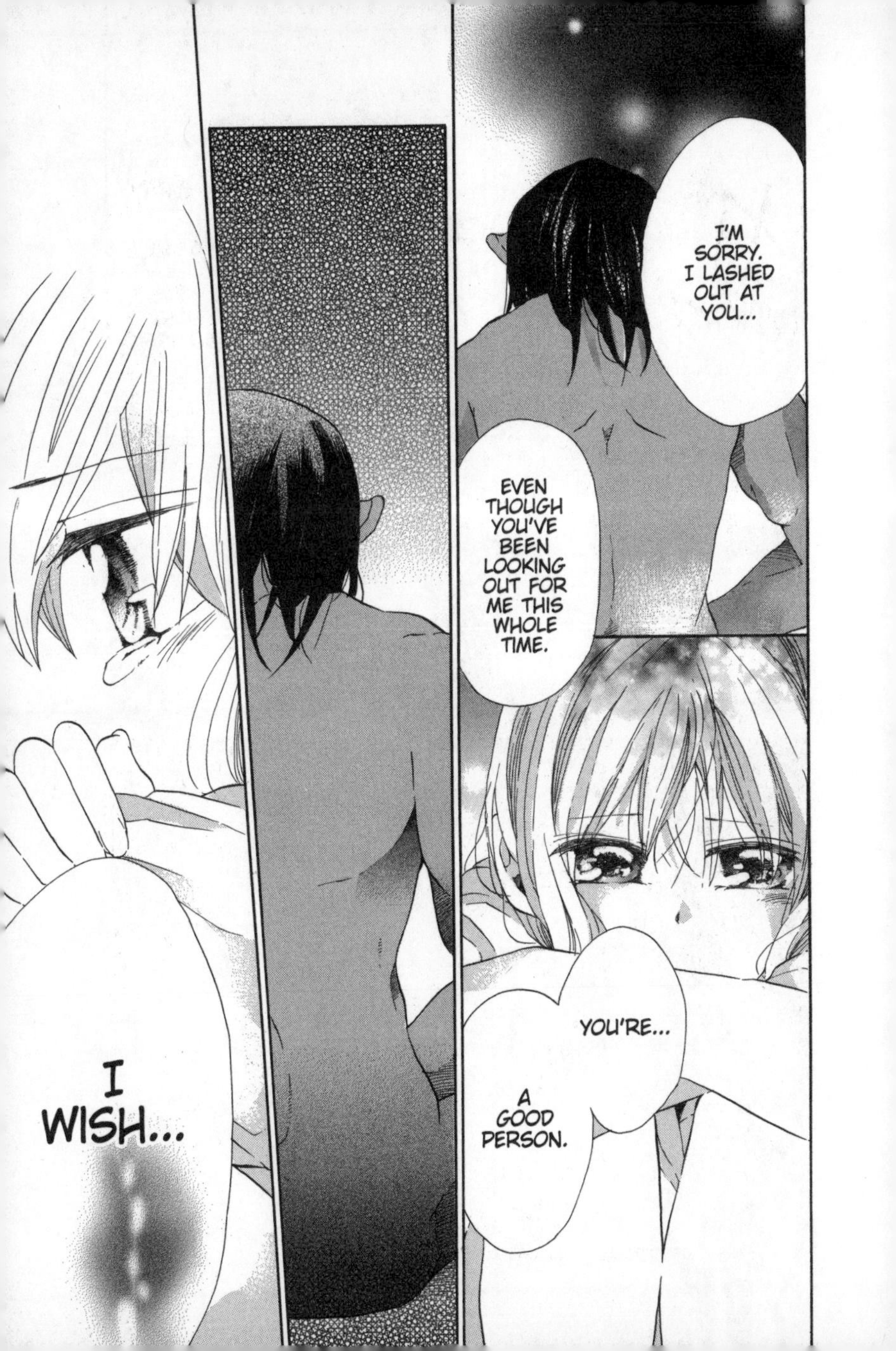
I'M SORRY. I LASHED OUT AT YOU...
EVEN THOUGH YOU'VE BEEN LOOKING OUT FOR ME THIS WHOLE TIME.
YOU'RE...
A GOOD PERSON.
I WISH...

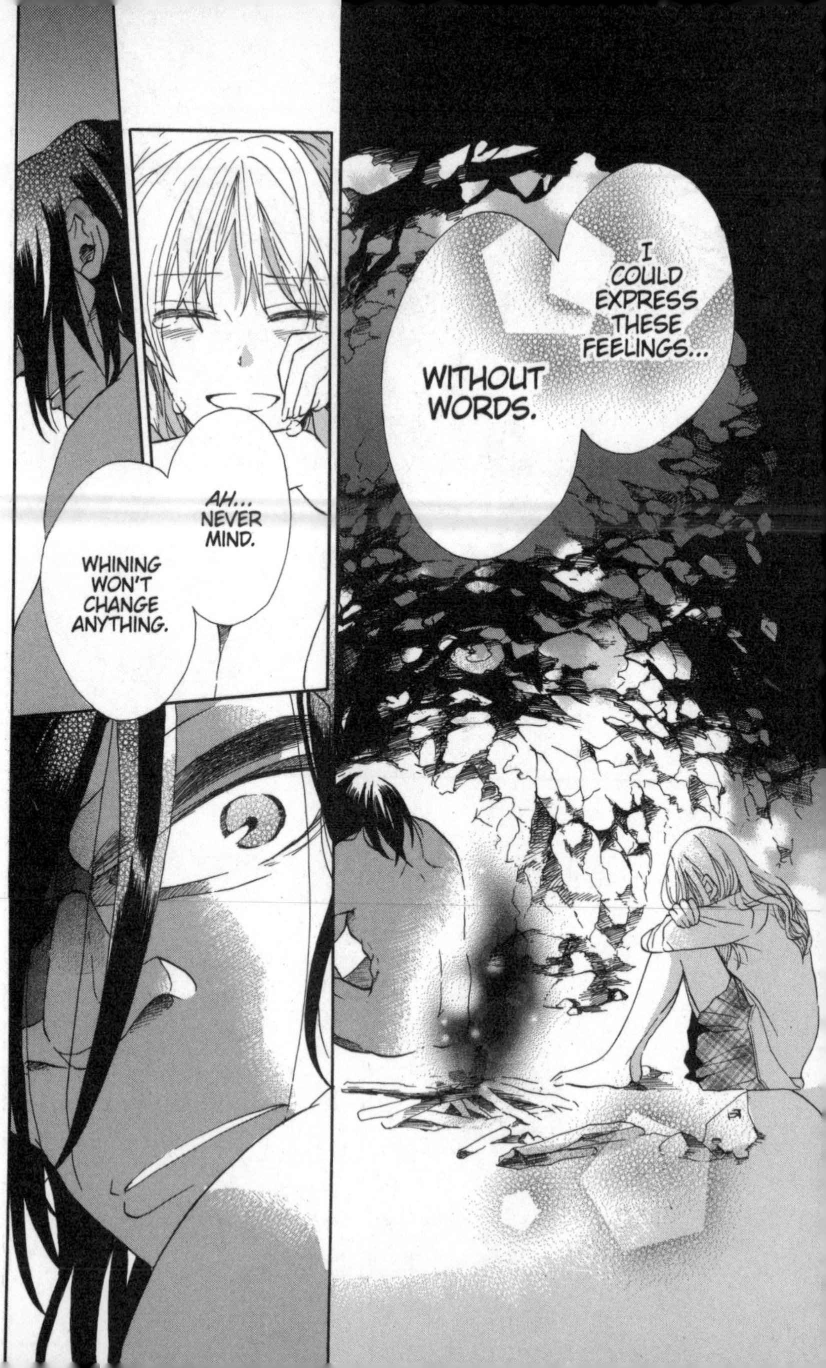
I COULD EXPRESS THESE FEELINGS...
WITHOUT WORDS.
AH... NEVER MIND.
WHINING WON'T CHANGE ANYTHING.

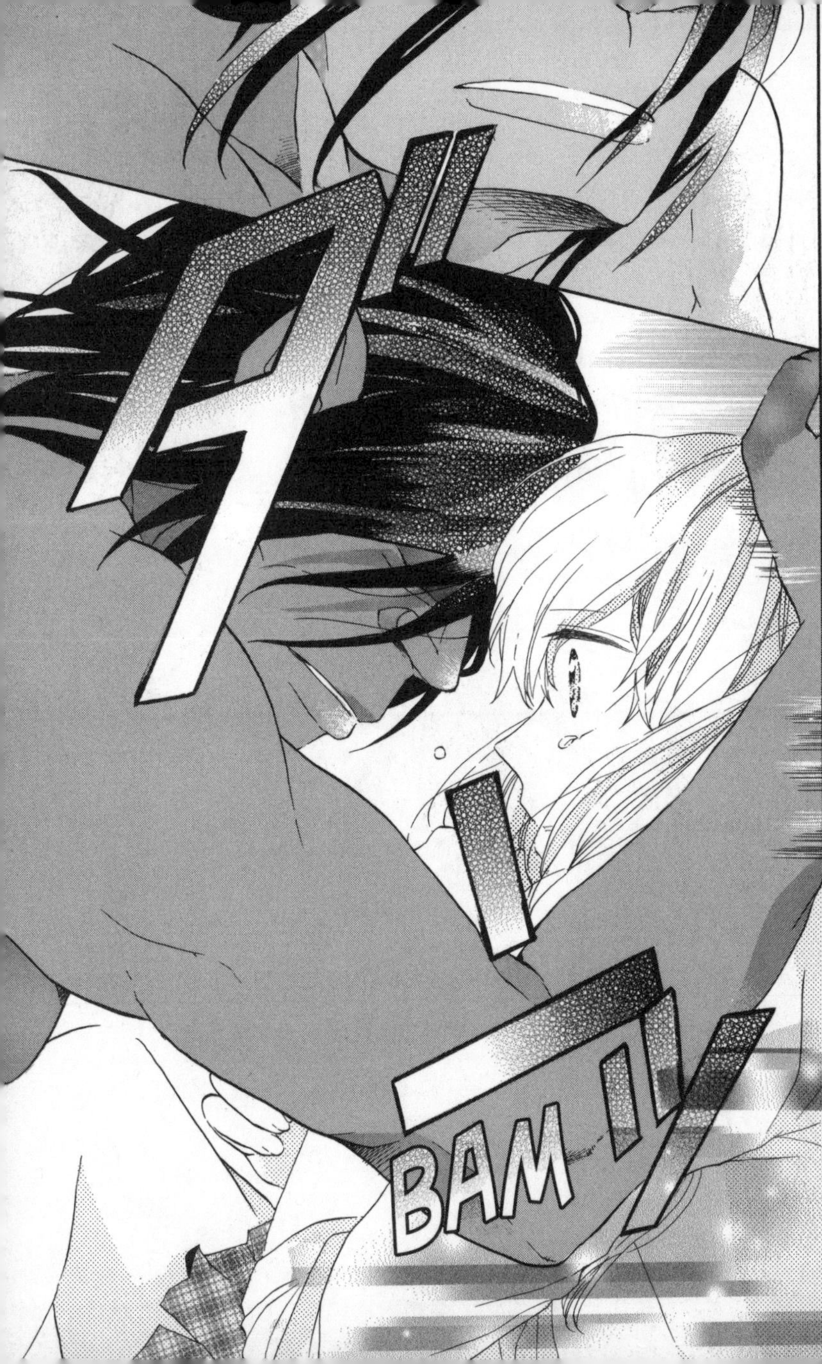
BAM!!

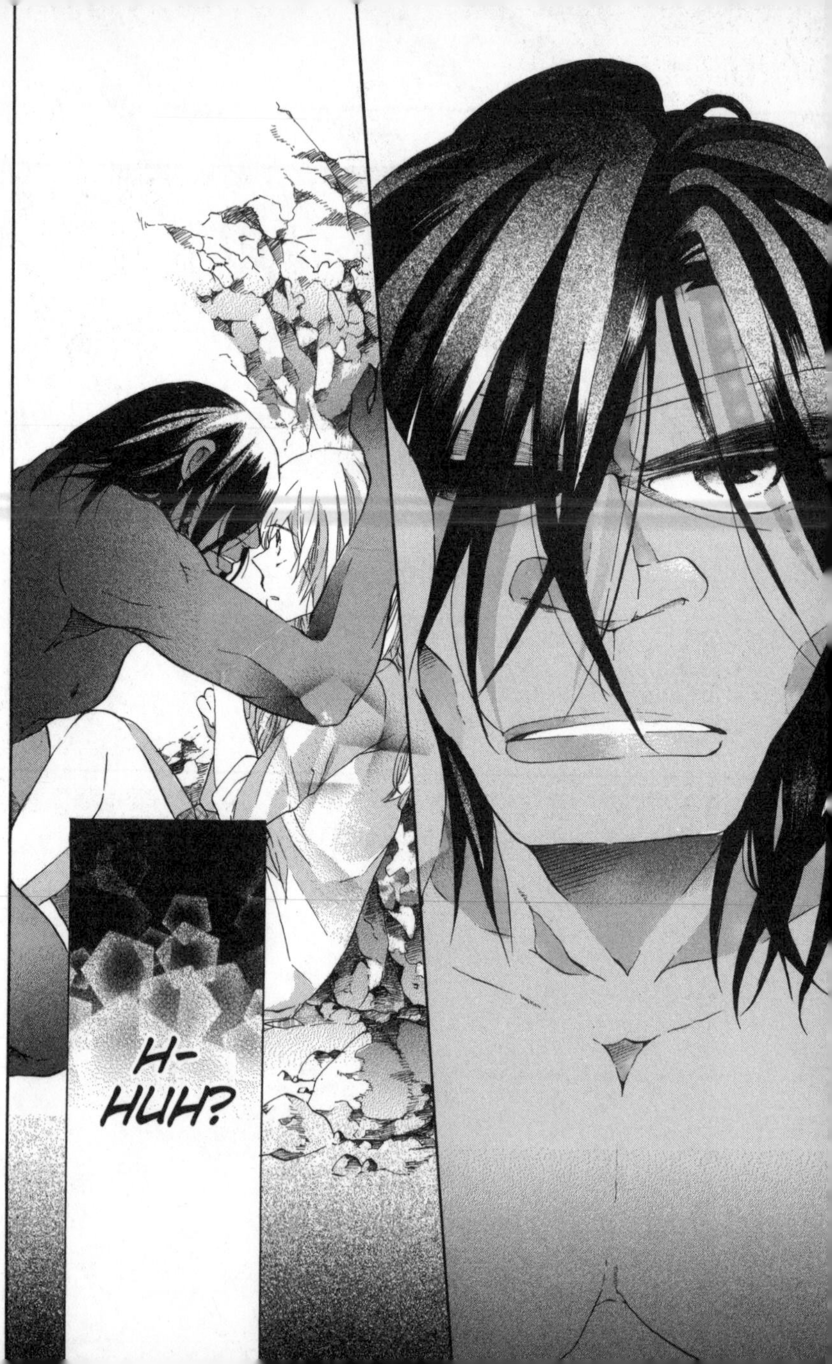
H-HUH?

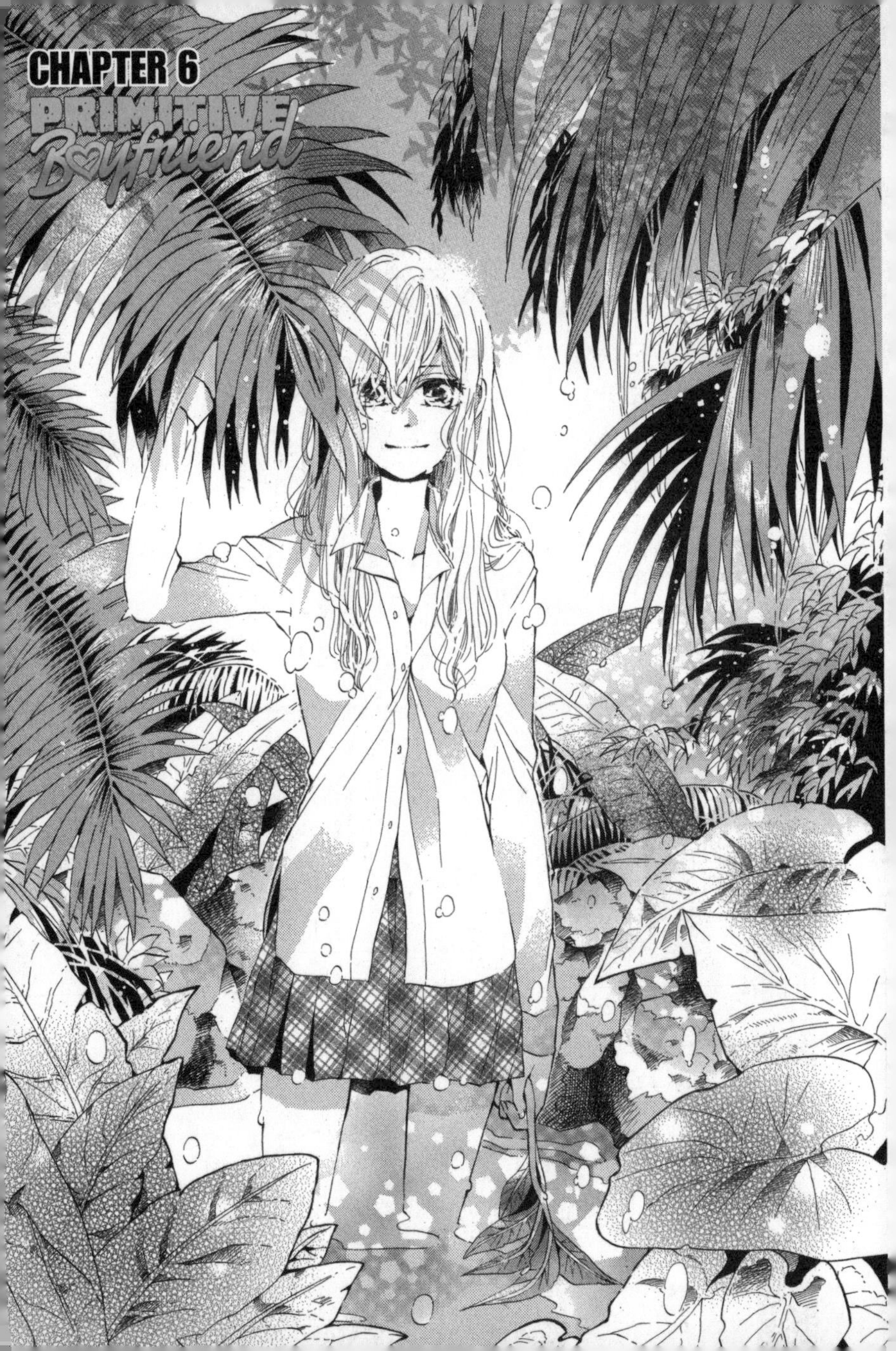
CHAPTER 6
PRIMITIVE Boyfriend

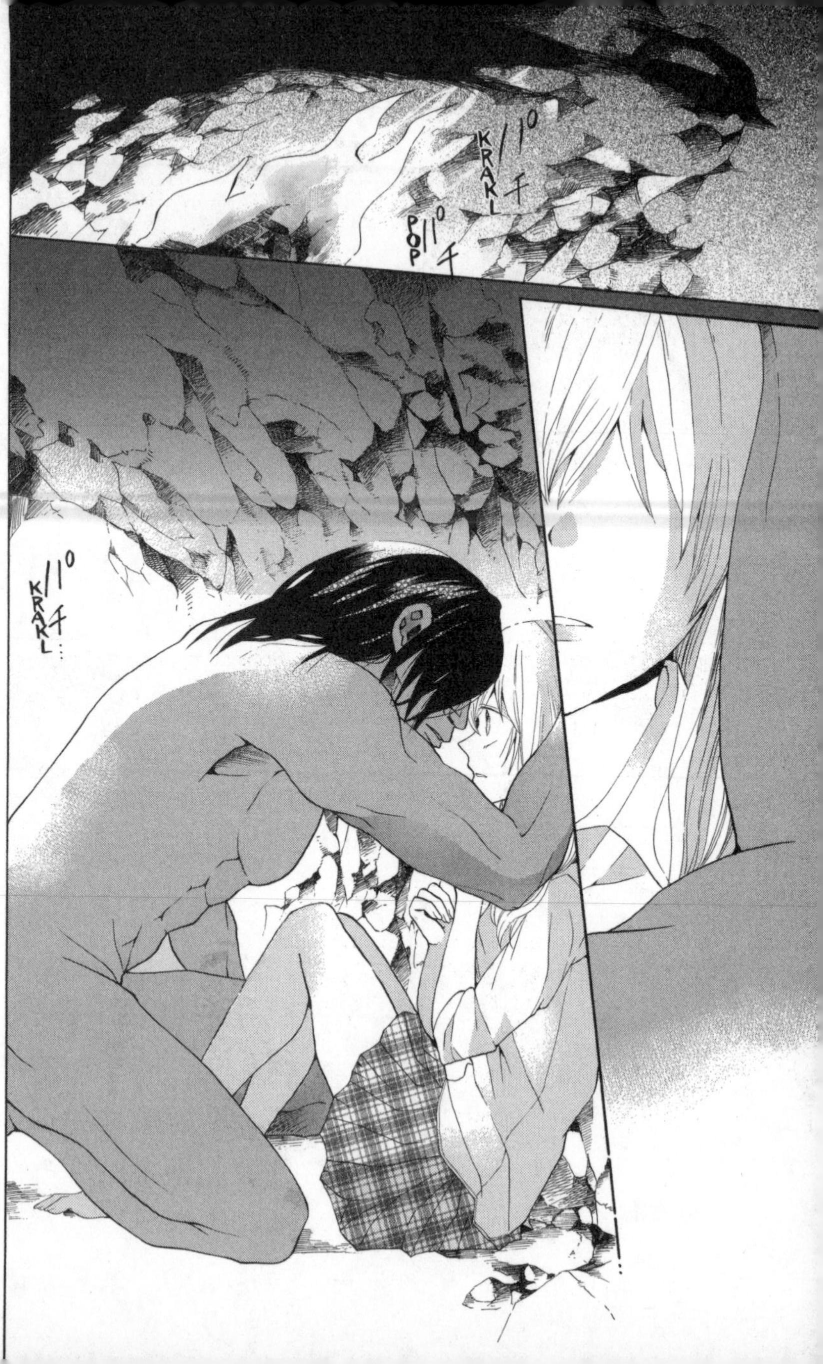
KRAKL
POP
KRAKL…

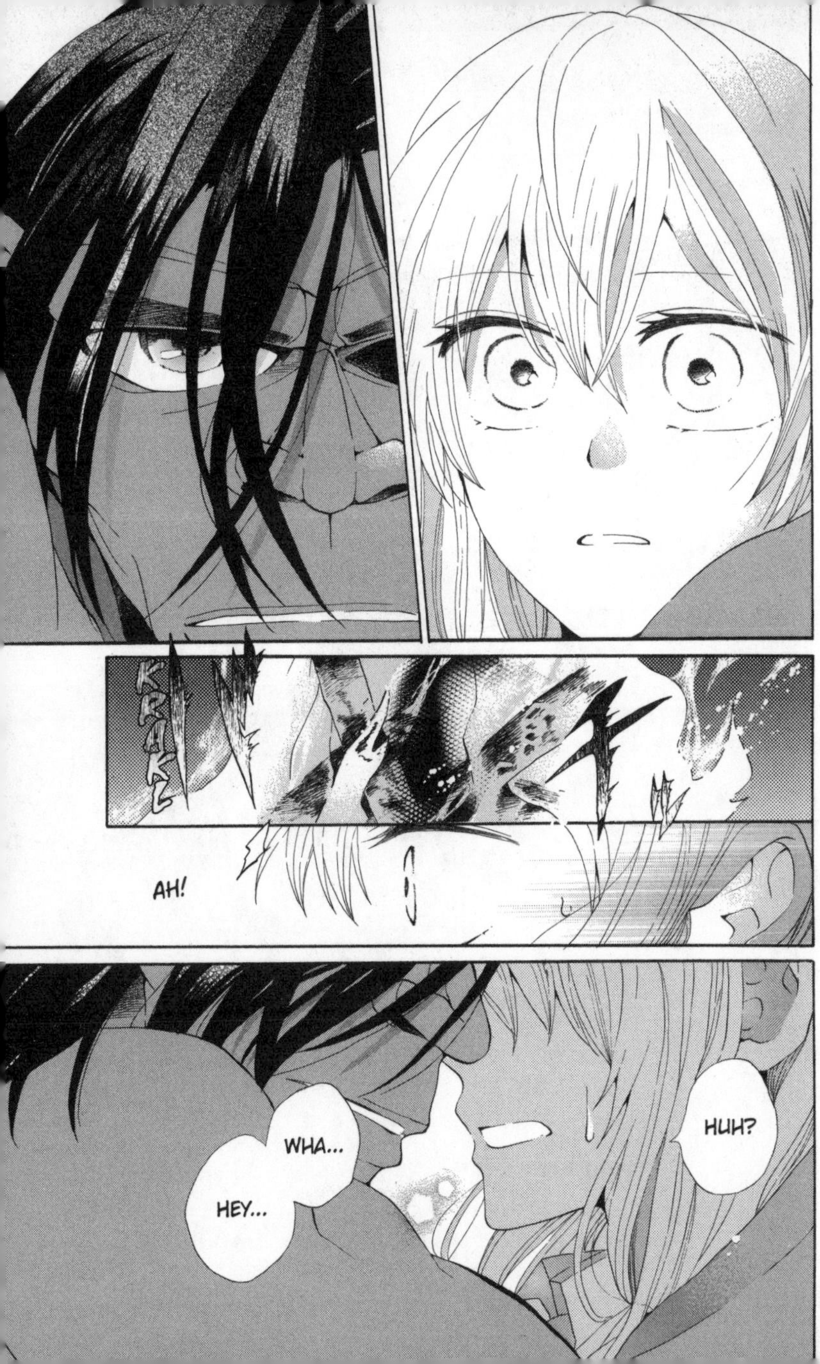
KRAKL
AH!
HUH?
WHA...
HEY...

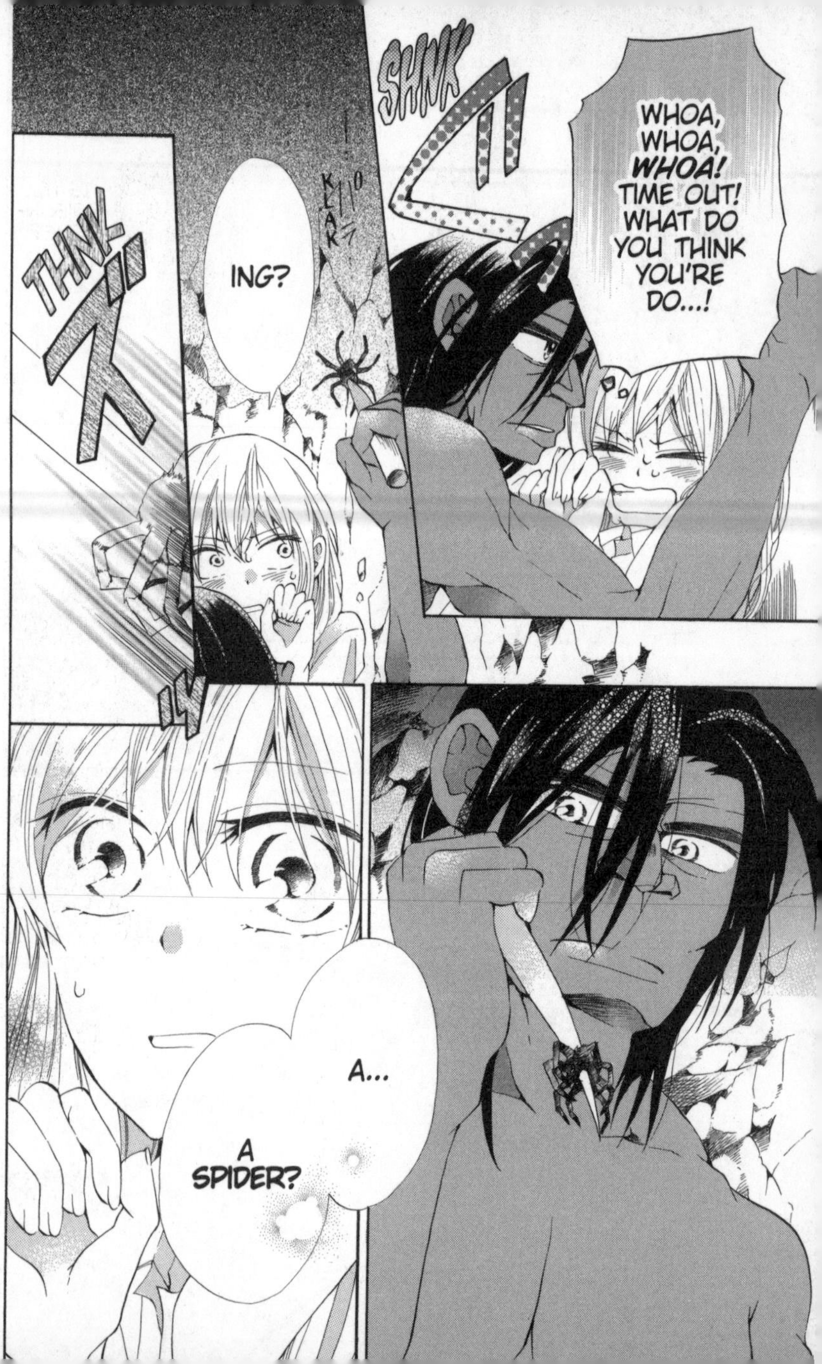
SHNK
WHOA, WHOA, WHOA! TIME OUT! WHAT DO YOU THINK YOU'RE DO...!
KLAR
ING?
THNK
A...
A SPIDER?

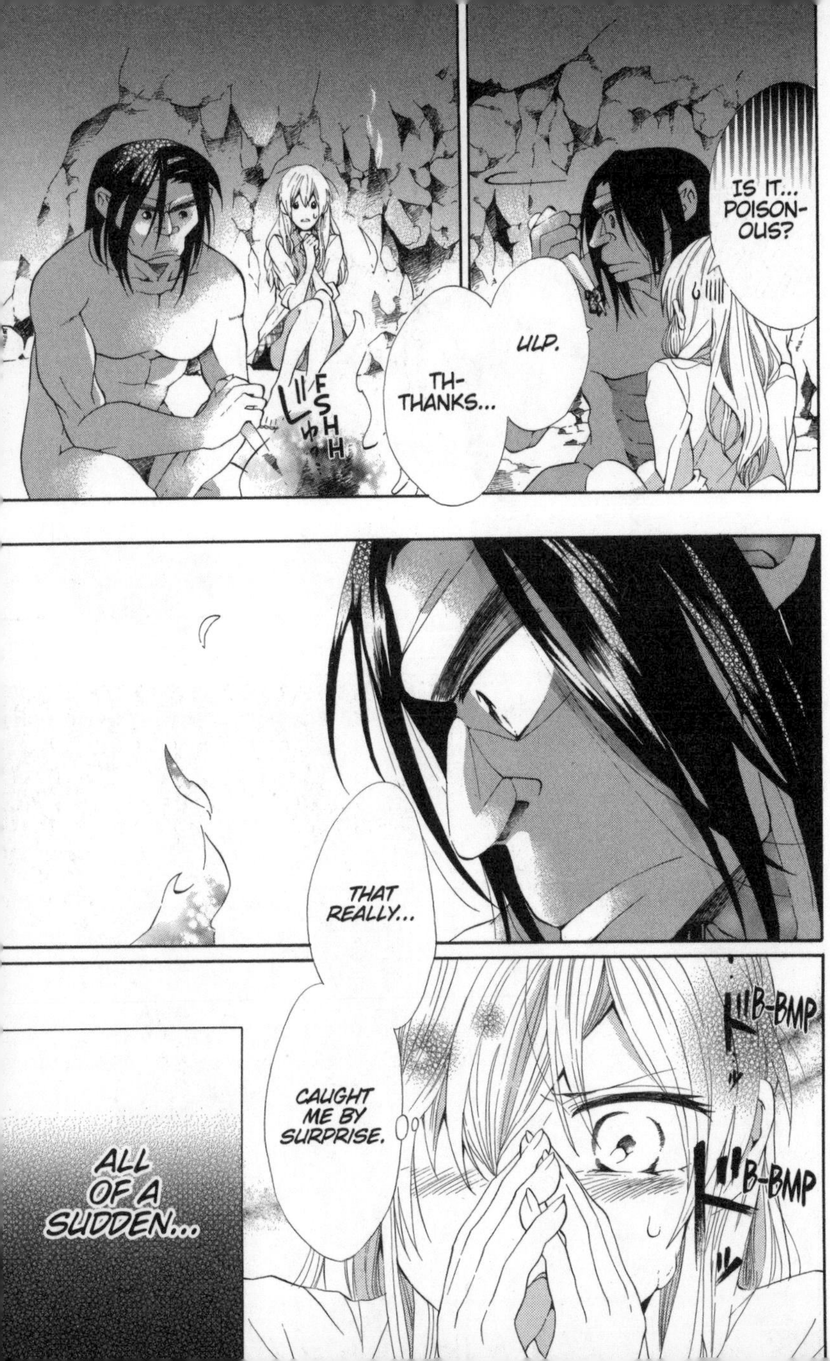
IS IT... POISONOUS?
ULP.
TH-THANKS...
FSHH
THAT REALLY...
B-BMP
CAUGHT ME BY SURPRISE.
B-BMP
ALL OF A SUDDEN...

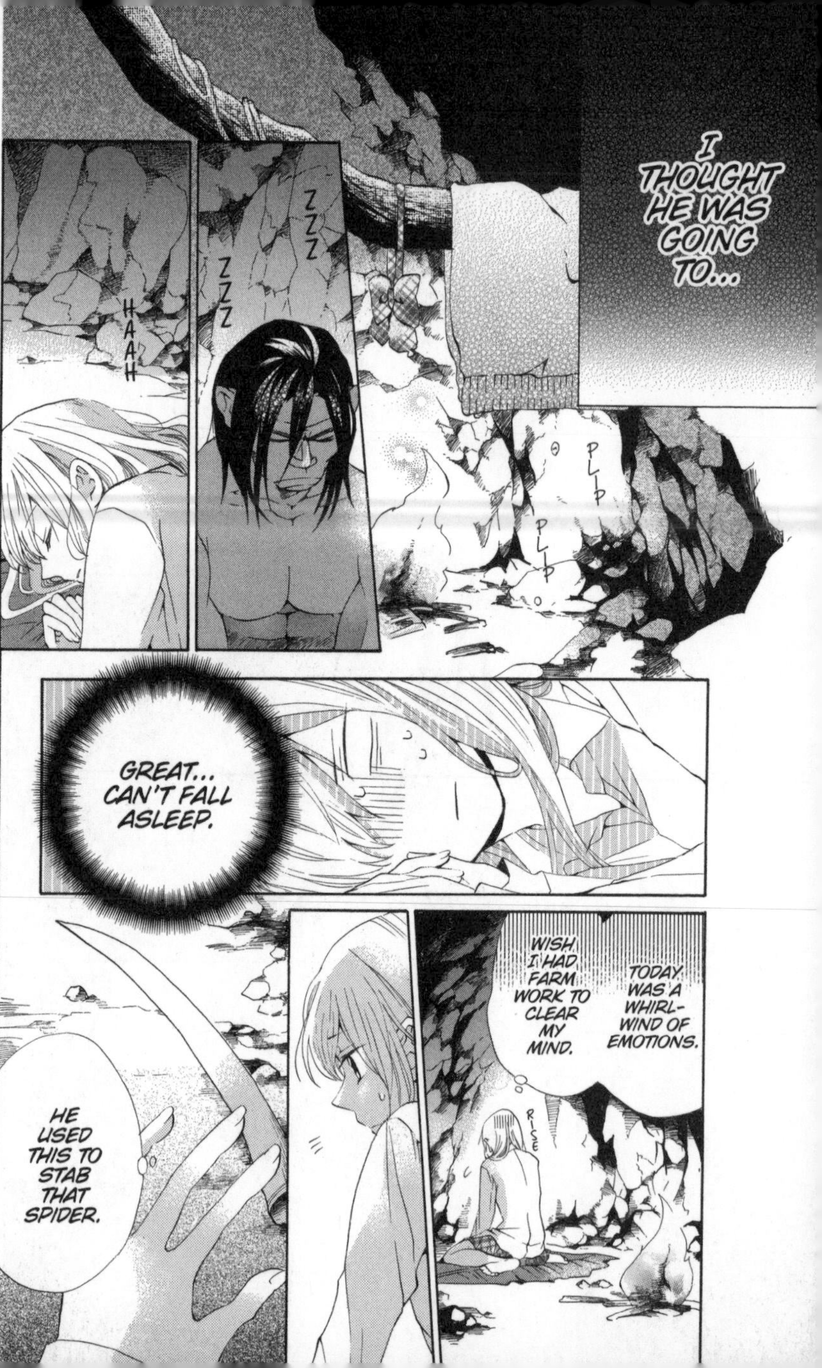

I THOUGHT HE WAS GOING TO...
PLIP
PLIP
ZZZ
ZZZ
HAAH
GREAT... CAN'T FALL ASLEEP.
TODAY WAS A WHIRLWIND OF EMOTIONS.
WISH I HAD FARM WORK TO CLEAR MY MIND.
RISE
HE USED THIS TO STAB THAT SPIDER.

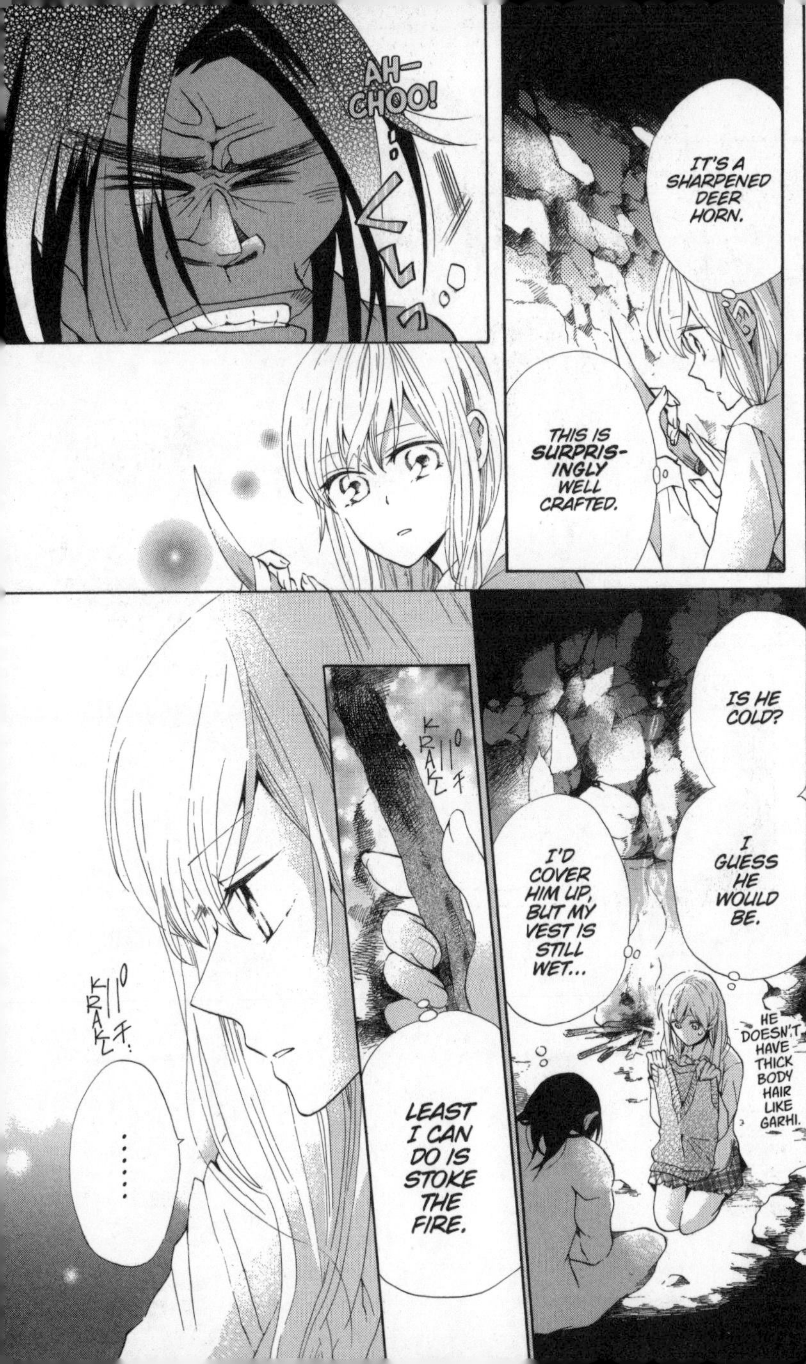
IT'S A SHARPENED DEER HORN.
THIS IS SURPRISINGLY WELL CRAFTED.
AH-CHOO!
IS HE COLD?
I GUESS HE WOULD BE.
HE DOESN'T HAVE THICK BODY HAIR LIKE GARHI.
I'D COVER HIM UP, BUT MY VEST IS STILL WET...
KRAKL
LEAST I CAN DO IS STOKE THE FIRE.
KRAKL
......

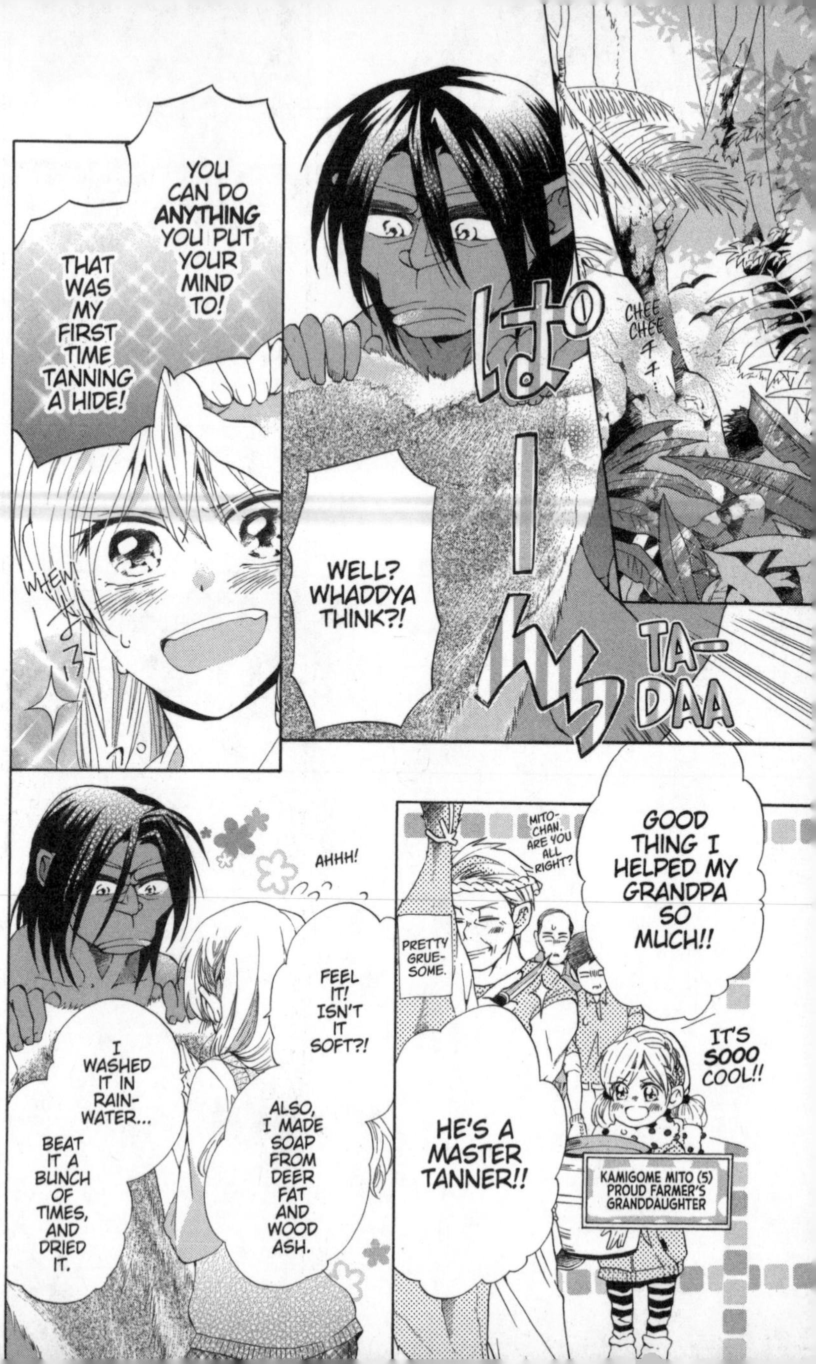

CHEE CHEE
チチ…
TA-DAA
WELL? WHADDYA THINK?!
YOU CAN DO ANYTHING YOU PUT YOUR MIND TO!
THAT WAS MY FIRST TIME TANNING A HIDE!
WHEW
GOOD THING I HELPED MY GRANDPA SO MUCH!!
MITO-CHAN, ARE YOU ALL RIGHT?
PRETTY GRUESOME.
IT'S SOOO COOL!!
HE'S A MASTER TANNER!!
KAMIGOME MITO (5) PROUD FARMER'S GRANDDAUGHTER
AHHH!
FEEL IT! ISN'T IT SOFT?!
I WASHED IT IN RAIN-WATER...
BEAT IT A BUNCH OF TIMES, AND DRIED IT.
ALSO, I MADE SOAP FROM DEER FAT AND WOOD ASH.

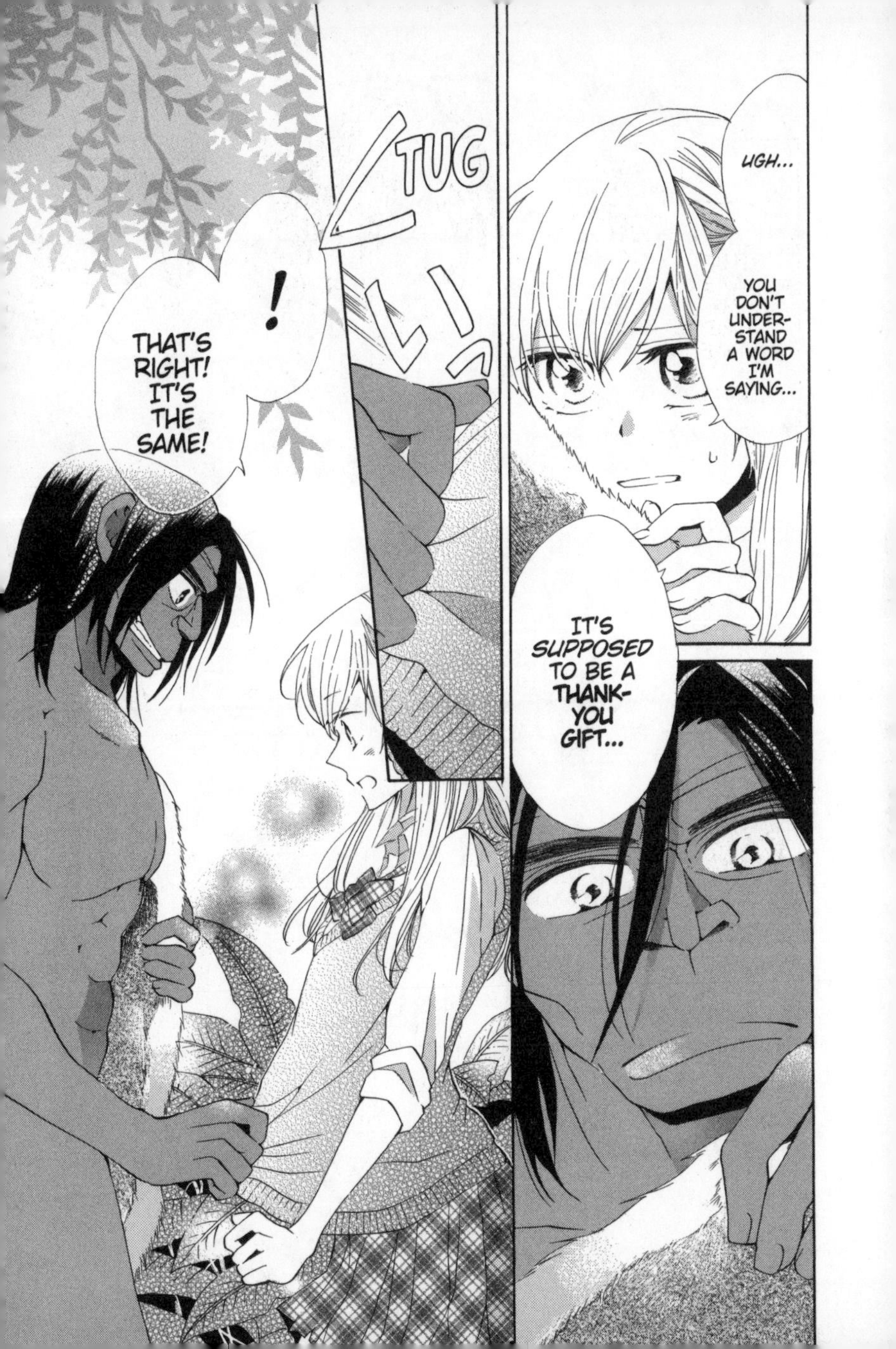
UGH...
YOU DON'T UNDERSTAND A WORD I'M SAYING...
IT'S SUPPOSED TO BE A THANK-YOU GIFT...
TUG
!
THAT'S RIGHT! IT'S THE SAME!

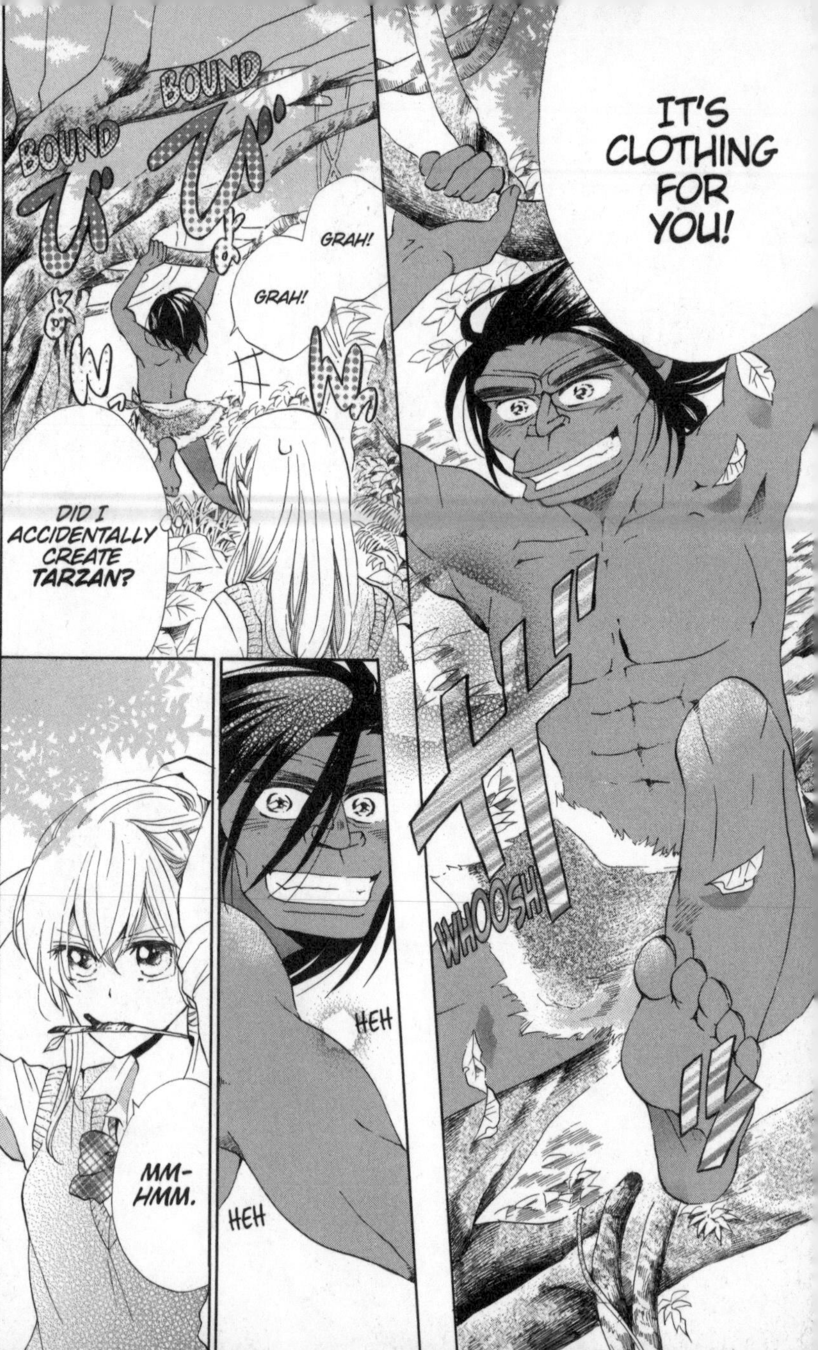

IT'S CLOTHING FOR YOU!
WHOOSH
BOUND
BOUND
GRAH!
GRAH!
DID I ACCIDENTALLY CREATE TARZAN?
HEH
HEH
MM-HMM.

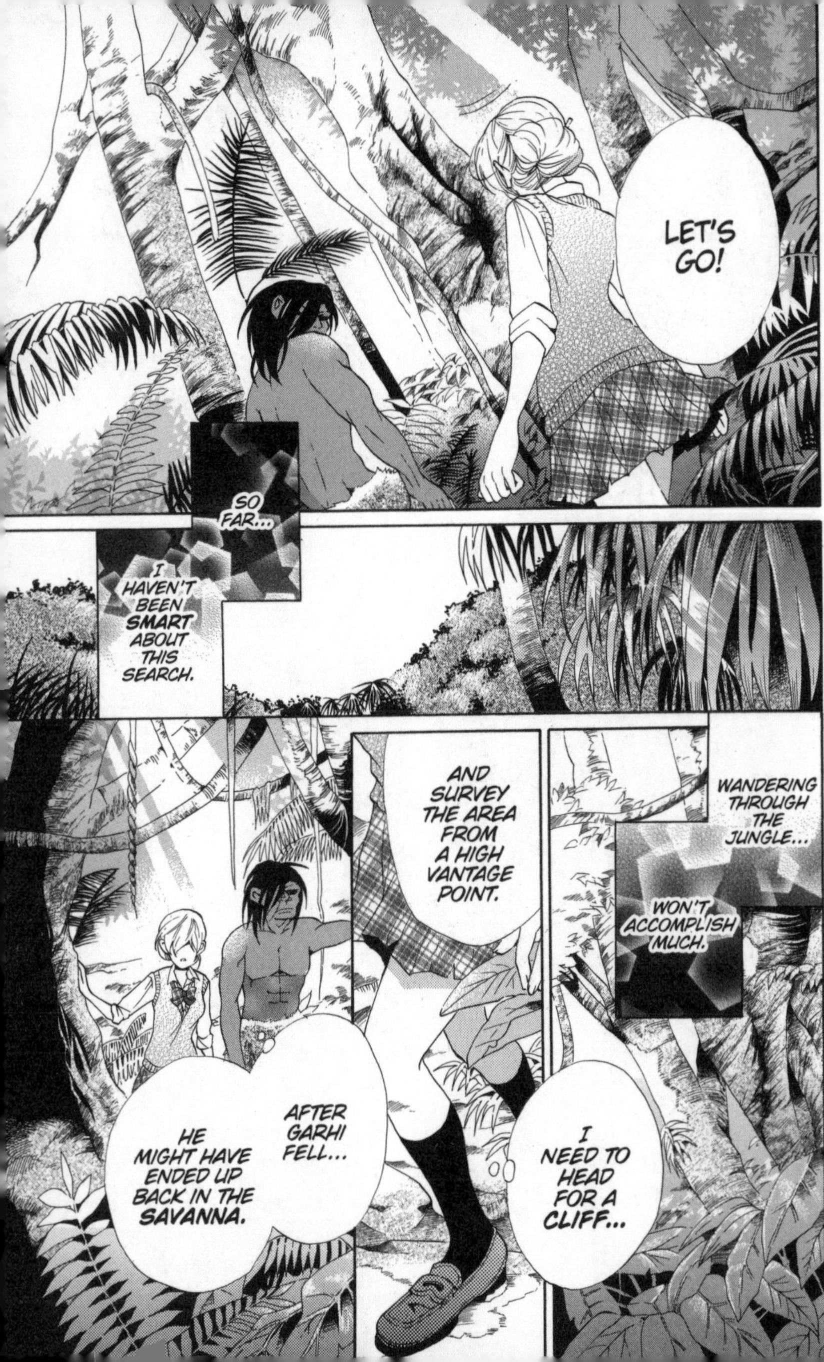
LET'S GO!
SO FAR...
I HAVEN'T BEEN SMART ABOUT THIS SEARCH.
WANDERING THROUGH THE JUNGLE...
WON'T ACCOMPLISH MUCH.
I NEED TO HEAD FOR A CLIFF...
AND SURVEY THE AREA FROM A HIGH VANTAGE POINT.
AFTER GARHI FELL...
HE MIGHT HAVE ENDED UP BACK IN THE SAVANNA.

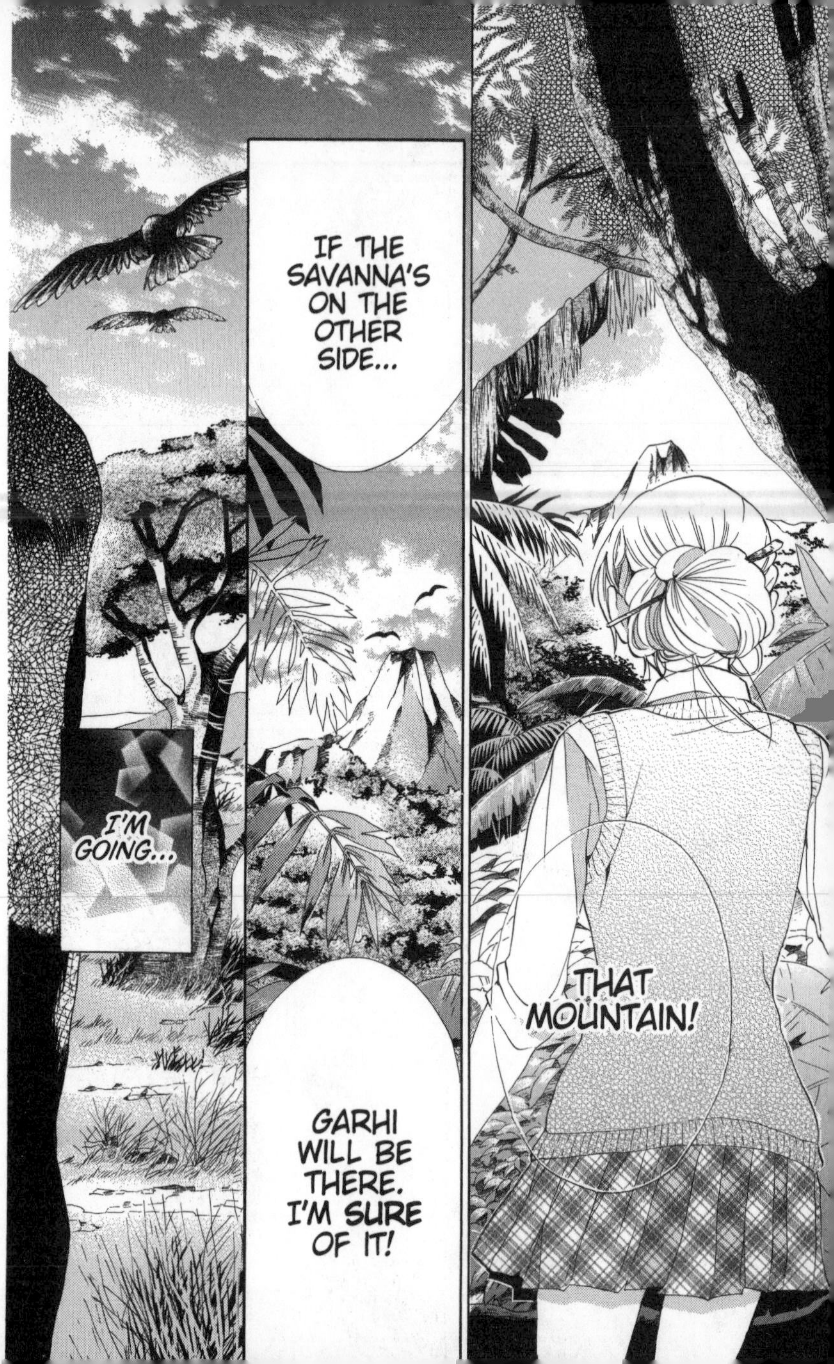
THAT MOUNTAIN!
IF THE SAVANNA'S ON THE OTHER SIDE...
GARHI WILL BE THERE. I'M SURE OF IT!
I'M GOING...

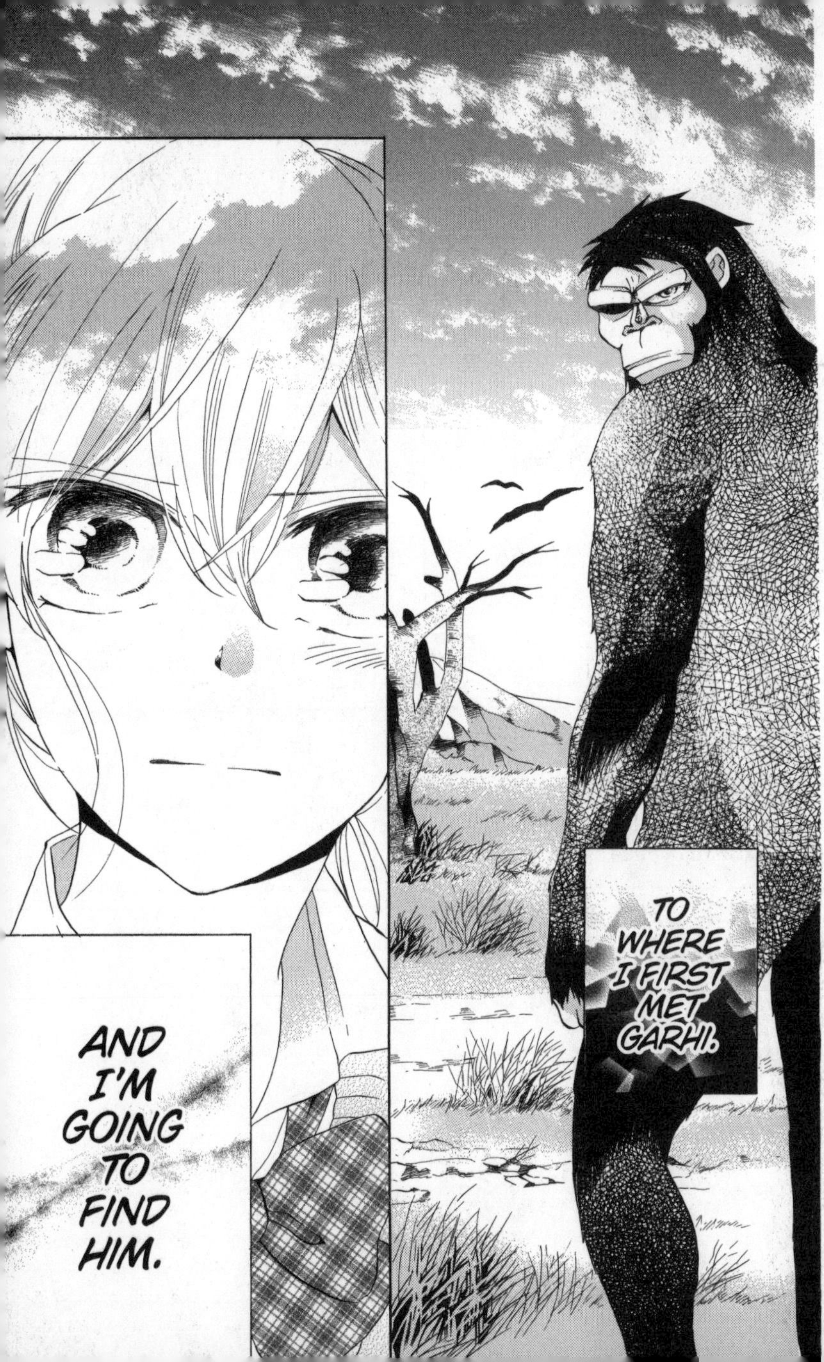
TO WHERE I FIRST MET GARHI.
AND I'M GOING TO FIND HIM.

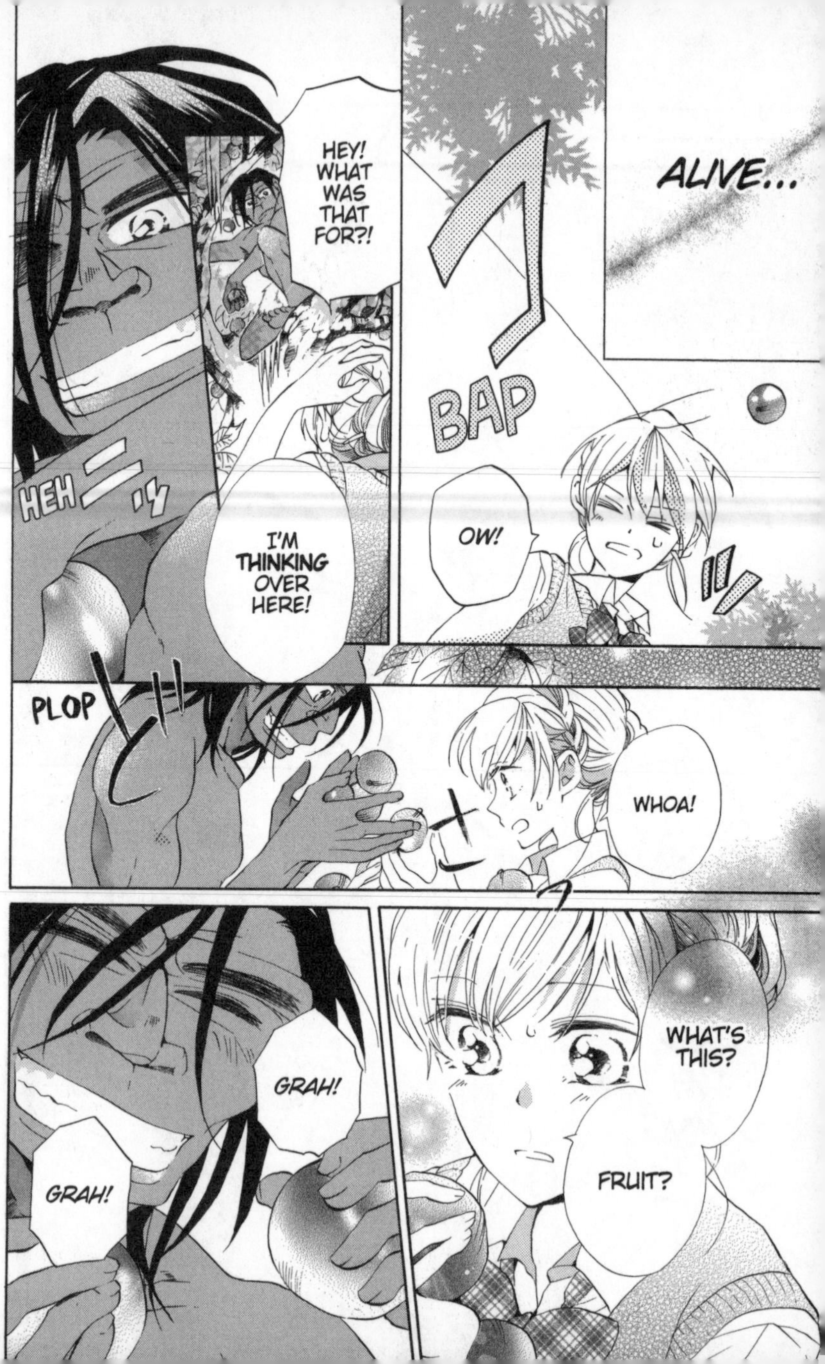
ALIVE...
BAP
OW!
HEY! WHAT WAS THAT FOR?!
HEH
I'M THINKING OVER HERE!
WHOA!
PLOP
WHAT'S THIS?
FRUIT?
GRAH!
GRAH!

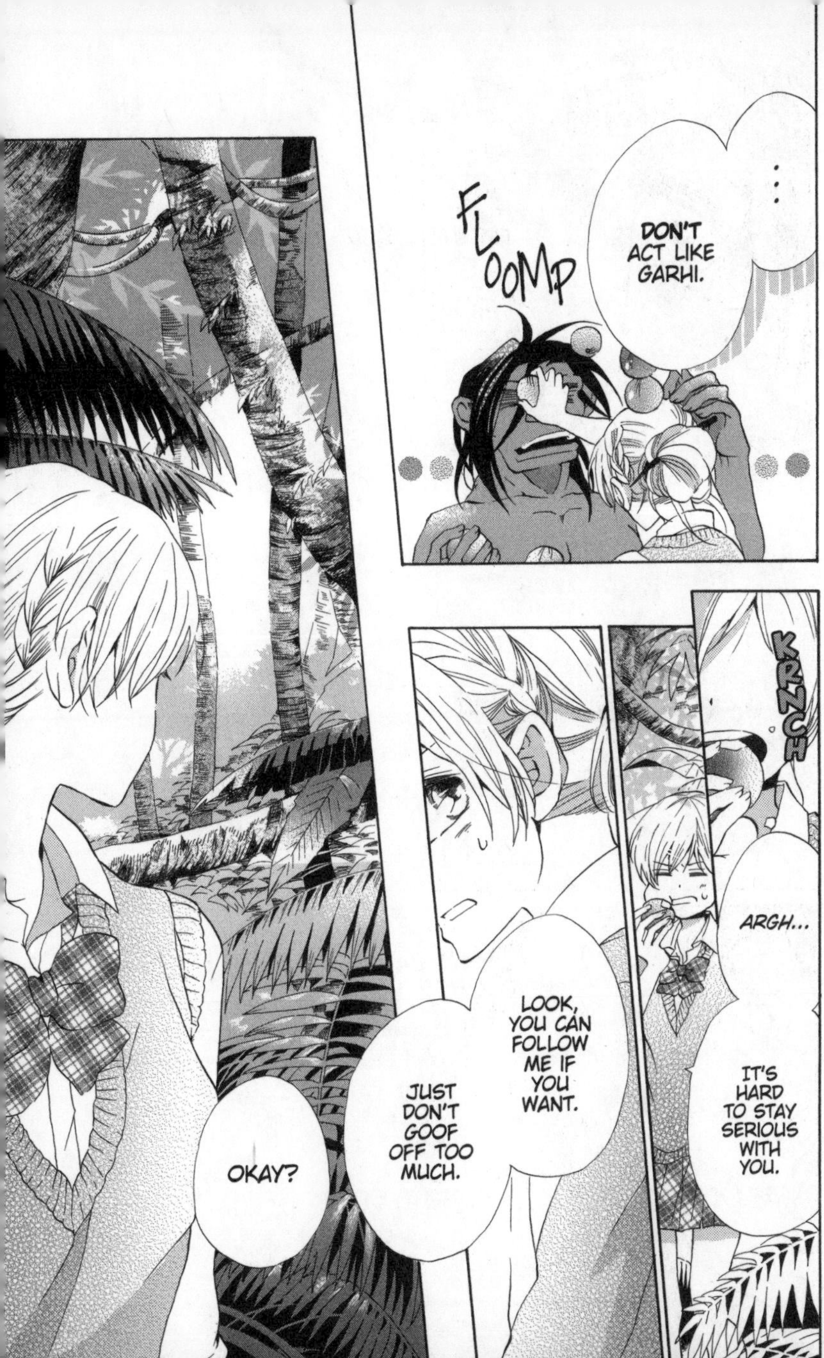
...
DON'T ACT LIKE GARHI.
FLOOMP
KRNCH
ARGH...
IT'S HARD TO STAY SERIOUS WITH YOU.
LOOK, YOU CAN FOLLOW ME IF YOU WANT.
JUST DON'T GOOF OFF TOO MUCH.
OKAY?

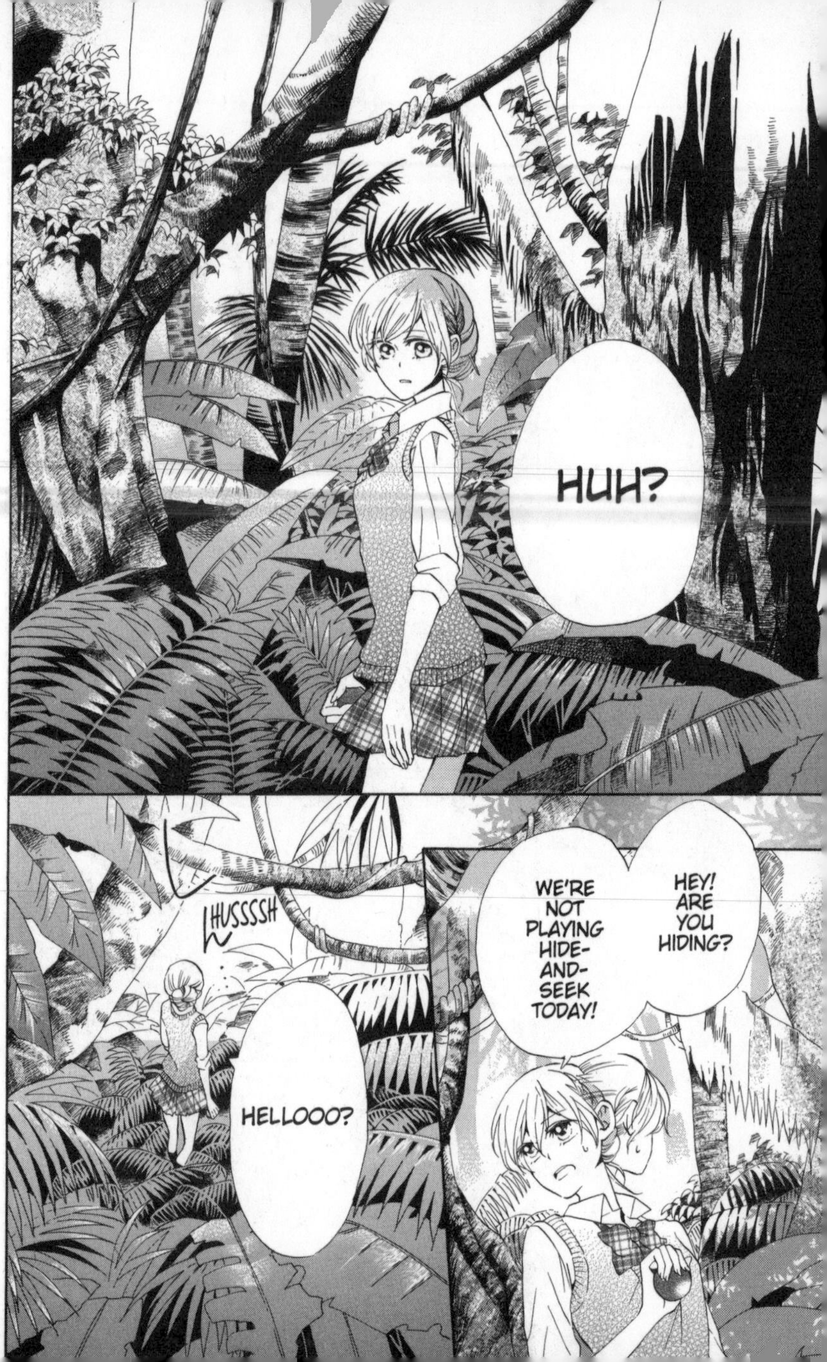
HUH?
HEY! ARE YOU HIDING?
WE'RE NOT PLAYING HIDE-AND-SEEK TODAY!
HUSSSSH
HELLOOO?

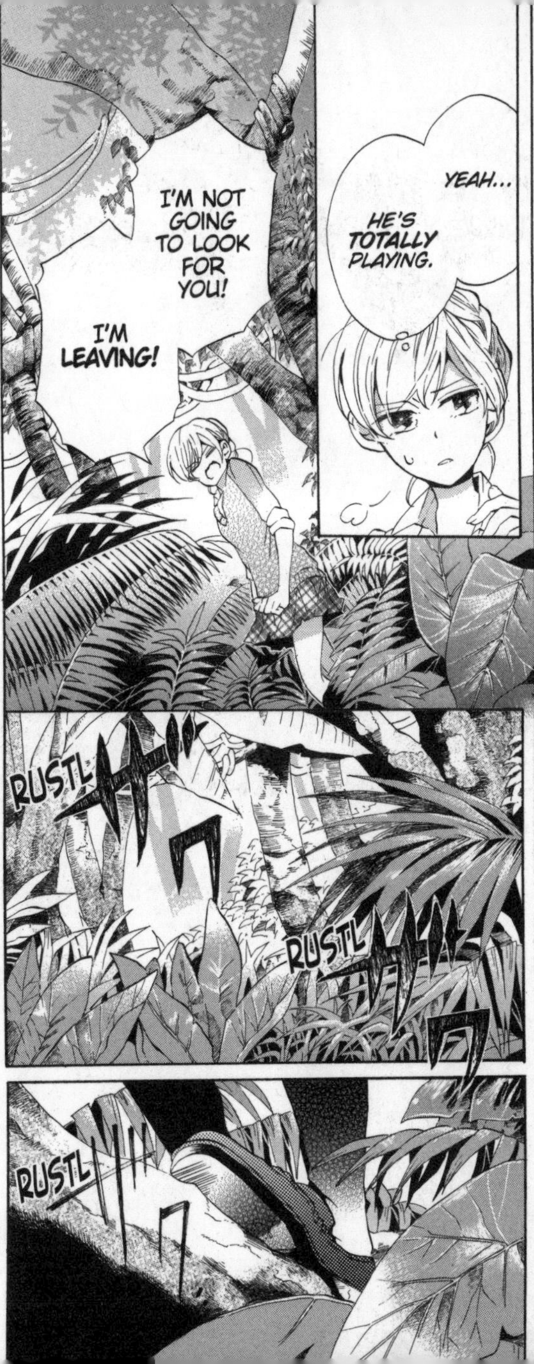
YEAH...
HE'S TOTALLY PLAYING.
I'M NOT GOING TO LOOK FOR YOU!
I'M LEAVING!
RUSTL
RUSTL
RUSTL

3

CHAPTER 6 IS WHEN I STARTED ENJOYING DRAWING THE JUNGLE.

MITO'S GOTTEN MORE EXPRESSIVE.

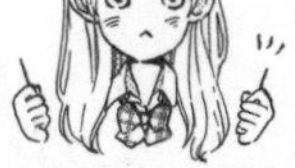

TO MAKE BRAIDS LIKE THIS...

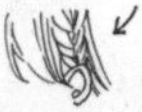

SHE ACTUALLY CARRIES HAIRPINS WITH HER.

SHE ALSO MAKES CLEVER USE OF TWIGS AND VINES.

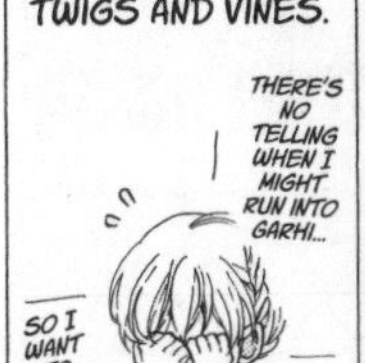
THERE'S NO TELLING WHEN I MIGHT RUN INTO GARHI...
SO I WANT TO LOOK AS CUTE AS I CAN!

THAT'S THE REASON.

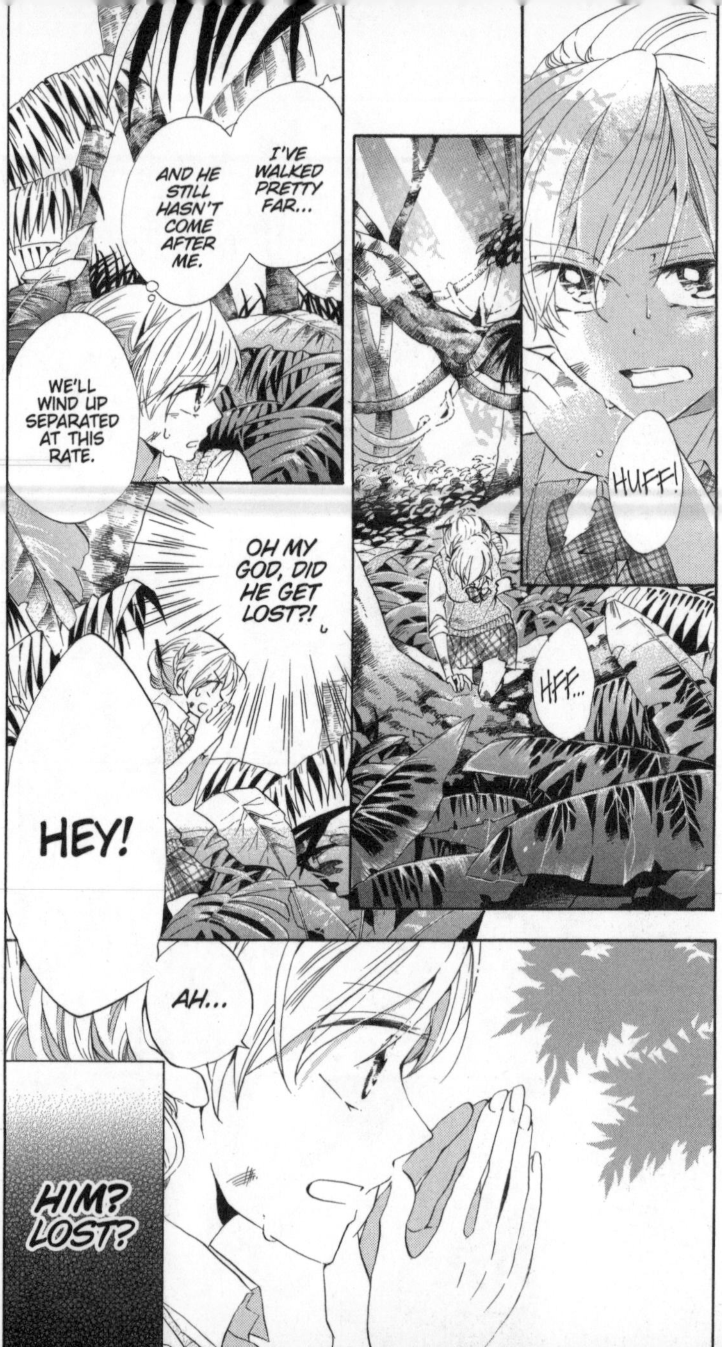
HUFF!
HFF...
I'VE WALKED PRETTY FAR...
AND HE STILL HASN'T COME AFTER ME.
WE'LL WIND UP SEPARATED AT THIS RATE.
OH MY GOD, DID HE GET LOST?!
HEY!
AH...
HIM? LOST?

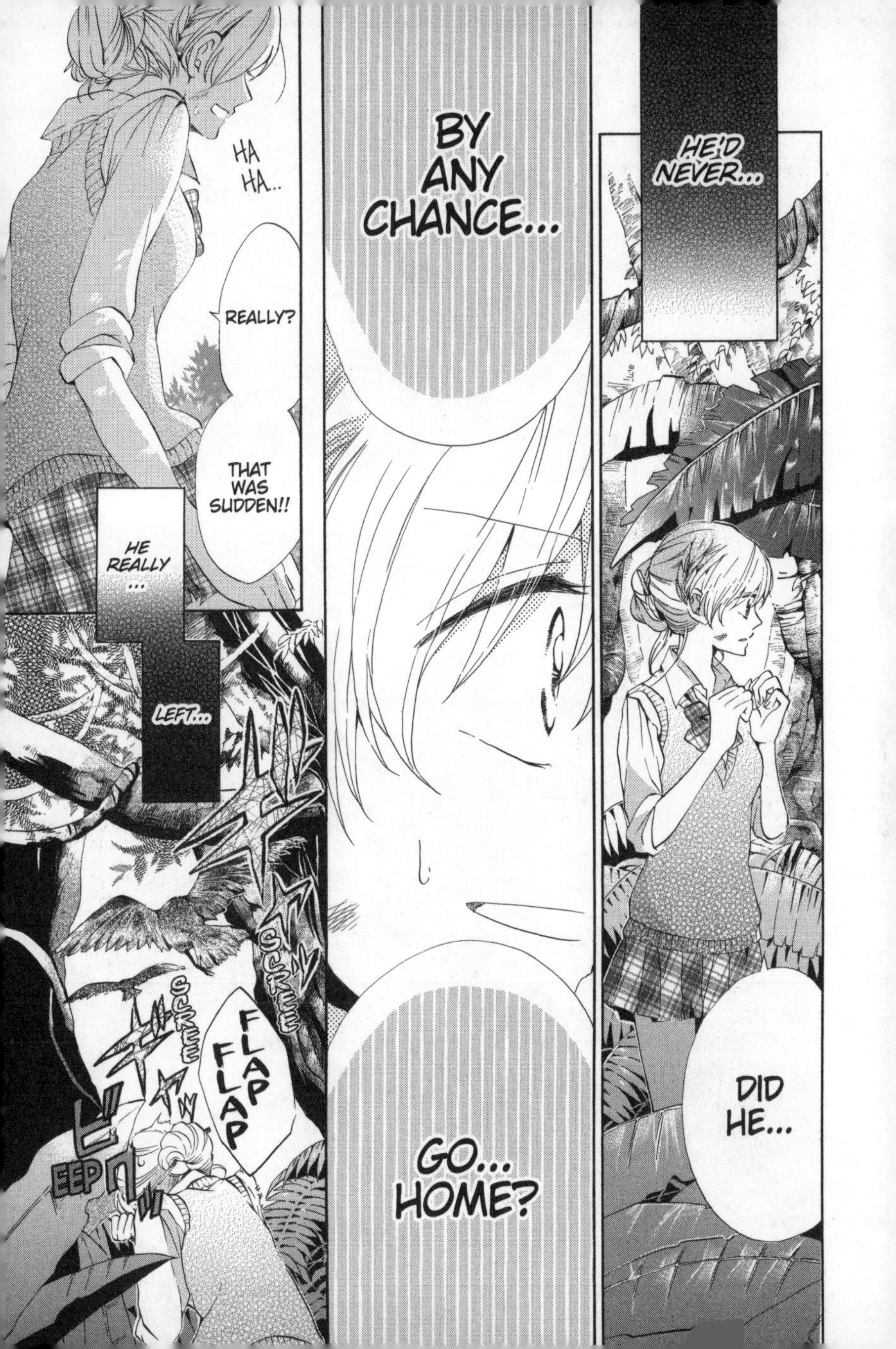

HE'D NEVER...
DID HE...
BY ANY CHANCE...
GO... HOME?
HA HA...
REALLY?
THAT WAS SUDDEN!!
HE REALLY ...
LEFT...
SCREE
FLAP FLAP
SCREE
EEP

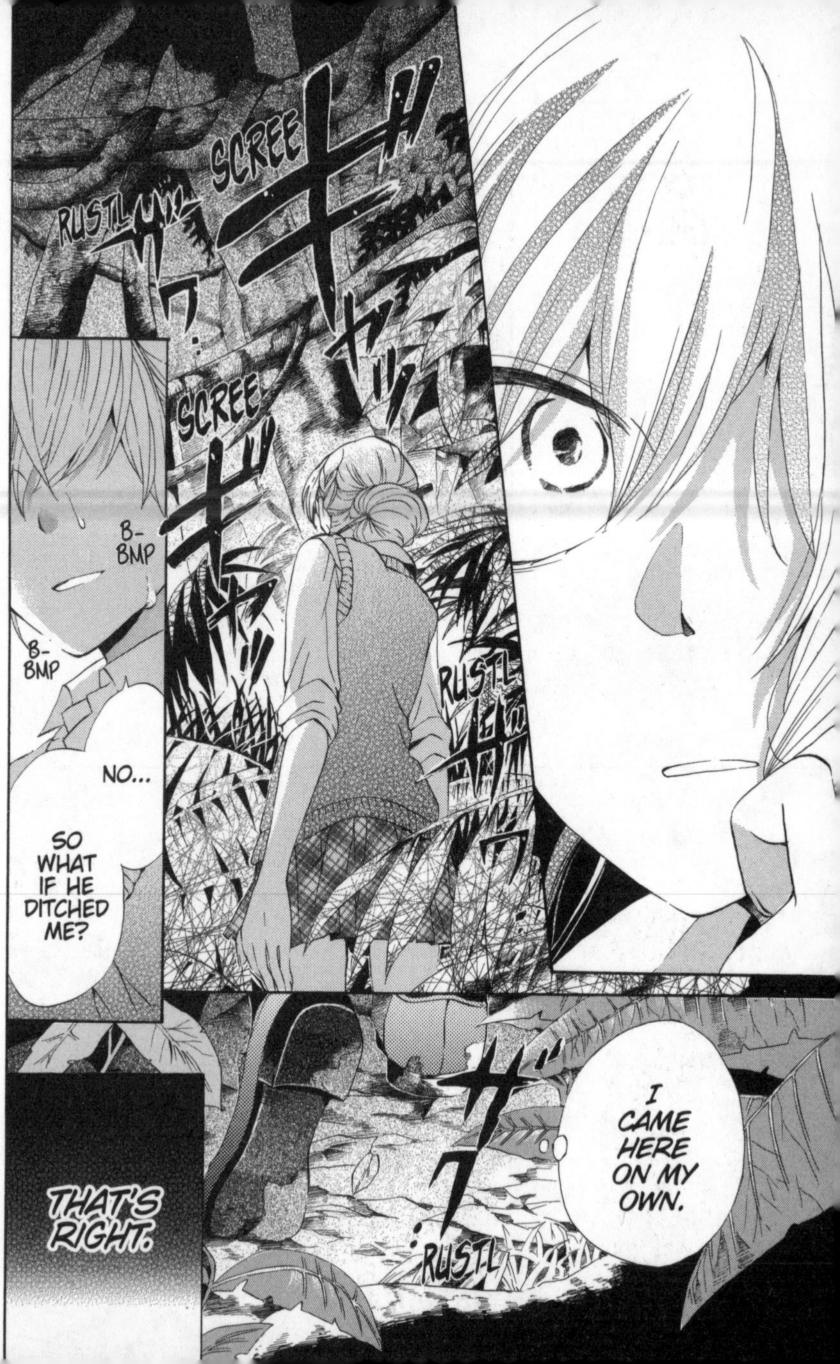
SCREE
RUSTL
SCREE
RUSTL
B-BMP
B-BMP
NO...
SO WHAT IF HE DITCHED ME?
I CAME HERE ON MY OWN.
RUSTL
THAT'S RIGHT.

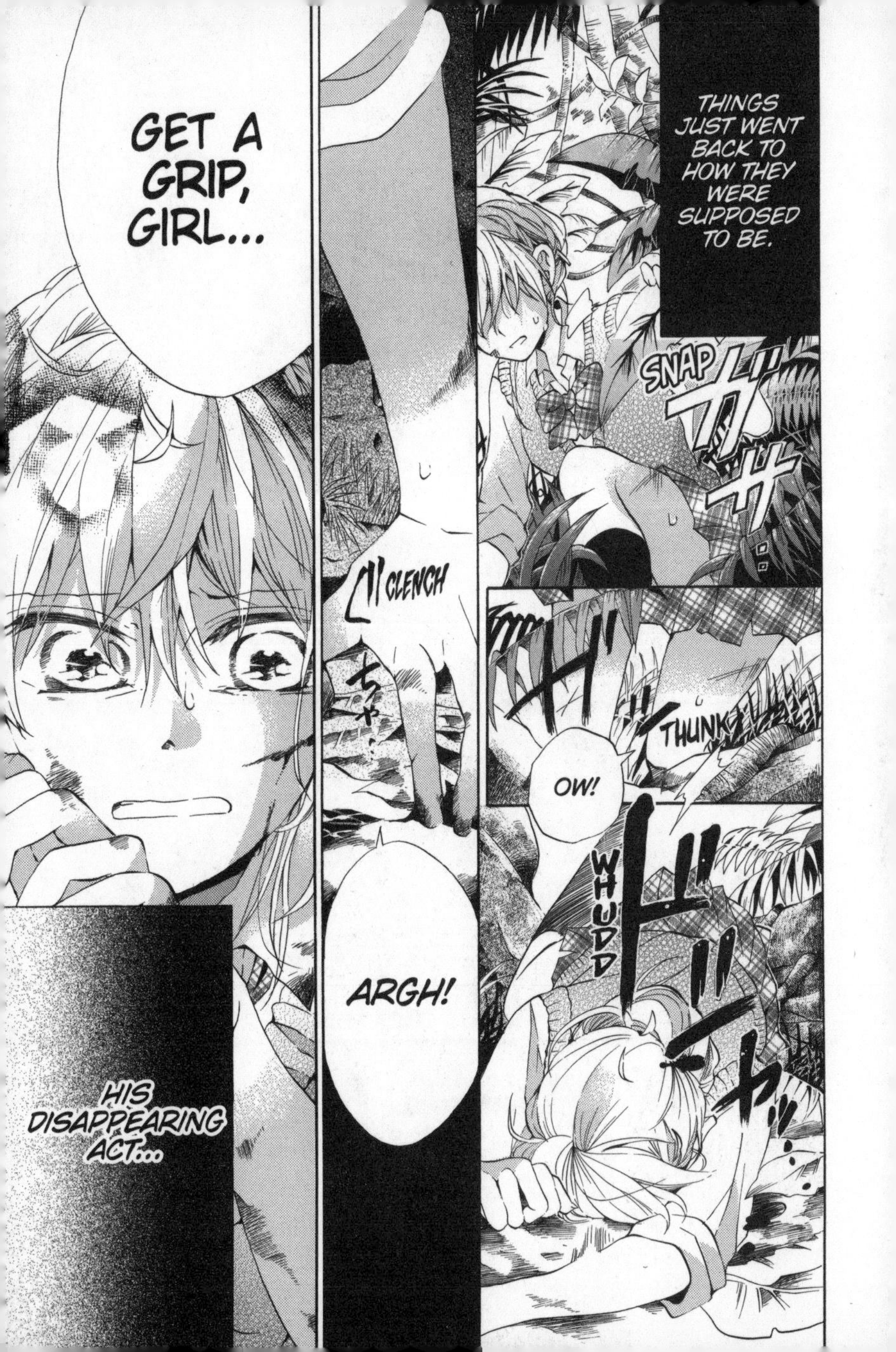
THINGS JUST WENT BACK TO HOW THEY WERE SUPPOSED TO BE.
SNAP
THUNK
OW!
WHUDD
CLENCH
ARGH!
GET A GRIP, GIRL...
HIS DISAPPEARING ACT...

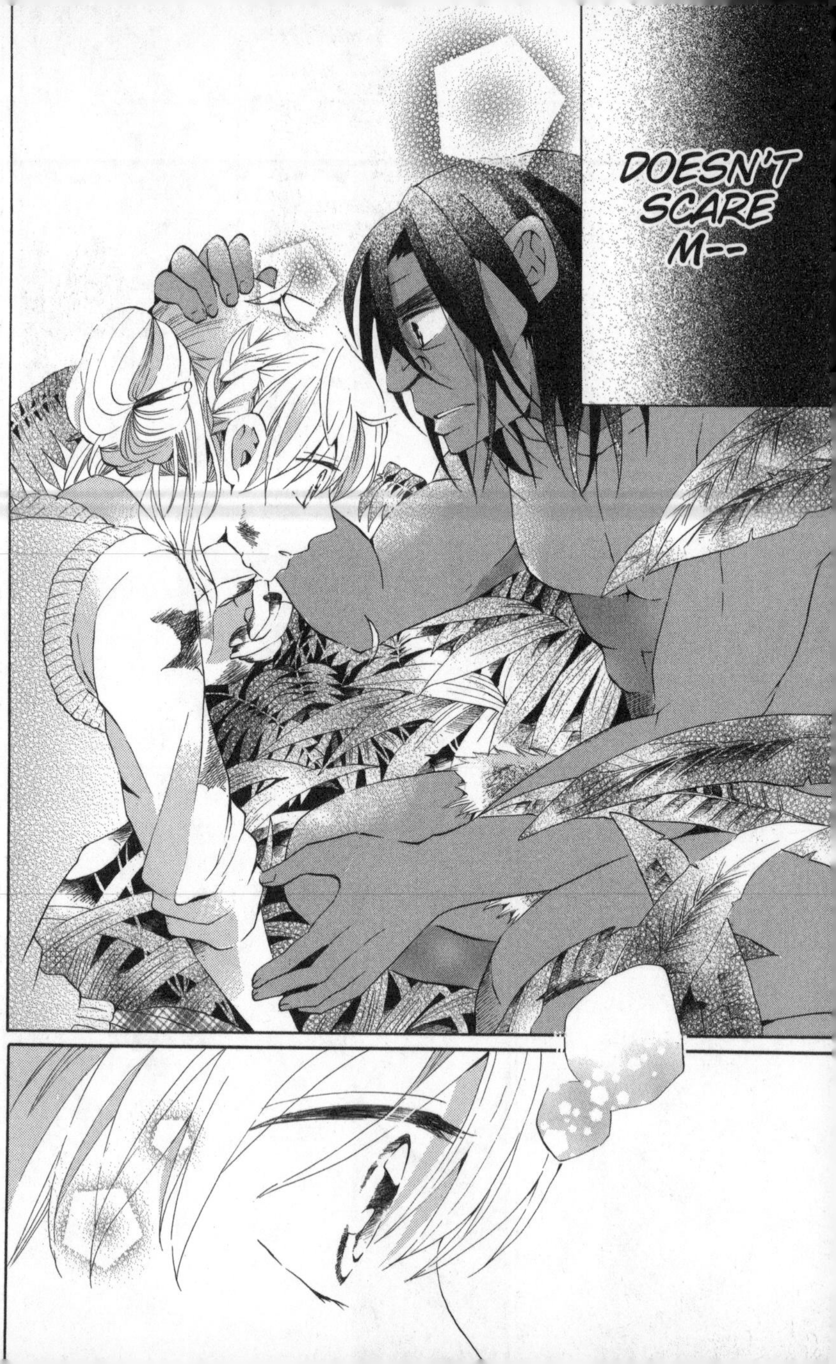
DOESN'T SCARE M--

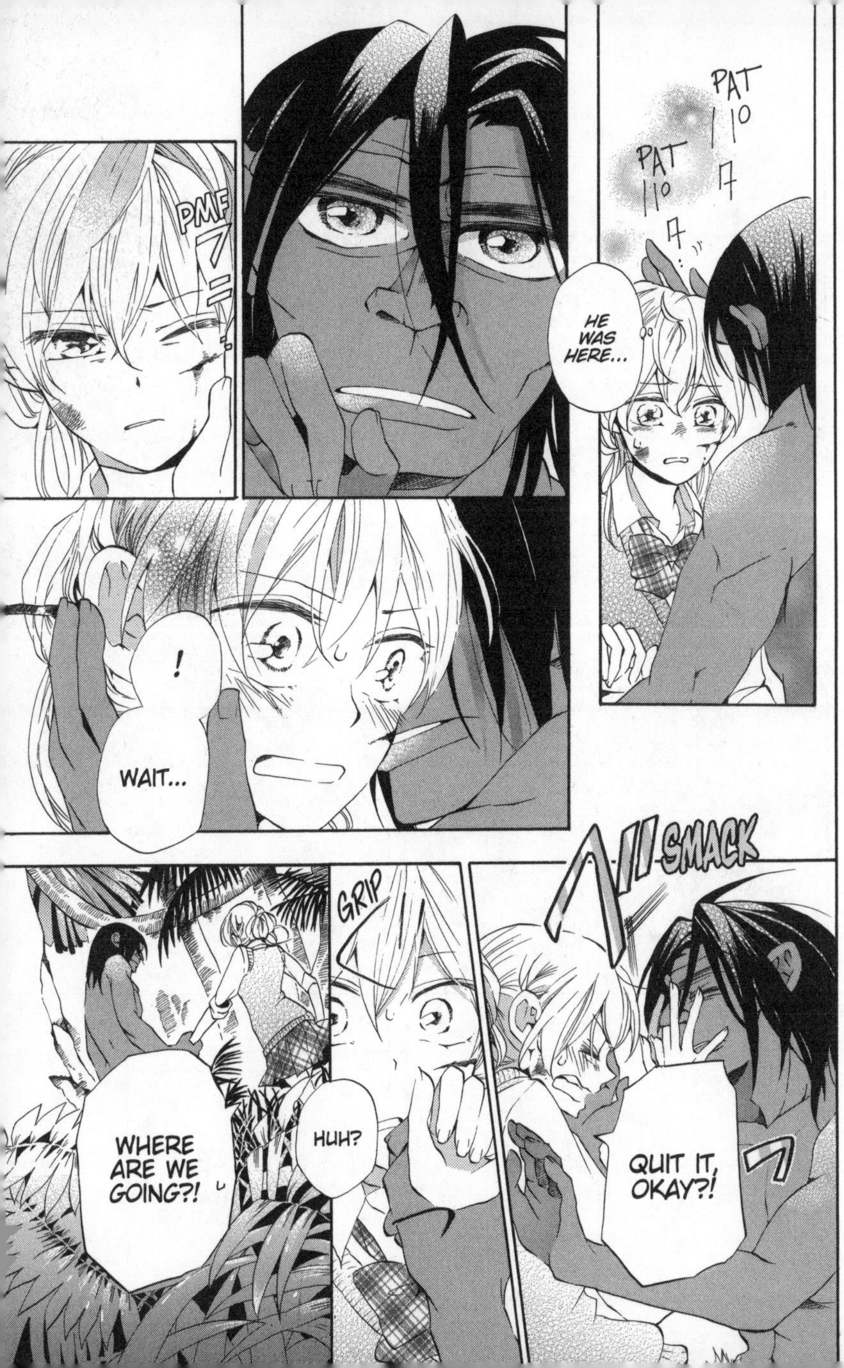
PAT
PAT
HE WAS HERE...
PMF
!
WAIT...
SMACK
QUIT IT, OKAY?!
GRIP
HUH?
WHERE ARE WE GOING?!

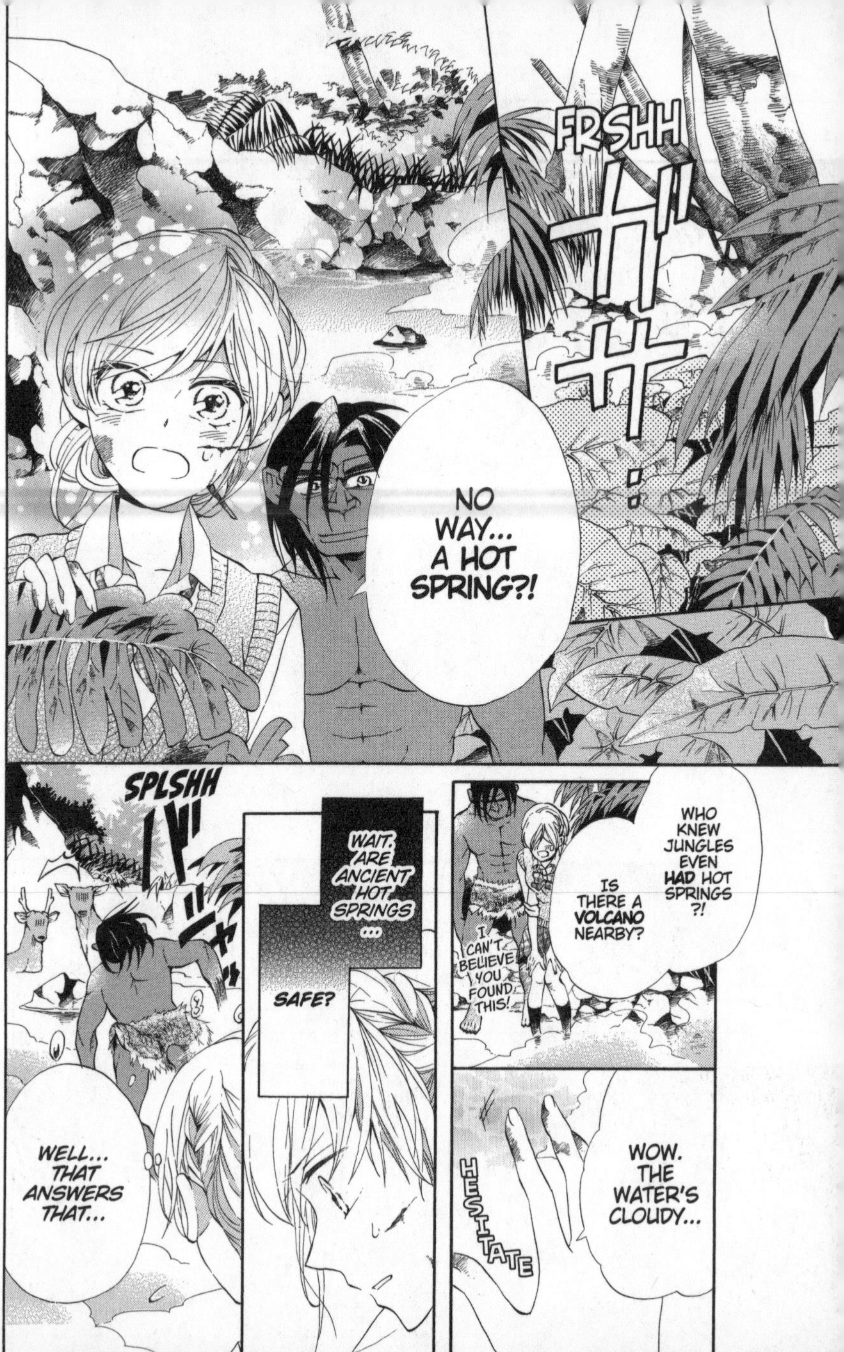
FRSHH
NO WAY... A HOT SPRING?!
WHO KNEW JUNGLES EVEN HAD HOT SPRINGS?!
IS THERE A VOLCANO NEARBY?
I CAN'T BELIEVE YOU FOUND THIS!
WOW. THE WATER'S CLOUDY...
HESITATE
WAIT. ARE ANCIENT HOT SPRINGS...
SAFE?
SPLSHH
WELL... THAT ANSWERS THAT...

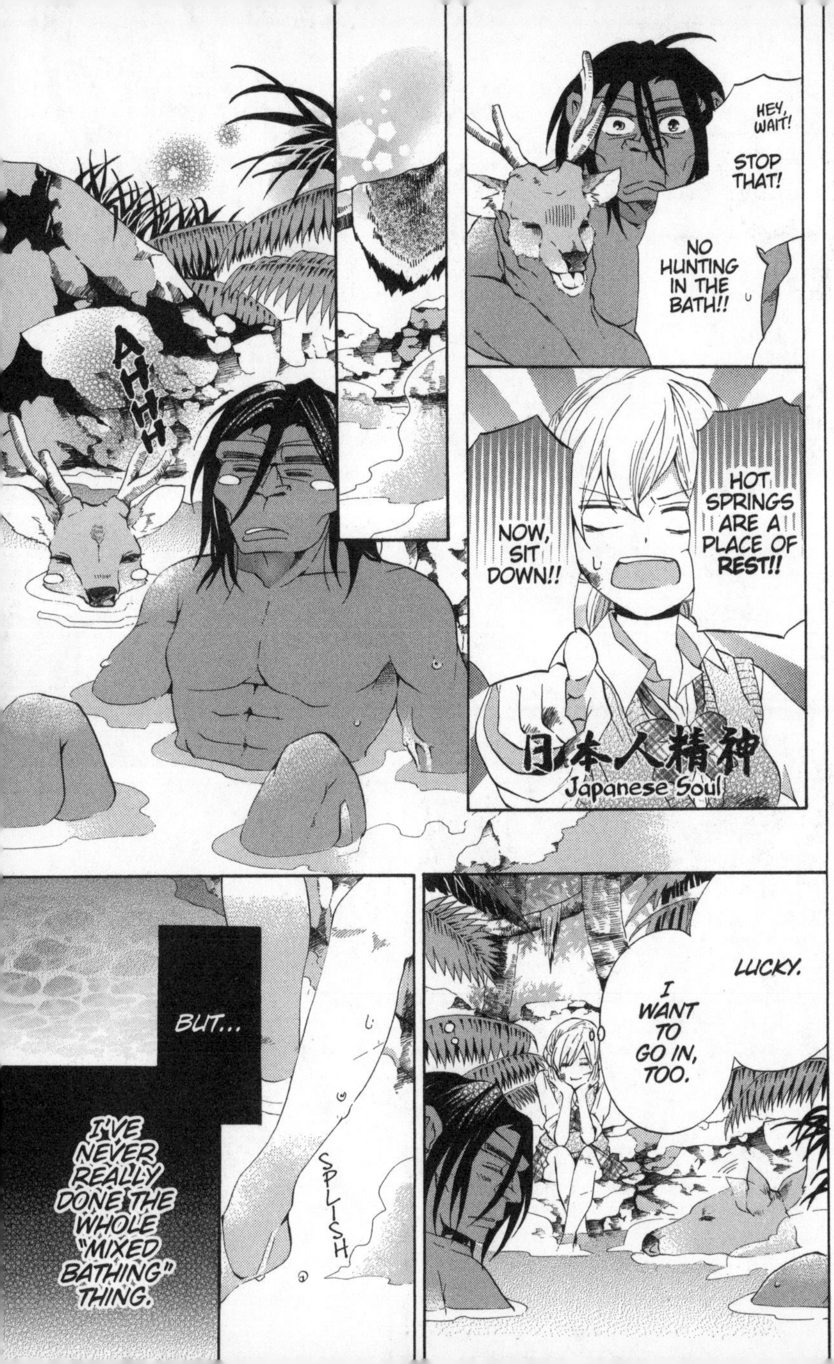
HEY, WAIT!
STOP THAT!
NO HUNTING IN THE BATH!!
HOT SPRINGS ARE A PLACE OF REST!!
NOW, SIT DOWN!!
日本人精神
Japanese Soul
AHHH
LUCKY.
I WANT TO GO IN, TOO.
SPLISH
BUT...
I'VE NEVER REALLY DONE THE WHOLE "MIXED BATHING" THING.

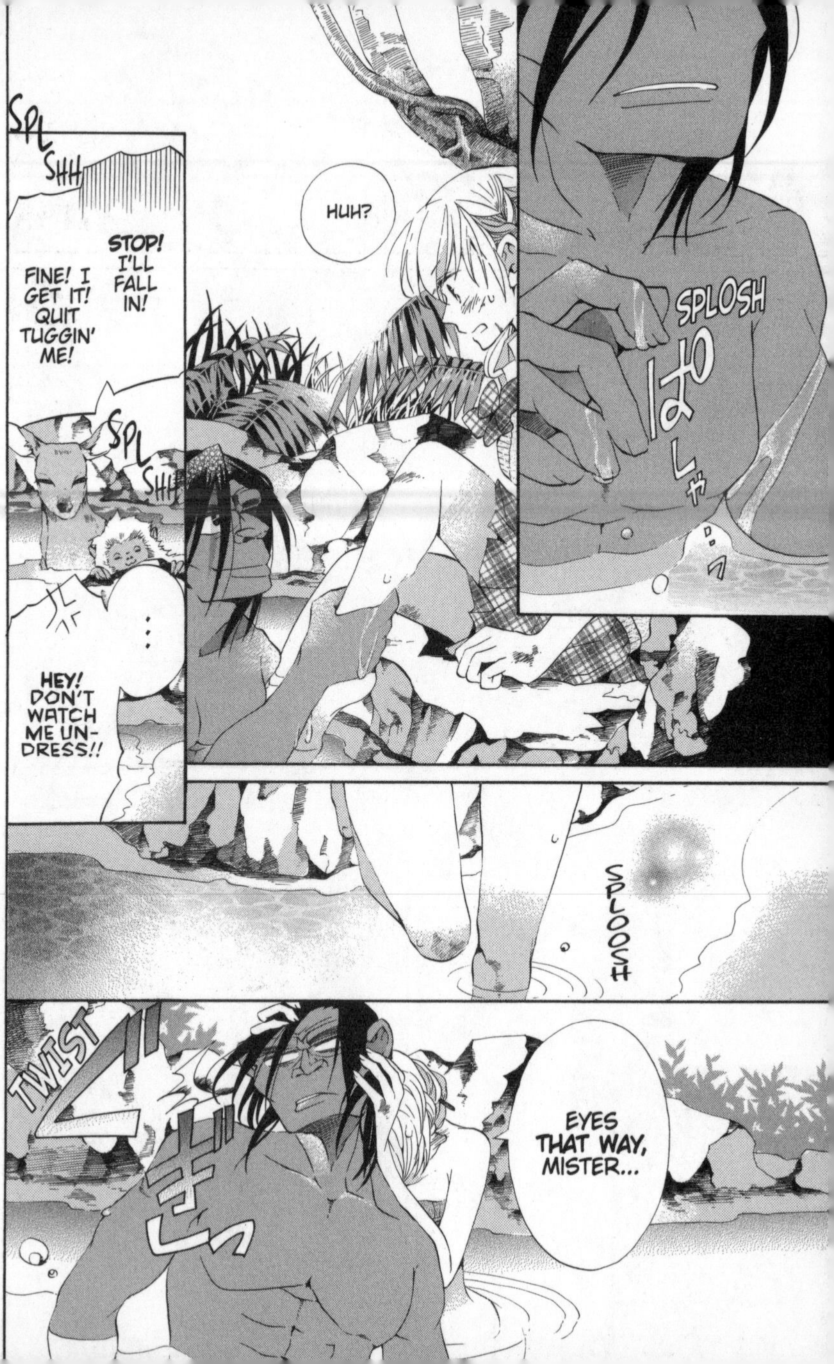
SPLOSH
ぱしゃっ
HUH?
SPL SHH
STOP! I'LL FALL IN!
FINE! I GET IT! QUIT TUGGIN' ME!
SPL SHH
...
HEY! DON'T WATCH ME UN-DRESS!!
SPLOOSH
EYES THAT WAY, MISTER...
TWIST
ぎゅっ

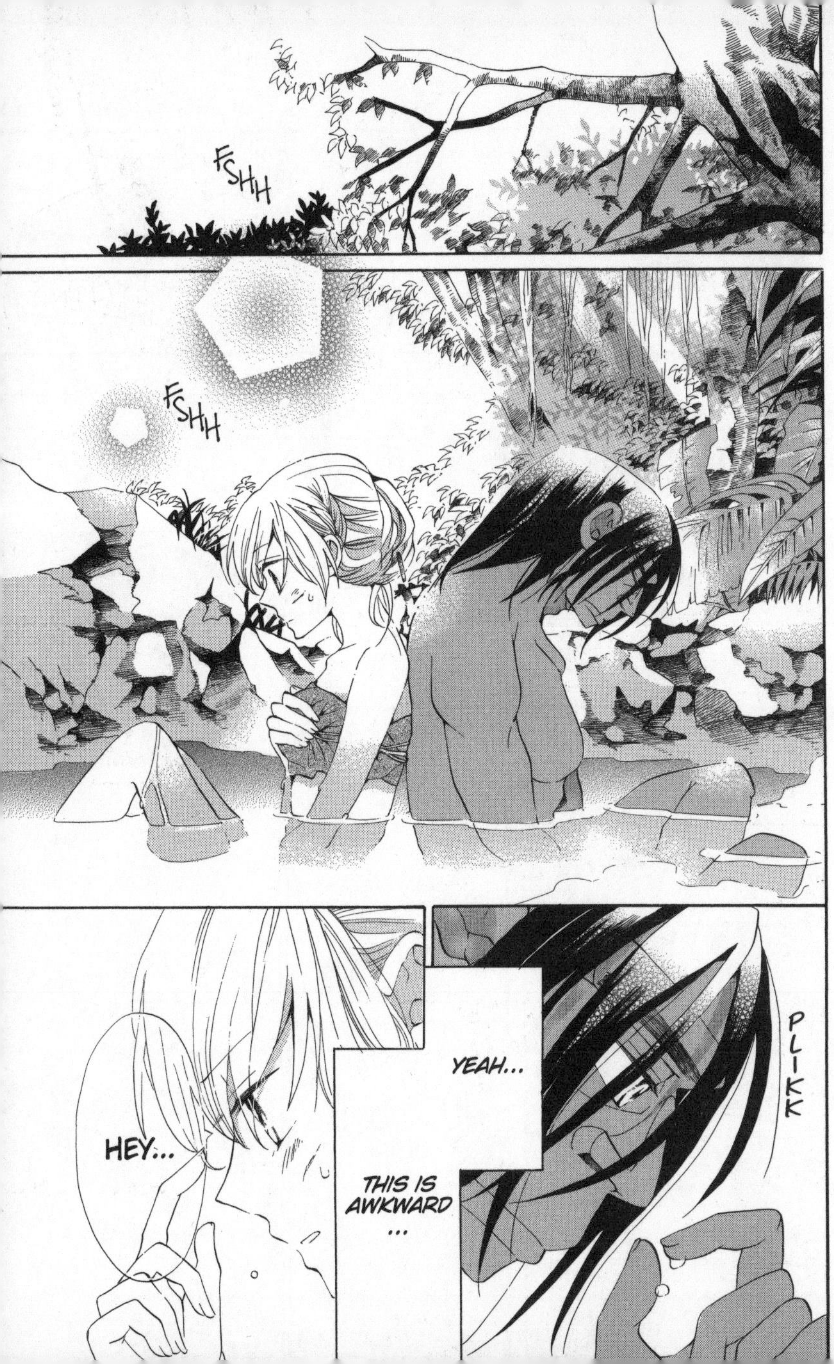
FSHH
FSHH
PLIKK
YEAH...
THIS IS AWKWARD ...
HEY...

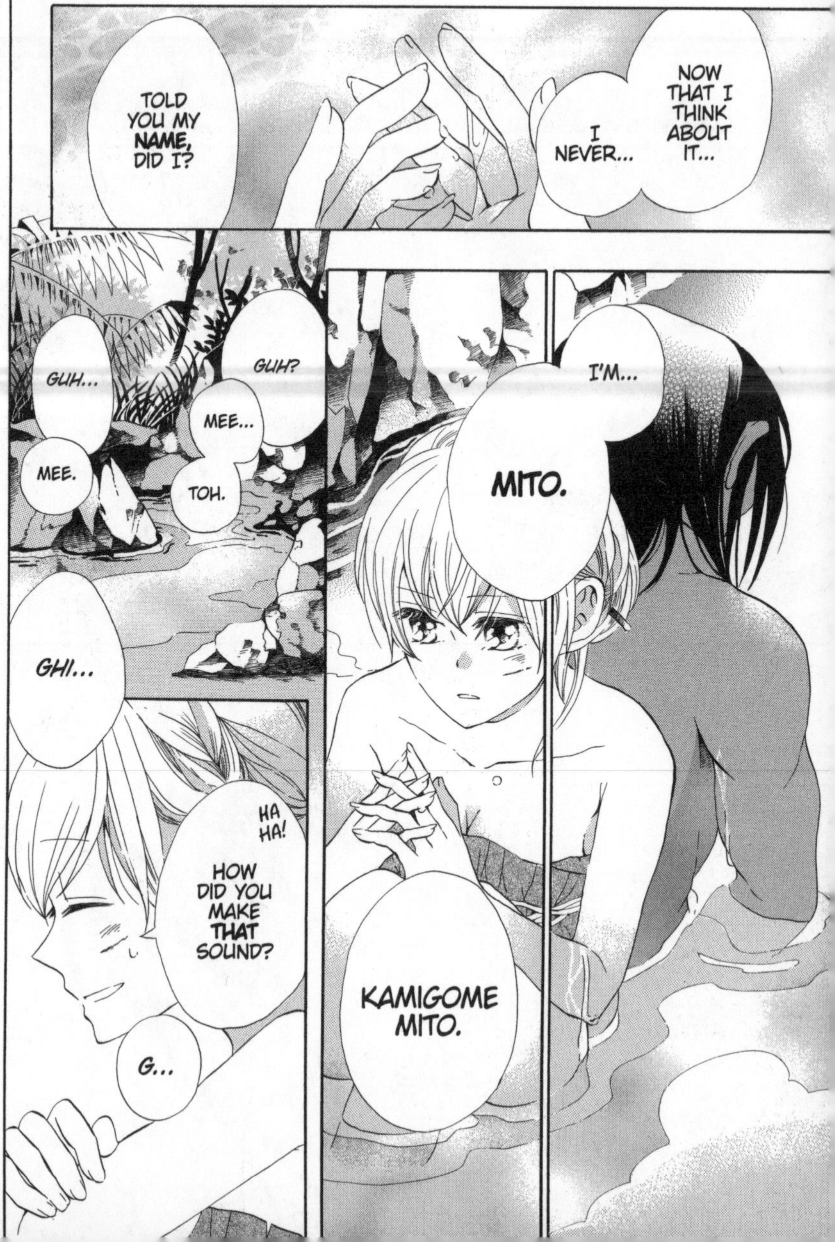
NOW THAT I THINK ABOUT IT...
I NEVER...
TOLD YOU MY NAME, DID I?
I'M...
MITO.
KAMIGOME MITO.
GUH?
GUH...
MEE...
MEE.
TOH.
GHI...
HA HA!
HOW DID YOU MAKE THAT SOUND?
G...

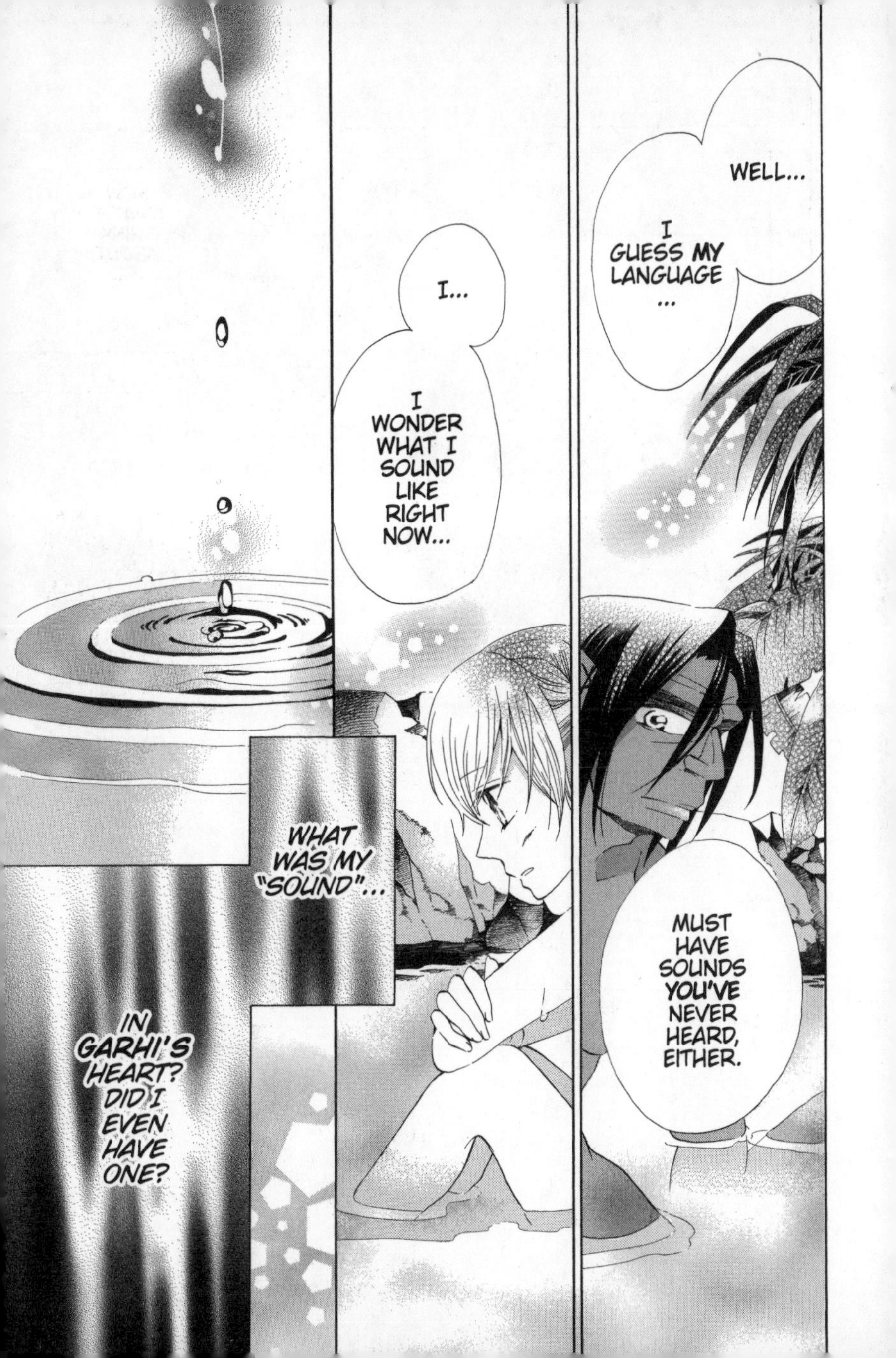
WELL...
I GUESS MY LANGUAGE ...
MUST HAVE SOUNDS YOU'VE NEVER HEARD, EITHER.
I...
I WONDER WHAT I SOUND LIKE RIGHT NOW...
WHAT WAS MY "SOUND"...
IN GARHI'S HEART? DID I EVEN HAVE ONE?

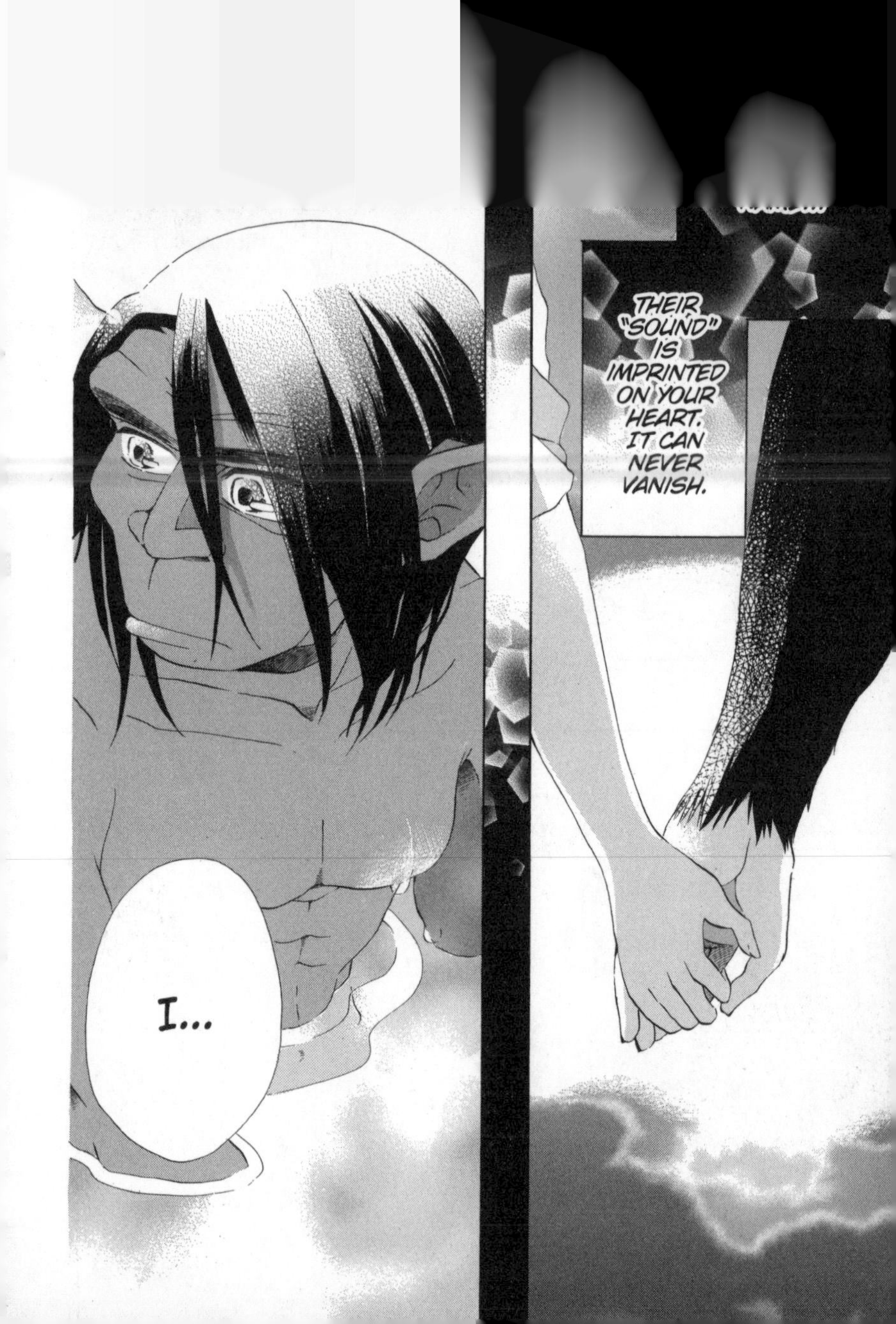
THEIR "SOUND" IS IMPRINTED ON YOUR HEART. IT CAN NEVER VANISH.
I...

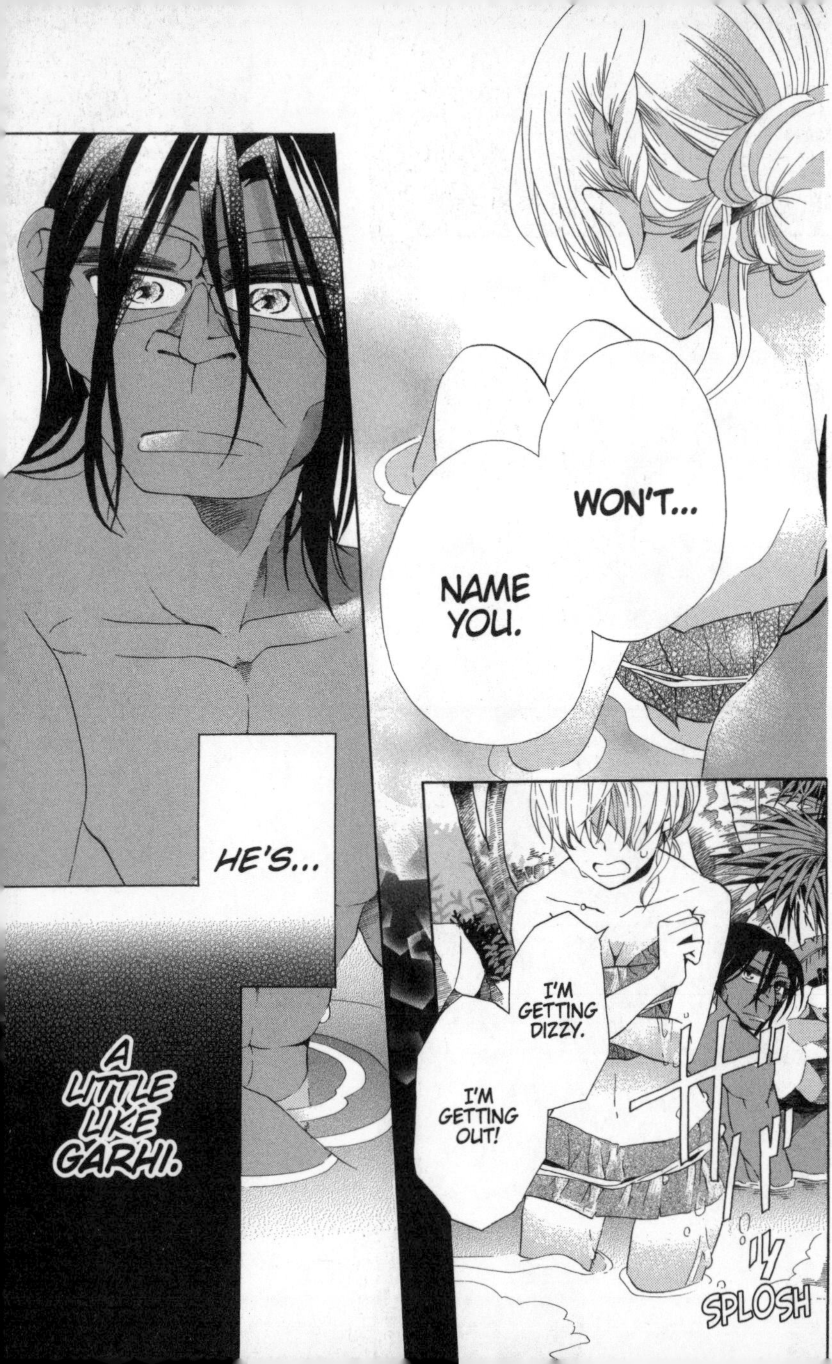
WON'T...
NAME YOU.
I'M GETTING DIZZY.
I'M GETTING OUT!
SPLOSH
HE'S...
A LITTLE LIKE GARHI.

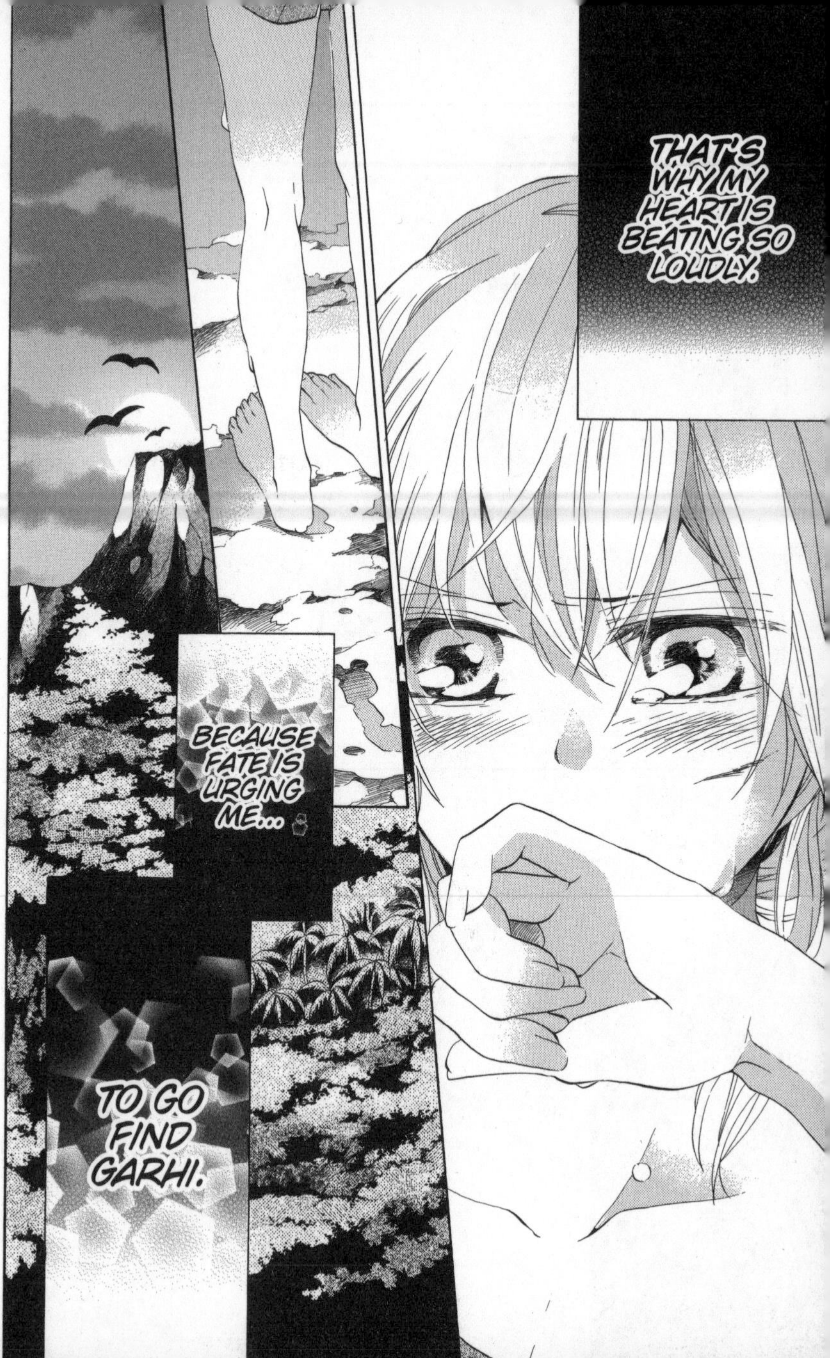
THAT'S WHY MY HEART IS BEATING SO LOUDLY.
BECAUSE FATE IS URGING ME...
TO GO FIND GARHI.

CHAPTER 7
PRIMITIVE Boyfriend

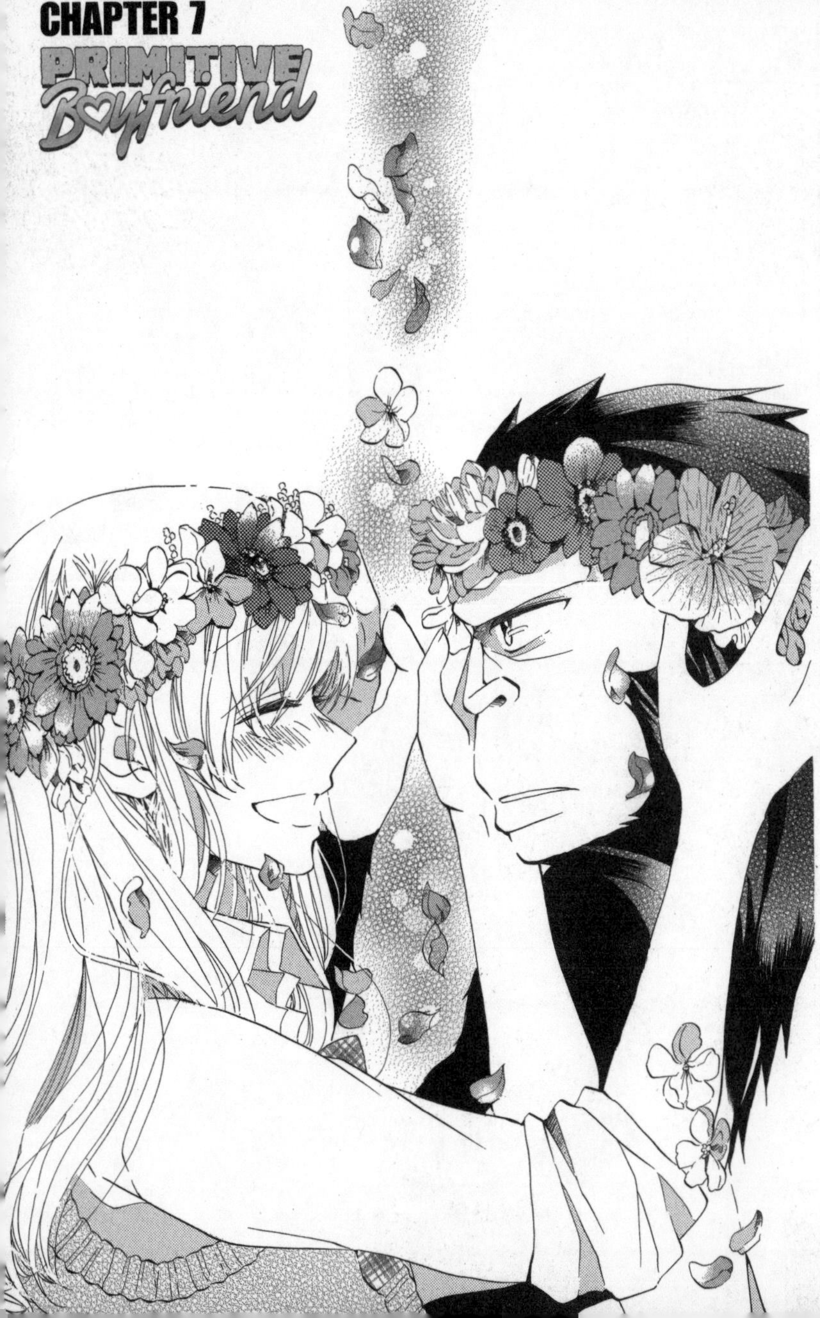

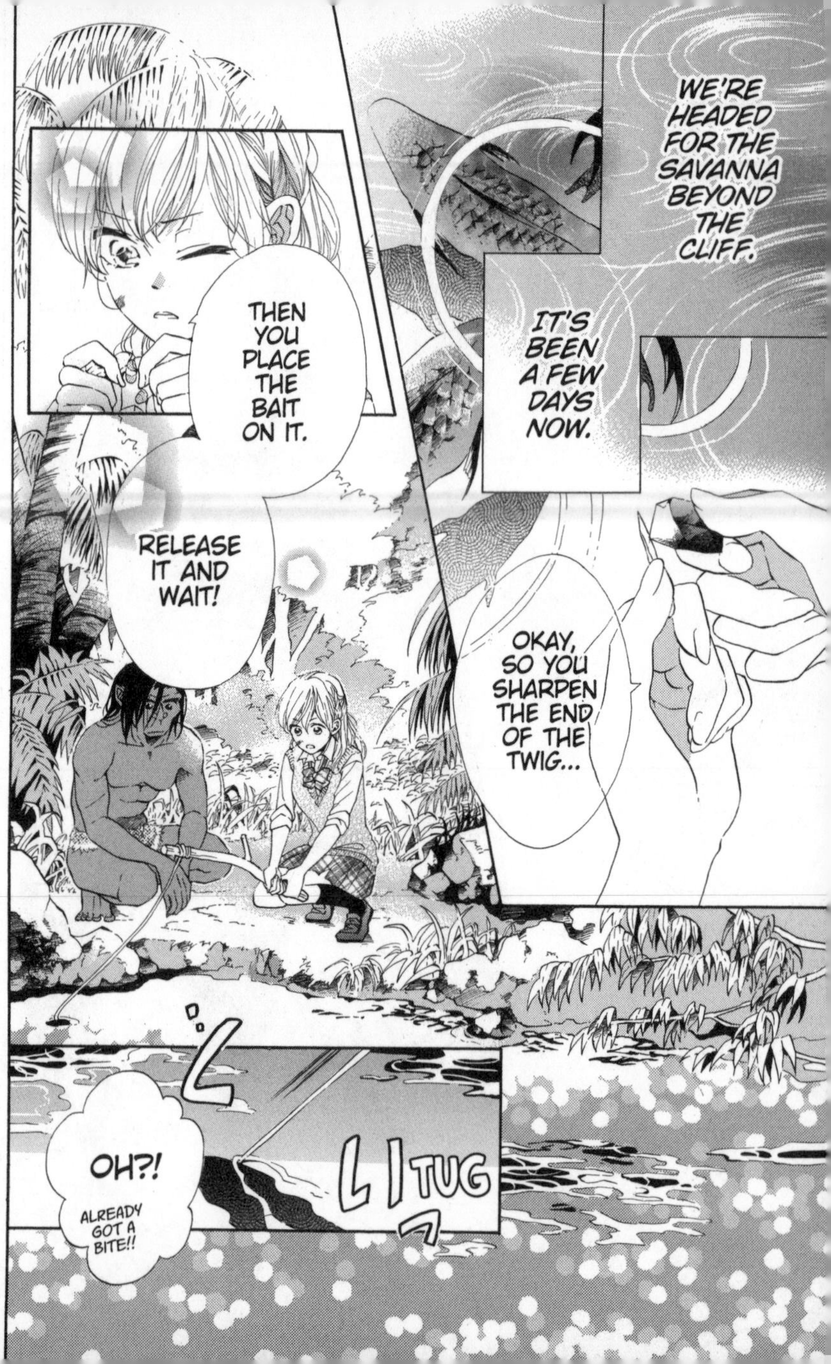
WE'RE HEADED FOR THE SAVANNA BEYOND THE CLIFF.
IT'S BEEN A FEW DAYS NOW.
OKAY, SO YOU SHARPEN THE END OF THE TWIG...
THEN YOU PLACE THE BAIT ON IT.
RELEASE IT AND WAIT!
TUG
OH?!
ALREADY GOT A BITE!!

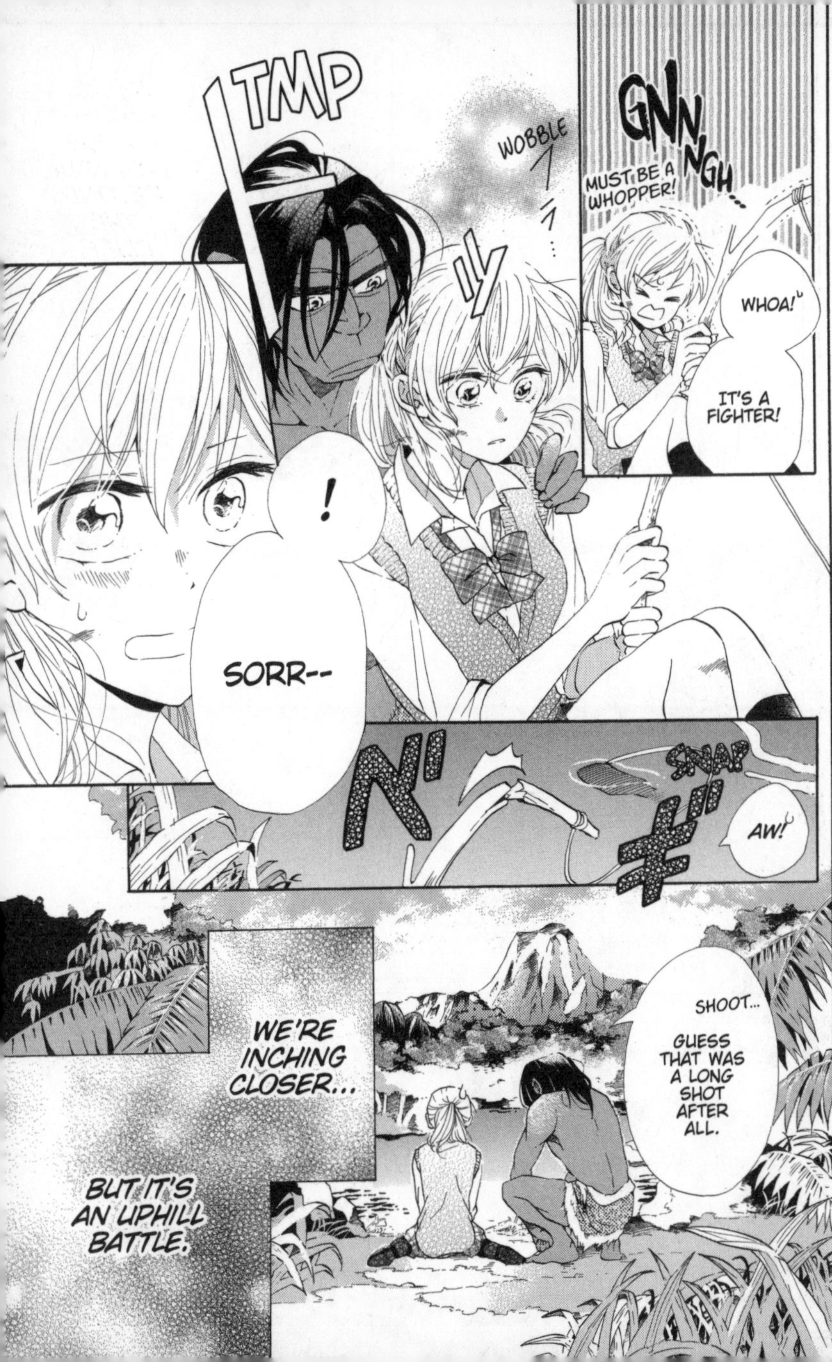
GNNNGH...
MUST BE A WHOPPER!
WHOA!
IT'S A FIGHTER!
TMP
WOBBLE
!
SORR--
SNAP
AW!
SHOOT...
GUESS THAT WAS A LONG SHOT AFTER ALL.
WE'RE INCHING CLOSER...
BUT IT'S AN UPHILL BATTLE.

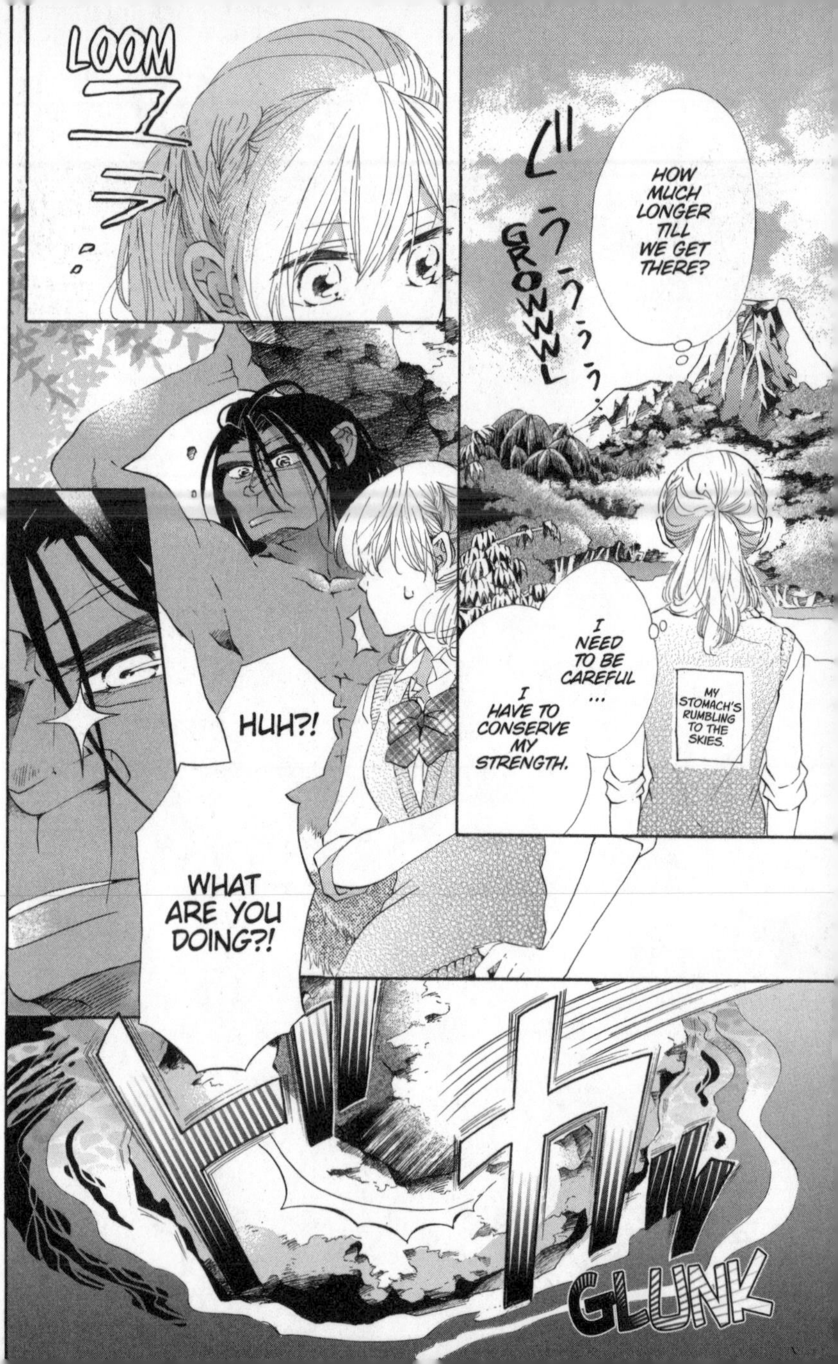
HOW MUCH LONGER TILL WE GET THERE?
GROWWWL
MY STOMACH'S RUMBLING TO THE SKIES.
I NEED TO BE CAREFUL ...
I HAVE TO CONSERVE MY STRENGTH.
LOOM
HUH?!
WHAT ARE YOU DOING?!
GLUNK

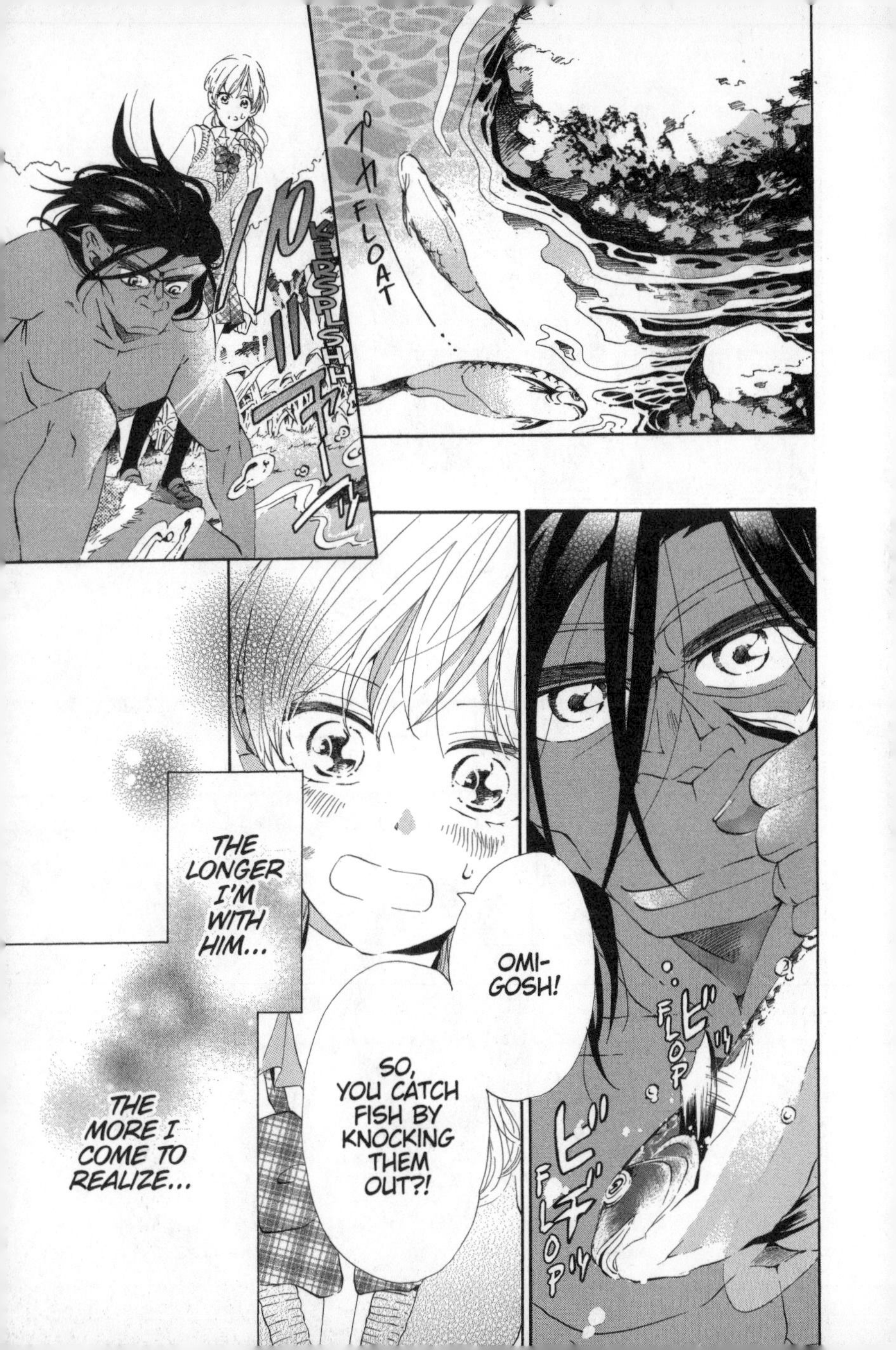
FLOAT
KERSPLSHHH
FLOP
FLOP
OMI-GOSH!
SO, YOU CATCH FISH BY KNOCKING THEM OUT?!
THE LONGER I'M WITH HIM...
THE MORE I COME TO REALIZE...

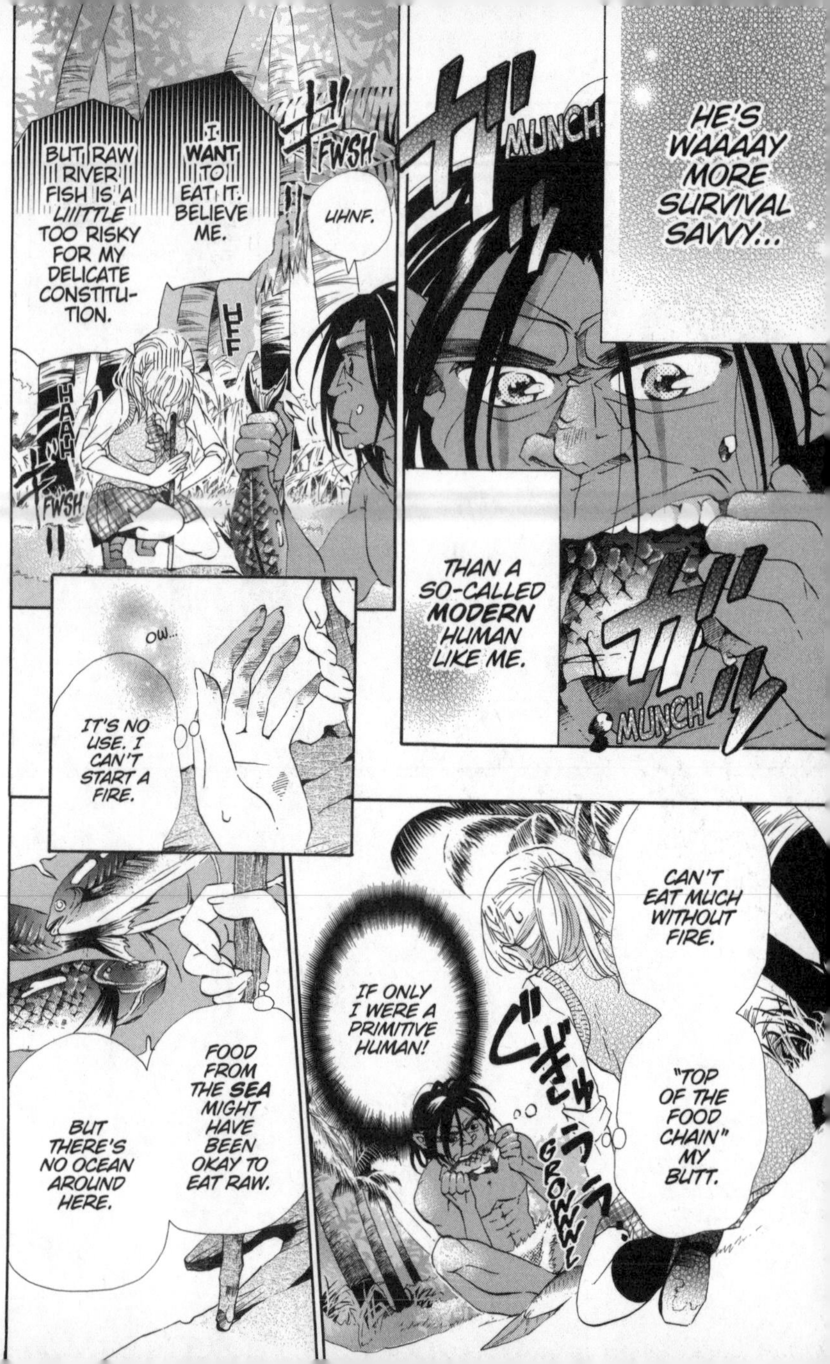
HE'S WAAAAY MORE SURVIVAL SAVVY...
MUNCH
THAN A SO-CALLED MODERN HUMAN LIKE ME.
MUNCH
I WANT TO EAT IT. BELIEVE ME.
BUT RAW RIVER FISH IS A LIIIITLE TOO RISKY FOR MY DELICATE CONSTITUTION.
FWSH
UHNF.
HUFF
HAAAH
FWSH
OW...
IT'S NO USE. I CAN'T START A FIRE.
CAN'T EAT MUCH WITHOUT FIRE.
"TOP OF THE FOOD CHAIN" MY BUTT.
IF ONLY I WERE A PRIMITIVE HUMAN!
GROWWL
FOOD FROM THE SEA MIGHT HAVE BEEN OKAY TO EAT RAW.
BUT THERE'S NO OCEAN AROUND HERE.

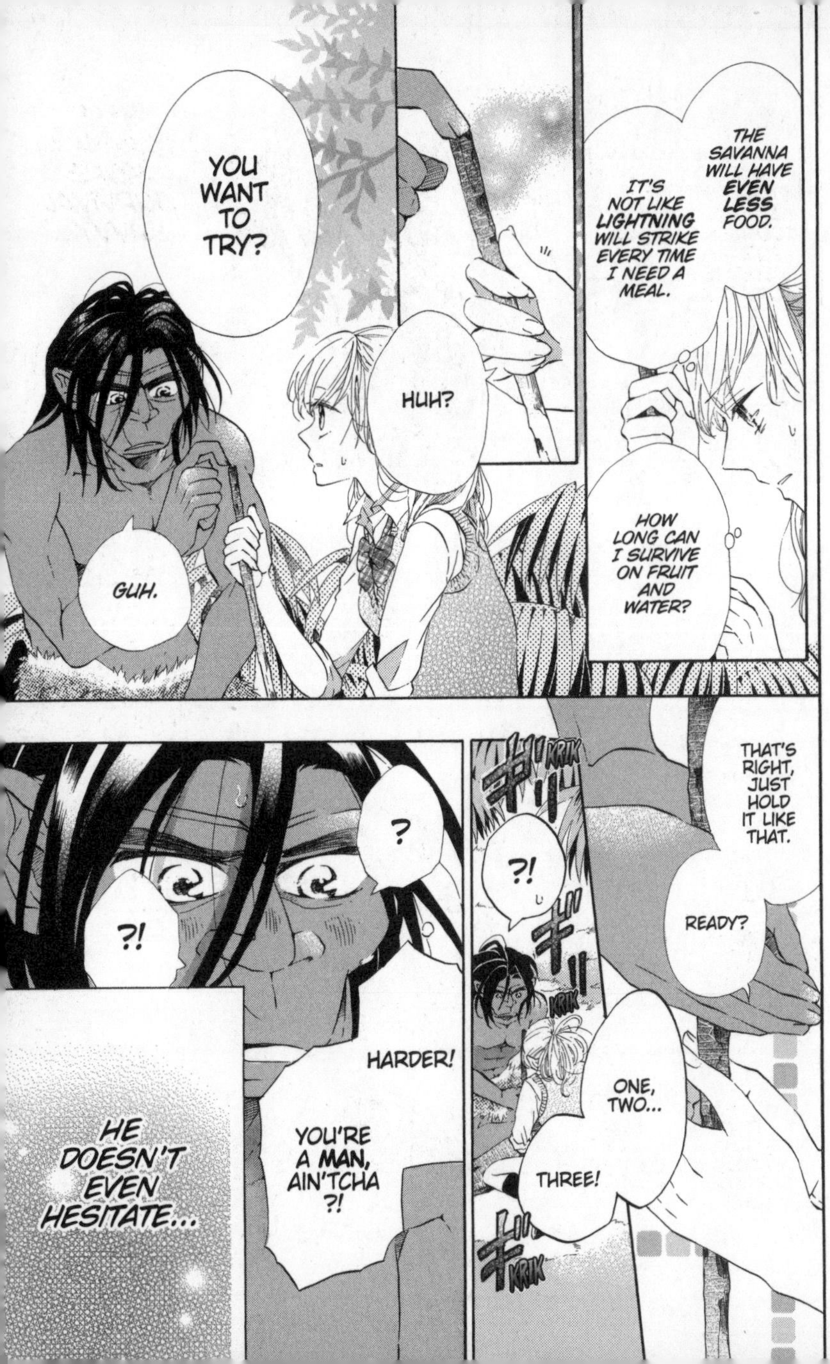
THE SAVANNA WILL HAVE EVEN LESS FOOD.
IT'S NOT LIKE LIGHTNING WILL STRIKE EVERY TIME I NEED A MEAL.
HOW LONG CAN I SURVIVE ON FRUIT AND WATER?
YOU WANT TO TRY?
HUH?
GUH.
THAT'S RIGHT, JUST HOLD IT LIKE THAT.
KRIK
?!
READY?
KRIK
ONE, TWO...
THREE!
KRIK
?
?!
HARDER!
YOU'RE A MAN, AIN'TCHA?!
HE DOESN'T EVEN HESITATE...

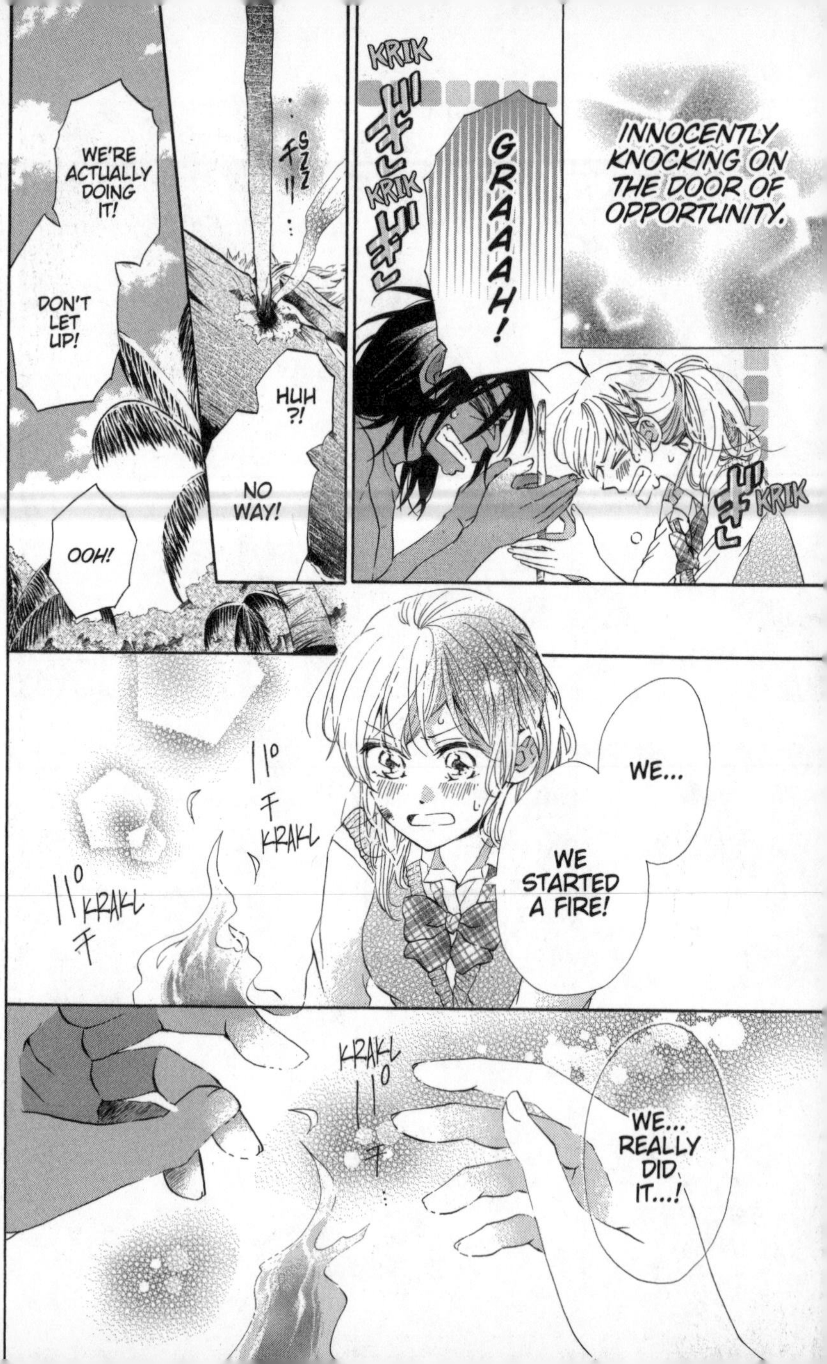

INNOCENTLY KNOCKING ON THE DOOR OF OPPORTUNITY.
KRIK
GRAAAAH!
KRIK
KRIK
WE'RE ACTUALLY DOING IT!
DON'T LET UP!
SZZ
HUH?!
NO WAY!
OOH!
WE...
WE STARTED A FIRE!
KRAKL
KRAKL
KRAKL
WE... REALLY DID IT...!

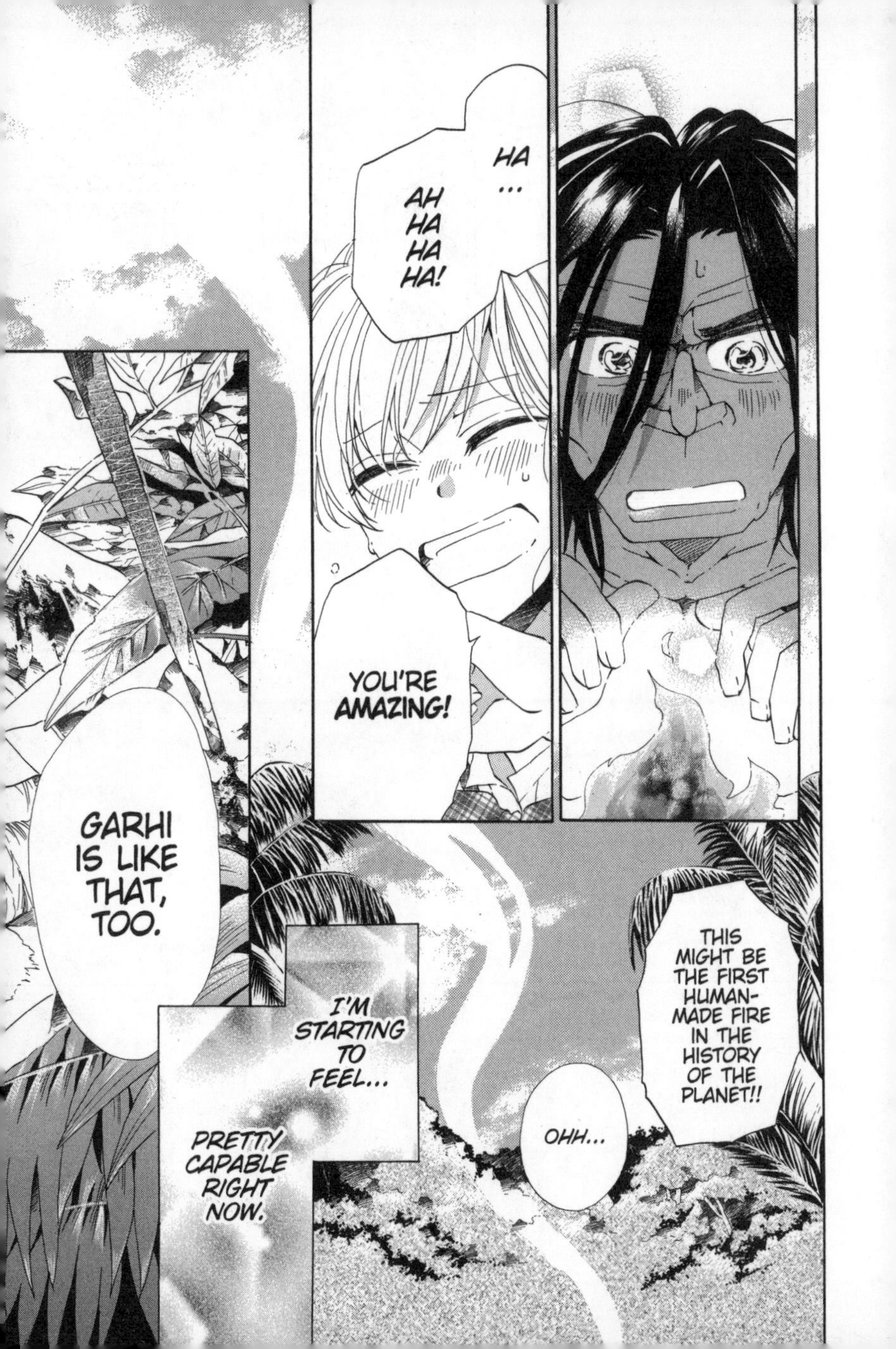
HA... AH HA HA HA!
YOU'RE AMAZING!
GARHI IS LIKE THAT, TOO.
THIS MIGHT BE THE FIRST HUMAN-MADE FIRE IN THE HISTORY OF THE PLANET!!
OHH...
I'M STARTING TO FEEL...
PRETTY CAPABLE RIGHT NOW.

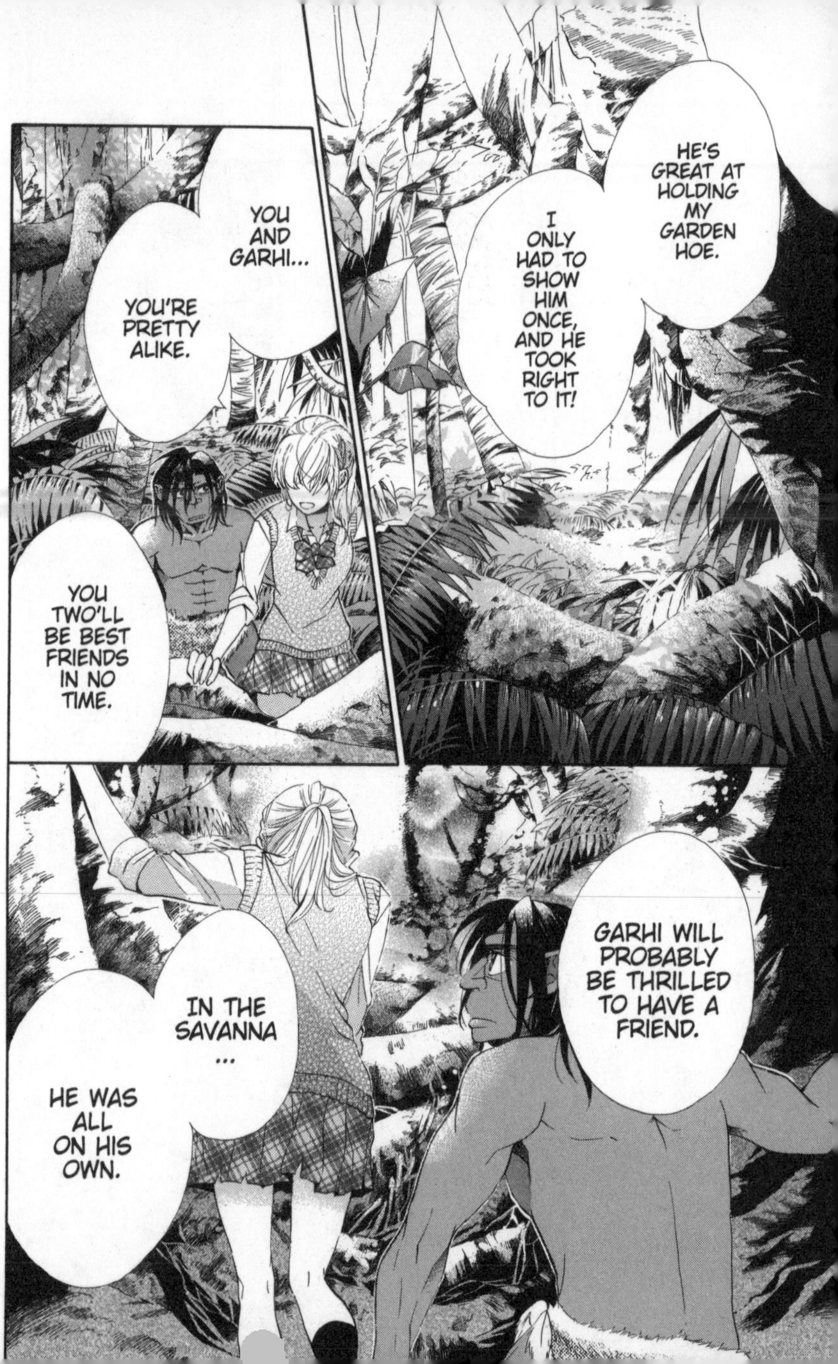
HE'S GREAT AT HOLDING MY GARDEN HOE.
I ONLY HAD TO SHOW HIM ONCE, AND HE TOOK RIGHT TO IT!
YOU AND GARHI...
YOU'RE PRETTY ALIKE.
YOU TWO'LL BE BEST FRIENDS IN NO TIME.
GARHI WILL PROBABLY BE THRILLED TO HAVE A FRIEND.
IN THE SAVANNA...
HE WAS ALL ON HIS OWN.

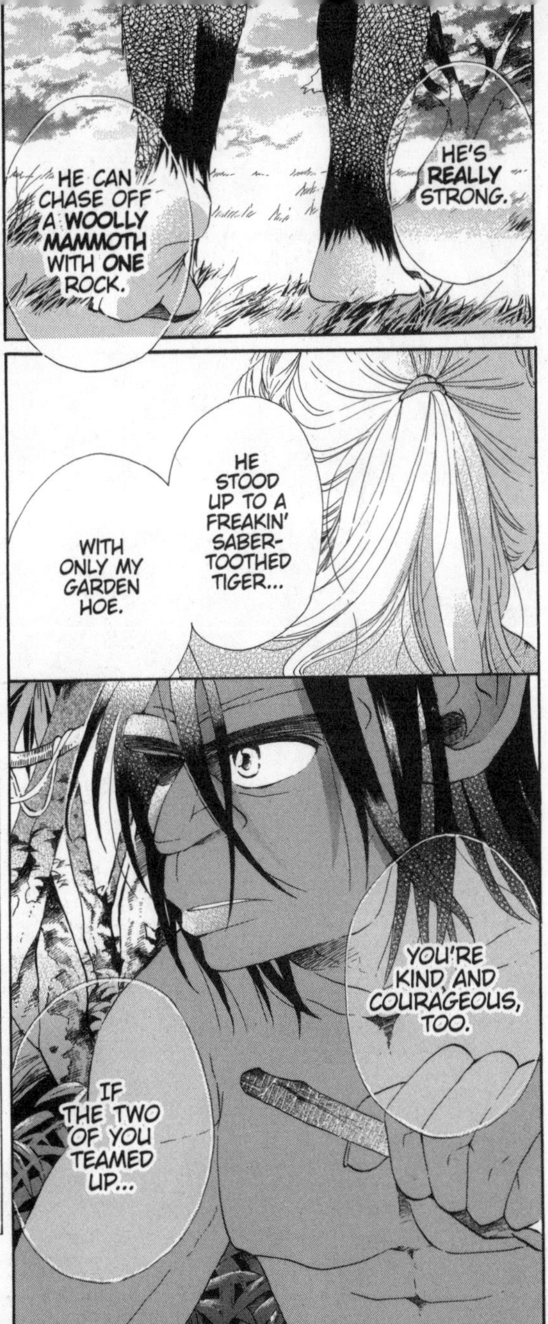
HE'S REALLY STRONG.
HE CAN CHASE OFF A WOOLLY MAMMOTH WITH ONE ROCK.
HE STOOD UP TO A FREAKIN' SABER-TOOTHED TIGER...
WITH ONLY MY GARDEN HOE.
YOU'RE KIND AND COURAGEOUS, TOO.
IF THE TWO OF YOU TEAMED UP...

4

CHAPTER 7

AT THIS POINT, I WAS COMPLETELY EXCITED BY THE JUNGLE ART. THE DOOR TO A NEW PASSION HAD BEEN OPENED.

I LOVE YOU, JUNGLE!!

ACCORDING TO THE NATIONAL MUSEUM OF NATURE AND SCIENCE IN TOKYO, ALL LIFE ON EARTH ORIGINATED FROM THE SAME CELL, APPROXIMATELY FOUR BILLION YEARS AGO.

THIS FILLED ME WITH NEWFOUND AWE, SO IN THIS CHAPTER, I EXPANDED ON THE WORLD SEEN BY MITO AND HER COMPANION.

I'LL BE BACK, MUSEUM!

(BECAUSE I ACCIDENTALLY DELETED ALL THE RESEARCH MATERIAL I'D SAVED ON MY IPAD...)

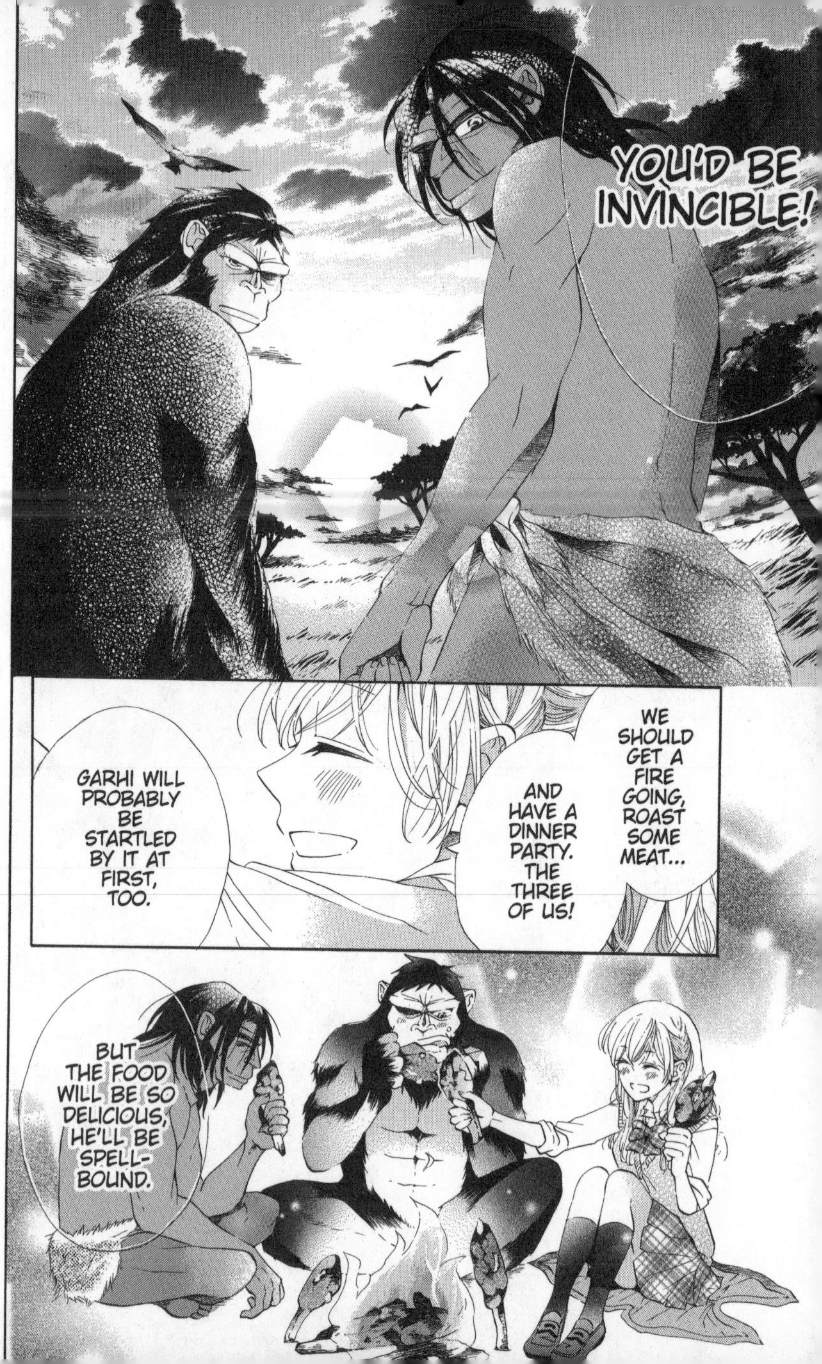
YOU'D BE INVINCIBLE!
WE SHOULD GET A FIRE GOING, ROAST SOME MEAT...
AND HAVE A DINNER PARTY. THE THREE OF US!
GARHI WILL PROBABLY BE STARTLED BY IT AT FIRST, TOO.
BUT THE FOOD WILL BE SO DELICIOUS, HE'LL BE SPELL-BOUND.

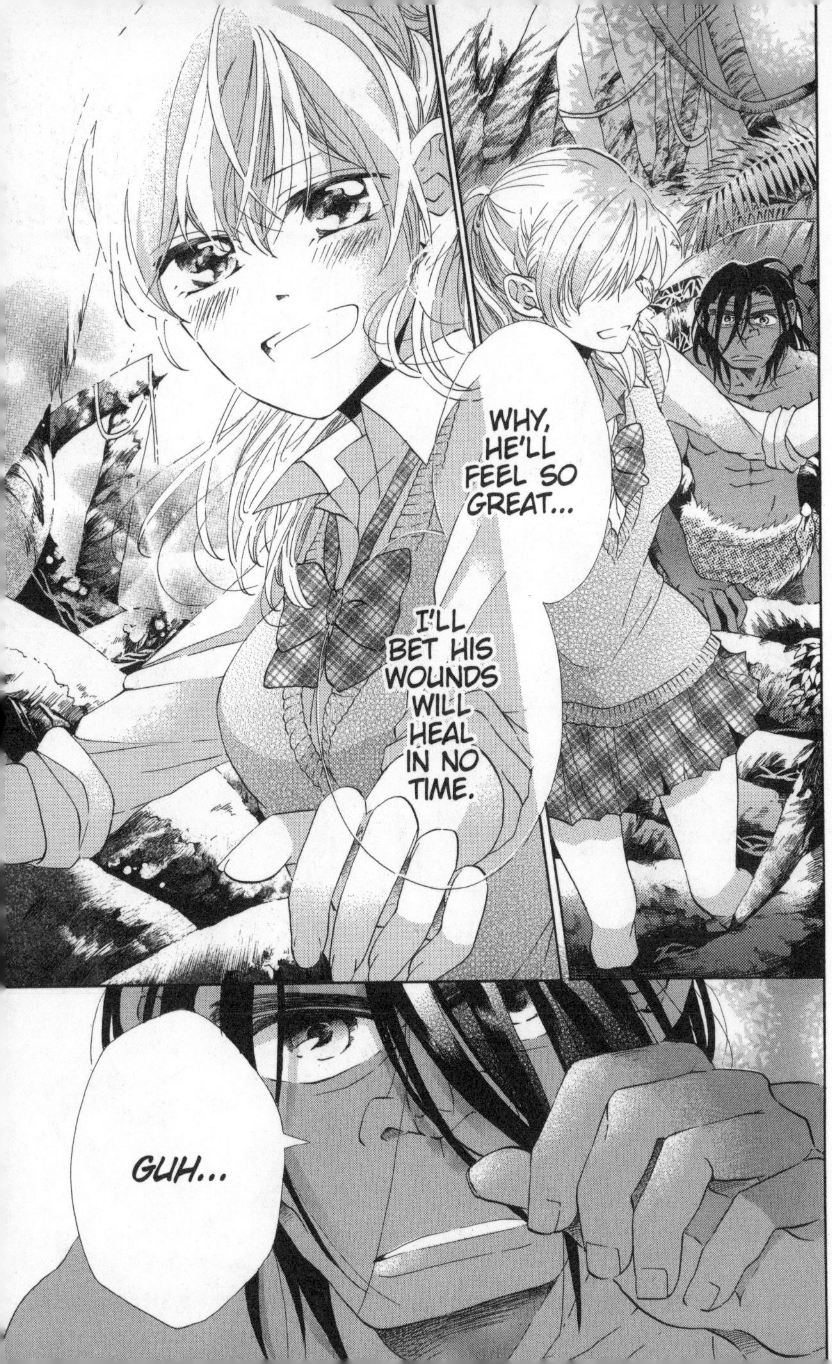
WHY, HE'LL FEEL SO GREAT...
I'LL BET HIS WOUNDS WILL HEAL IN NO TIME.
GUH...

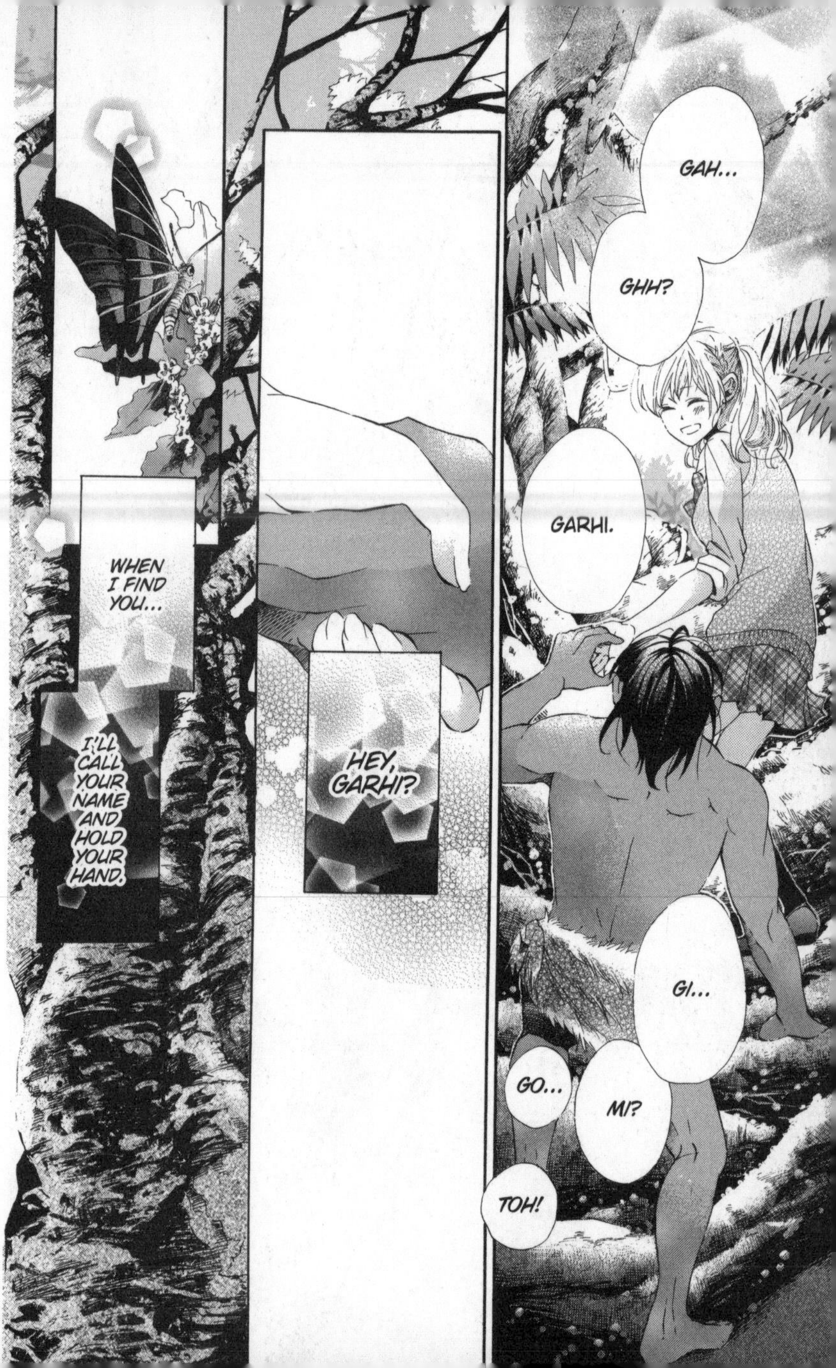
GAH...
GHH?
GARHI.
GI...
MI?
GO...
TOH!
HEY, GARHI?
WHEN I FIND YOU...
I'LL CALL YOUR NAME AND HOLD YOUR HAND.

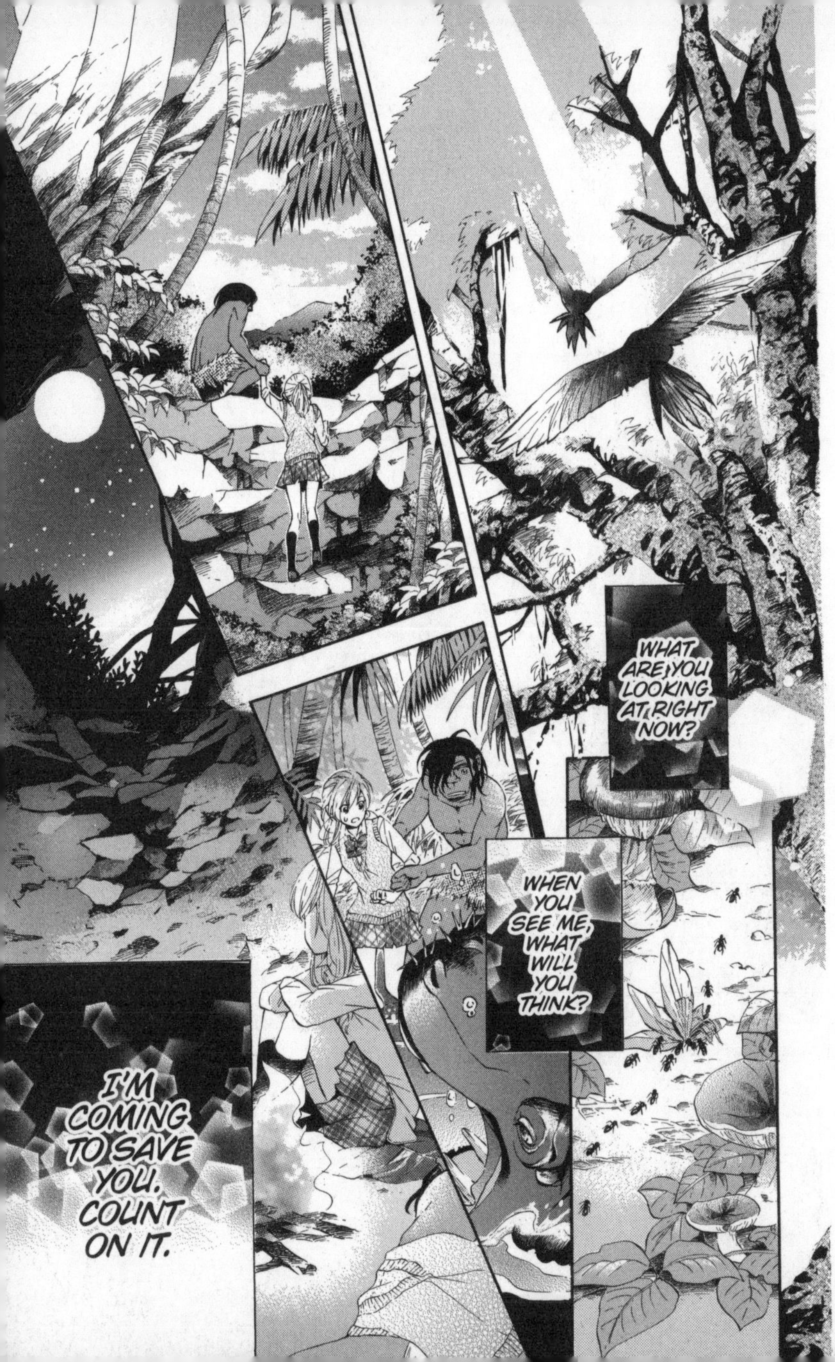
WHAT ARE YOU LOOKING AT RIGHT NOW?
WHEN YOU SEE ME, WHAT WILL YOU THINK?
I'M COMING TO SAVE YOU. COUNT ON IT.

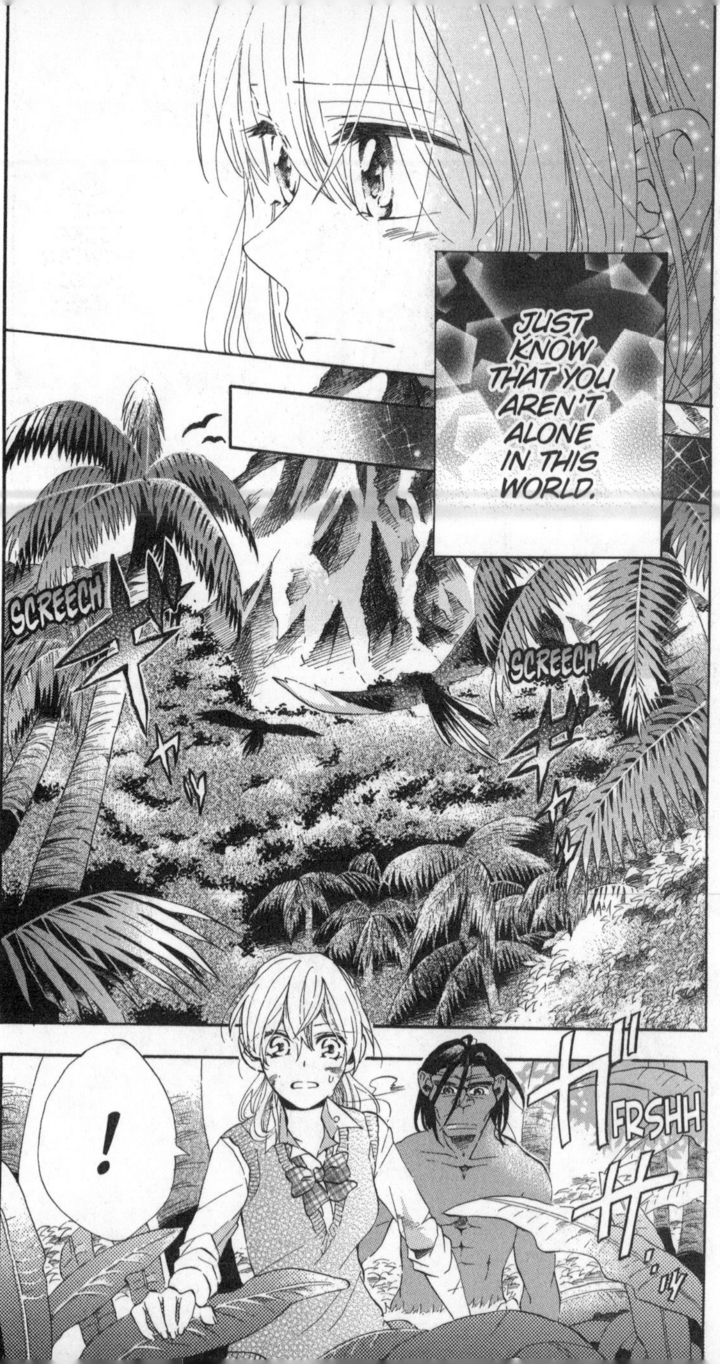
JUST KNOW THAT YOU AREN'T ALONE IN THIS WORLD.
SCREECH
SCREECH
FRSHH
!

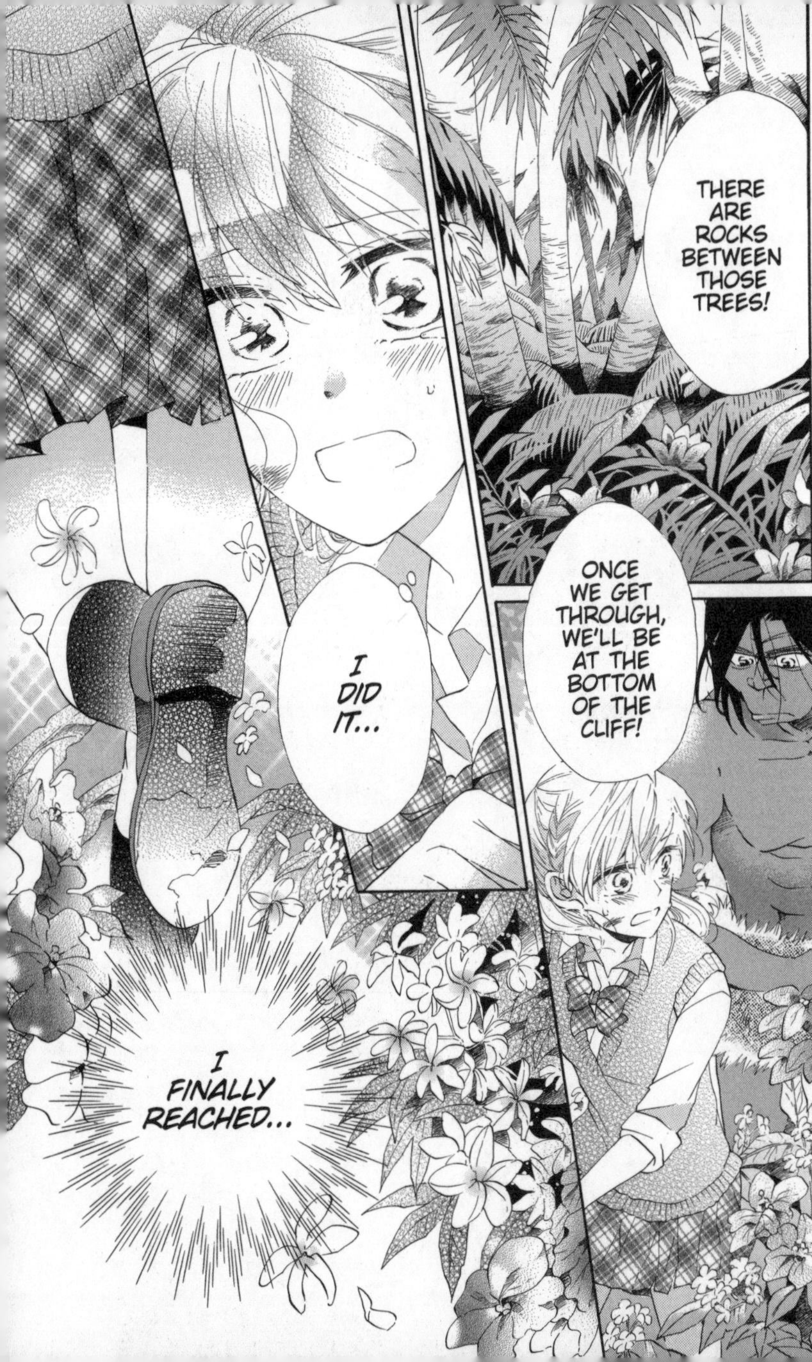
THERE ARE ROCKS BETWEEN THOSE TREES!
ONCE WE GET THROUGH, WE'LL BE AT THE BOTTOM OF THE CLIFF!
I DID IT...
I FINALLY REACHED...

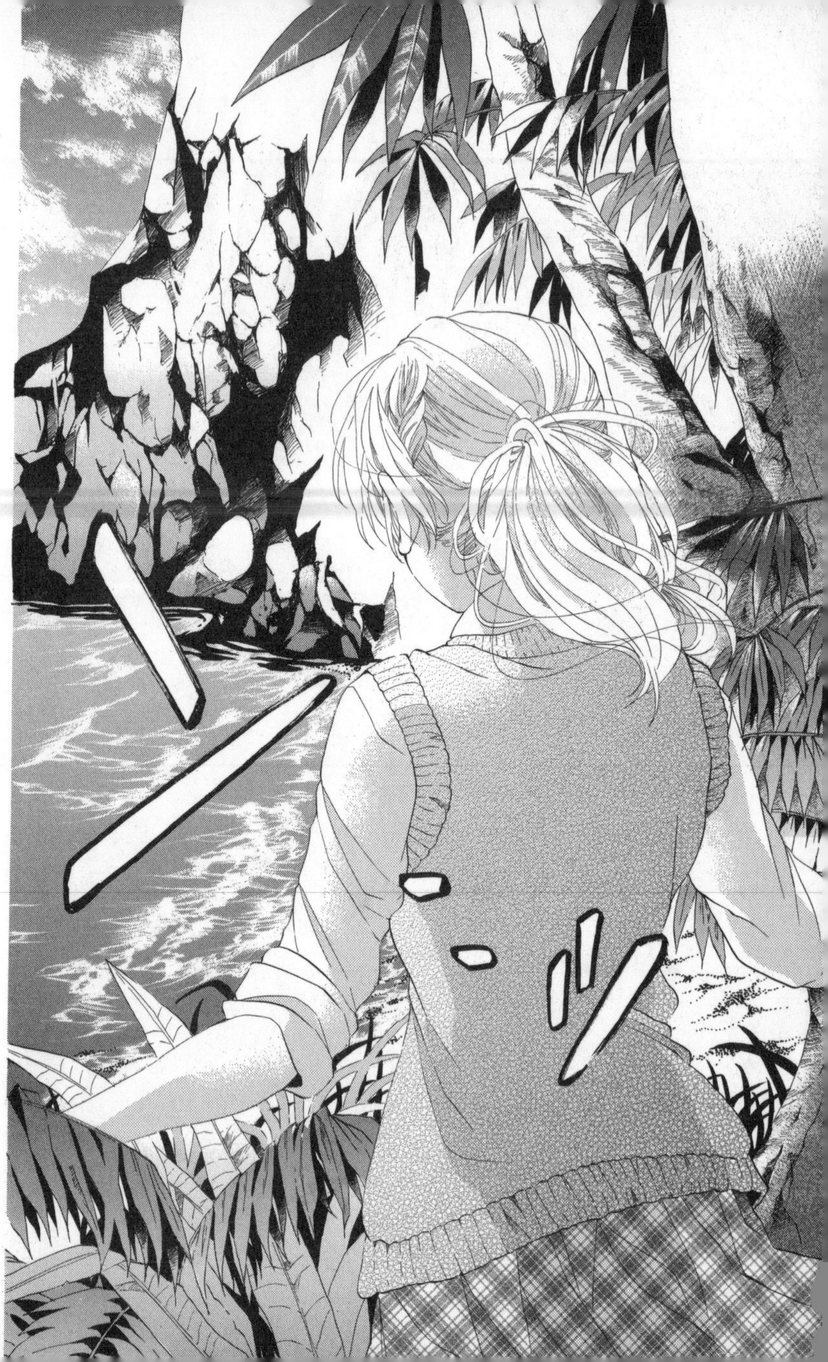
ザッ

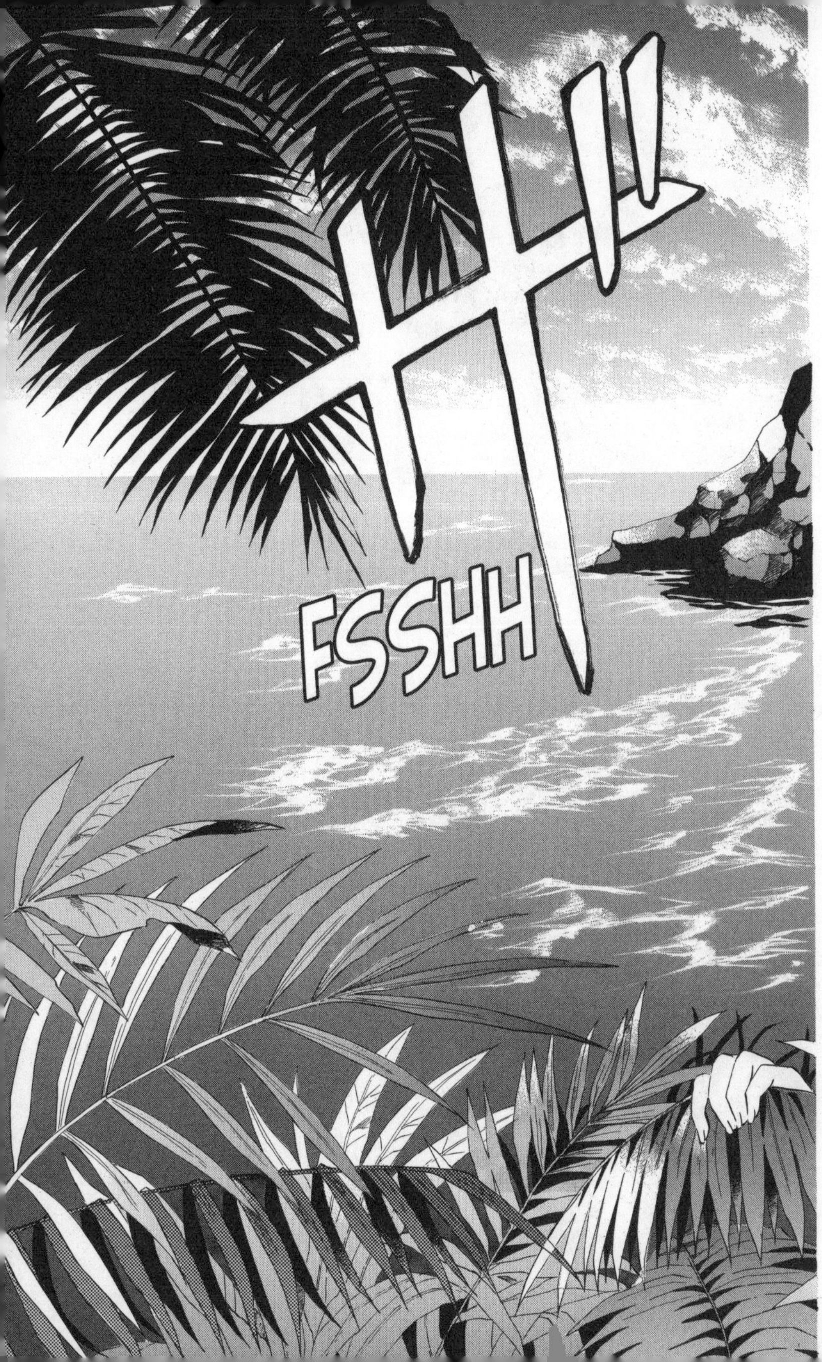
FSSHH

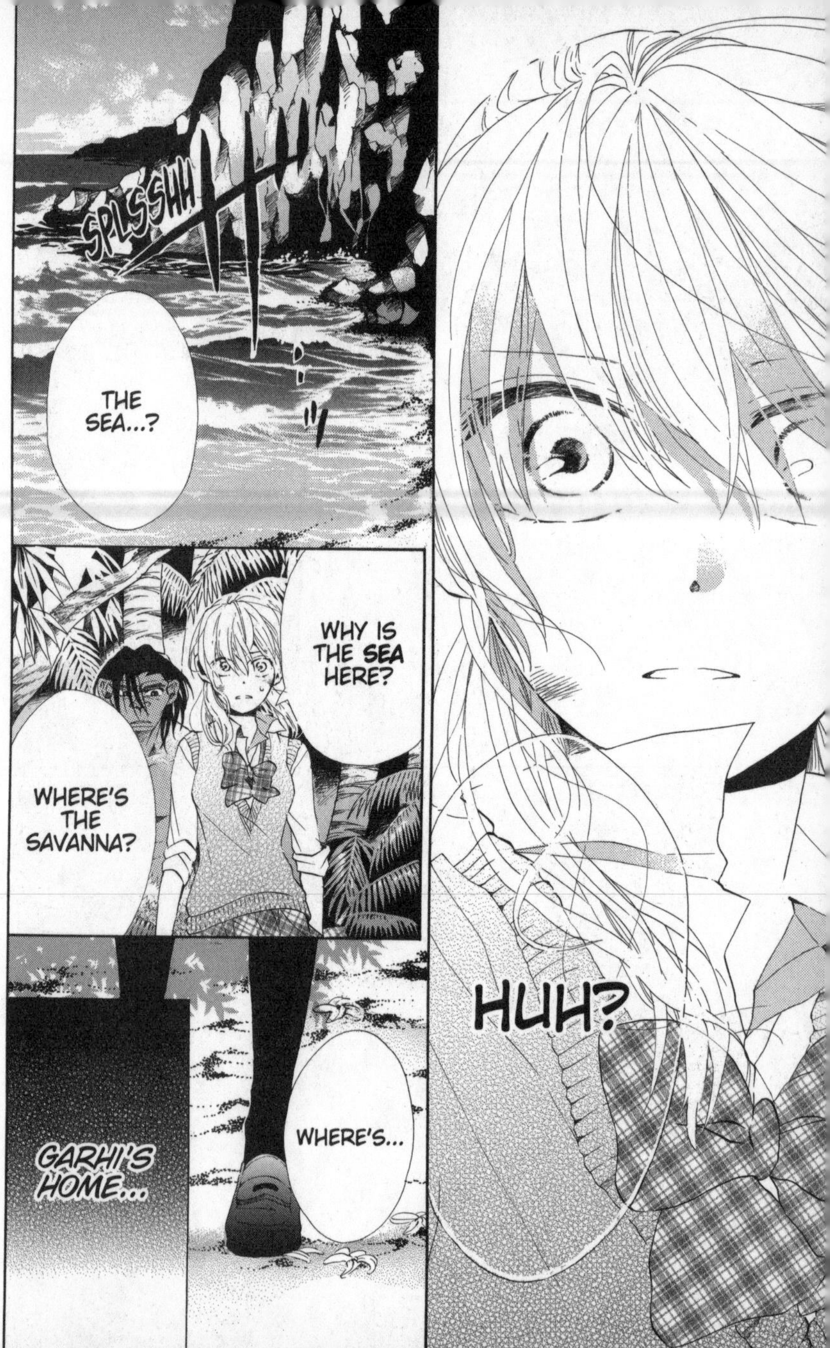
HUH?
SPLSSHH
THE SEA...?
WHY IS THE SEA HERE?
WHERE'S THE SAVANNA?
WHERE'S...
GARHI'S HOME...

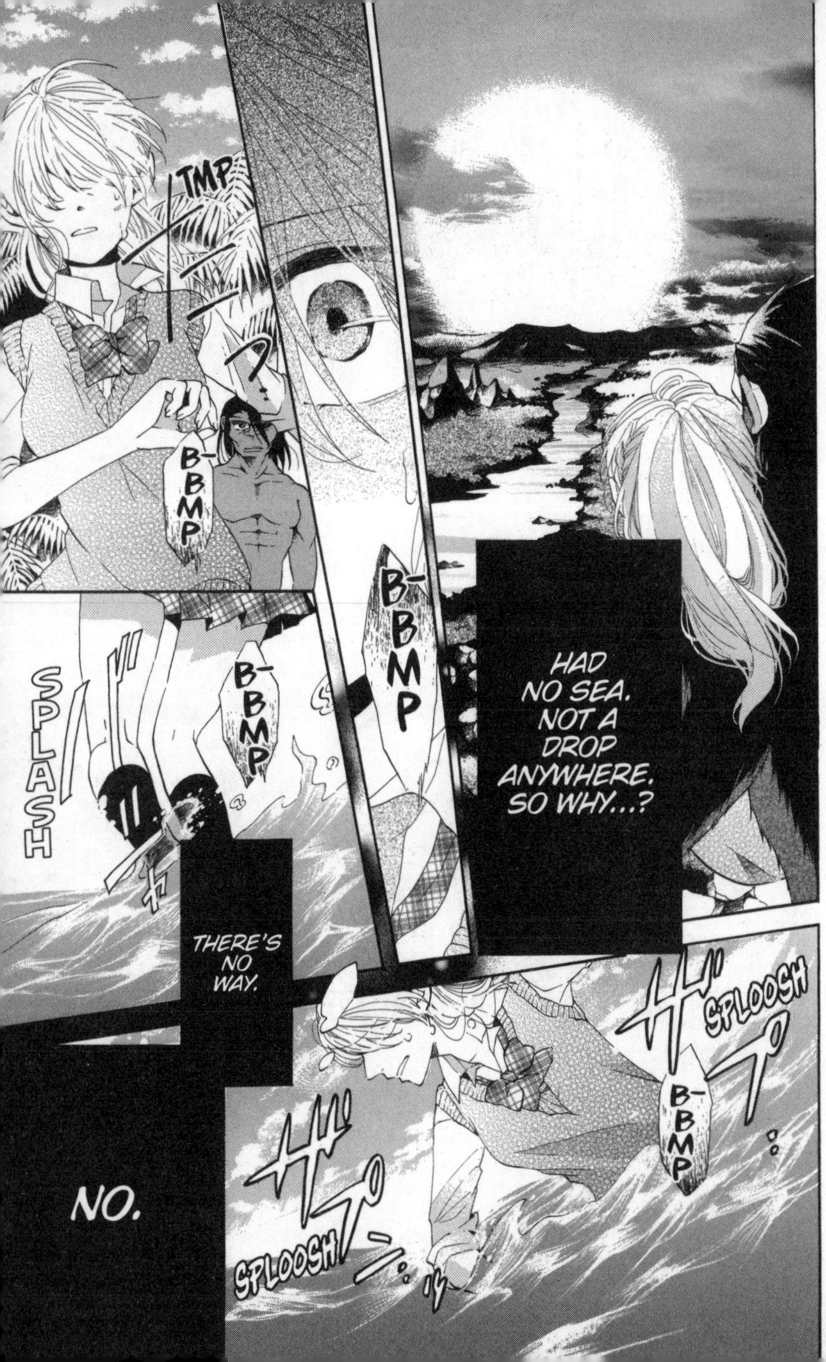
HAD NO SEA. NOT A DROP ANYWHERE. SO WHY...?
B-BBMP
TMP
B-BBMP
B-BBMP
SPLASH
THERE'S NO WAY.
SPLOOSH
B-BBMP
SPLOOSH
NO.

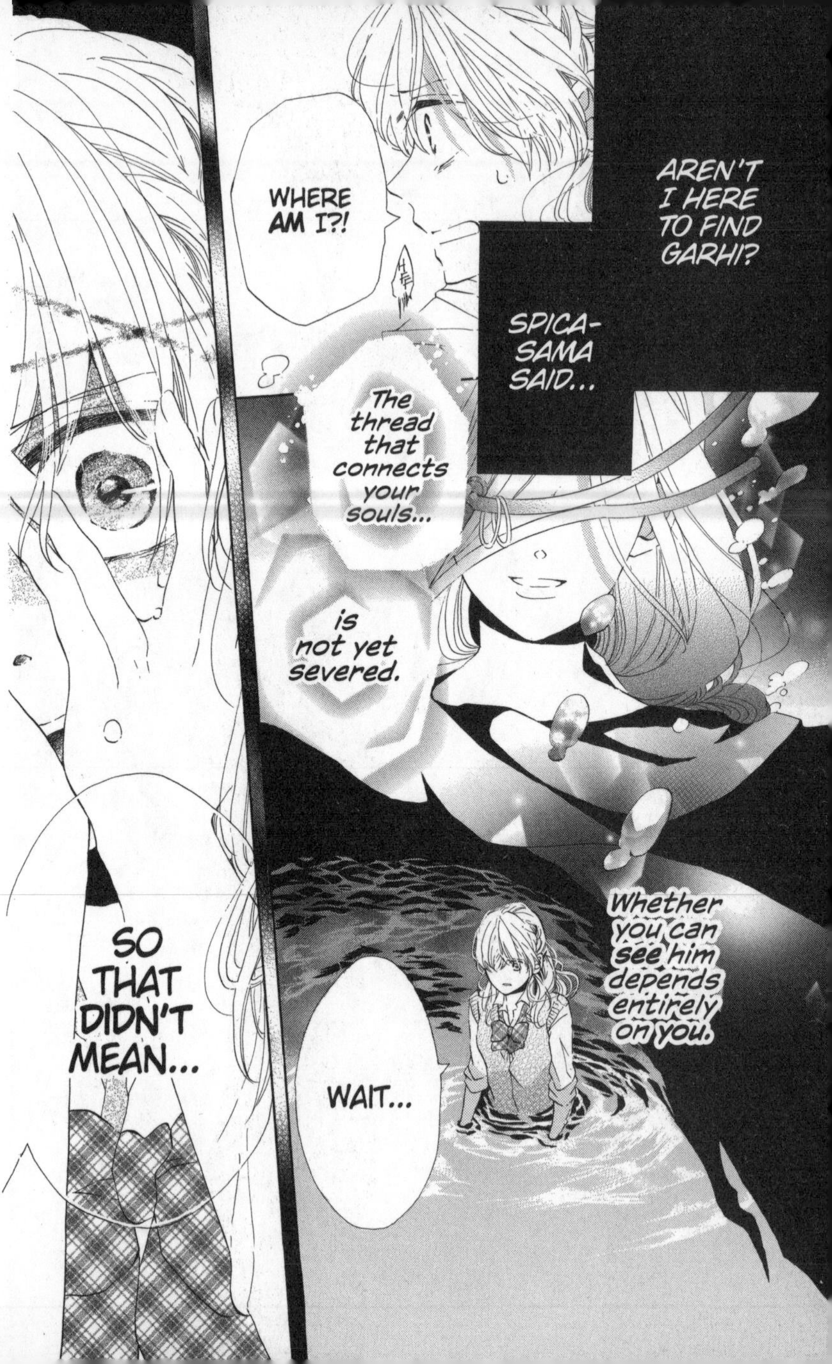

AREN'T I HERE TO FIND GARHI?
WHERE AM I?!
SPICA-SAMA SAID...
The thread that connects your souls...
is not yet severed.
Whether you can see him depends entirely on you.
WAIT...
SO THAT DIDN'T MEAN...

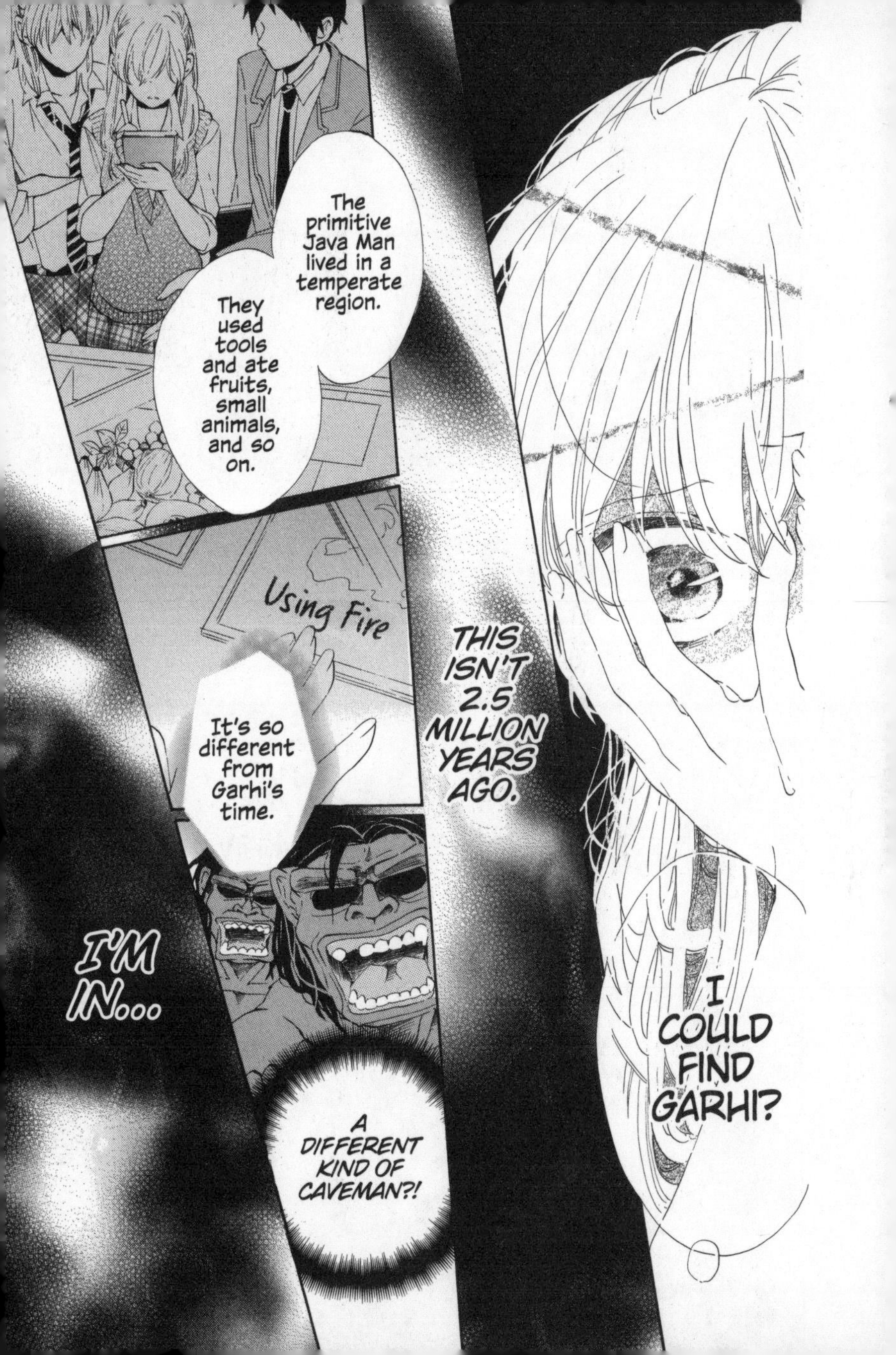
THIS ISN'T 2.5 MILLION YEARS AGO.
I COULD FIND GARHI?
The primitive Java Man lived in a temperate region.
They used tools and ate fruits, small animals, and so on.
Using Fire
It's so different from Garhi's time.
A DIFFERENT KIND OF CAVEMAN?!
I'M IN...

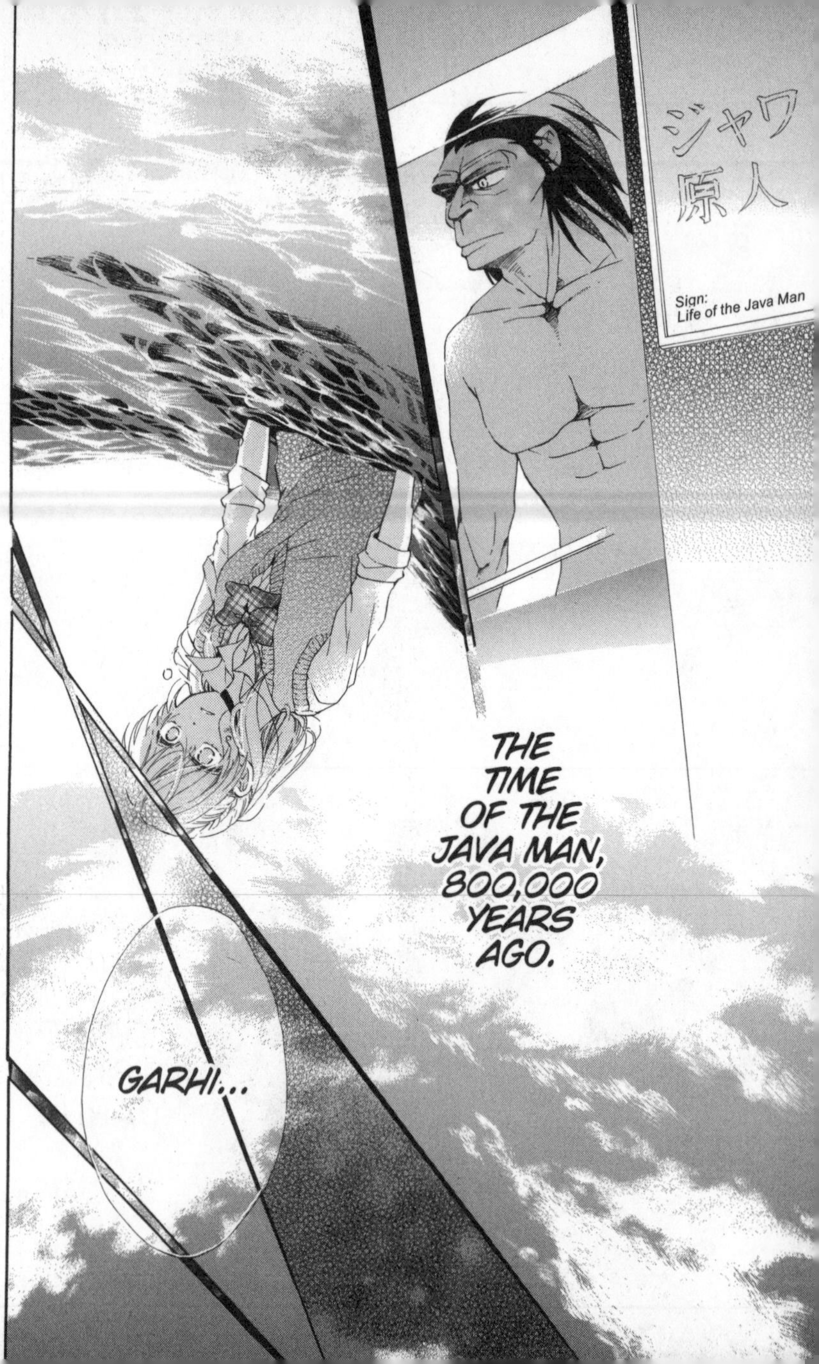
ジャワ原人
Sign:
Life of the Java Man
THE TIME OF THE JAVA MAN, 800,000 YEARS AGO.
GARHI...

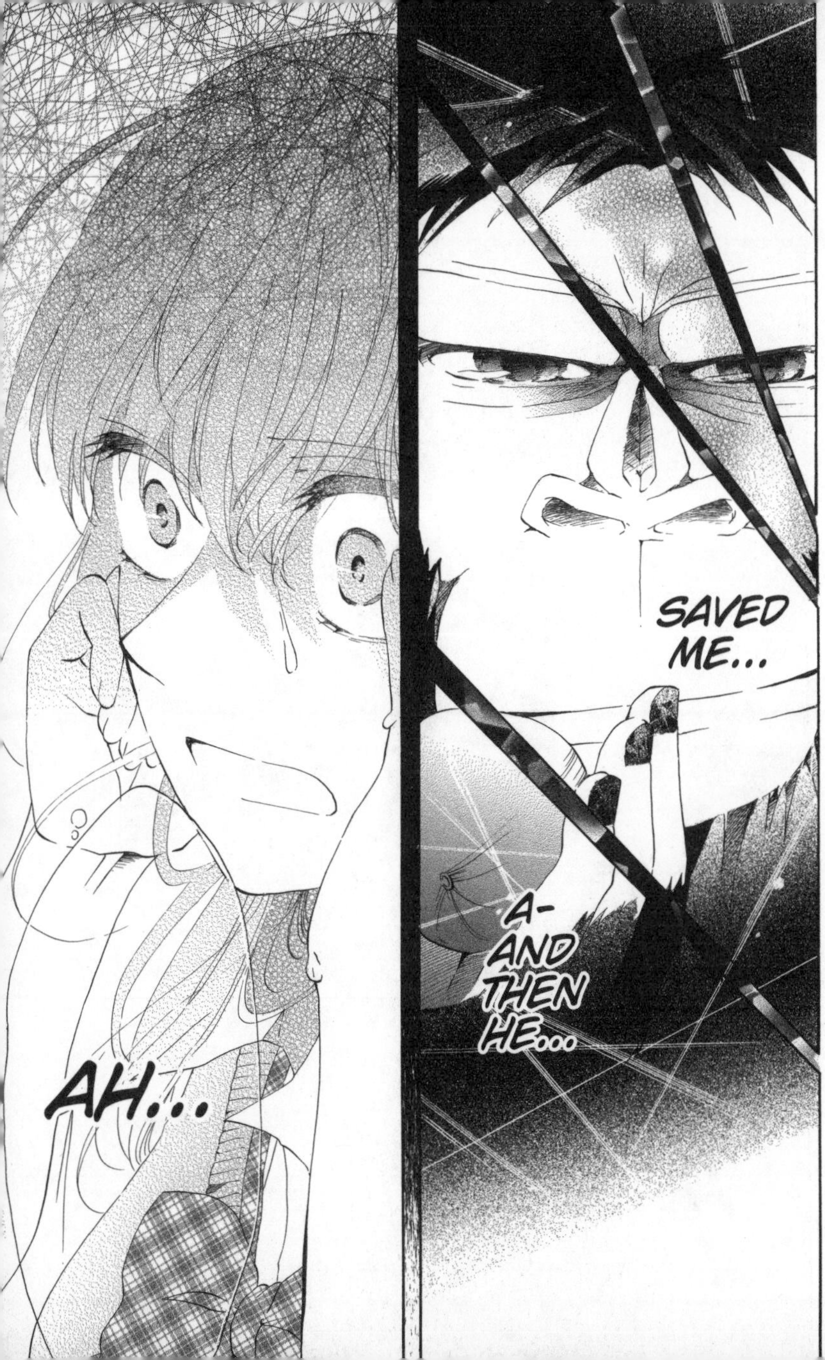
SAVED ME...
A- AND THEN HE...
AH...

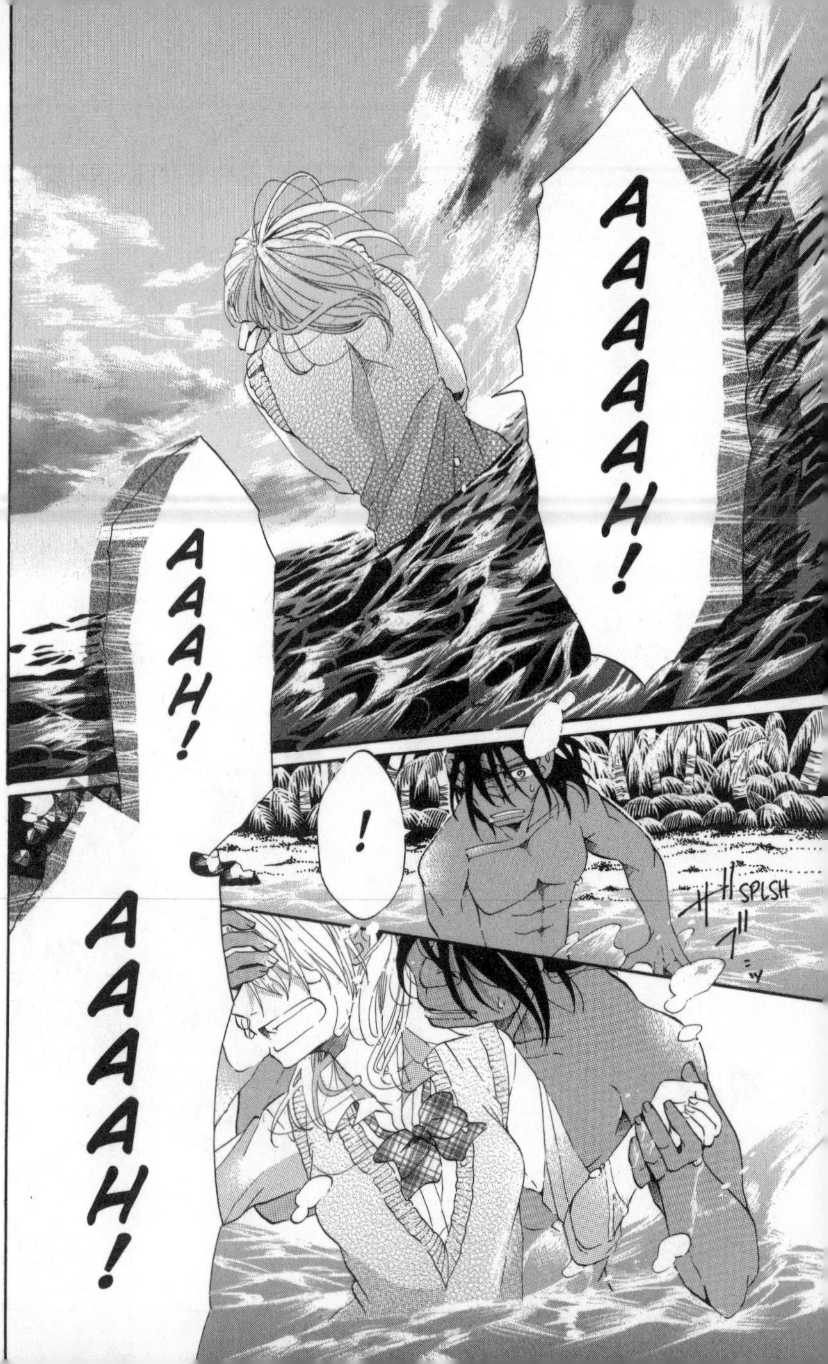
AAAAAH!
AAAH!
!
SPLSH
AAAAH!

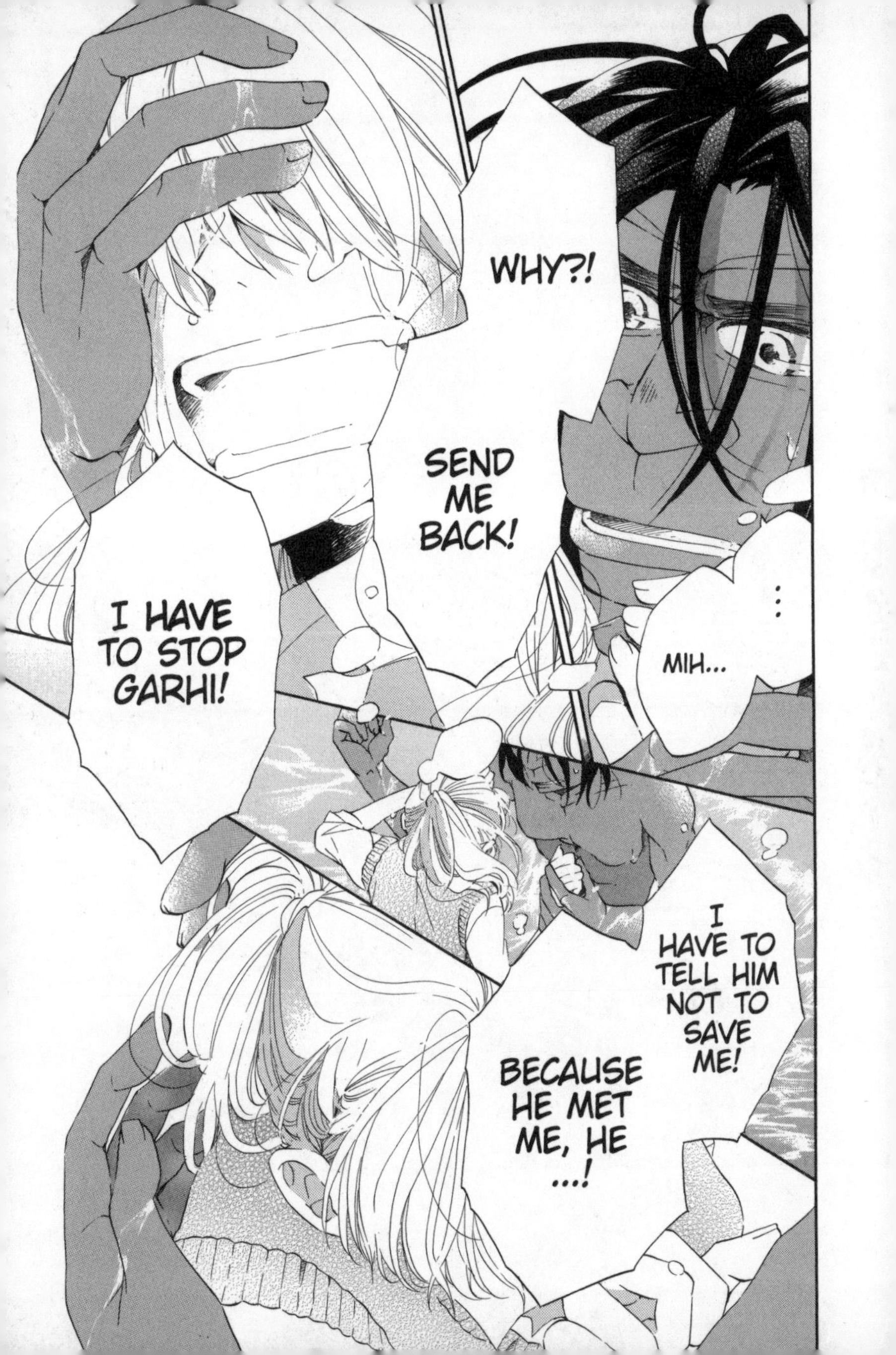
WHY?!
SEND ME BACK!
...
MIH...
I HAVE TO STOP GARHI!
I HAVE TO TELL HIM NOT TO SAVE ME!
BECAUSE HE MET ME, HE ...!

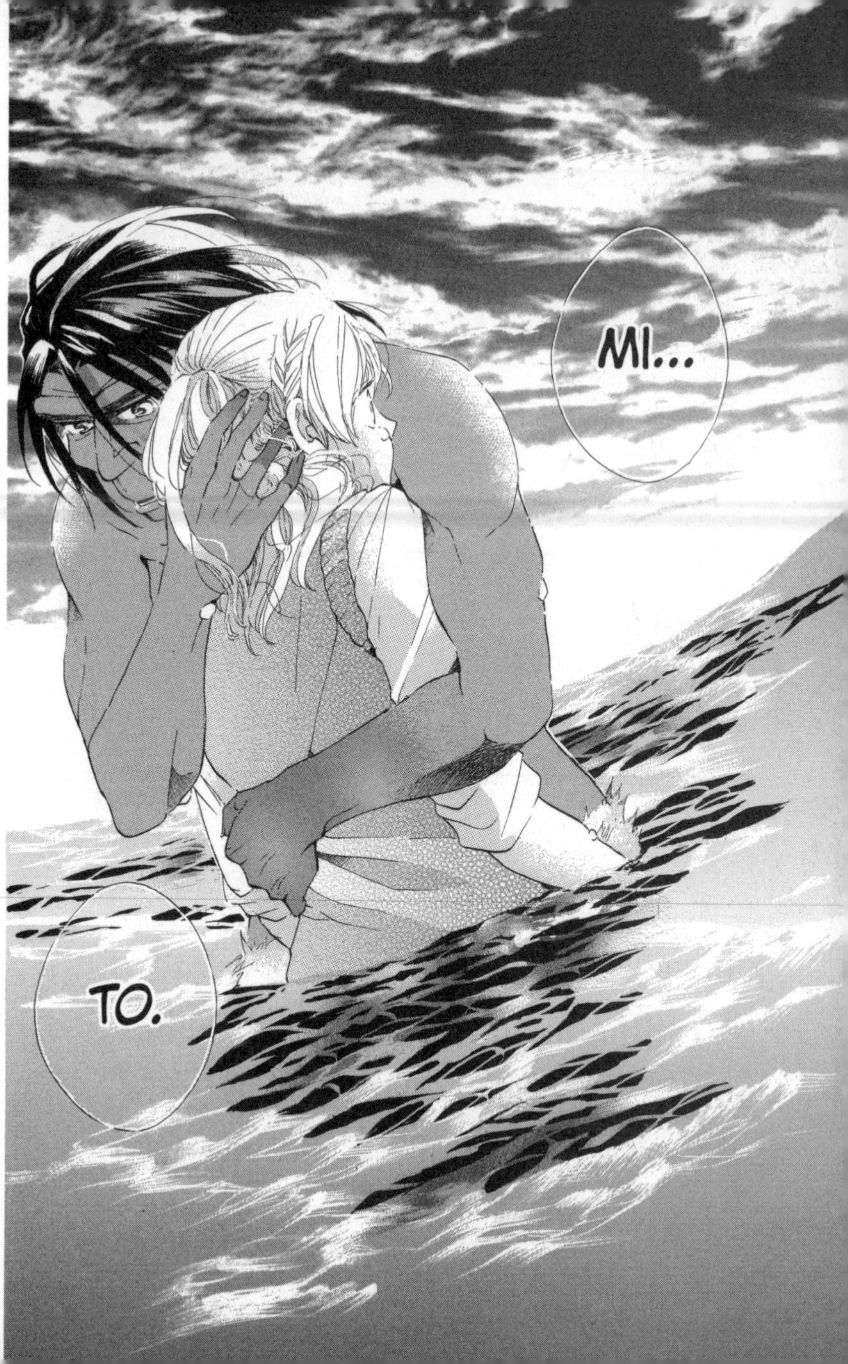
MI...
TO.

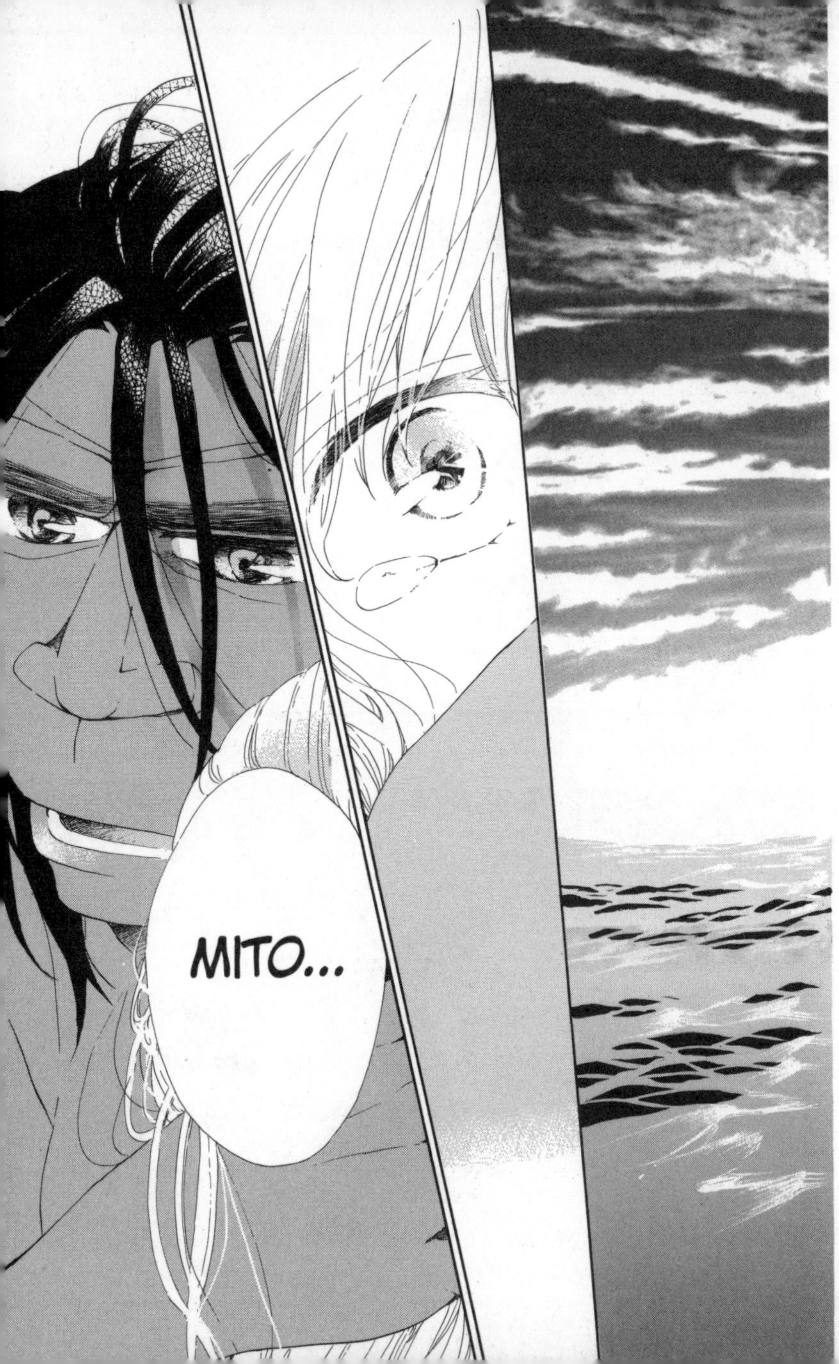
MITO...

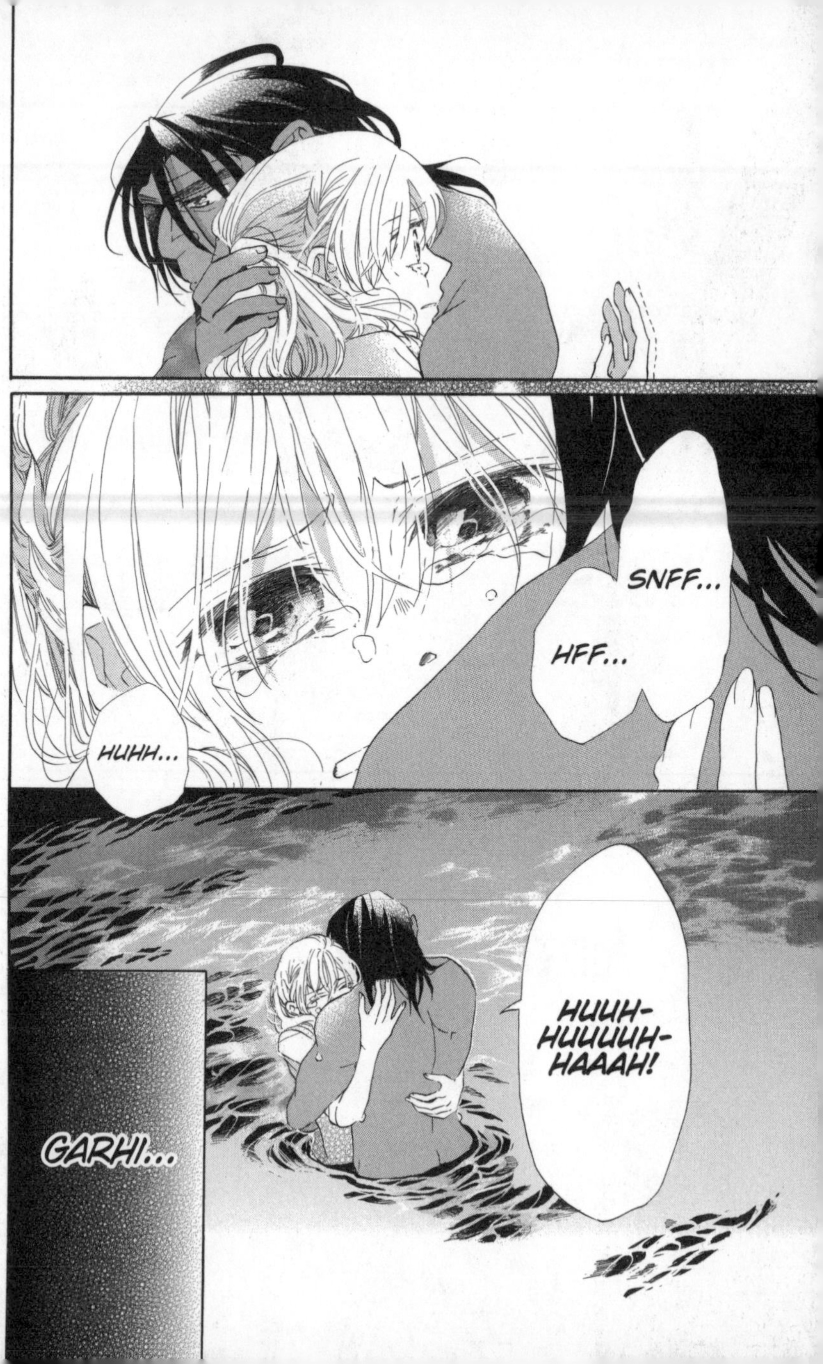
SNFF...
HFF...
HUHH...
HUUH-HUUUUH-HAAAH!
GARHI...

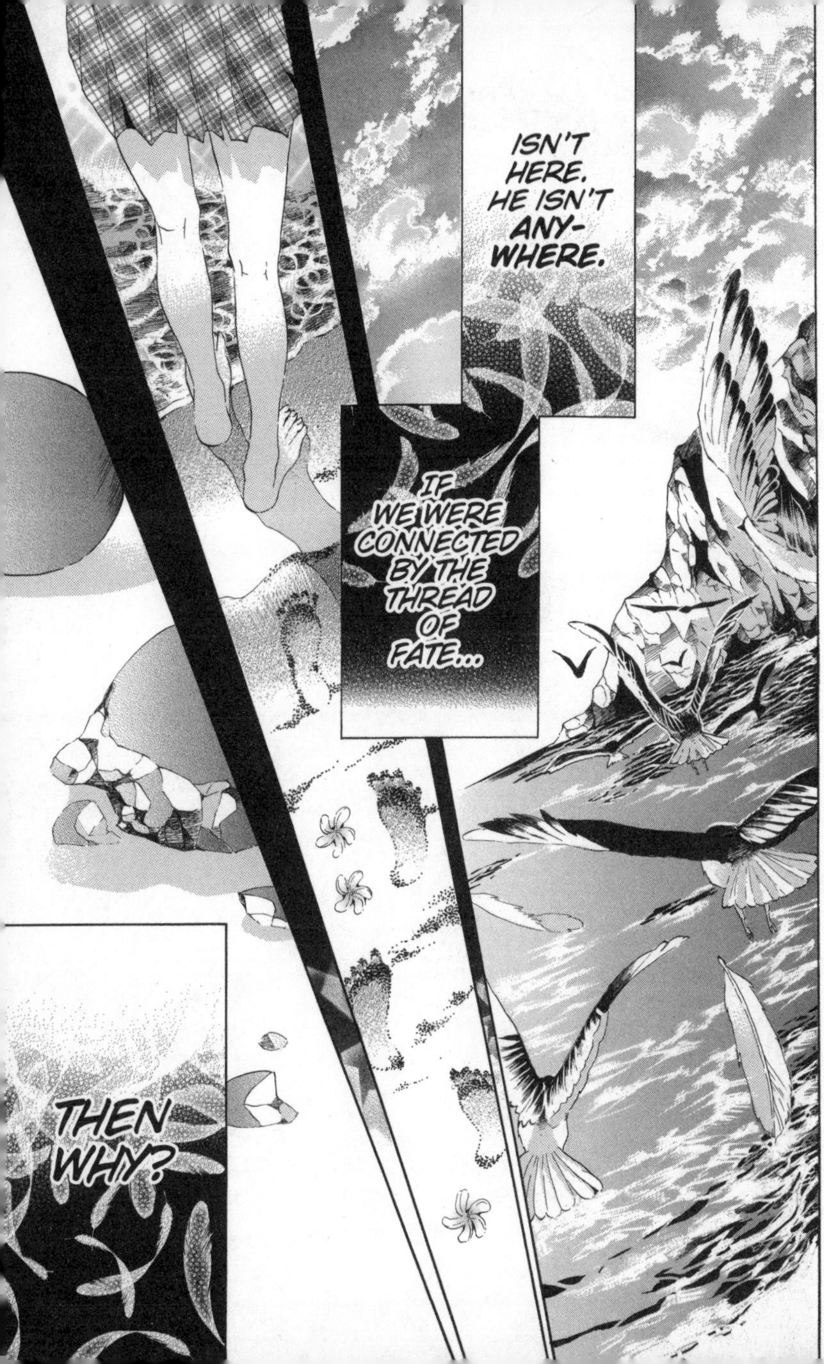
ISN'T HERE. HE ISN'T ANYWHERE.
IF WE WERE CONNECTED BY THE THREAD OF FATE...
THEN WHY?

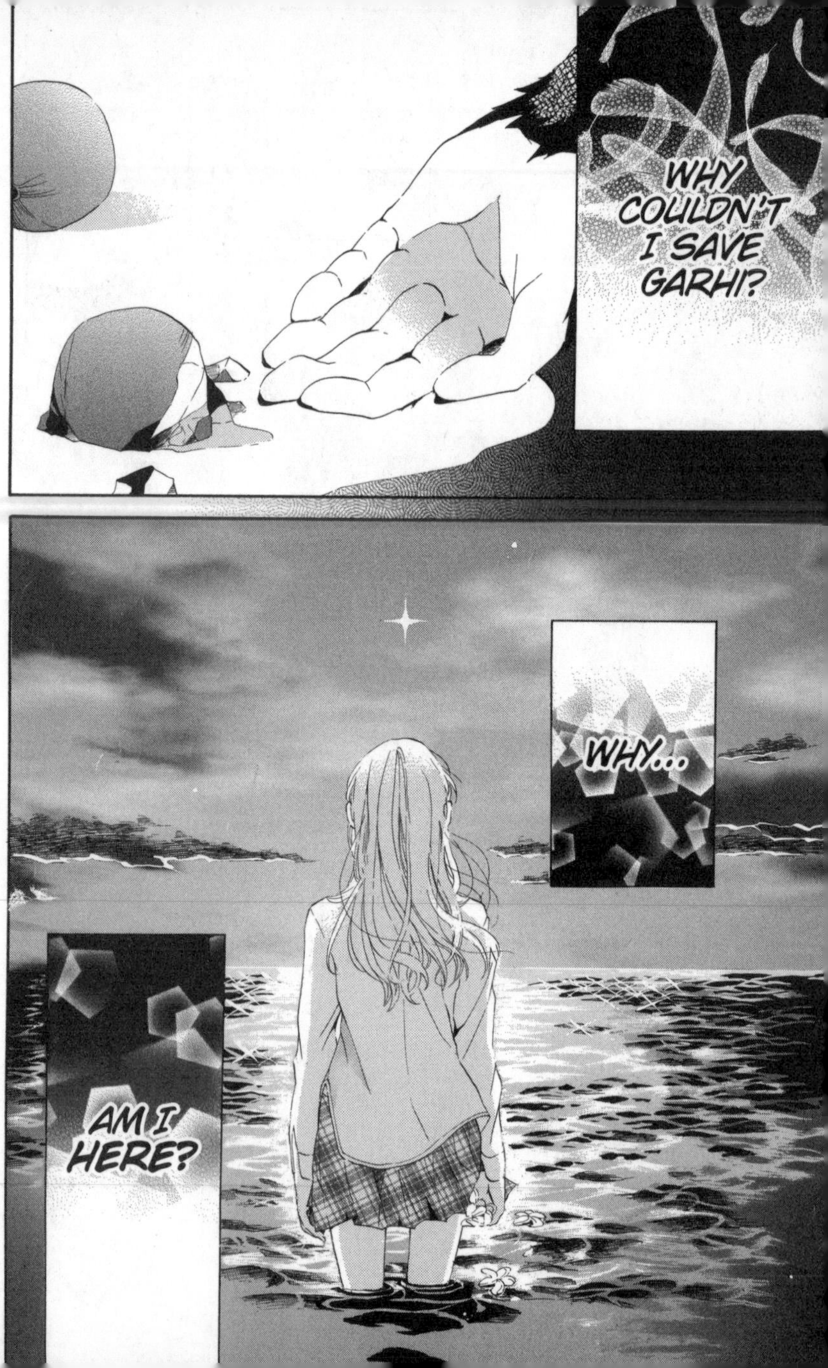
WHY COULDN'T I SAVE GARHI?
WHY...
AM I HERE?

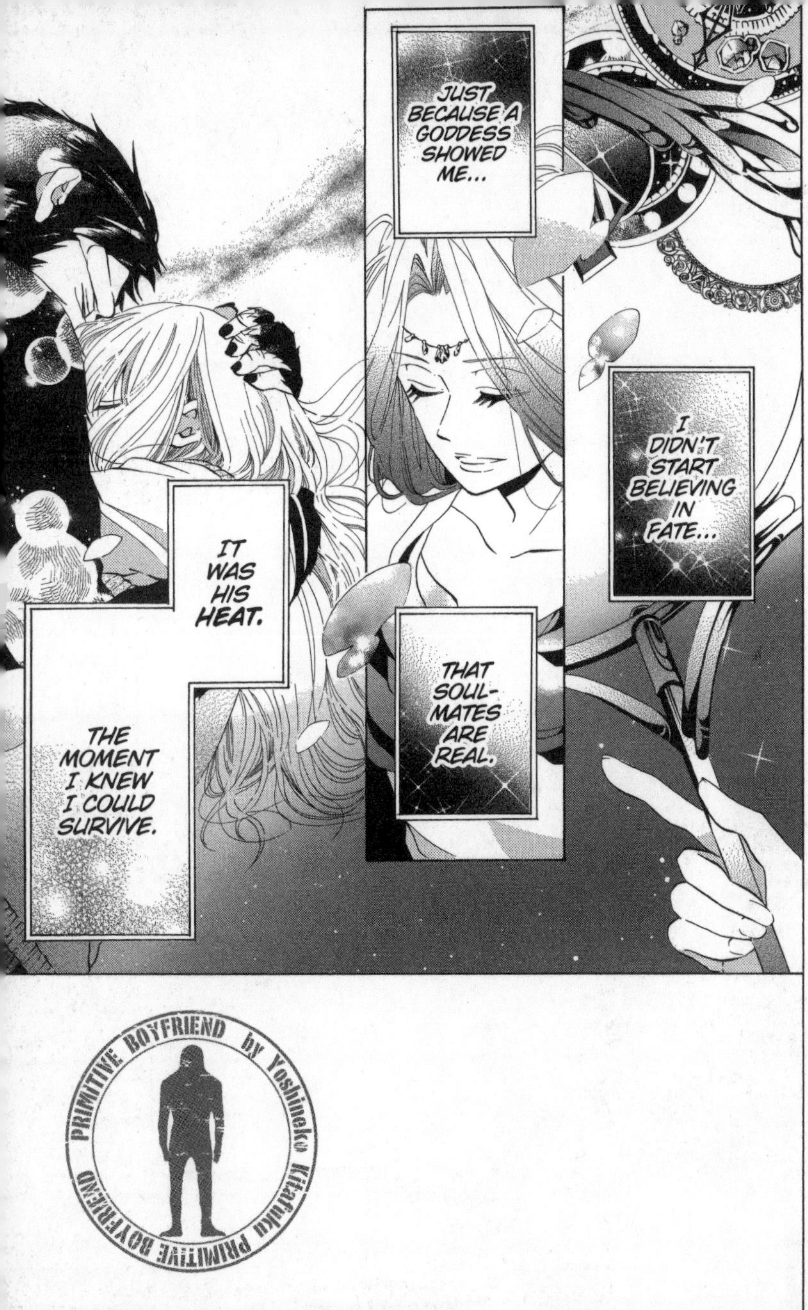
JUST BECAUSE A GODDESS SHOWED ME...
I DIDN'T START BELIEVING IN FATE...
THAT SOUL-MATES ARE REAL.
IT WAS HIS HEAT.
THE MOMENT I KNEW I COULD SURVIVE.

PRIMITIVE BOYFRIEND by Yoshineko Kitafuku PRIMITIVE BOYFRIEND

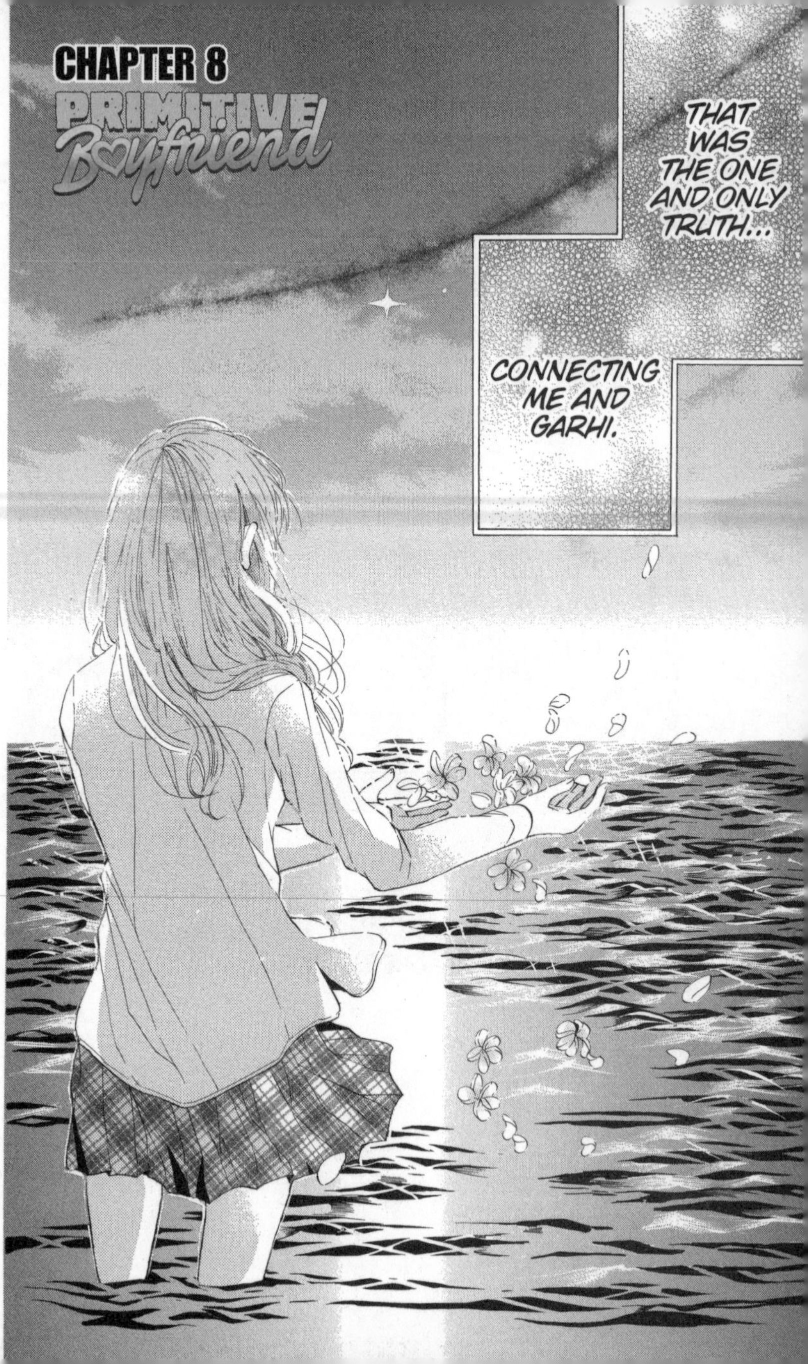
CHAPTER 8
PRIMITIVE Boyfriend
THAT WAS THE ONE AND ONLY TRUTH...
CONNECTING ME AND GARHI.

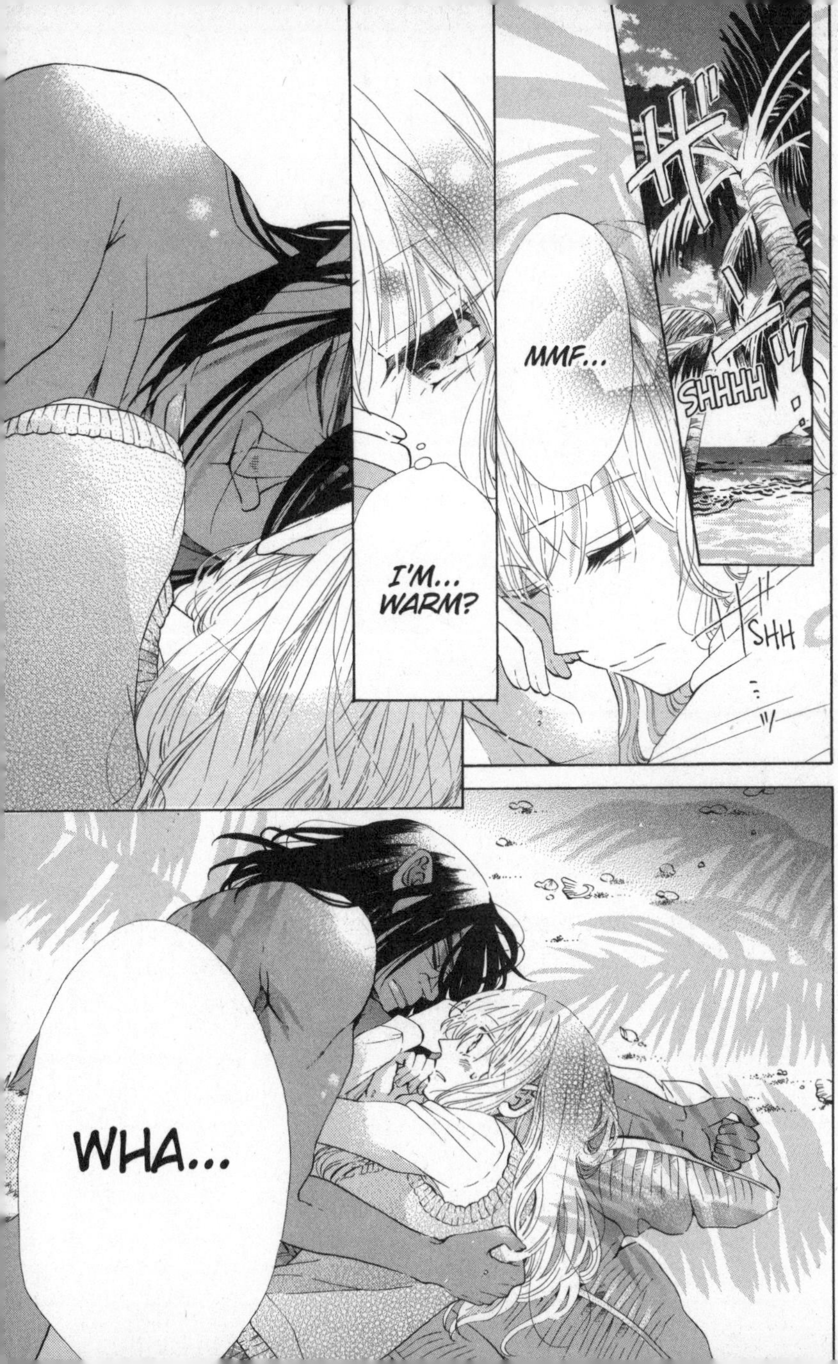
SHHHH
MMF...
SHH
I'M... WARM?
WHA...

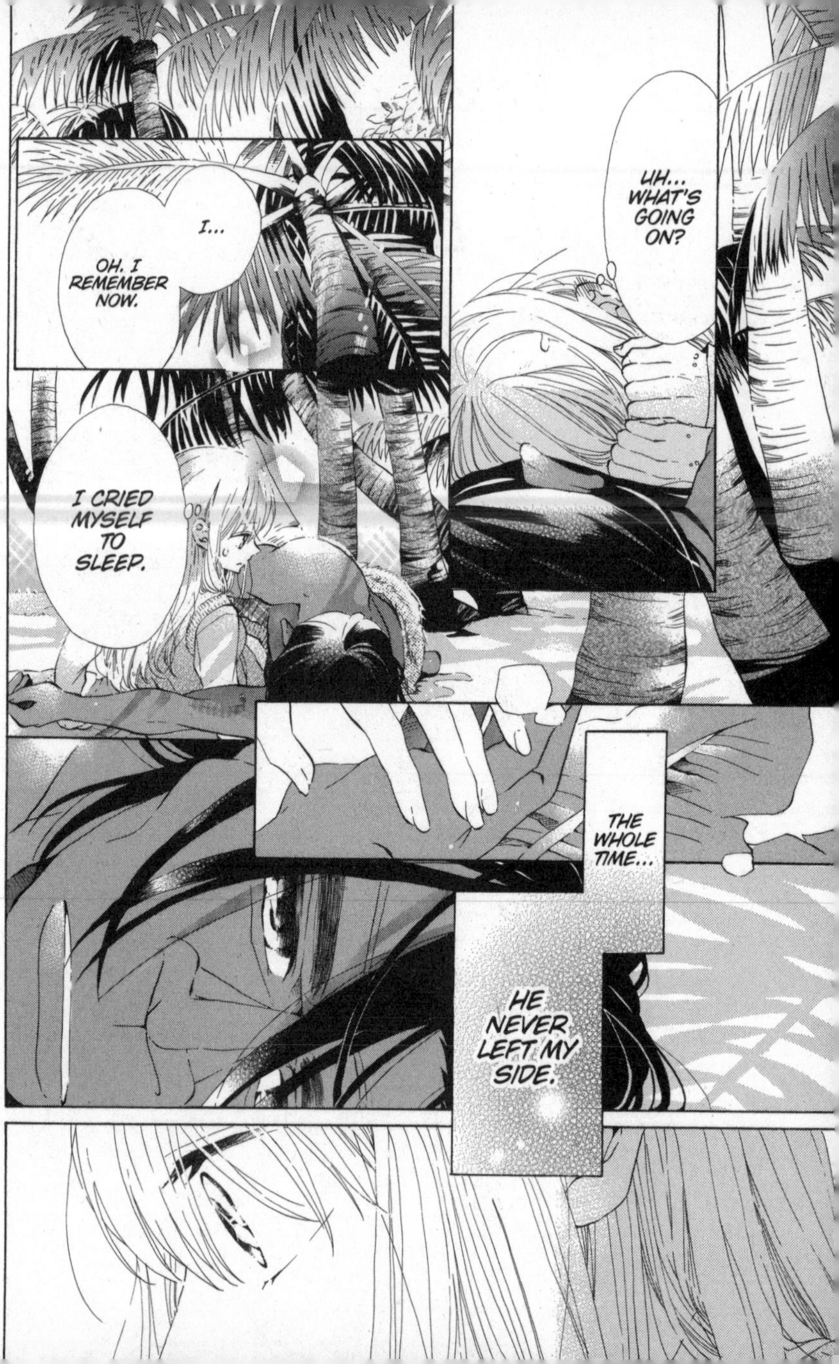
UH... WHAT'S GOING ON?
I...
OH. I REMEMBER NOW.
I CRIED MYSELF TO SLEEP.
THE WHOLE TIME...
HE NEVER LEFT MY SIDE.

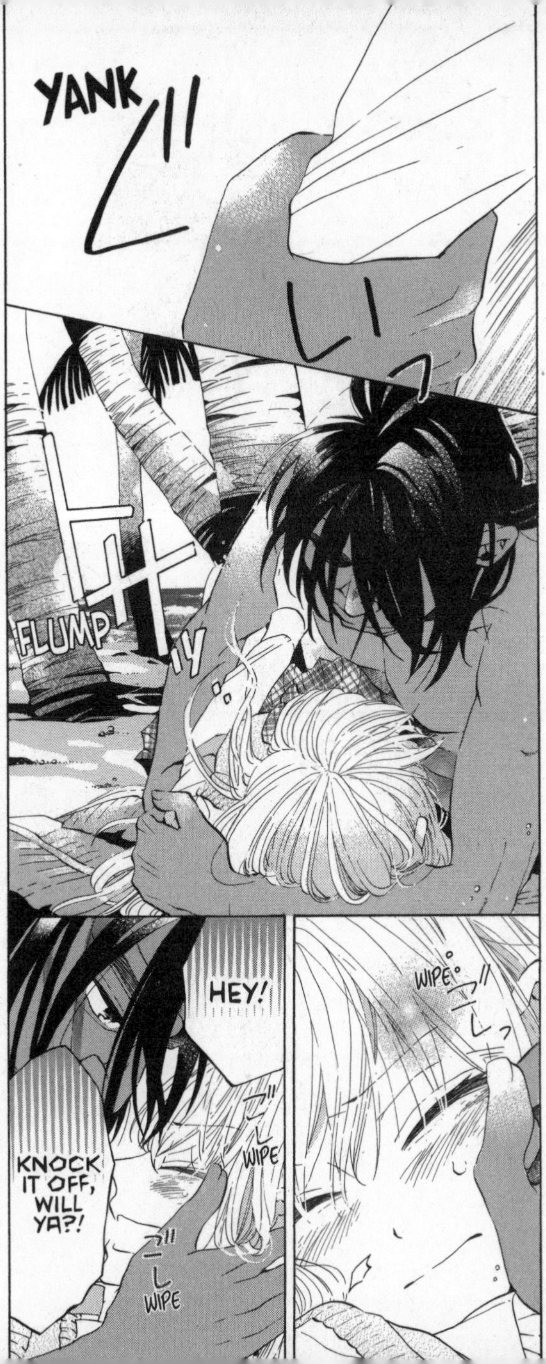
YANK
FLUMP
WIPE
HEY!
WIPE
KNOCK IT OFF, WILL YA?!
WIPE

5

I OFTEN GET MY MOTHER TO HELP ME. IN CHAPTER 8, HER SCREENTONE TECHNIQUE LEVELED UP EVEN MORE.

SHE PASTES THE SCREENTONES FOR MITO'S UNIFORM, ETC. RECENTLY, WHEN I ASK...

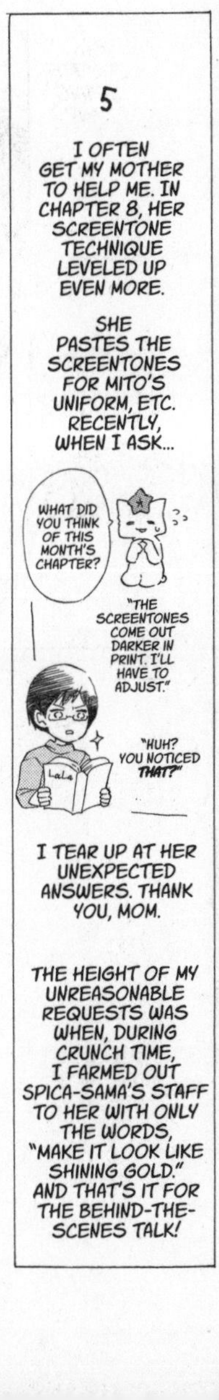
WHAT DID YOU THINK OF THIS MONTH'S CHAPTER?
"THE SCREENTONES COME OUT DARKER IN PRINT. I'LL HAVE TO ADJUST."
"HUH? YOU NOTICED ***THAT?***"
LaLa

I TEAR UP AT HER UNEXPECTED ANSWERS. THANK YOU, MOM.

THE HEIGHT OF MY UNREASONABLE REQUESTS WAS WHEN, DURING CRUNCH TIME, I FARMED OUT SPICA-SAMA'S STAFF TO HER WITH ONLY THE WORDS, "MAKE IT LOOK LIKE SHINING GOLD." AND THAT'S IT FOR THE BEHIND-THE-SCENES TALK!

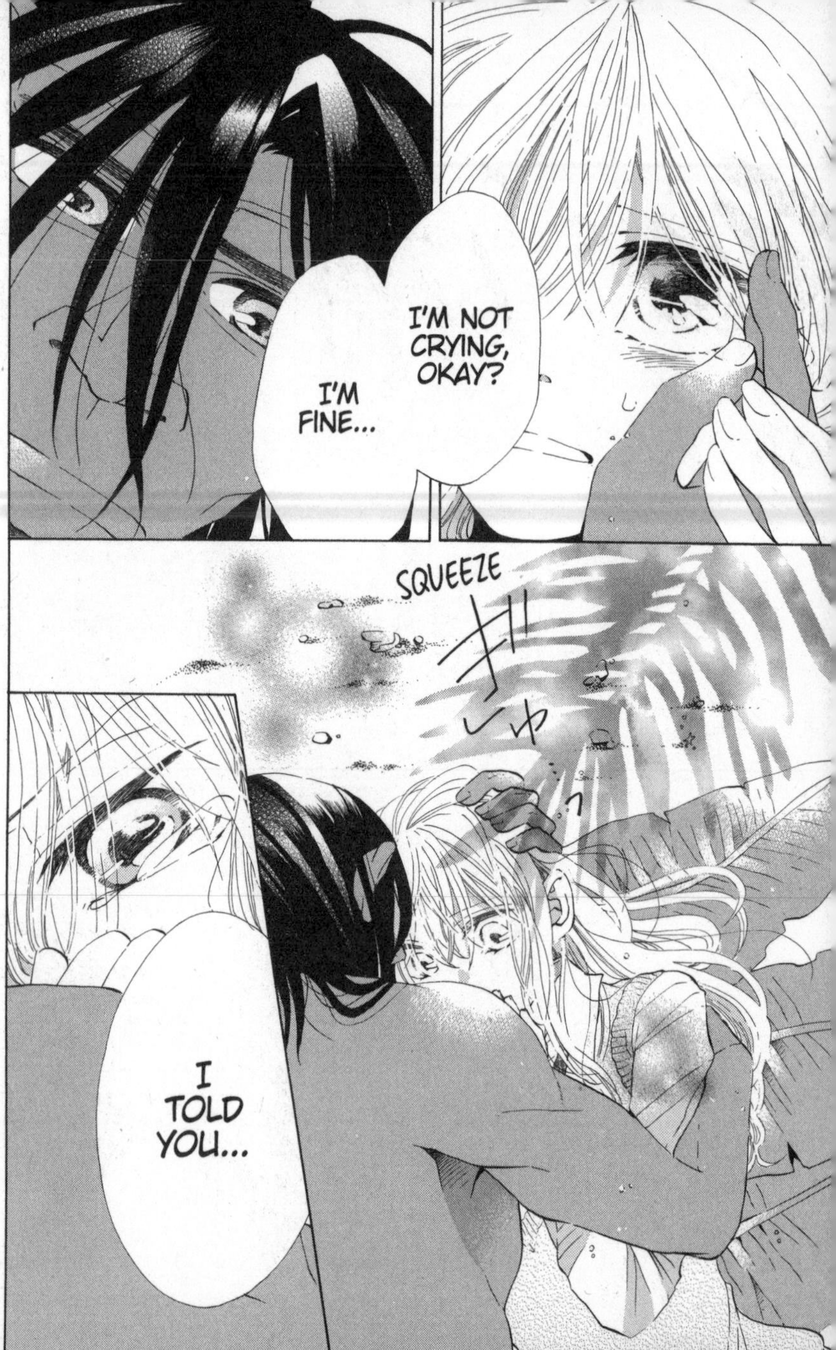
I'M NOT CRYING, OKAY?
I'M FINE...
SQUEEZE
ぎゅっ
I TOLD YOU...

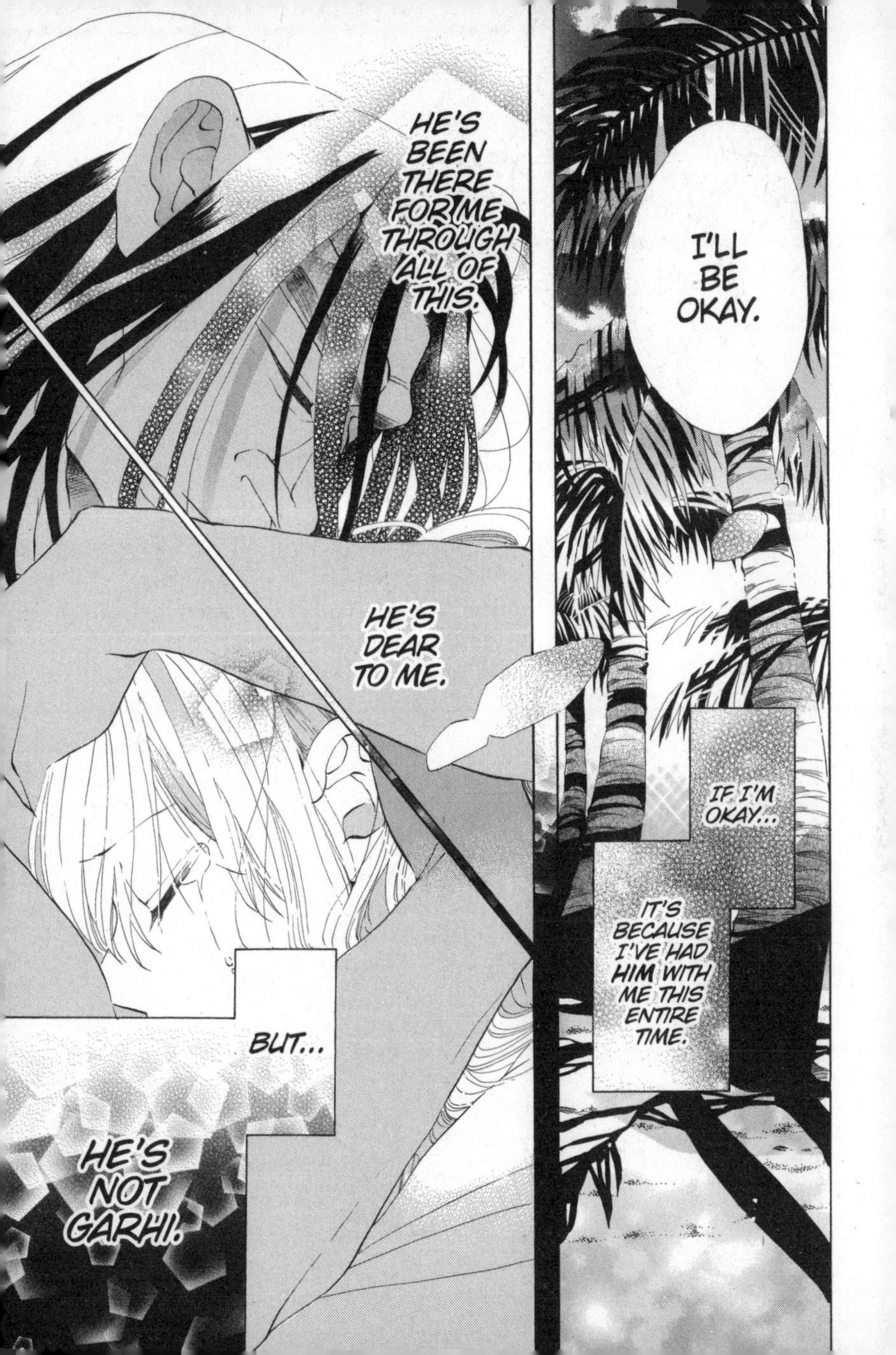
I'LL BE OKAY.
IF I'M OKAY...
IT'S BECAUSE I'VE HAD HIM WITH ME THIS ENTIRE TIME.
HE'S BEEN THERE FOR ME THROUGH ALL OF THIS.
HE'S DEAR TO ME.
BUT...
HE'S NOT GARHI.

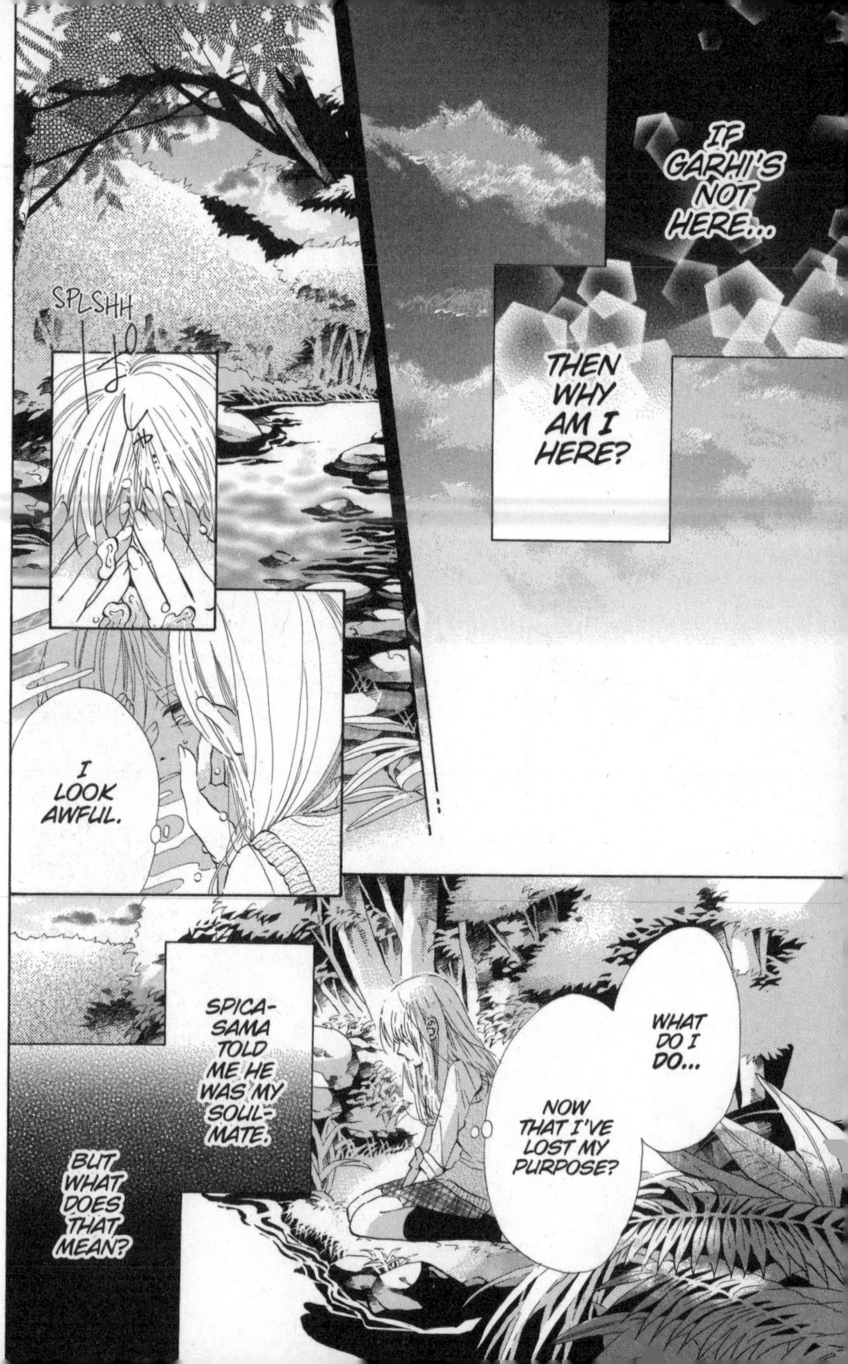
IF GARHI'S NOT HERE...
THEN WHY AM I HERE?
SPLSHH
I LOOK AWFUL.
WHAT DO I DO...
NOW THAT I'VE LOST MY PURPOSE?
SPICA-SAMA TOLD ME HE WAS MY SOUL-MATE.
BUT WHAT DOES THAT MEAN?

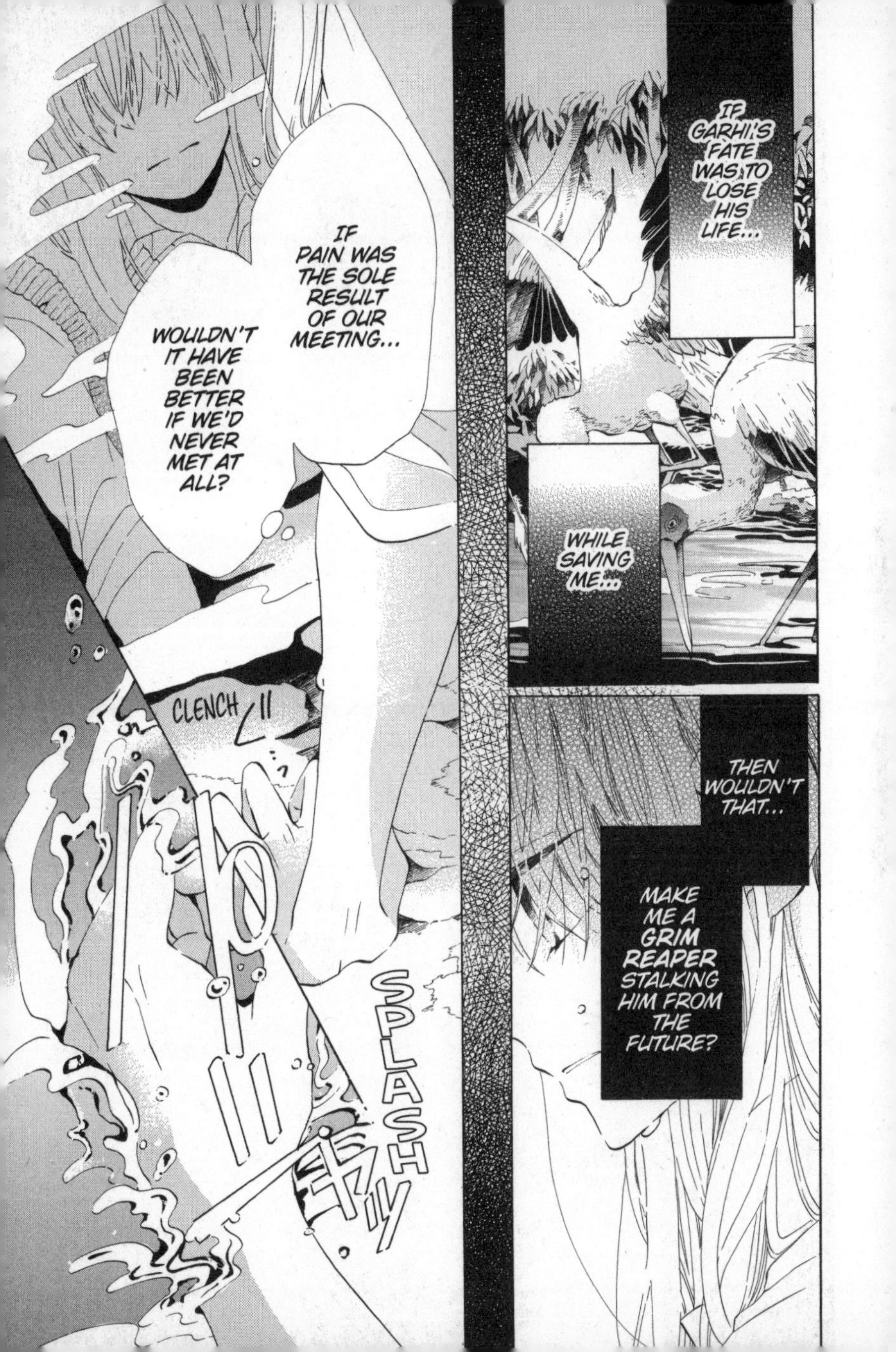
IF GARHII'S FATE WAS TO LOSE HIS LIFE...
WHILE SAVING ME...
THEN WOULDN'T THAT...
MAKE ME A GRIM REAPER STALKING HIM FROM THE FUTURE?
IF PAIN WAS THE SOLE RESULT OF OUR MEETING...
WOULDN'T IT HAVE BEEN BETTER IF WE'D NEVER MET AT ALL?
CLENCH
SPLASH

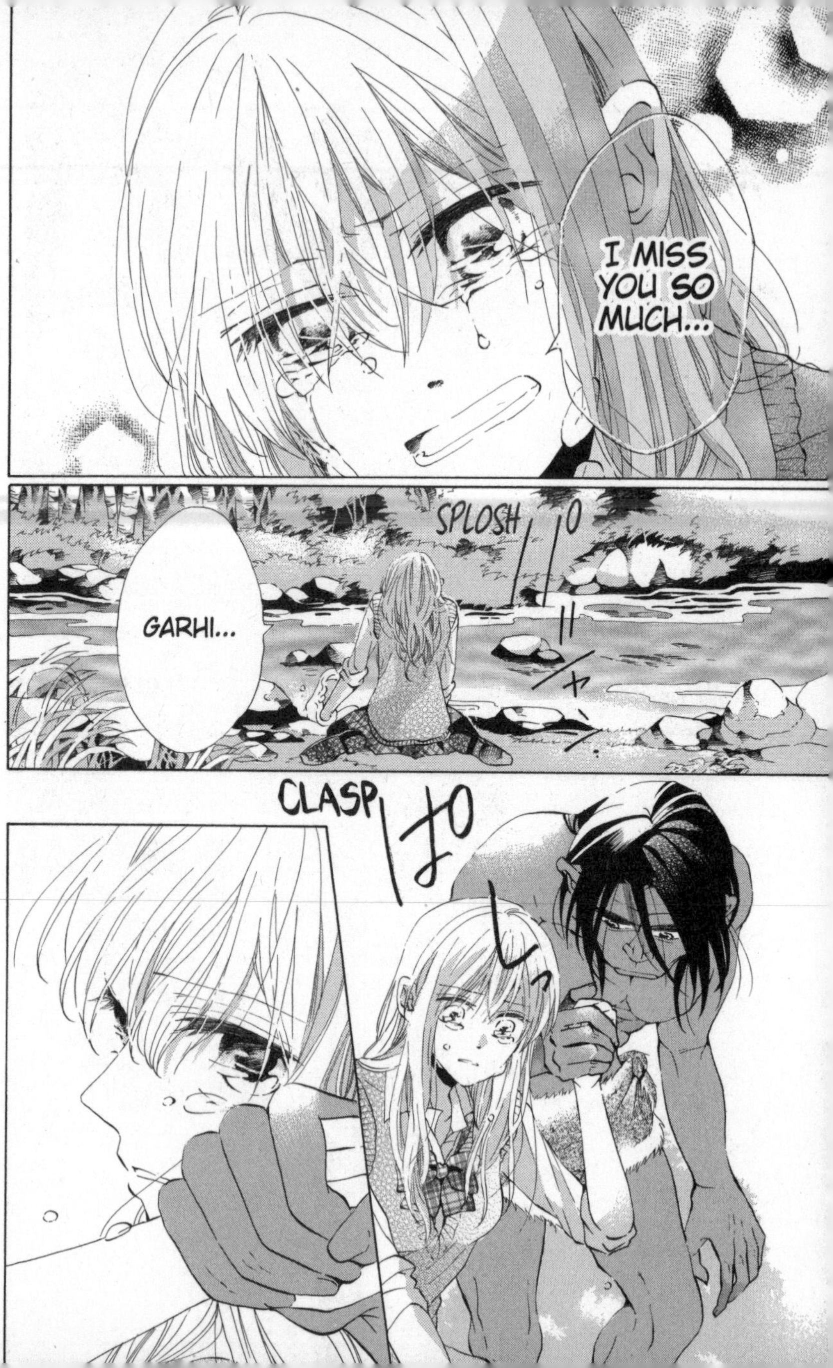
I MISS YOU SO MUCH...
SPLOSH
GARHI...
CLASP

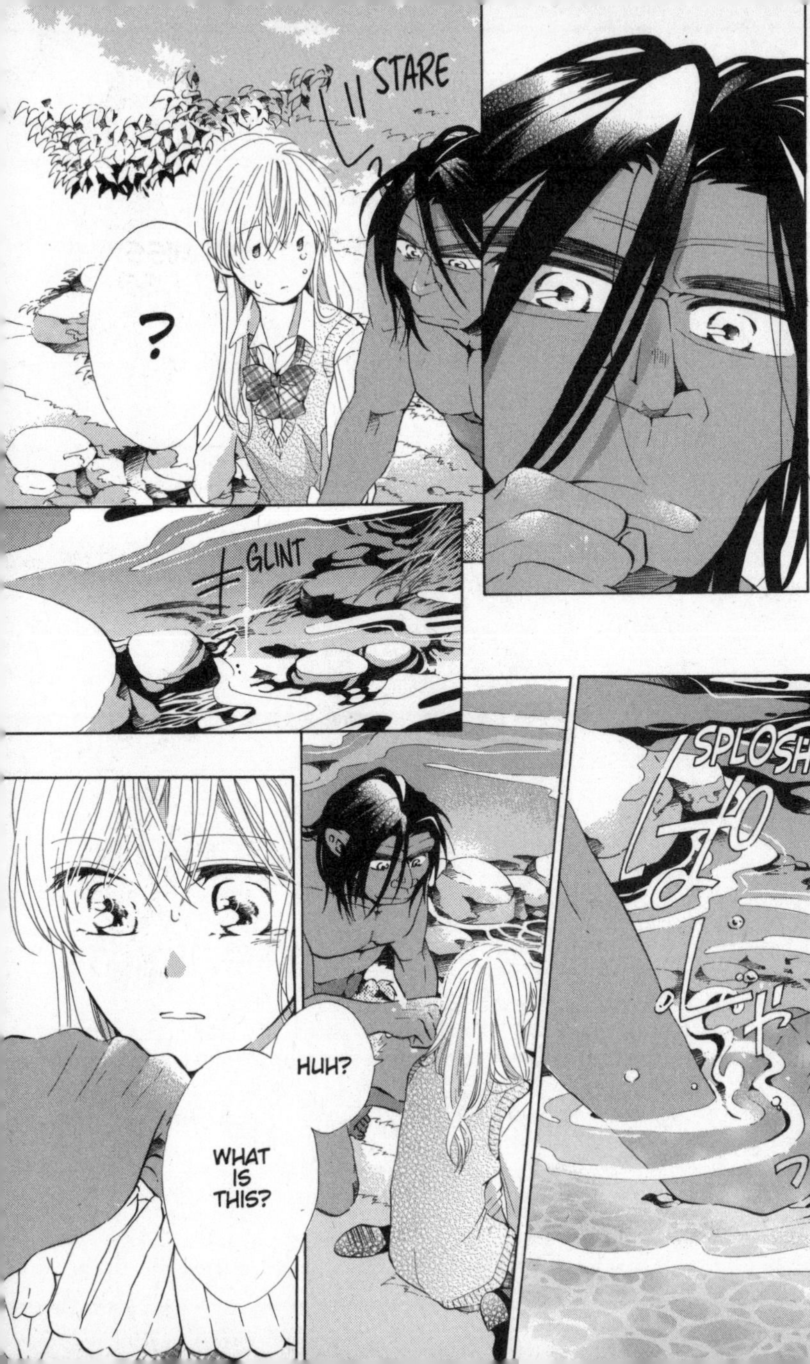
STARE
?
GLINT
SPLOSH
HUH?
WHAT IS THIS?

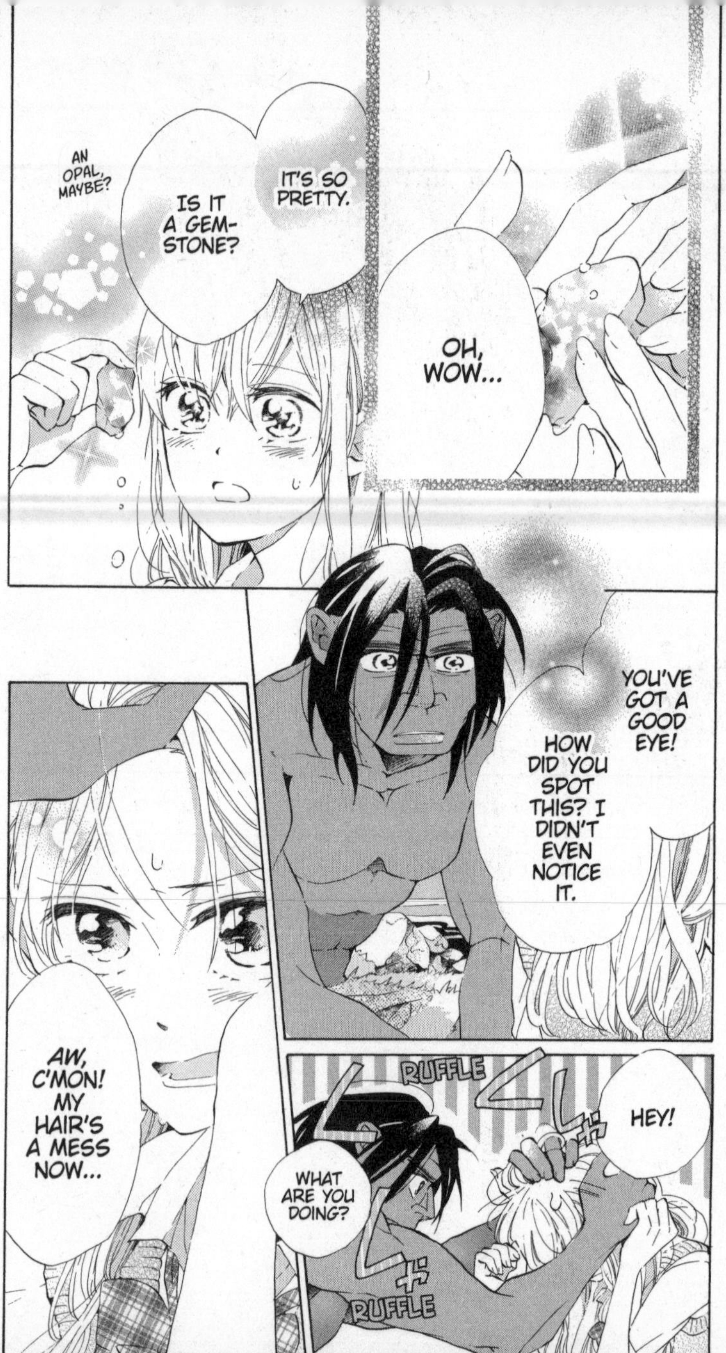

OH, WOW...
IT'S SO PRETTY.
IS IT A GEMSTONE?
AN OPAL, MAYBE?
YOU'VE GOT A GOOD EYE!
HOW DID YOU SPOT THIS? I DIDN'T EVEN NOTICE IT.
RUFFLE
HEY!
WHAT ARE YOU DOING?
RUFFLE
AW, C'MON! MY HAIR'S A MESS NOW...

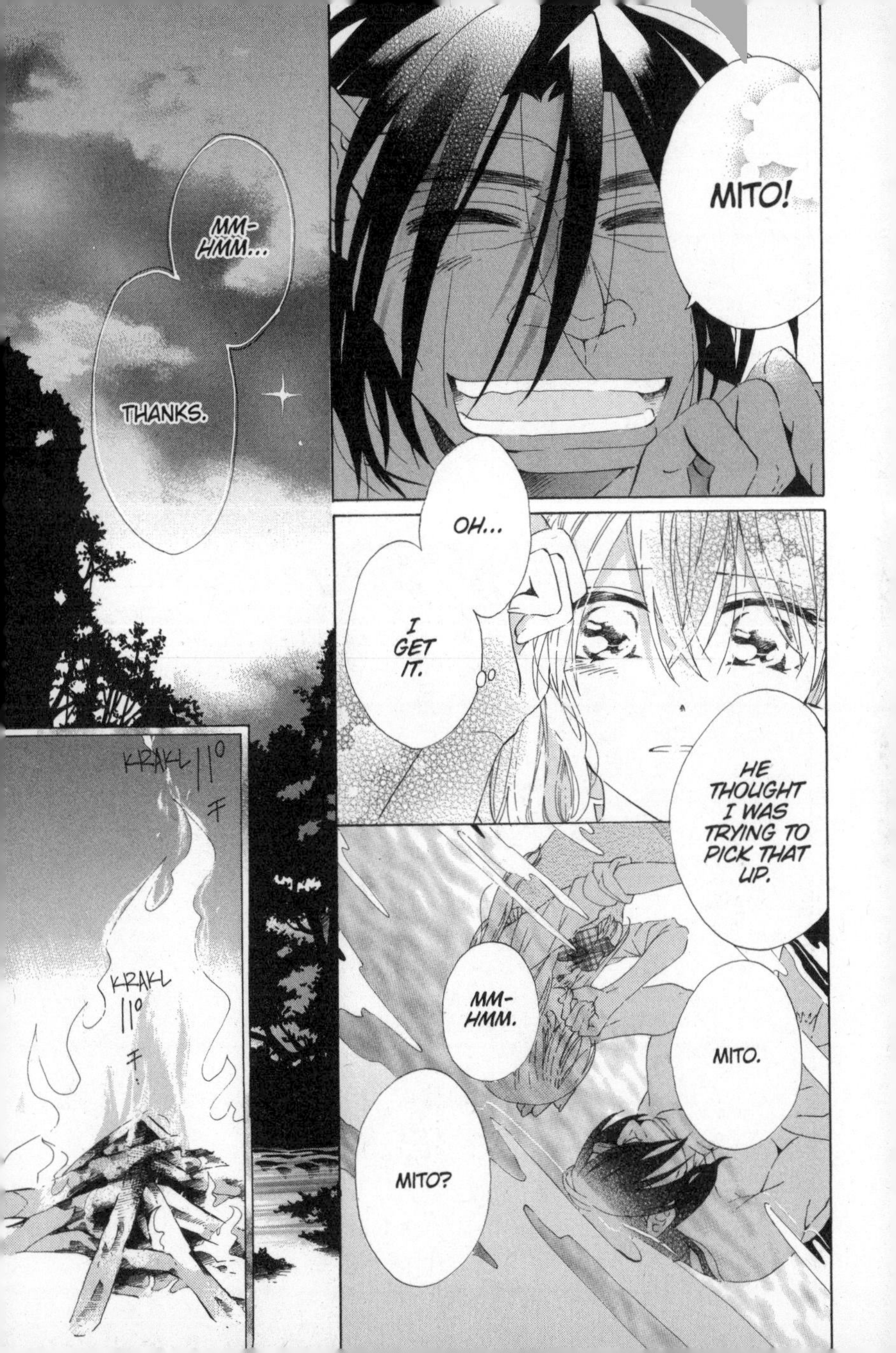
MITO!
OH...
I GET IT.
HE THOUGHT I WAS TRYING TO PICK THAT UP.
MITO.
MM-HMM.
MITO?
MM-HMM...
THANKS.
KRAKL
KRAKL

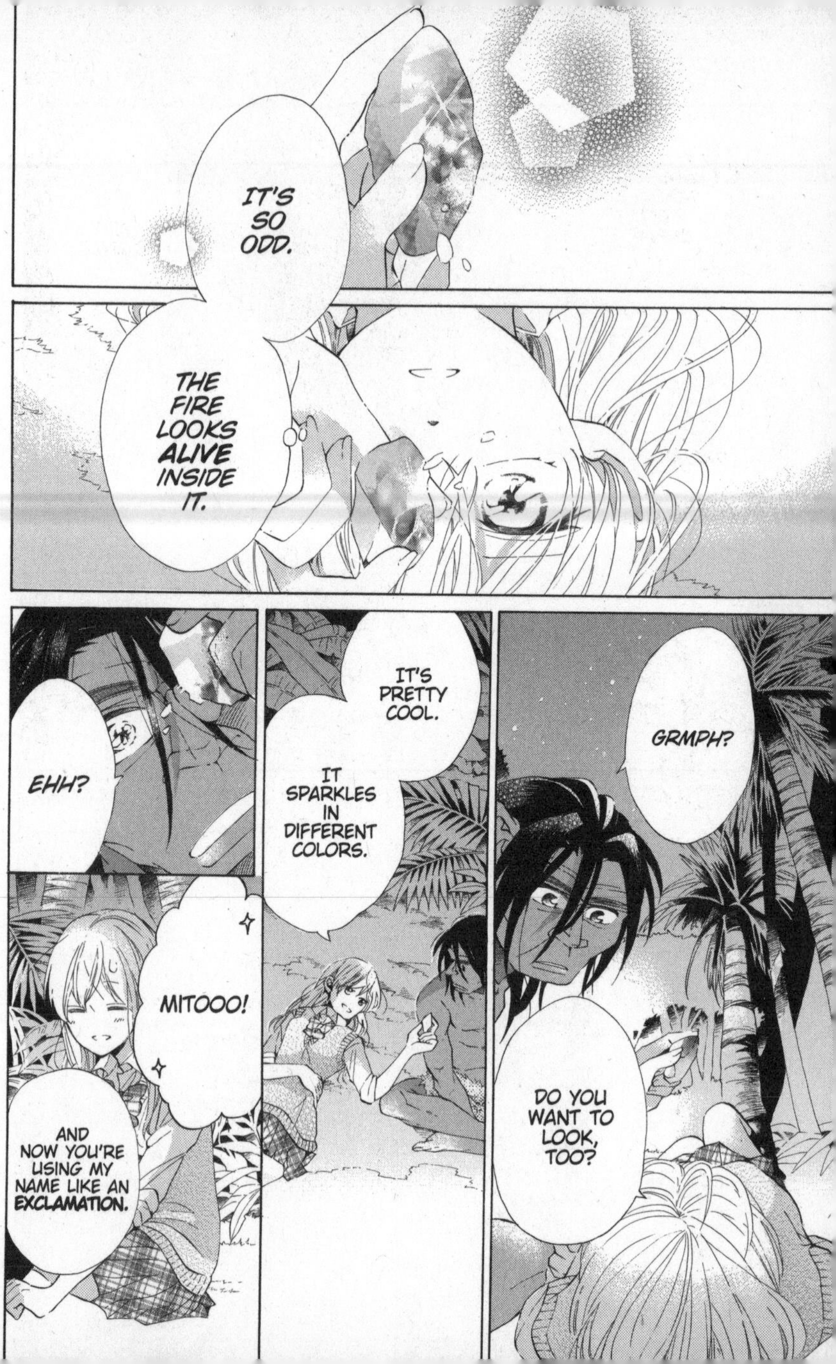
IT'S SO ODD.
THE FIRE LOOKS **ALIVE** INSIDE IT.
GRMPH?
DO YOU WANT TO LOOK, TOO?
IT'S PRETTY COOL.
IT SPARKLES IN DIFFERENT COLORS.
EHH?
MITOOO!
AND NOW YOU'RE USING MY NAME LIKE AN **EXCLAMATION.**

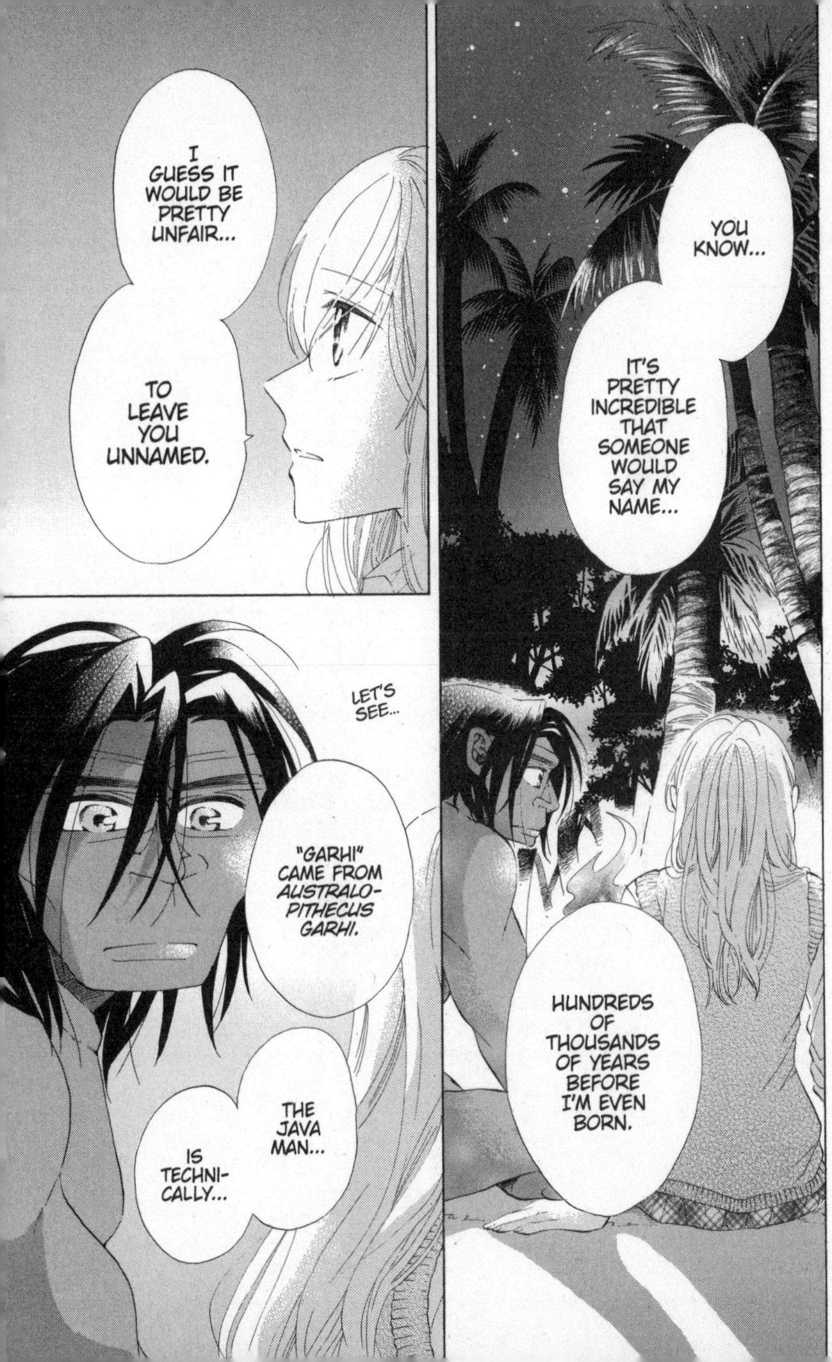
YOU KNOW...
IT'S PRETTY INCREDIBLE THAT SOMEONE WOULD SAY MY NAME...
HUNDREDS OF THOUSANDS OF YEARS BEFORE I'M EVEN BORN.
I GUESS IT WOULD BE PRETTY UNFAIR...
TO LEAVE YOU UNNAMED.
LET'S SEE...
"GARHI" CAME FROM AUSTRALOPITHECUS GARHI.
THE JAVA MAN...
IS TECHNICALLY...

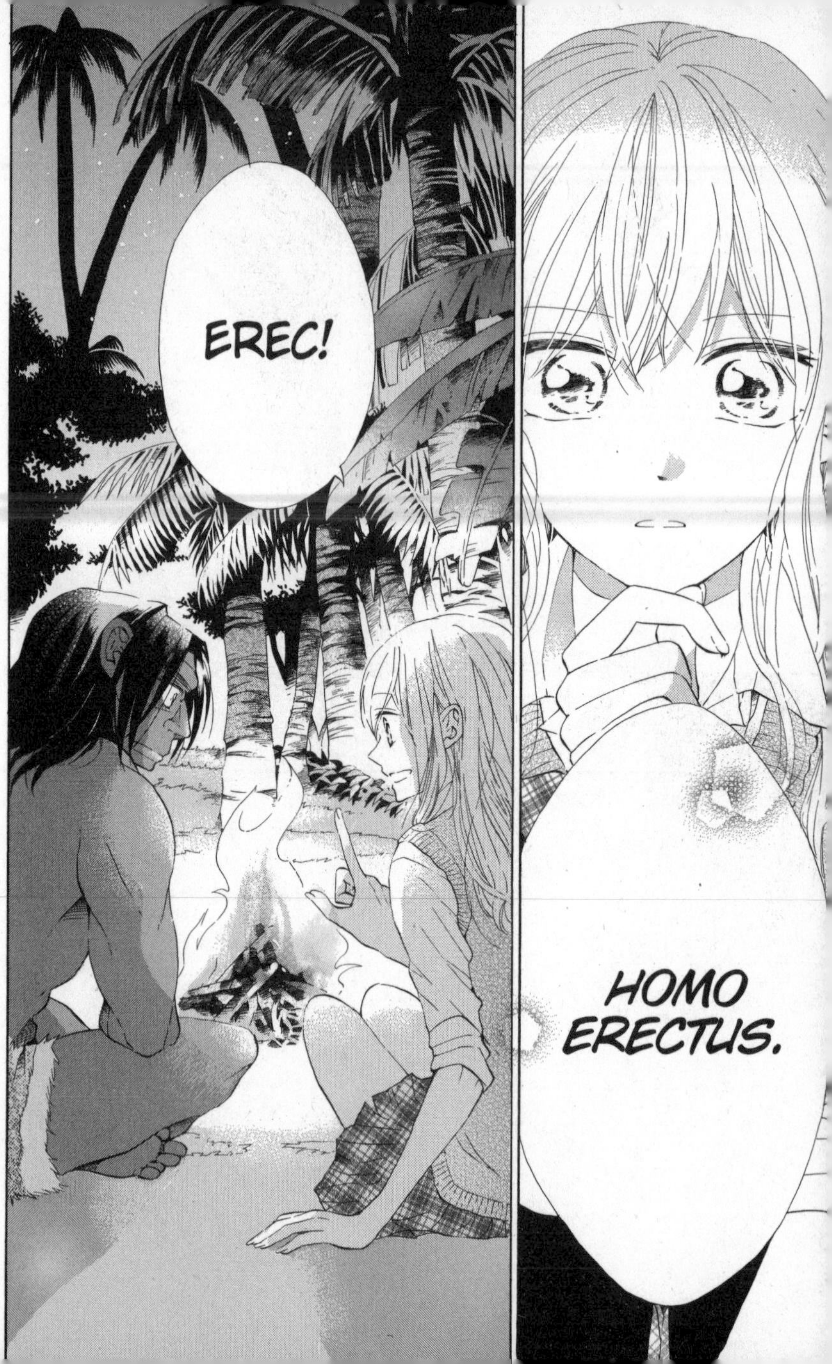
HOMO ERECTUS.
EREC!

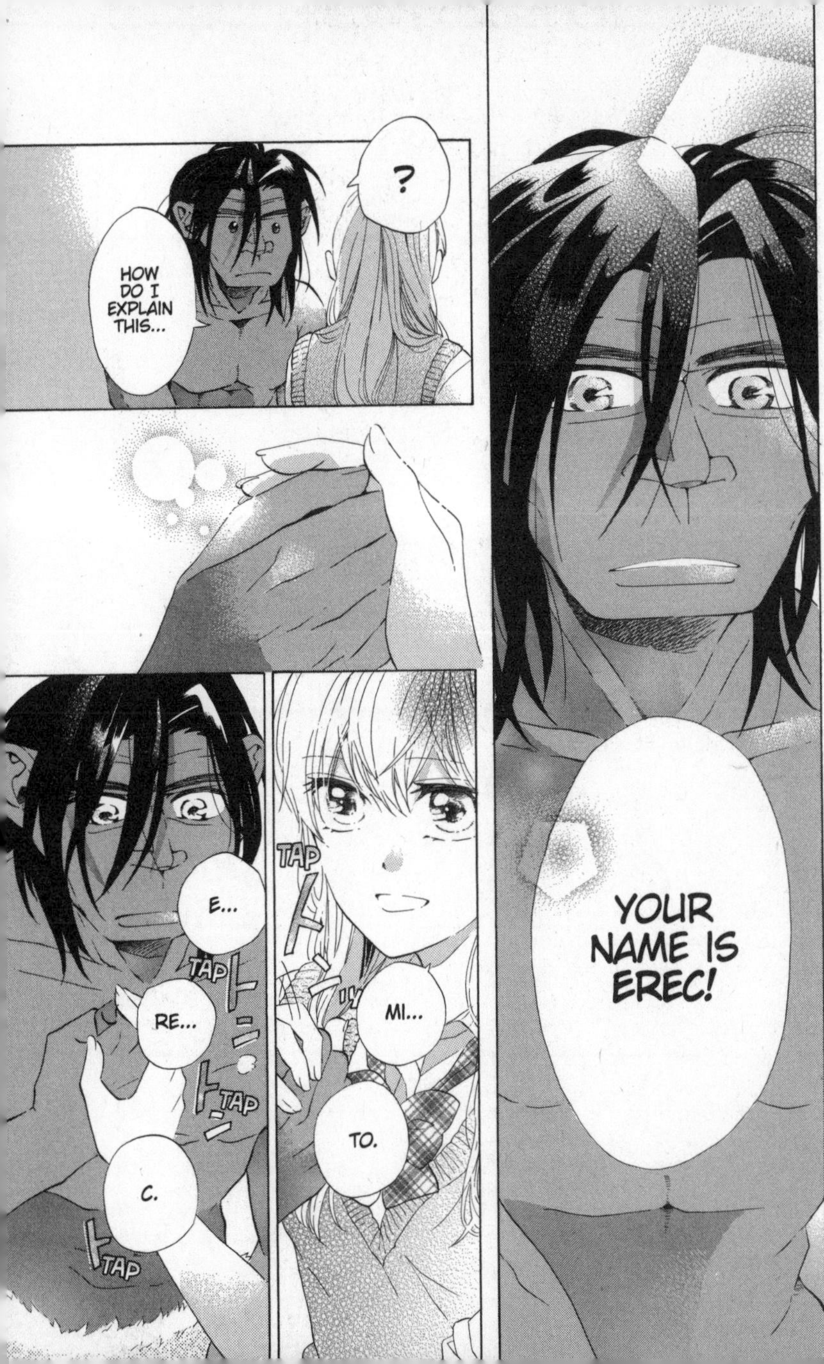
YOUR NAME IS EREC!
?
HOW DO I EXPLAIN THIS...
TAP
MI...
TO.
E...
TAP
RE...
TAP
C.
TAP

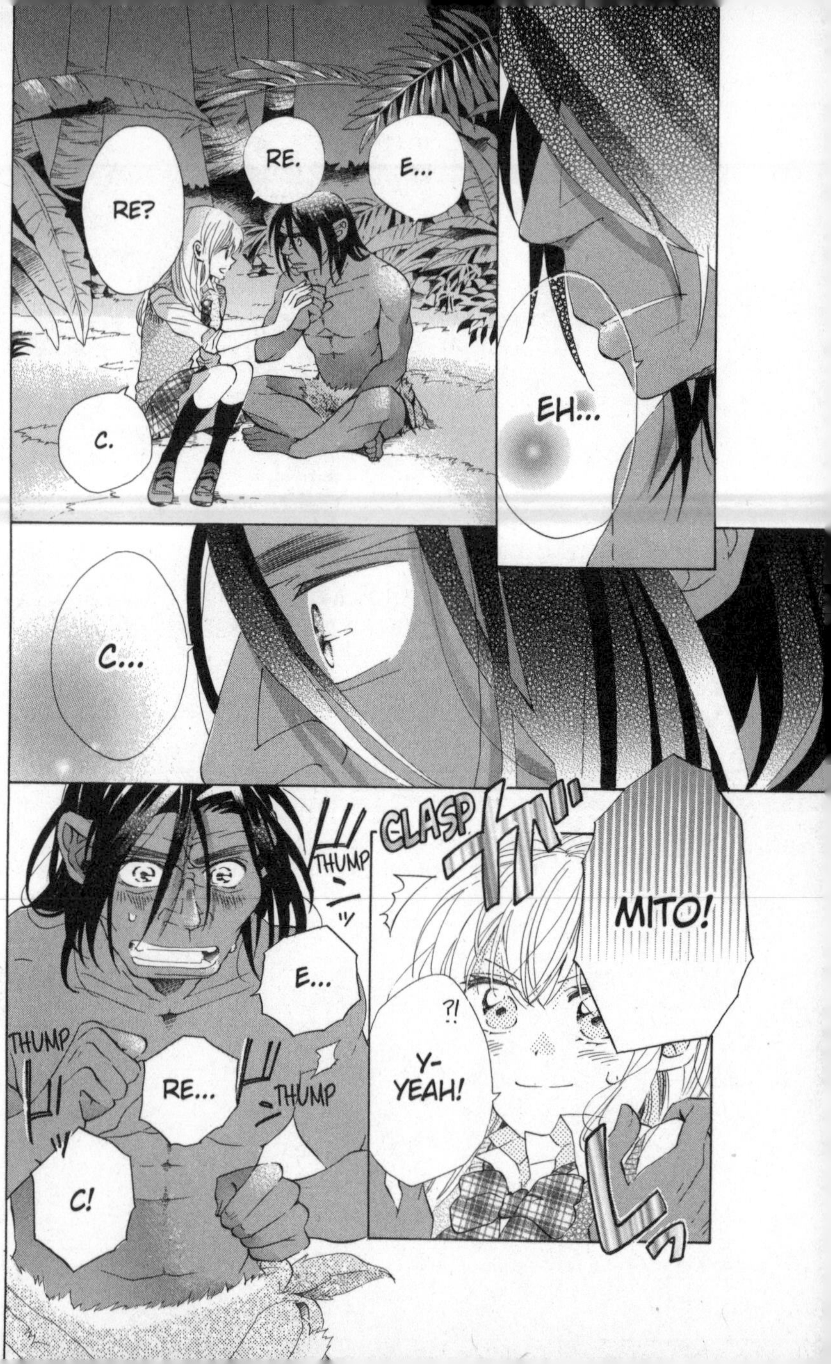
EH...
E...
RE.
RE?
C.
C...
MITO!
CLASP
?!
Y-YEAH!
THUMP
E...
THUMP
RE...
THUMP
C!

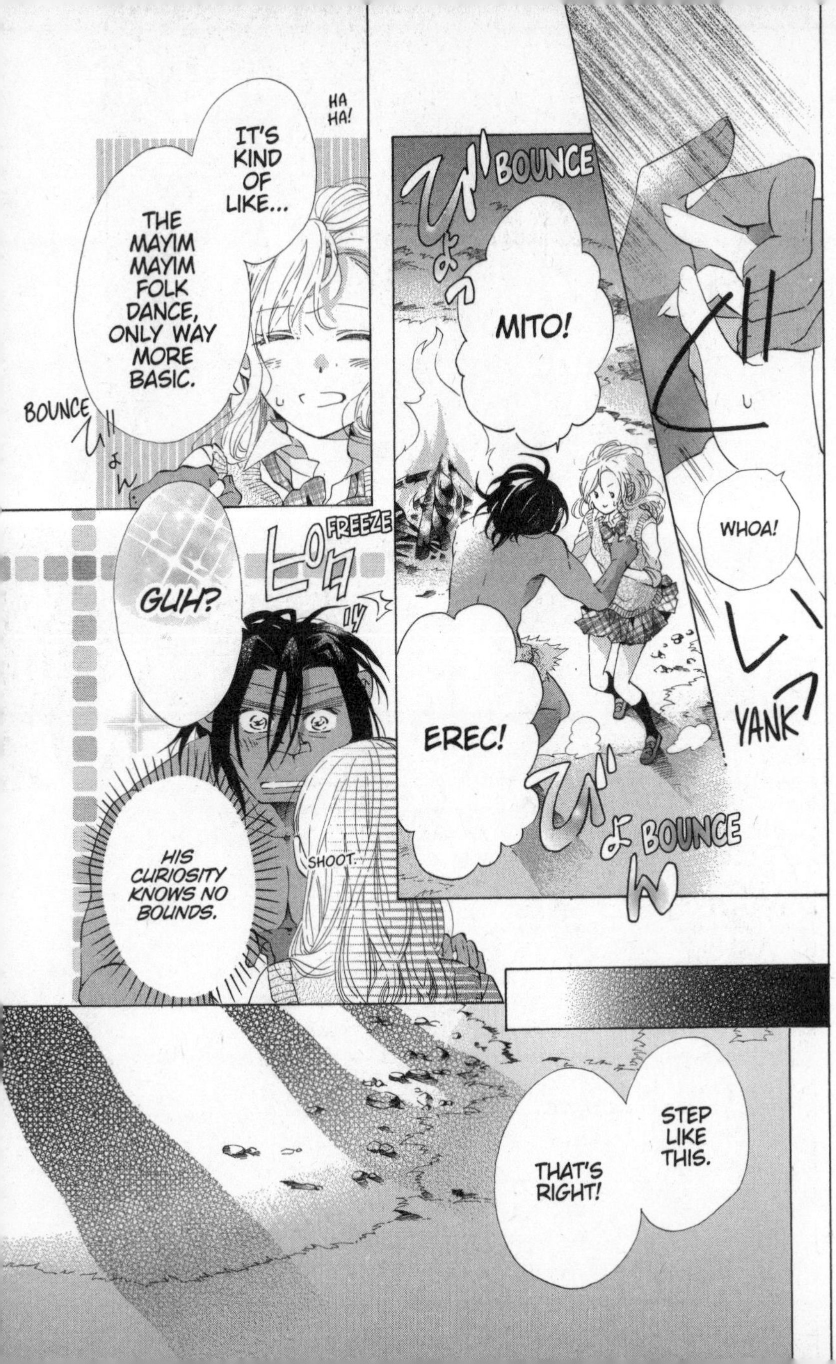
WHOA!
YANK
BOUNCE
MITO!
EREC!
BOUNCE
HA HA!
IT'S KIND OF LIKE...
THE MAYIM MAYIM FOLK DANCE, ONLY WAY MORE BASIC.
BOUNCE
FREEZE
GUH?
SHOOT.
HIS CURIOSITY KNOWS NO BOUNDS.
STEP LIKE THIS.
THAT'S RIGHT!

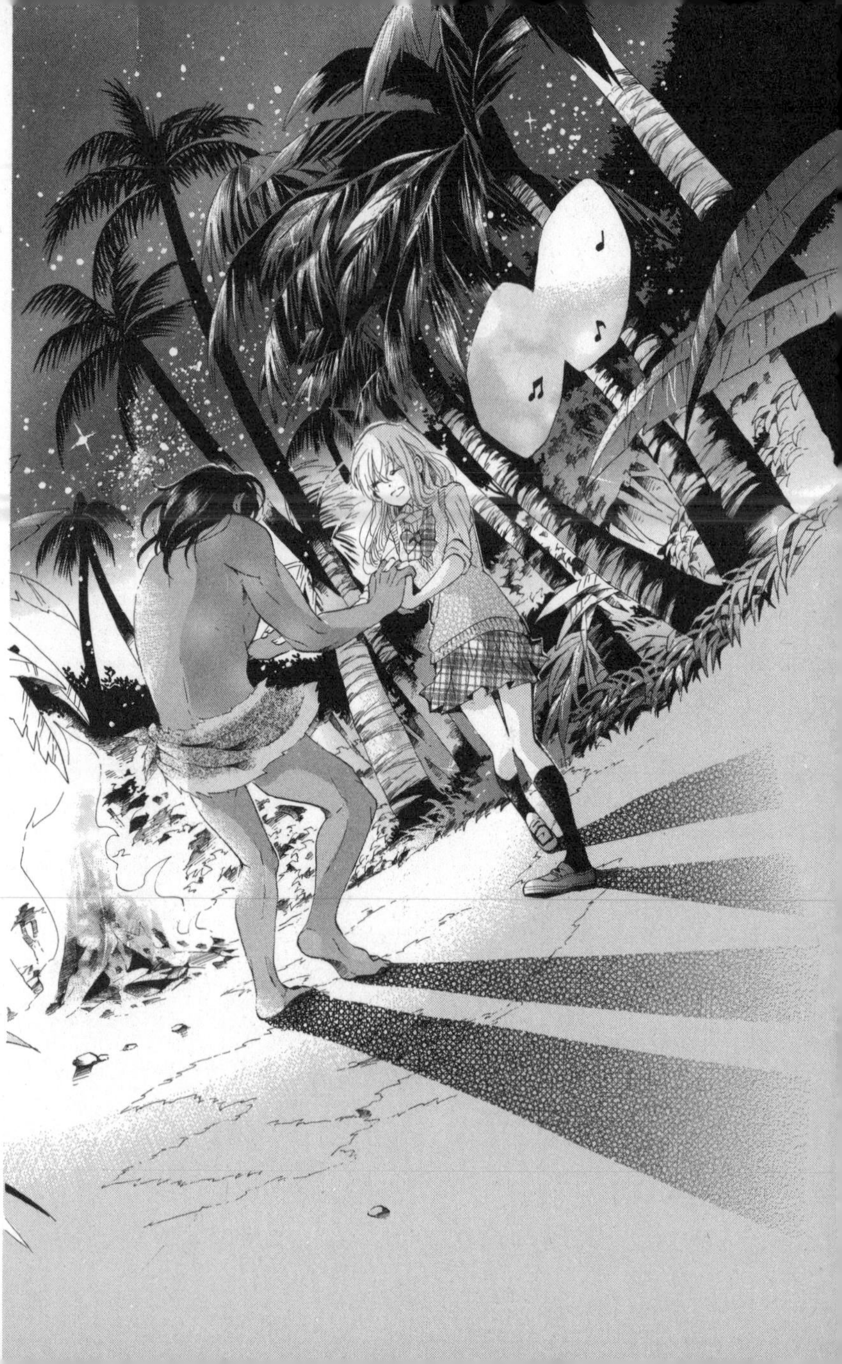

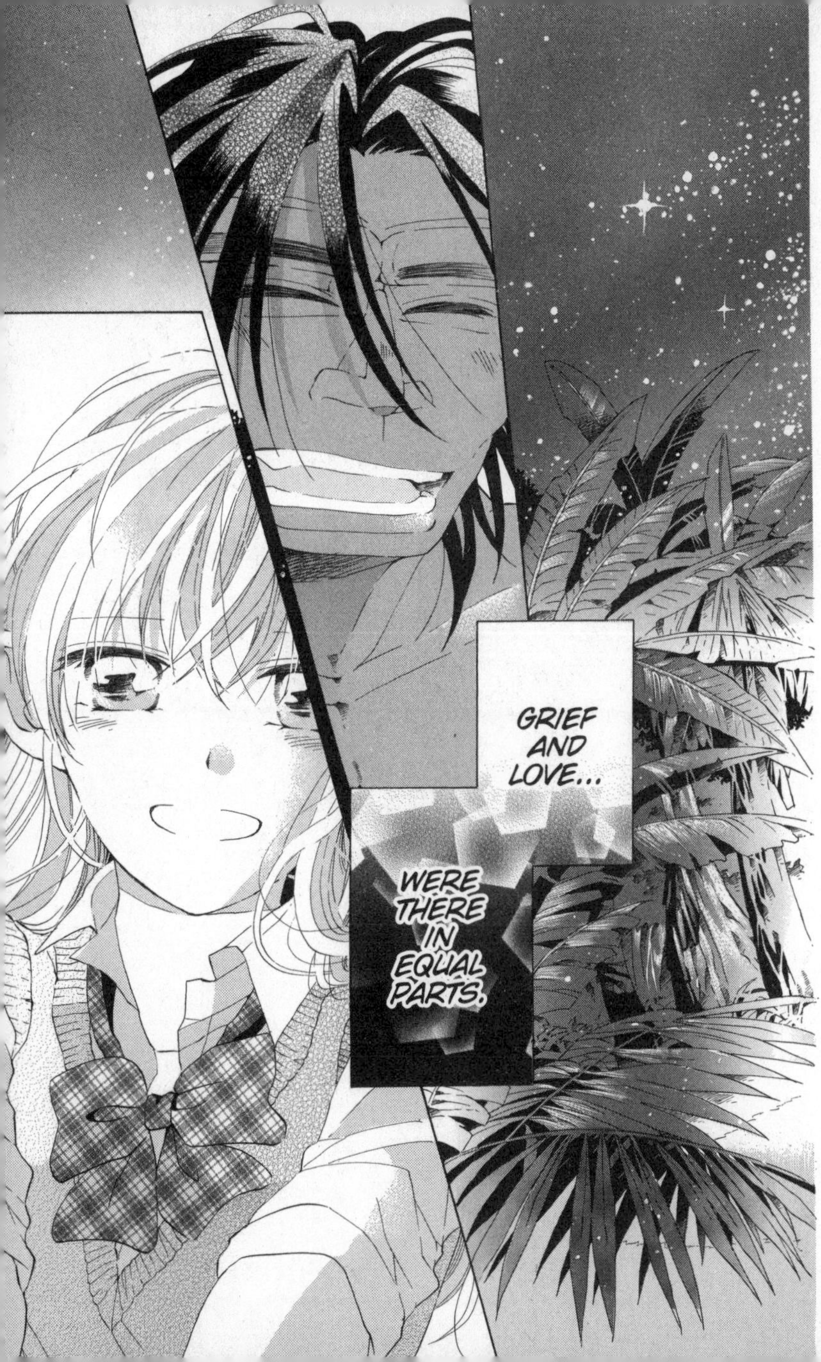
GRIEF AND LOVE...
WERE THERE IN EQUAL PARTS.

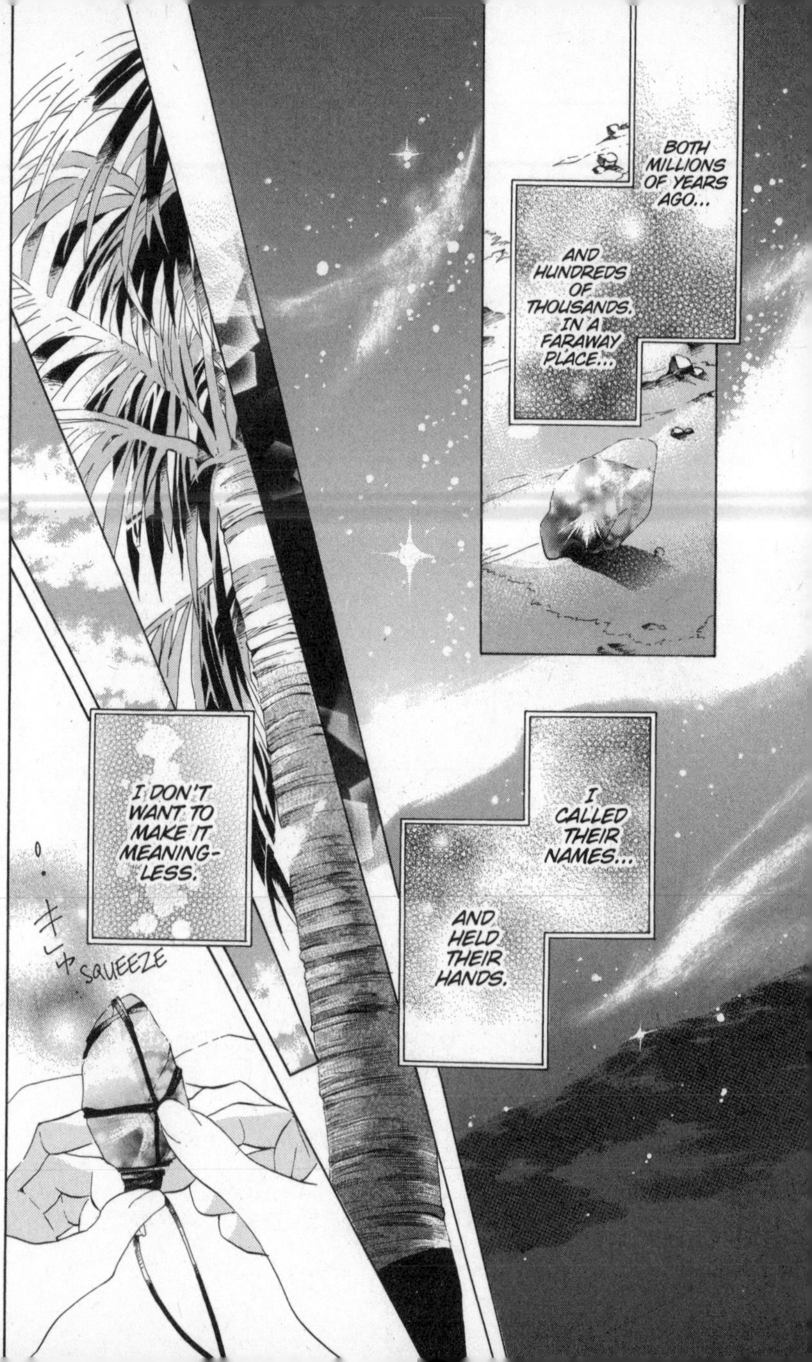
BOTH MILLIONS OF YEARS AGO...
AND HUNDREDS OF THOUSANDS. IN A FARAWAY PLACE...
I CALLED THEIR NAMES...
AND HELD THEIR HANDS.
I DON'T WANT TO MAKE IT MEANING-LESS.
キュッ
SQUEEZE

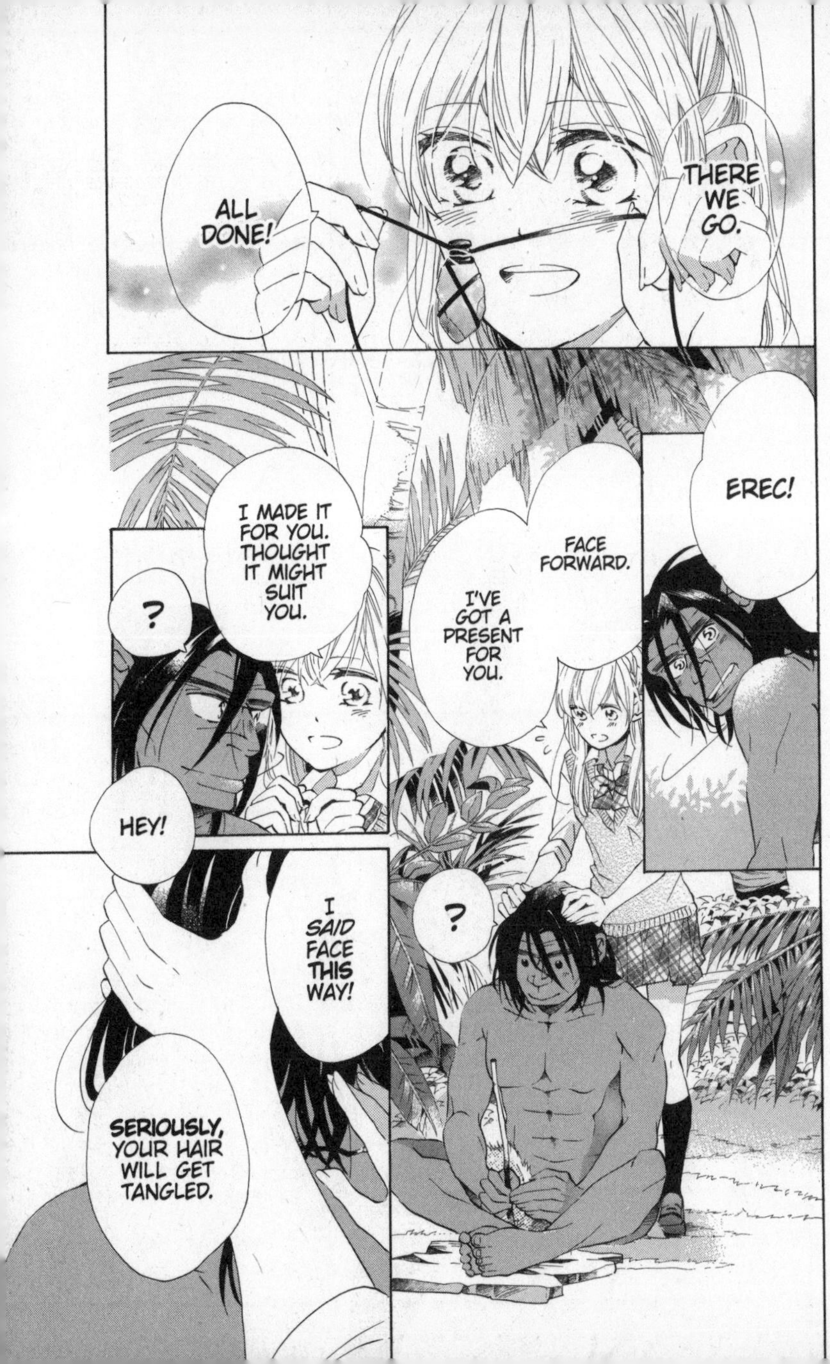
THERE WE GO.
ALL DONE!
EREC!
FACE FORWARD.
I'VE GOT A PRESENT FOR YOU.
I MADE IT FOR YOU. THOUGHT IT MIGHT SUIT YOU.
?
HEY!
?
I SAID FACE THIS WAY!
SERIOUSLY, YOUR HAIR WILL GET TANGLED.

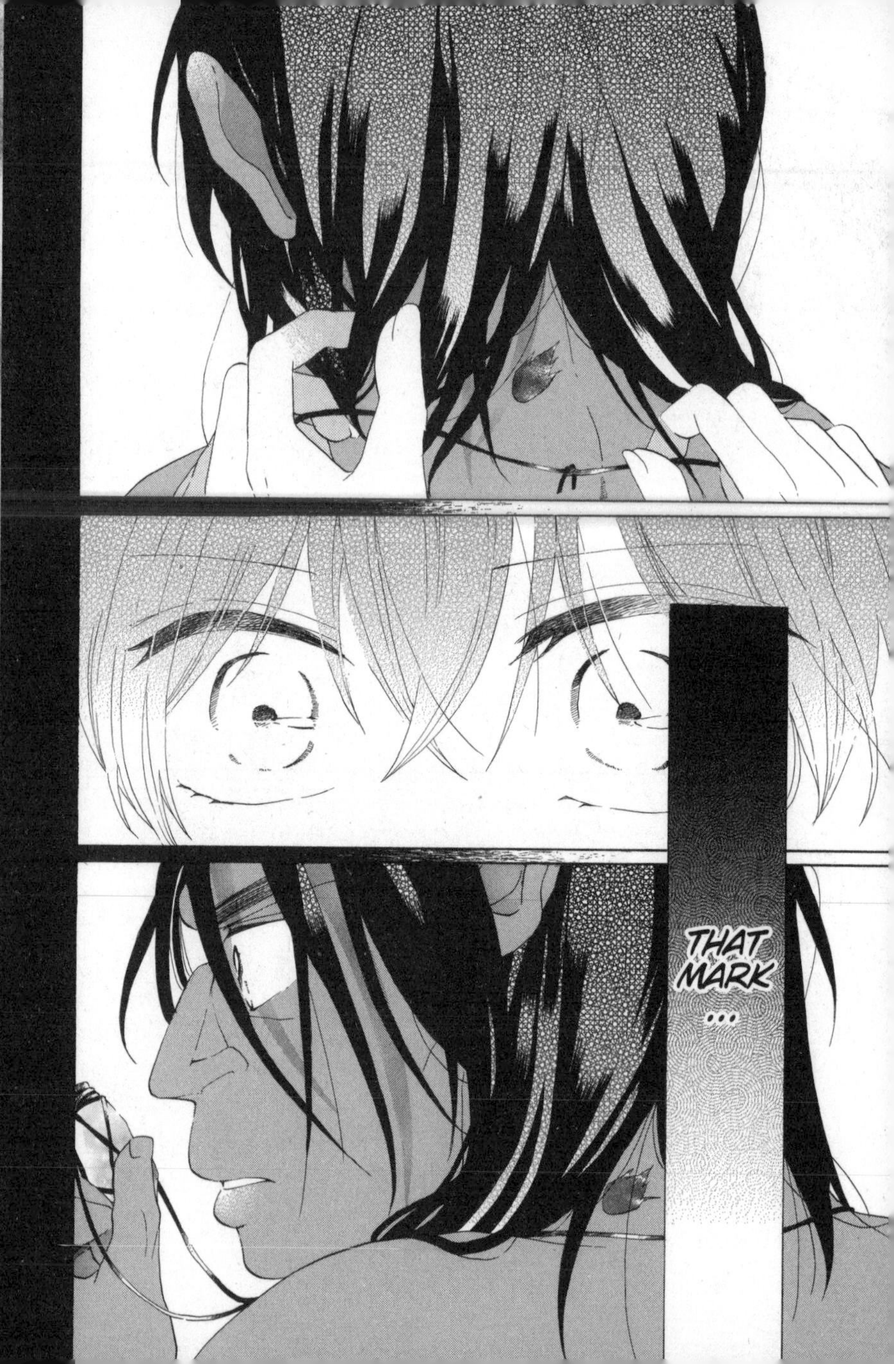
THAT MARK ...

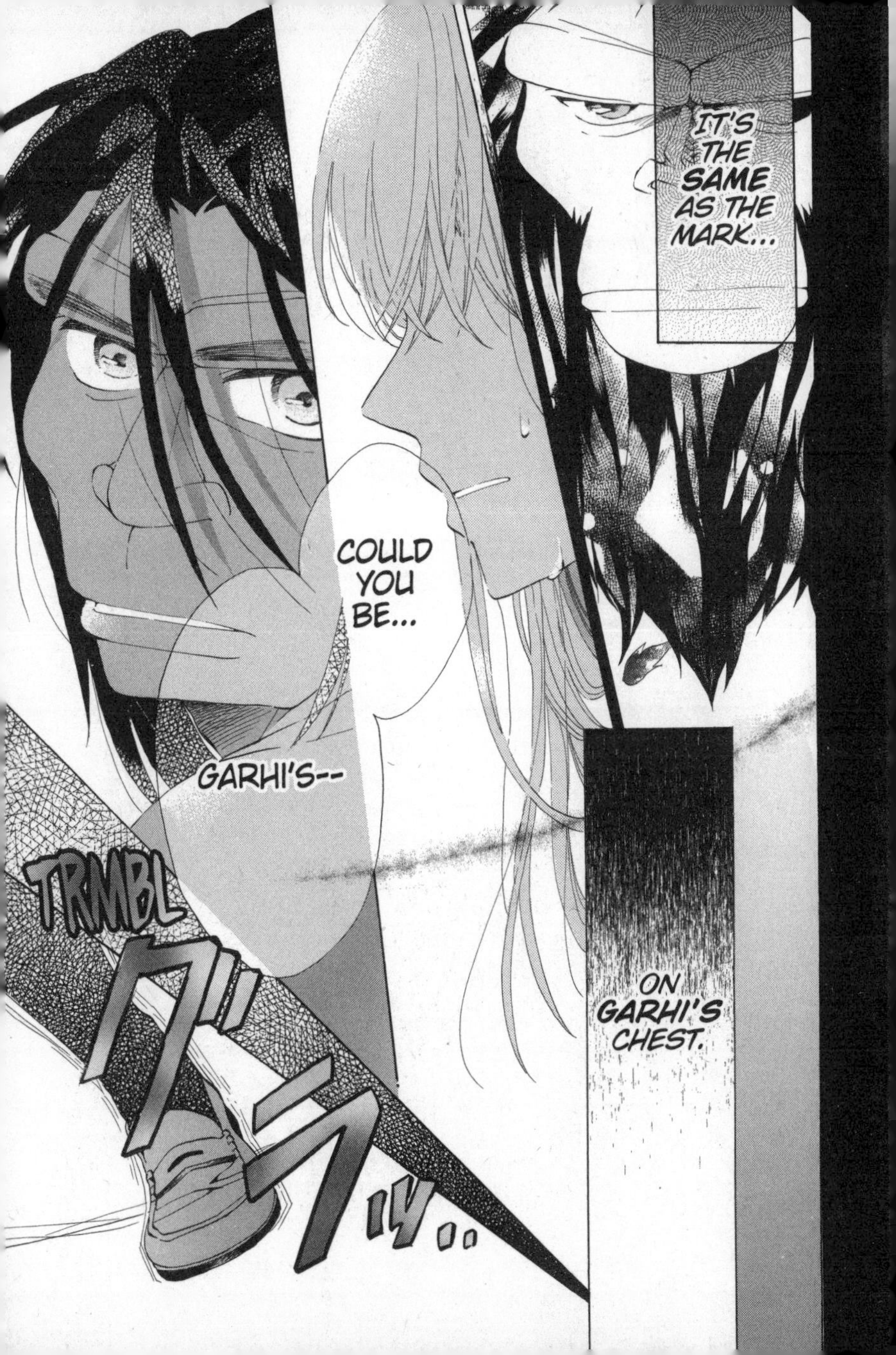
IT'S THE SAME AS THE MARK...
ON GARHI'S CHEST.
COULD YOU BE...
GARHI'S--
TRMBL

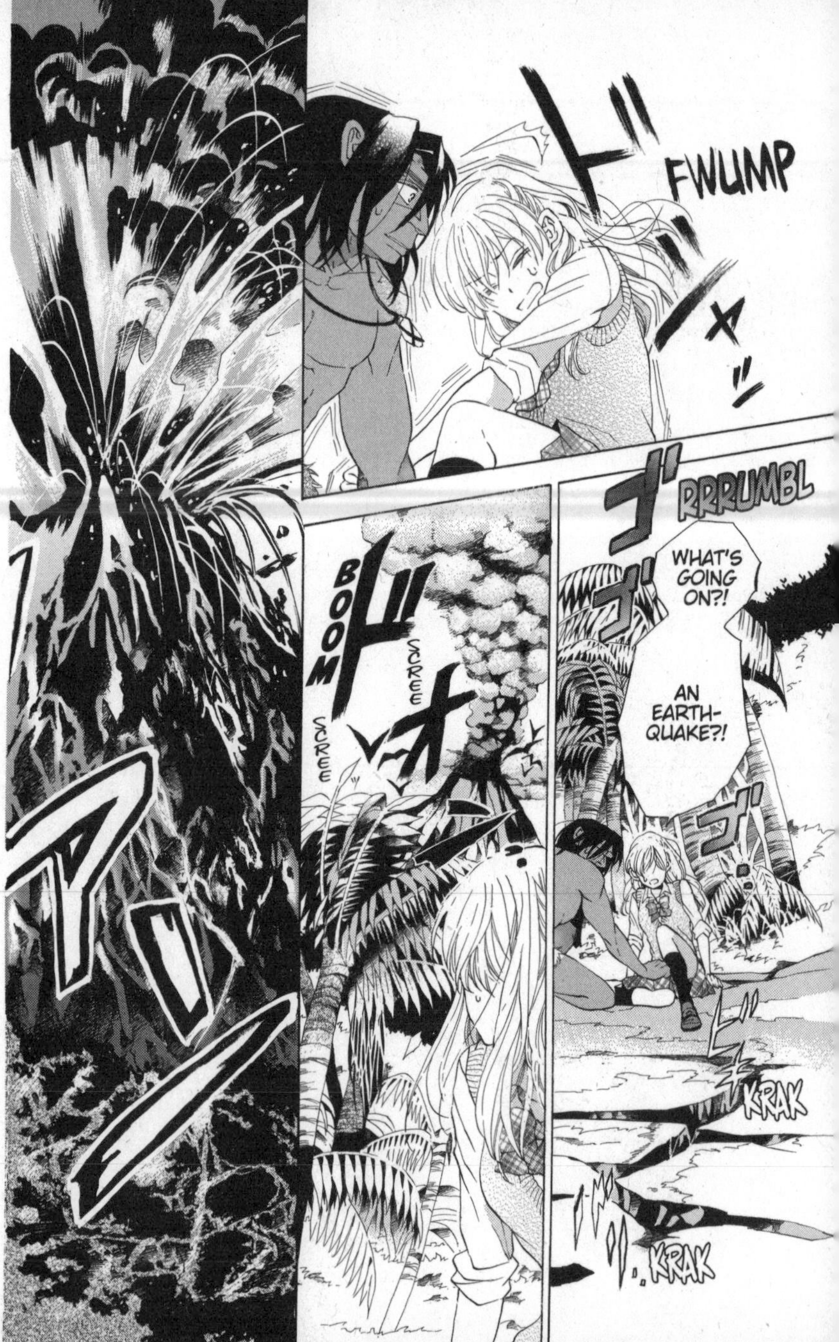
FWUMP
RRRUMBL
WHAT'S GOING ON?!
AN EARTH-QUAKE?!
KRAK
KRAK
BOOOM
SCREE
SCREE

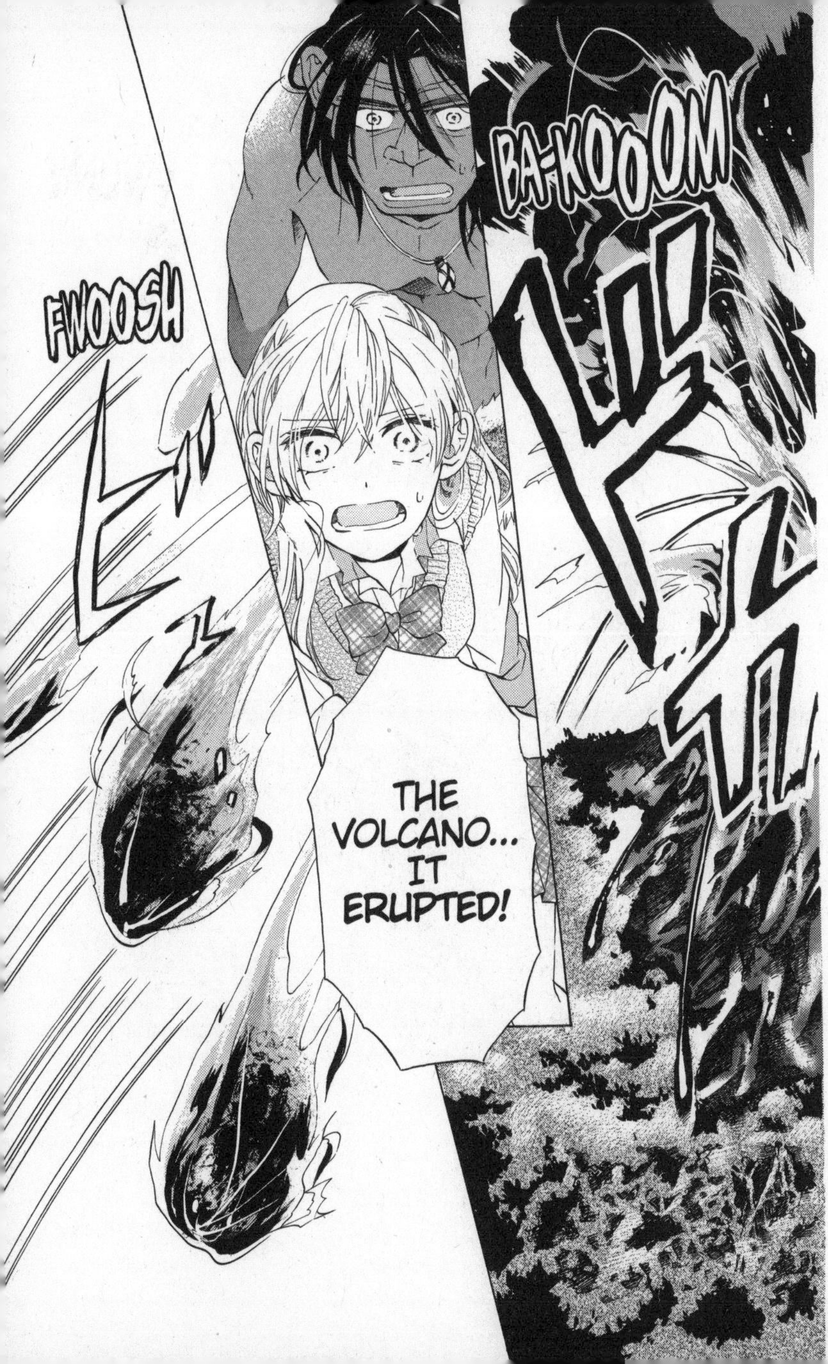
BA-KOOOM
THE VOLCANO... IT ERUPTED!
FWOOSH

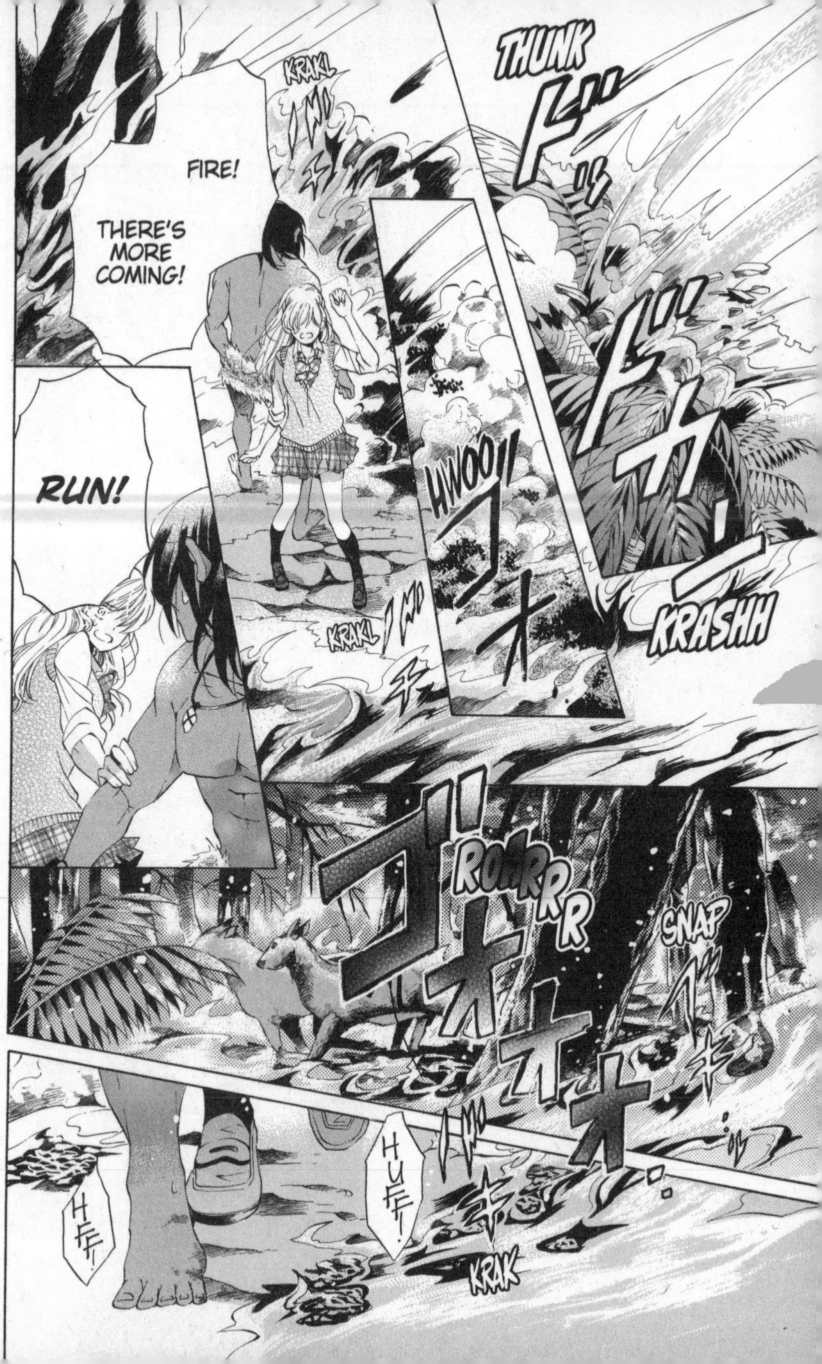
THUNK
KRASHH
HWOO
KRAKL
KRAKL
FIRE!
THERE'S MORE COMING!
RUN!
ROARRR
SNAP
KRAK
HUFF!
HFF!

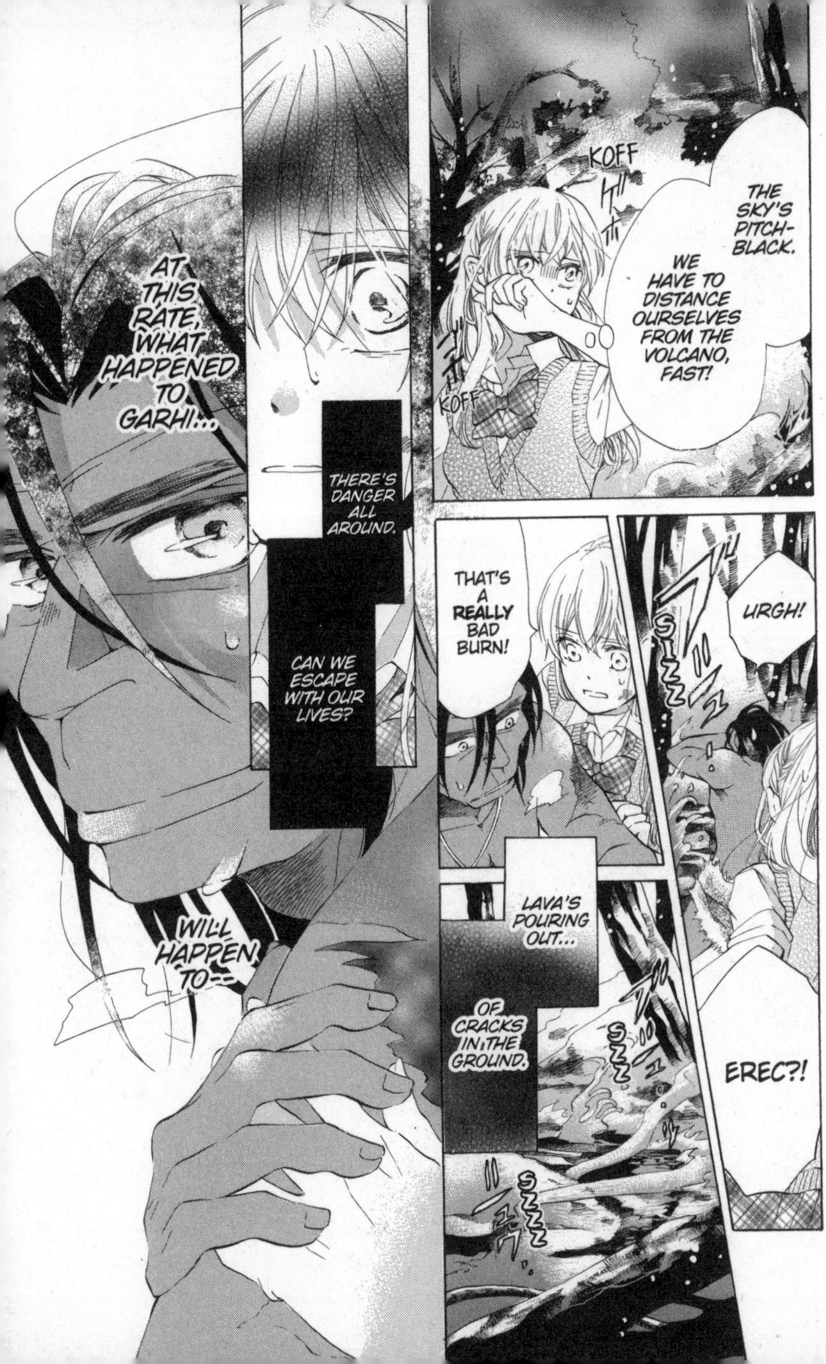
KOFF
THE SKY'S PITCH-BLACK.
WE HAVE TO DISTANCE OURSELVES FROM THE VOLCANO, FAST!
KOFF
URGH!
SIZZ
EREC?!
THAT'S A **REALLY** BAD BURN!
LAVA'S POURING OUT...
OF CRACKS IN THE GROUND.
SIZZ
SZZZ
THERE'S DANGER ALL AROUND.
CAN WE ESCAPE WITH OUR LIVES?
AT THIS RATE, WHAT HAPPENED TO GARHI...
WILL HAPPEN TO--

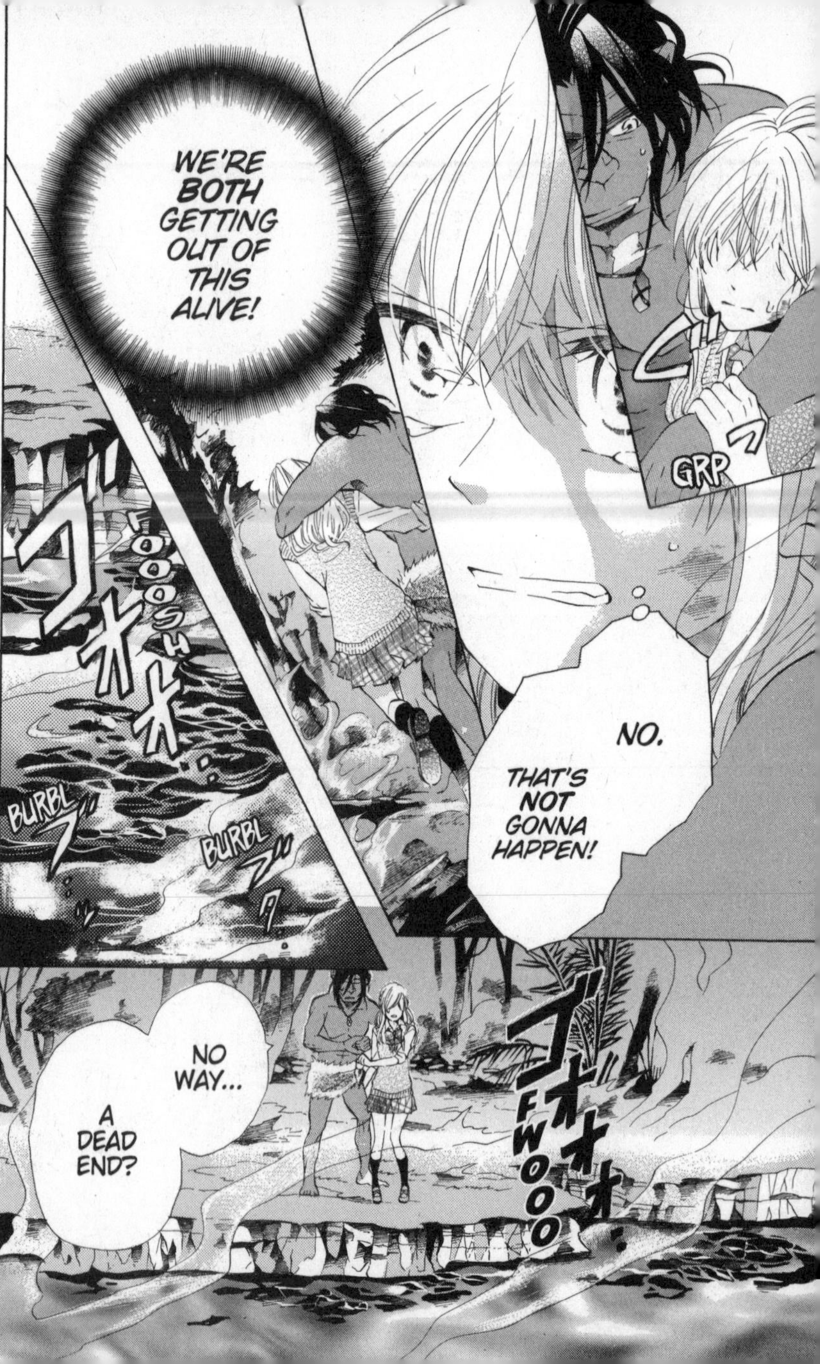
GRP
NO.
THAT'S NOT GONNA HAPPEN!
WE'RE BOTH GETTING OUT OF THIS ALIVE!
FOOOOSH
BURBL
BURBL
FWOOOO
NO WAY...
A DEAD END?

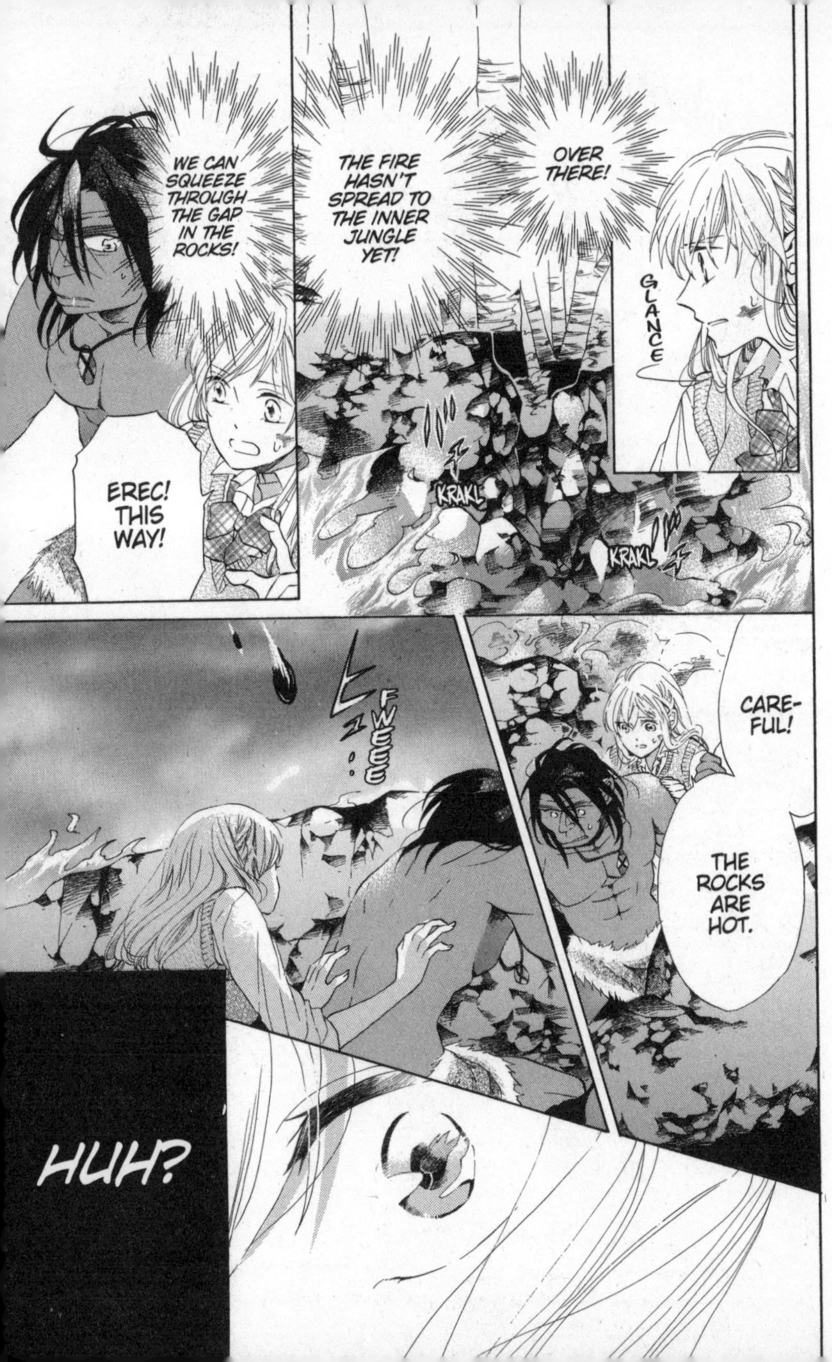
GLANCE
OVER THERE!
THE FIRE HASN'T SPREAD TO THE INNER JUNGLE YET!
KRAKL
KRAKL
WE CAN SQUEEZE THROUGH THE GAP IN THE ROCKS!
EREC! THIS WAY!
CARE-FUL!
THE ROCKS ARE HOT.
FWEEE
HUH?

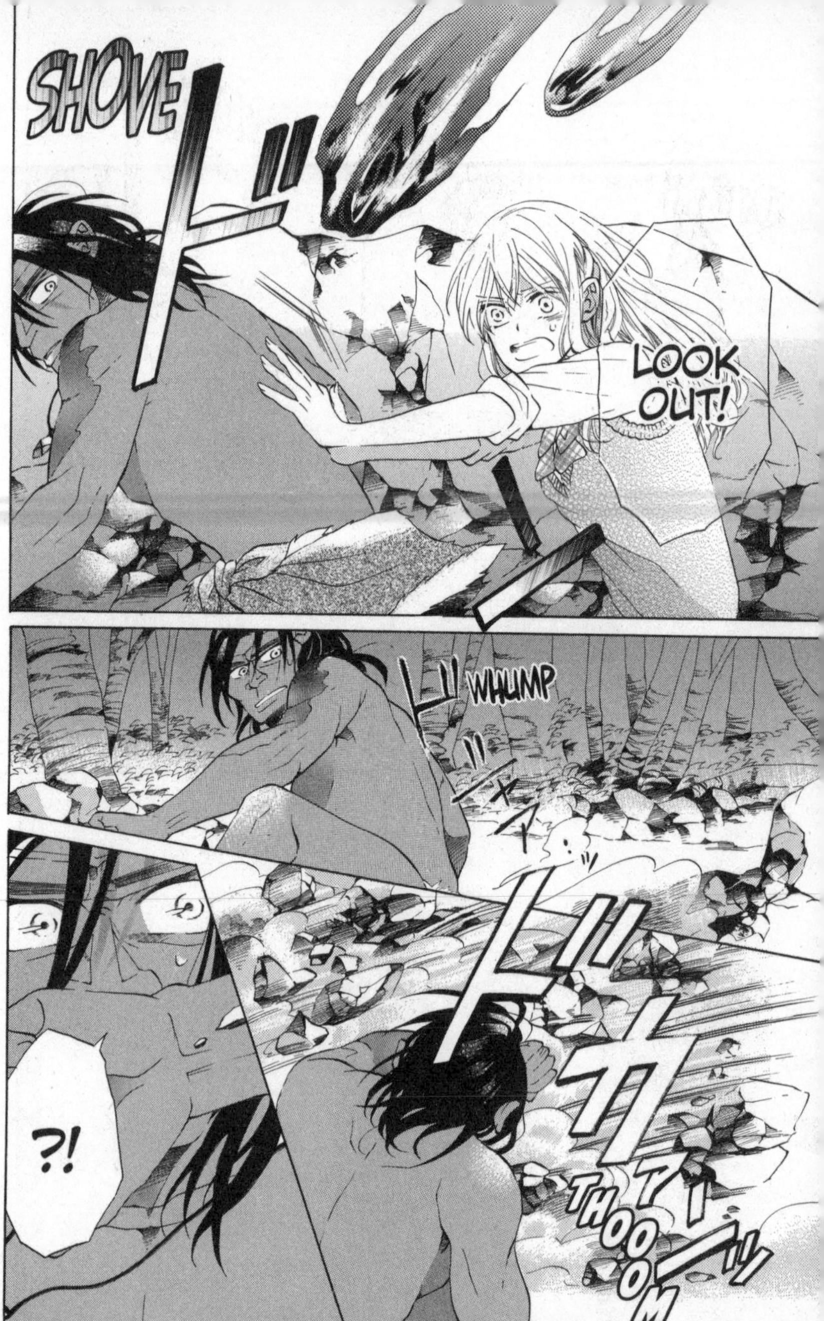
LOOK OUT!
SHOVE
WHUMP
THOOOOM
?!

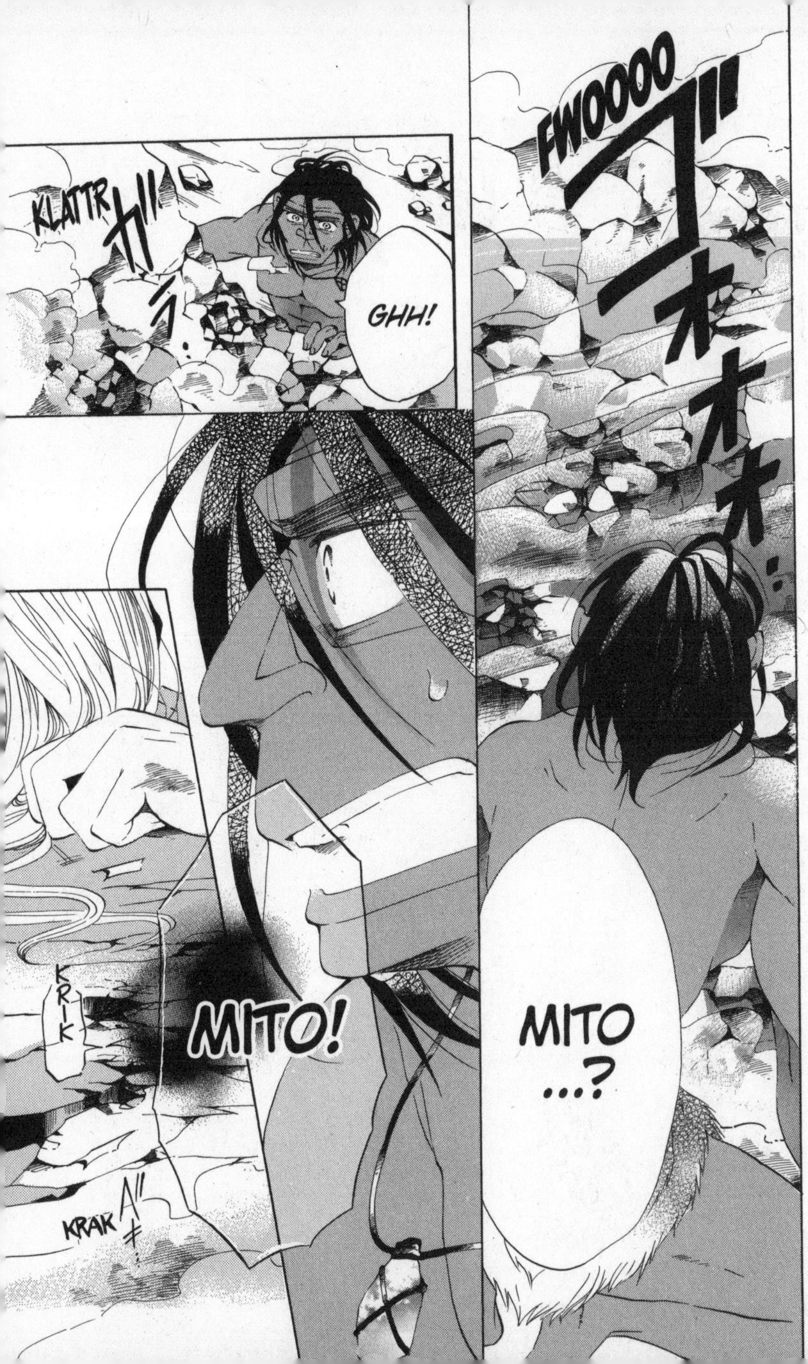
FWOOOO
ゴオオオ…
MITO ...?
KLATTR
GHH!
MITO!
KRIK
KRAK

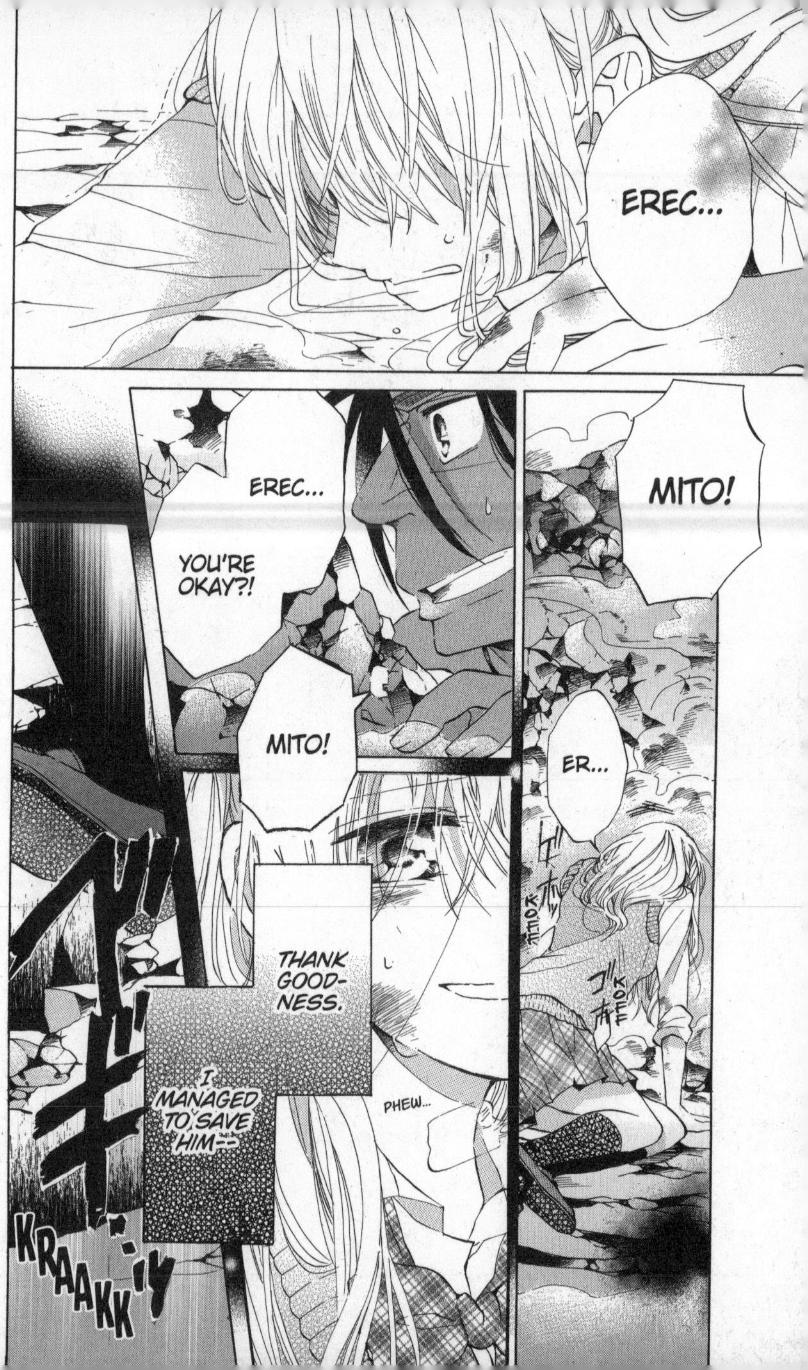
EREC...
MITO!
ER...
KOFF
KOFF
EREC...
YOU'RE OKAY?!
MITO!
THANK GOODNESS.
I MANAGED TO SAVE HIM--
PHEW...
KRAAKK!!

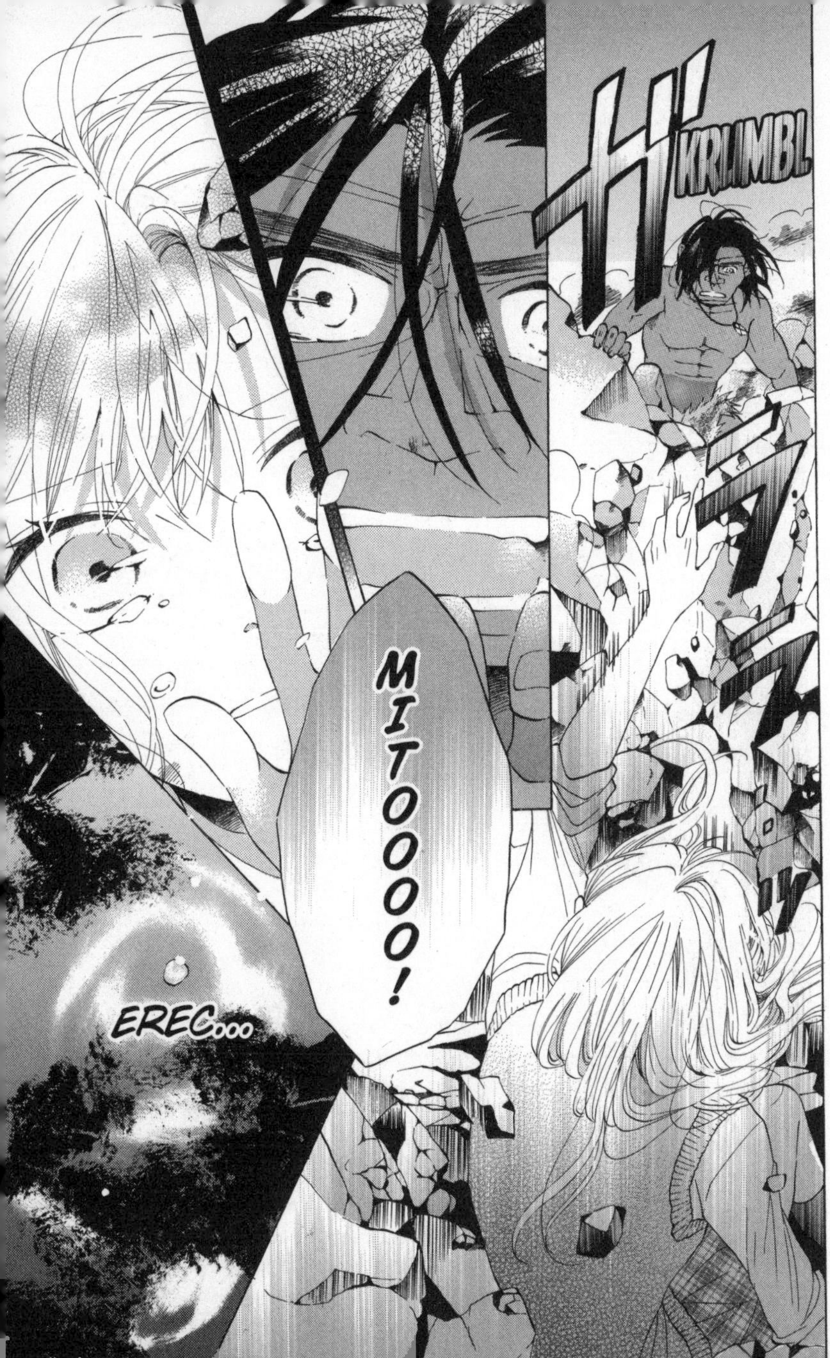
KRUMBL
MITOOOOO!
EREC...

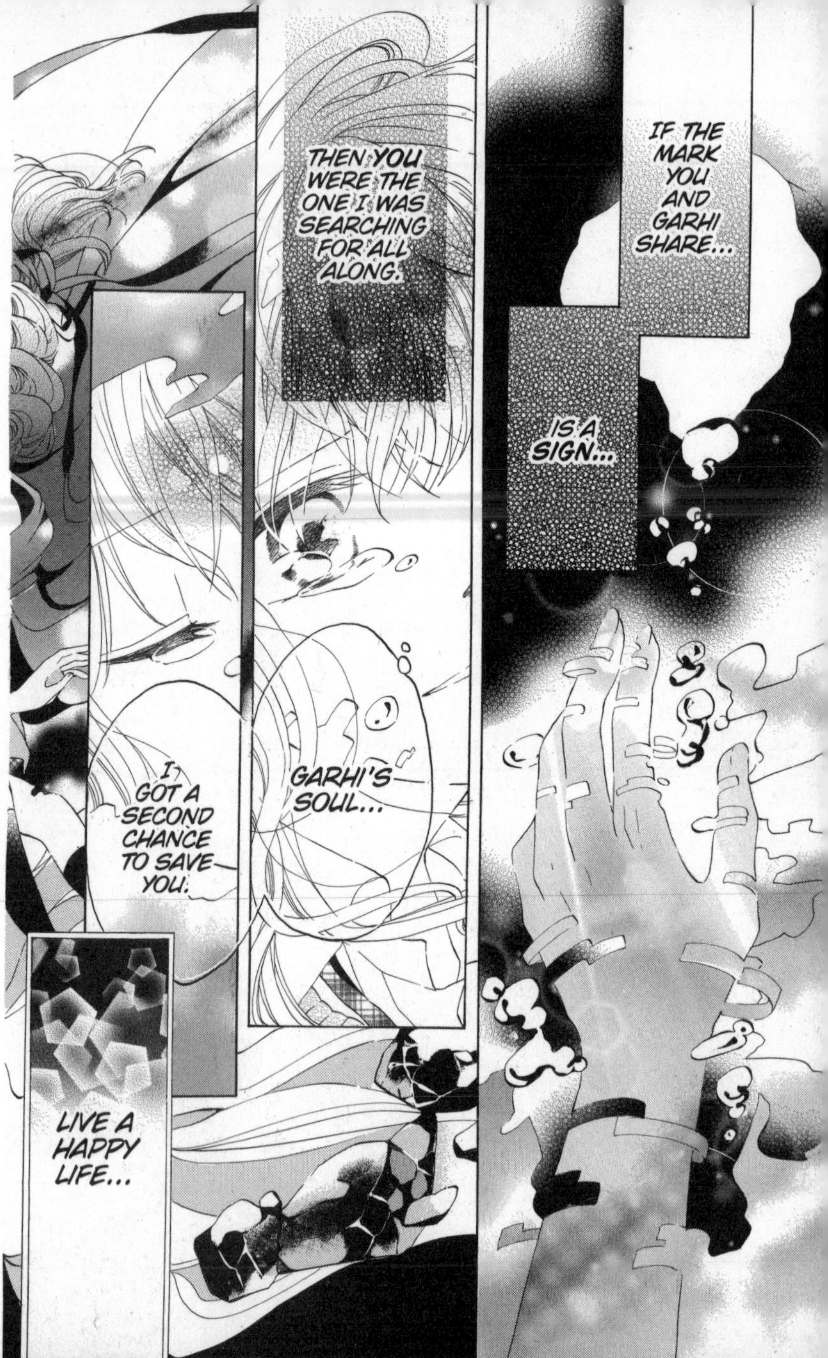
IF THE MARK YOU AND GARHI SHARE...
IS A SIGN...
THEN YOU WERE THE ONE I WAS SEARCHING FOR ALL ALONG.
GARHI'S SOUL...
I GOT A SECOND CHANCE TO SAVE YOU.
LIVE A HAPPY LIFE...

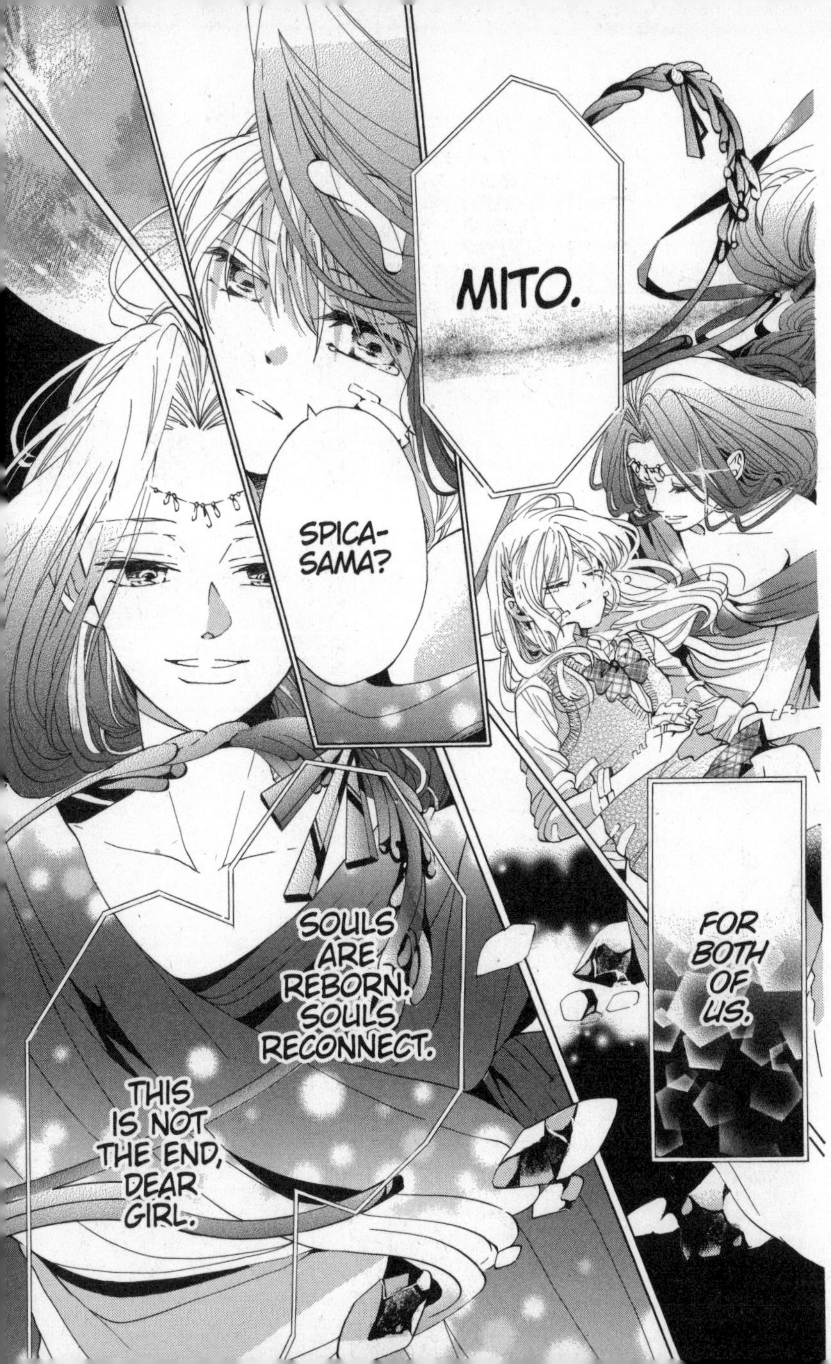
MITO.
SPICA-SAMA?
FOR BOTH OF US.
SOULS ARE REBORN. SOULS RECONNECT.
THIS IS NOT THE END, DEAR GIRL.

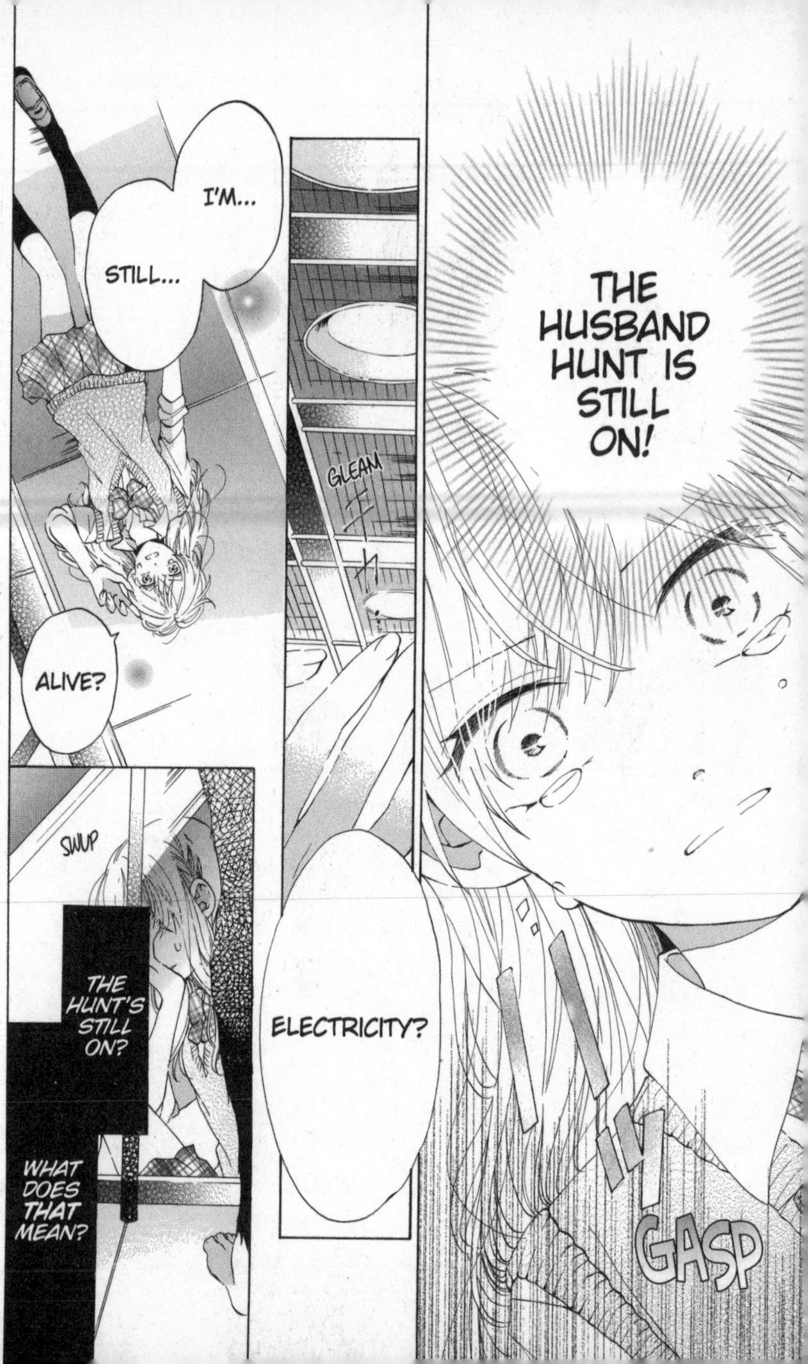
THE HUSBAND HUNT IS STILL ON!
GASP
GLEAM
ELECTRICITY?
I'M...
STILL...
ALIVE?
SWUP
THE HUNT'S STILL ON?
WHAT DOES THAT MEAN?

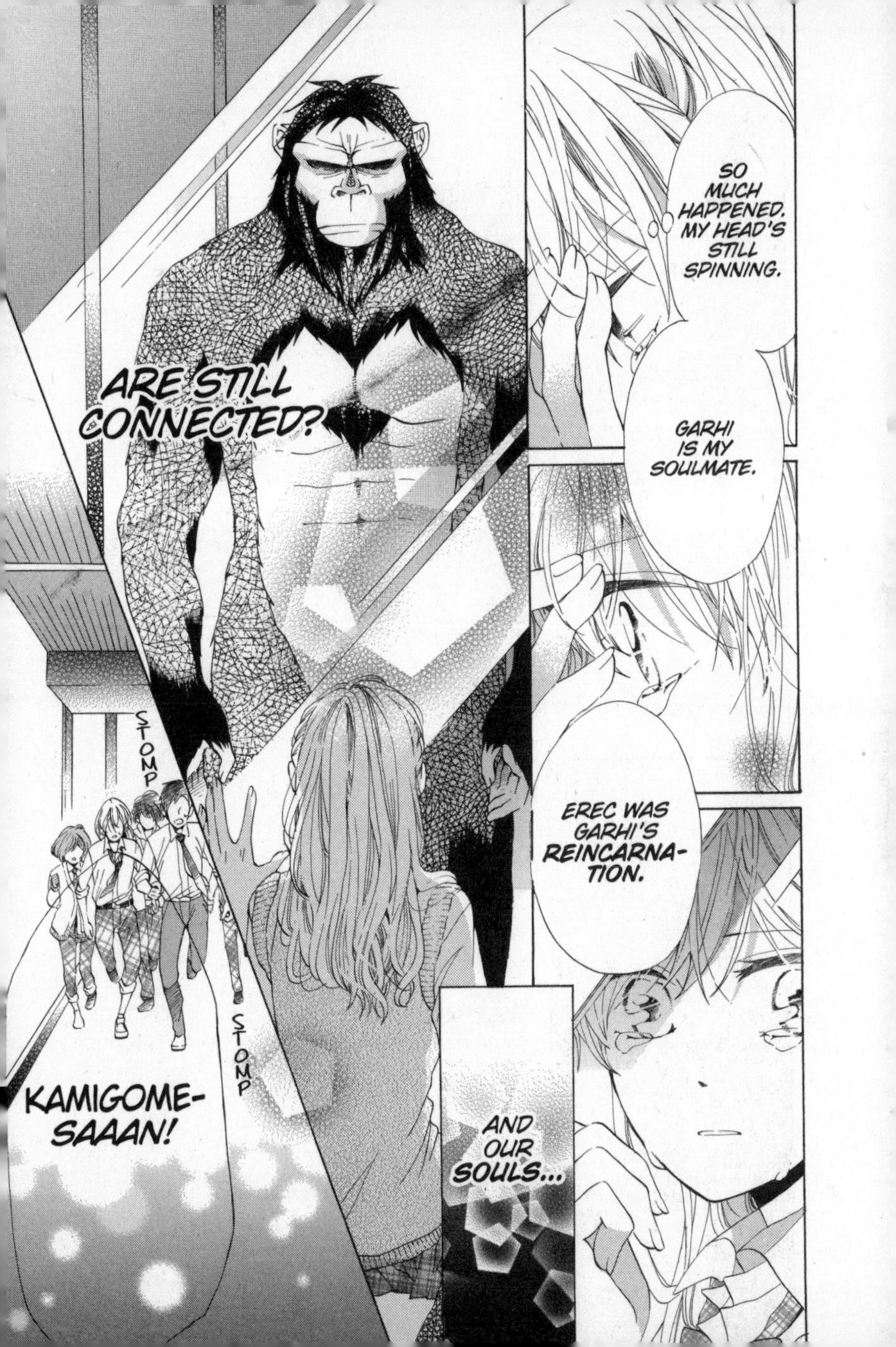
SO MUCH HAPPENED. MY HEAD'S STILL SPINNING.
GARHI IS MY SOULMATE.
EREC WAS GARHI'S REINCARNATION.
AND OUR SOULS...
ARE STILL CONNECTED?
STOMP
STOMP
KAMIGOME-SAAAN!

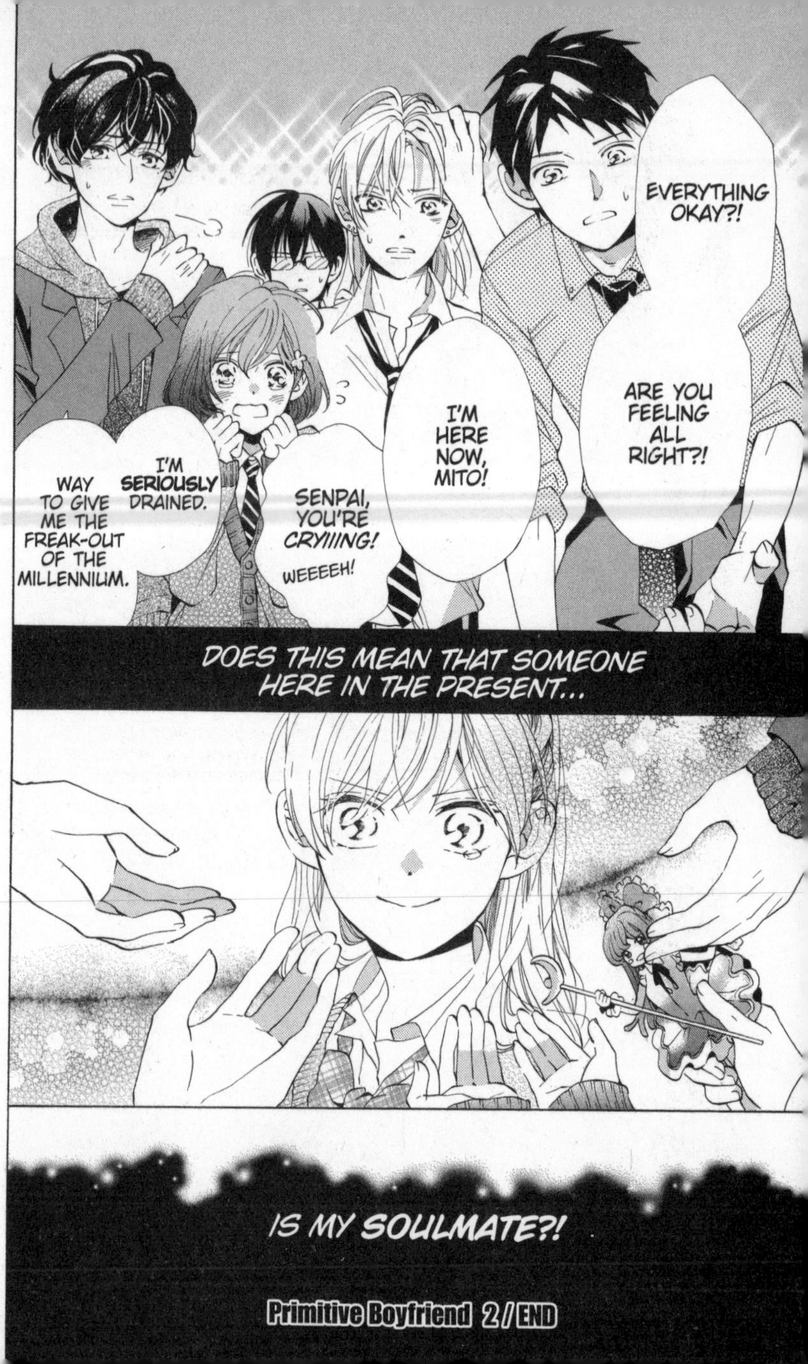
EVERYTHING OKAY?!
ARE YOU FEELING ALL RIGHT?!
I'M HERE NOW, MITO!
SENPAI, YOU'RE CRYIIING!
WEEEEH!
I'M SERIOUSLY DRAINED.
WAY TO GIVE ME THE FREAK-OUT OF THE MILLENNIUM.
DOES THIS MEAN THAT SOMEONE HERE IN THE PRESENT...
IS MY SOULMATE?!
Primitive Boyfriend 2 / END

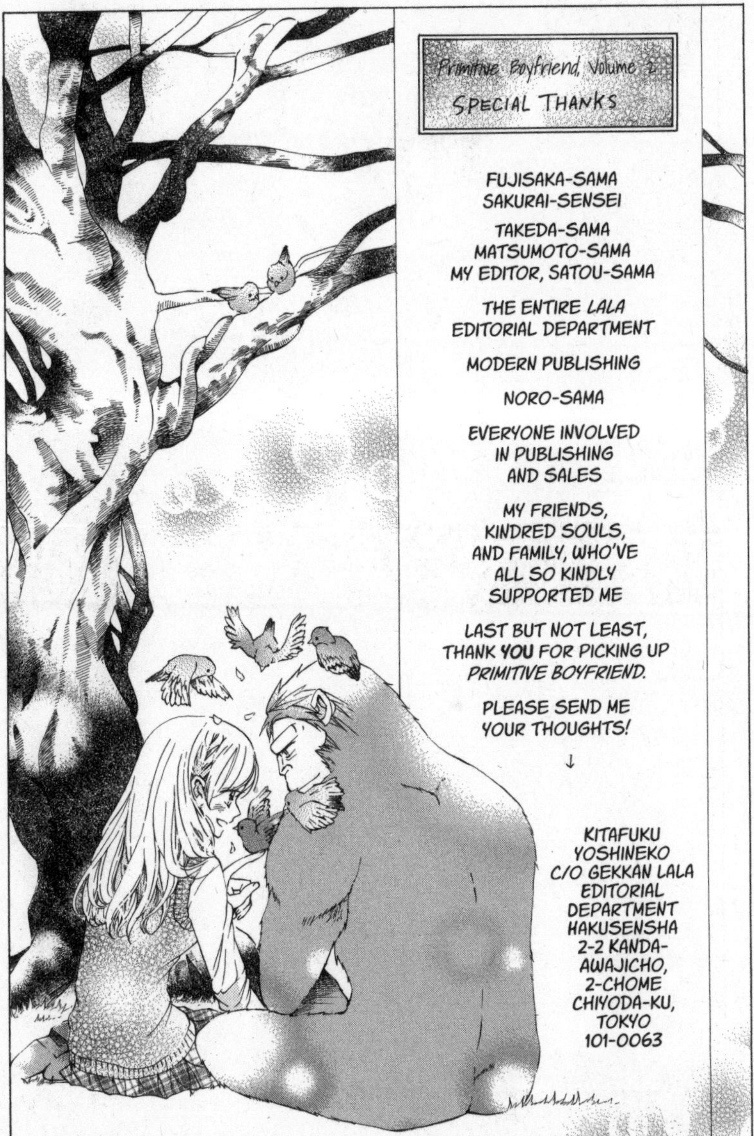

Primitive Boyfriend, Volume 2

SPECIAL THANKS

FUJISAKA-SAMA
SAKURAI-SENSEI

TAKEDA-SAMA
MATSUMOTO-SAMA
MY EDITOR, SATOU-SAMA

THE ENTIRE *LALA* EDITORIAL DEPARTMENT

MODERN PUBLISHING

NORO-SAMA

EVERYONE INVOLVED IN PUBLISHING AND SALES

MY FRIENDS, KINDRED SOULS, AND FAMILY, WHO'VE ALL SO KINDLY SUPPORTED ME

LAST BUT NOT LEAST, THANK **YOU** FOR PICKING UP *PRIMITIVE BOYFRIEND.*

PLEASE SEND ME YOUR THOUGHTS!

↓

KITAFUKU YOSHINEKO
C/O GEKKAN LALA EDITORIAL DEPARTMENT
HAKUSENSHA
2-2 KANDA-AWAJICHO, 2-CHOME
CHIYODA-KU, TOKYO
101-0063

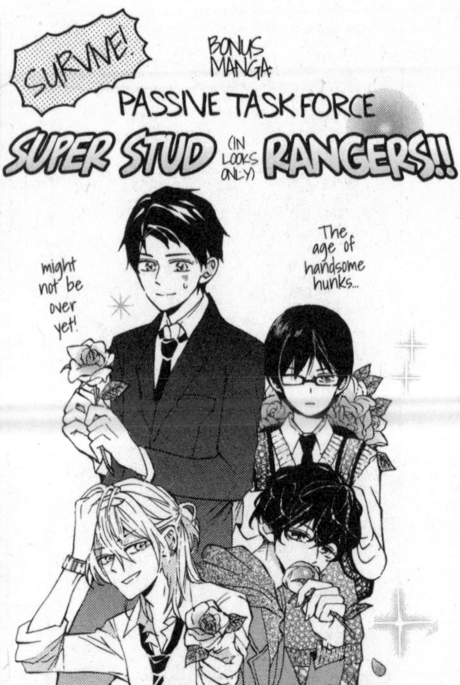
SURVIVE!
BONUS MANGA
PASSIVE TASK FORCE
SUPER STUD (IN LOOKS ONLY) RANGERS!!
The age of handsome hunks...
might not be over yet!

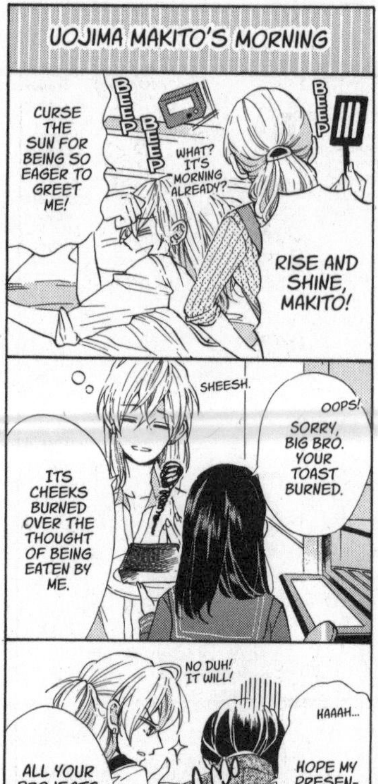
UOJIMA MAKITO'S MORNING
BEEP BEEP
RISE AND SHINE, MAKITO!
WHAT? IT'S MORNING ALREADY?
BEEP BEEP
CURSE THE SUN FOR BEING SO EAGER TO GREET ME!
OOPS! SORRY, BIG BRO. YOUR TOAST BURNED.
SHEESH.
ITS CHEEKS BURNED OVER THE THOUGHT OF BEING EATEN BY ME.
HAAAH... HOPE MY PRESENTATION GOES WELL...
NO DUH! IT WILL!
SMACK
ALL YOUR PROJECTS TURN OUT GREAT... JUST LOOK AT ME!
SHEESH.
I'M HEADING OUT.
SORRY I KEPT YOU WAITING, WORLD!
KA-CHAK
HAVE A GOOD DAY!
THERE GOES OUR DORK.

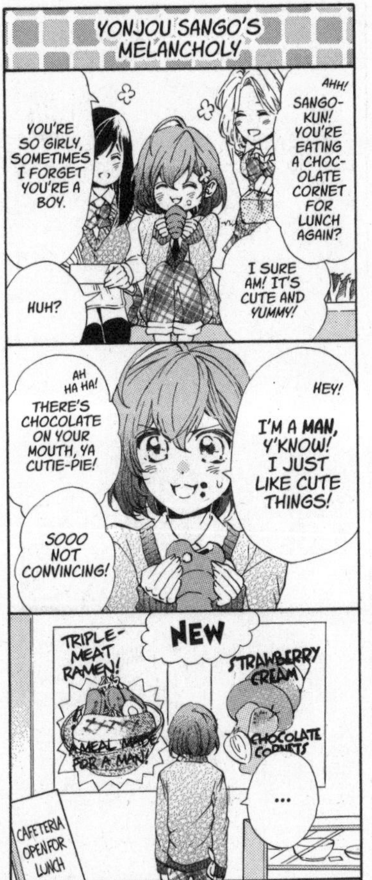
YONJOU SANGO'S MELANCHOLY
AHH! SANGO-KUN! YOU'RE EATING A CHOCOLATE CORNET FOR LUNCH AGAIN?
I SURE AM! IT'S CUTE AND YUMMY!
YOU'RE SO GIRLY, SOMETIMES I FORGET YOU'RE A BOY.
HUH?
HEY!
I'M A MAN, Y'KNOW! I JUST LIKE CUTE THINGS!
AH HA HA! THERE'S CHOCOLATE ON YOUR MOUTH, YA CUTIE-PIE!
SOOO NOT CONVINCING!
NEW
STRAWBERRY CREAM
CHOCOLATE CORNETS
TRIPLE-MEAT RAMEN!
A MEAL MADE FOR A MAN!
...
CAFETERIA OPEN FOR LUNCH
HUH?
RAMEN TODAY, SANGO-KUN?
YOU LOOK LIKE A RABBIT EATING THAT! SO CUUUTE!
WHYYY?

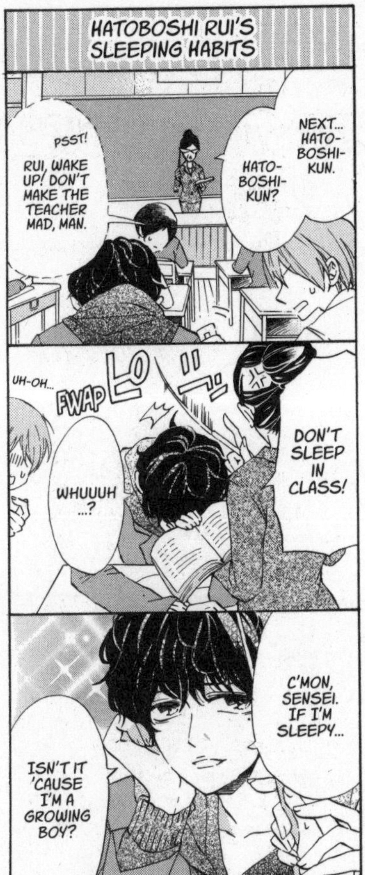
HATOBOSHI RUI'S SLEEPING HABITS
NEXT... HATO-BOSHI-KUN.
HATO-BOSHI-KUN?
PSST!
RUI, WAKE UP! DON'T MAKE THE TEACHER MAD, MAN.
DON'T SLEEP IN CLASS!
FWAP
WHUUUH ...?
UH-OH...
C'MON, SENSEI. IF I'M SLEEPY...
ISN'T IT 'CAUSE I'M A GROWING BOY?
G...
GOOD QUESTION.
IF YOU'RE FEELING ILL, GO TO THE NURSE'S OFFICE.
NAH...
I DON'T WANNA MISS CLASS. I'LL SLEEP HERE.
OH, REALLY?
SENSEIII!!

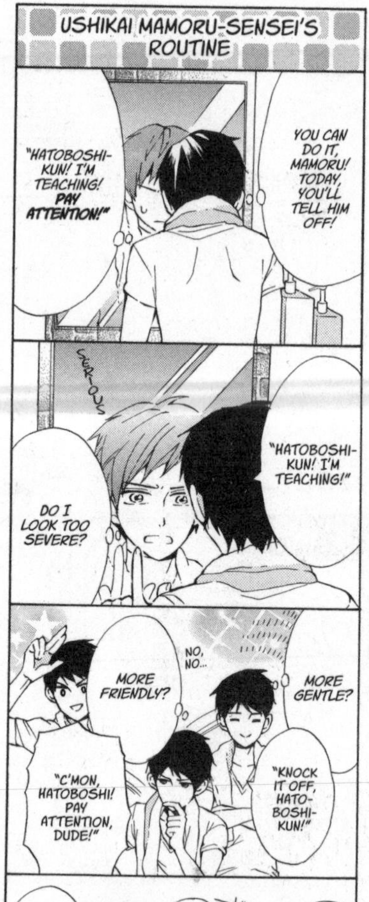
USHIKAI MAMORU-SENSEI'S ROUTINE
YOU CAN DO IT, MAMORU! TODAY, YOU'LL TELL HIM OFF!
"HATOBOSHI-KUN! I'M TEACHING! PAY ATTENTION!"
"HATOBOSHI-KUN! I'M TEACHING!"
SERIOUS
DO I LOOK TOO SEVERE?
MORE GENTLE?
"KNOCK IT OFF, HATOBOSHI-KUN!"
NO, NO...
MORE FRIENDLY?
"C'MON, HATOBOSHI! PAY ATTENTION, DUDE!"
MORNIN', USHIKAI-CHAN.
HA...
ERR... HOW YOU DOIN'?
TO...
WHAT'S WITH YOUR FACE?

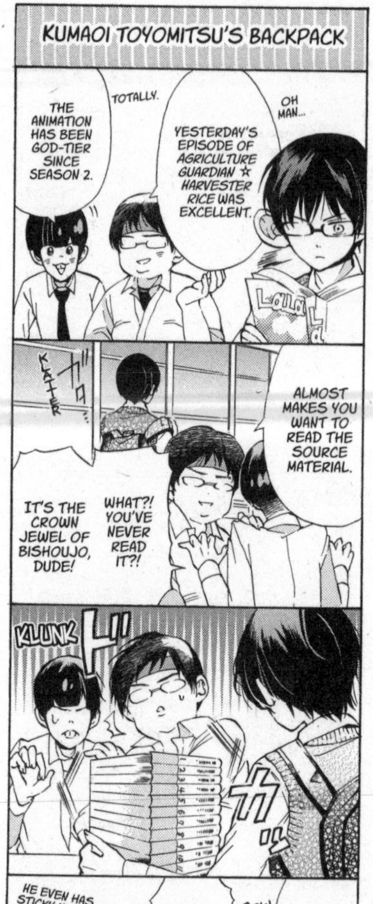
KUMAOI TOYOMITSU'S BACKPACK
OH MAN...
YESTERDAY'S EPISODE OF AGRICULTURE GUARDIAN ☆ HARVESTER RICE WAS EXCELLENT.
TOTALLY.
THE ANIMATION HAS BEEN GOD-TIER SINCE SEASON 2.
ALMOST MAKES YOU WANT TO READ THE SOURCE MATERIAL.
KLATTER
WHAT?! YOU'VE NEVER READ IT?!
IT'S THE CROWN JEWEL OF BISHOUJO, DUDE!
KLUNK
IF YOU NEED THE ORIGINAL MAGAZINE RUN, LET ME KNOW.
BOW
FIRST EDITIONS, COMPLETE WITH THE DISCARDABLE MARKETING BLURBS?!
HE EVEN HAS STICKY NOTES FOR THE DIFFERENCES BETWEEN THE MANGA AND THE ANIME!!!

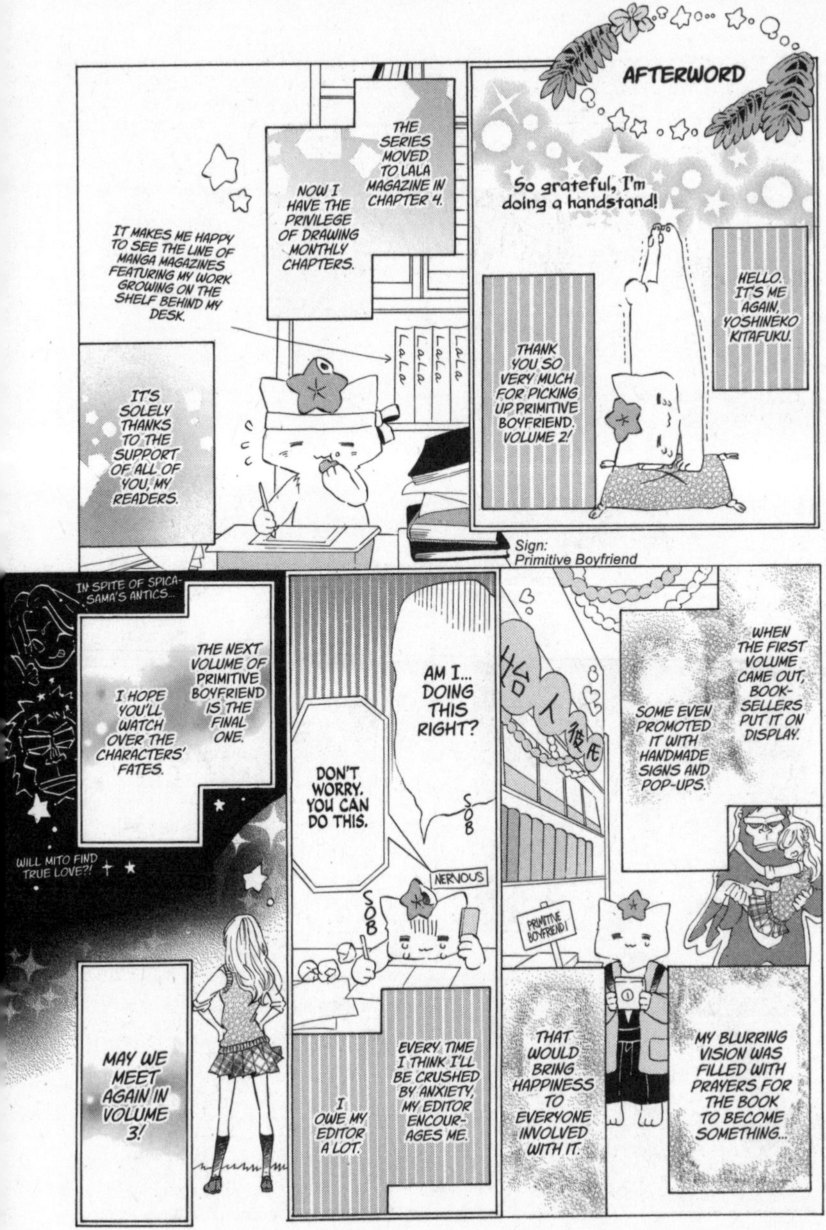
AFTERWORD
So grateful, I'm doing a handstand!
HELLO. IT'S ME AGAIN, YOSHINEKO KITAFUKU.
THANK YOU SO VERY MUCH FOR PICKING UP PRIMITIVE BOYFRIEND. VOLUME 2!
Sign: Primitive Boyfriend
THE SERIES MOVED TO LALA MAGAZINE IN CHAPTER 4.
NOW I HAVE THE PRIVILEGE OF DRAWING MONTHLY CHAPTERS.
IT MAKES ME HAPPY TO SEE THE LINE OF MANGA MAGAZINES FEATURING MY WORK GROWING ON THE SHELF BEHIND MY DESK.
LaLa
LaLa
LaLa
LaLa
IT'S SOLELY THANKS TO THE SUPPORT OF ALL OF YOU, MY READERS.
WHEN THE FIRST VOLUME CAME OUT, BOOK-SELLERS PUT IT ON DISPLAY.
SOME EVEN PROMOTED IT WITH HANDMADE SIGNS AND POP-UPS.
PRIMITIVE BOYFRIEND 1
MY BLURRING VISION WAS FILLED WITH PRAYERS FOR THE BOOK TO BECOME SOMETHING...
THAT WOULD BRING HAPPINESS TO EVERYONE INVOLVED WITH IT.
AM I... DOING THIS RIGHT?
DON'T WORRY. YOU CAN DO THIS.
SOB
NERVOUS
SOB
EVERY TIME I THINK I'LL BE CRUSHED BY ANXIETY, MY EDITOR ENCOUR-AGES ME.
I OWE MY EDITOR A LOT.
IN SPITE OF SPICA-SAMA'S ANTICS...
THE NEXT VOLUME OF PRIMITIVE BOYFRIEND IS THE FINAL ONE.
I HOPE YOU'LL WATCH OVER THE CHARACTERS' FATES.
WILL MITO FIND TRUE LOVE?!
MAY WE MEET AGAIN IN VOLUME 3!

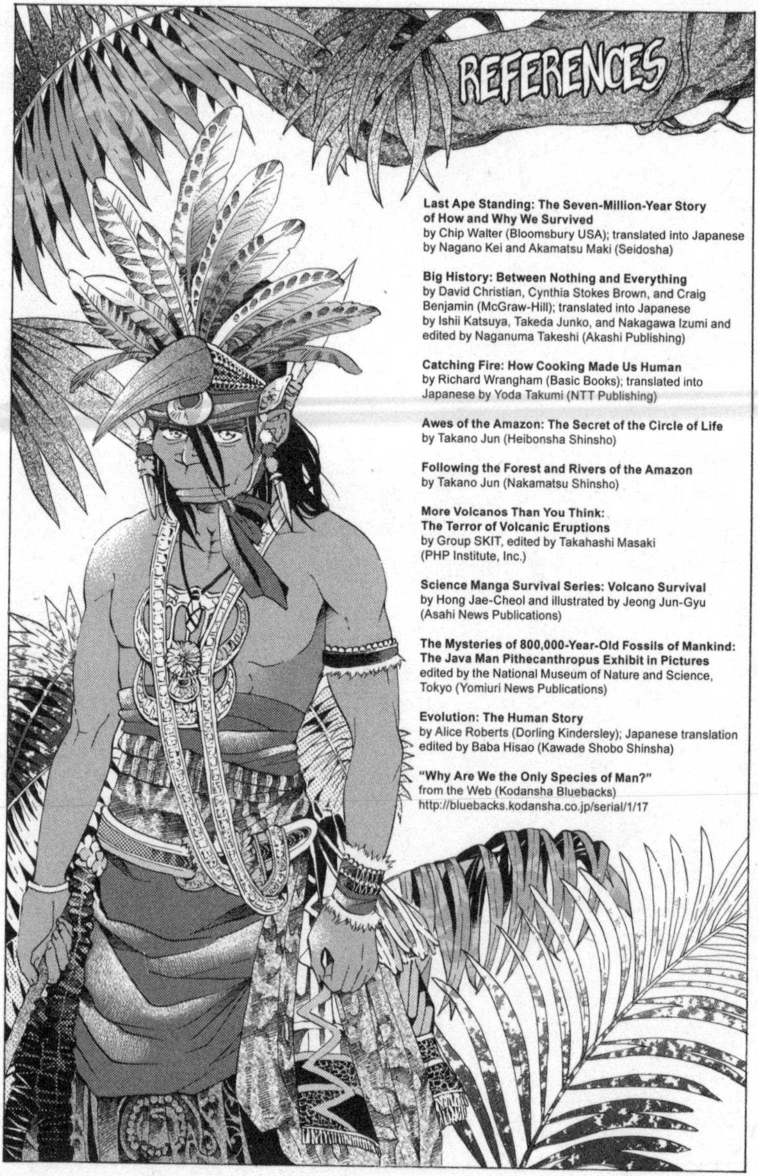

REFERENCES

Last Ape Standing: The Seven-Million-Year Story of How and Why We Survived
by Chip Walter (Bloomsbury USA); translated into Japanese by Nagano Kei and Akamatsu Maki (Seidosha)

Big History: Between Nothing and Everything
by David Christian, Cynthia Stokes Brown, and Craig Benjamin (McGraw-Hill); translated into Japanese by Ishii Katsuya, Takeda Junko, and Nakagawa Izumi and edited by Naganuma Takeshi (Akashi Publishing)

Catching Fire: How Cooking Made Us Human
by Richard Wrangham (Basic Books); translated into Japanese by Yoda Takumi (NTT Publishing)

Awes of the Amazon: The Secret of the Circle of Life
by Takano Jun (Heibonsha Shinsho)

Following the Forest and Rivers of the Amazon
by Takano Jun (Nakamatsu Shinsho)

More Volcanos Than You Think: The Terror of Volcanic Eruptions
by Group SKIT, edited by Takahashi Masaki (PHP Institute, Inc.)

Science Manga Survival Series: Volcano Survival
by Hong Jae-Cheol and illustrated by Jeong Jun-Gyu (Asahi News Publications)

The Mysteries of 800,000-Year-Old Fossils of Mankind: The Java Man Pithecanthropus Exhibit in Pictures
edited by the National Museum of Nature and Science, Tokyo (Yomiuri News Publications)

Evolution: The Human Story
by Alice Roberts (Dorling Kindersley); Japanese translation edited by Baba Hisao (Kawade Shobo Shinsha)

"Why Are We the Only Species of Man?"
from the Web (Kodansha Bluebacks)
http://bluebacks.kodansha.co.jp/serial/1/17